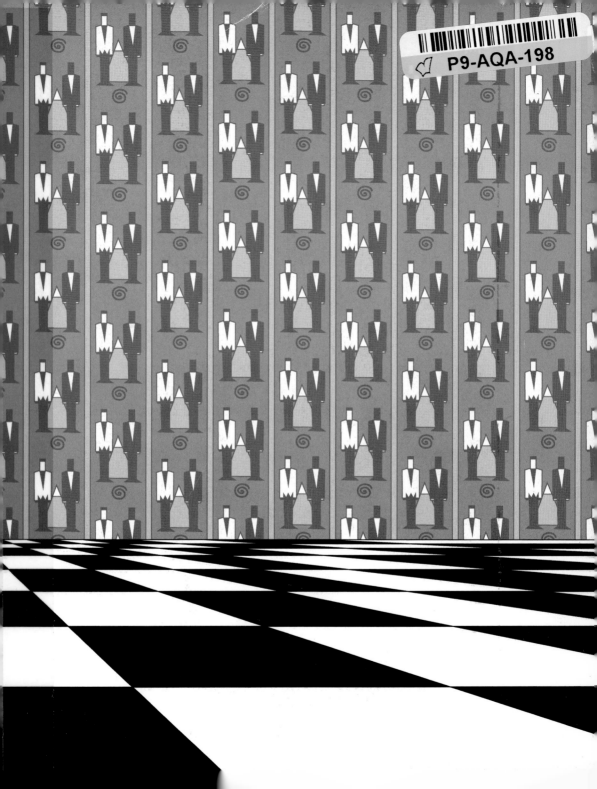

Ceci n'est pas un Gump.

THE LOUCHE AND INSALUBRIOUS ESCAPADES OF
ART d'ECCO

ANDREW AND ROGER LANGRIDGE

FANTAGRAPHICS BOOKS

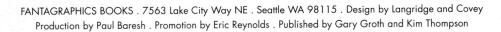

FANTAGRAPHICS BOOKS . 7563 Lake City Way NE . Seattle WA 98115 . Design by Langridge and Covey
Production by Paul Baresh . Promotion by Eric Reynolds . Published by Gary Groth and Kim Thompson

This book contains material that has previously appeared in *Art Dekko* Volume 1 #1-3, *Art d'Ecco* Volume 2 #1-4, *Zoot!* #1, *Craccum* 1989 and *The New Zealand Comics Gazette Yearbook* 1988. All characters, stories, and artwork ©2006 Andrew and Roger Langridge.

To receive a free catalog of comics, call 1-800-657-1100 or write us at the address above. Also view our catalog at www.fantagraphics.com. Visit Roger Langridge's website at www.hotelfred.com

Distributed in the U.S. by W.W. Norton and Company, Inc. (212-354-5500) . Distributed in Canada by Raincoast Books (800-663-5714) . Distributed in the United Kingdom by Turnaround Distribution (208-829-3009) .

First printing: July 2006 . ISBN10: 1-56097-796-5 . ISBN13: 978-1-56097-796-4 . Printed in Singapore

INTRODUCTION

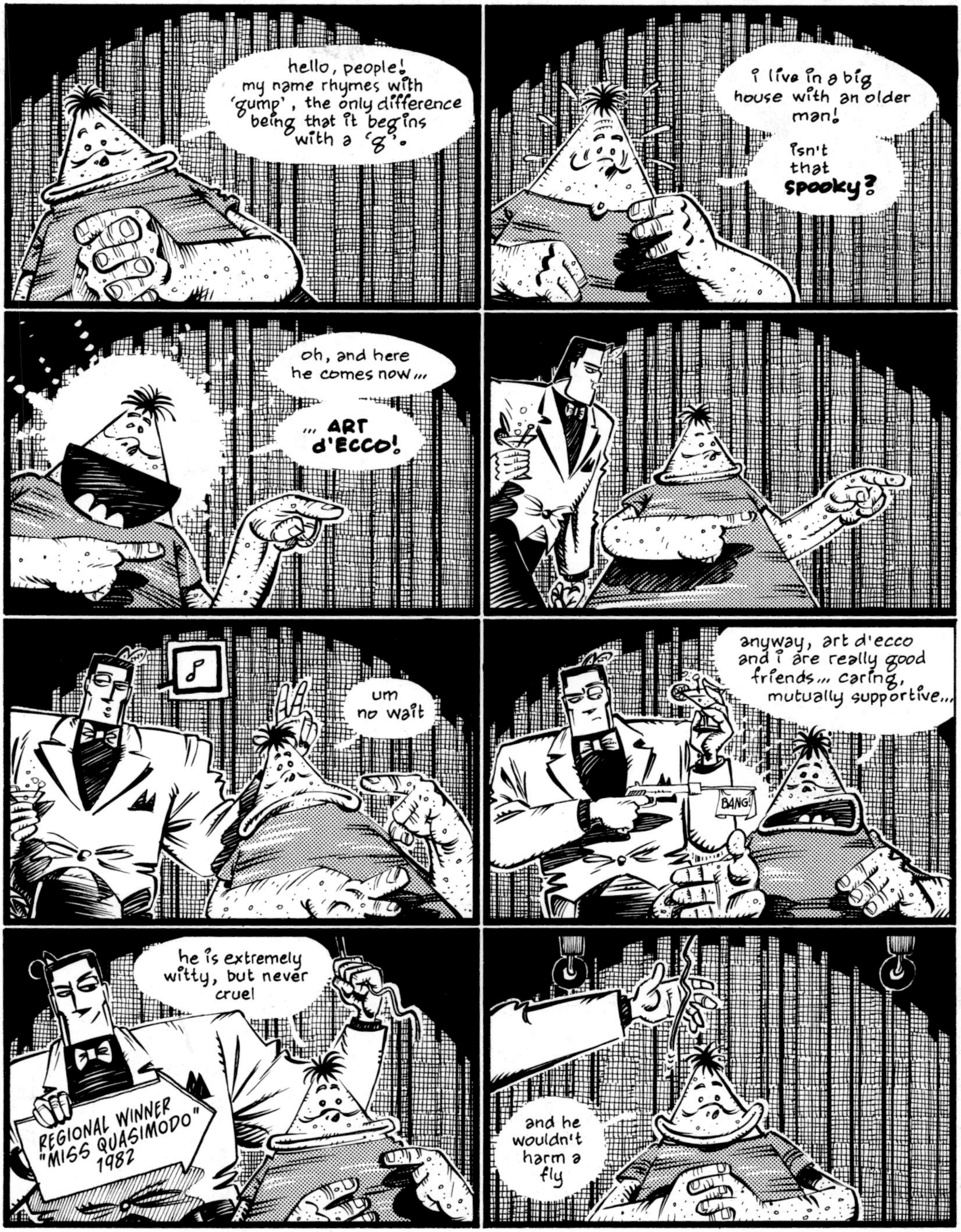
hello, people! my name rhymes with 'gump', the only difference being that it begins with a 'g'.
i live in a big house with an older man!
isn't that spooky?
oh, and here he comes now...
... ART d'ECCO!
um no wait
anyway, art d'ecco and i are really good friends... caring, mutually supportive...
BANG!
he is extremely witty, but never cruel
REGIONAL WINNER "MISS QUASIMODO" 1982
and he wouldn't harm a fly

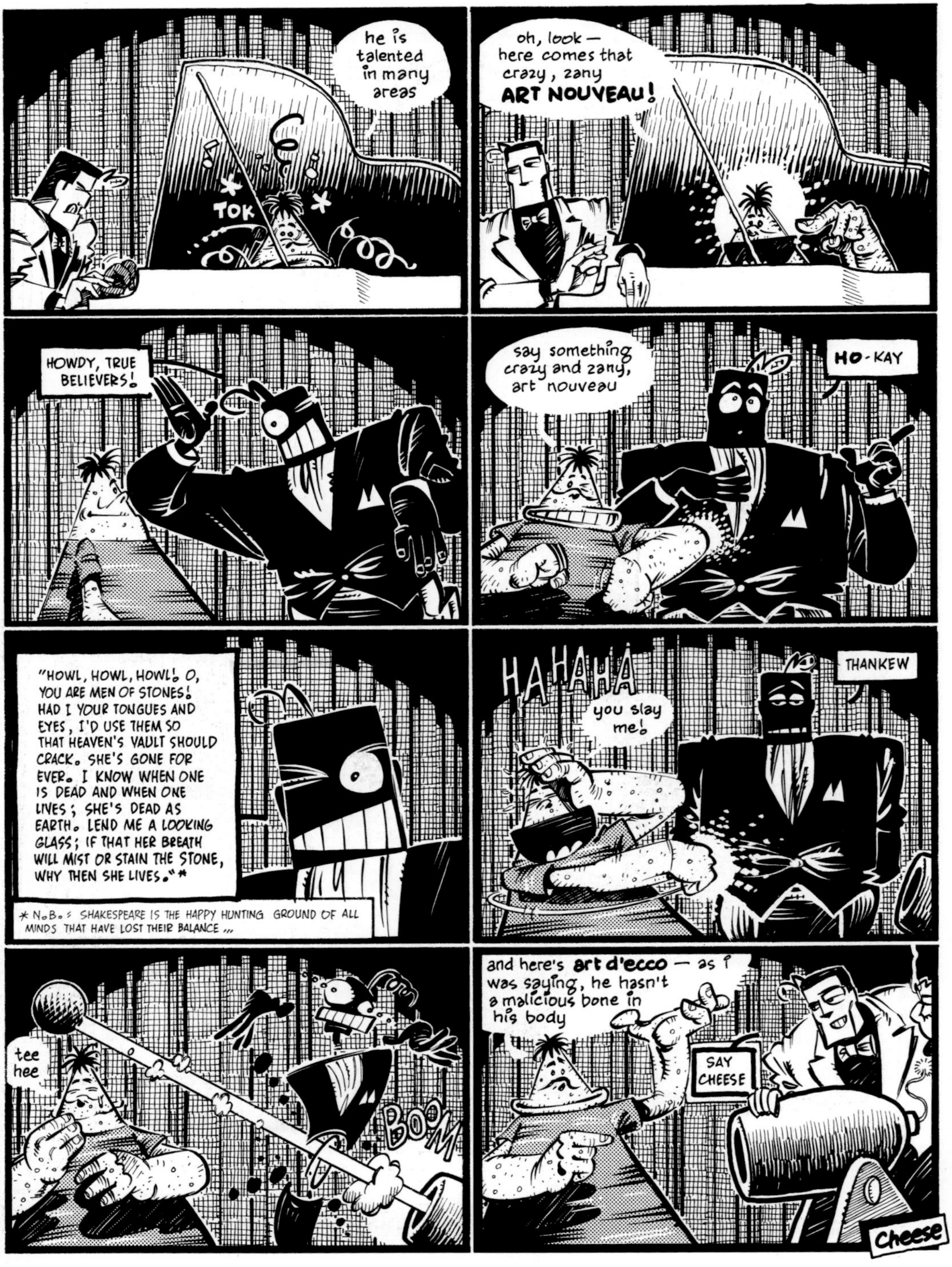
he is talented in many areas
TOK
oh, look — here comes that crazy, zany ART NOUVEAU!
HOWDY, TRUE BELIEVERS!
say something crazy and zany, art nouveau
HO-KAY
"HOWL, HOWL, HOWL! O, YOU ARE MEN OF STONES! HAD I YOUR TONGUES AND EYES, I'D USE THEM SO THAT HEAVEN'S VAULT SHOULD CRACK. SHE'S GONE FOR EVER. I KNOW WHEN ONE IS DEAD AND WHEN ONE LIVES; SHE'S DEAD AS EARTH. LEND ME A LOOKING GLASS; IF THAT HER BREATH WILL MIST OR STAIN THE STONE, WHY THEN SHE LIVES." *
* N.B.: SHAKESPEARE IS THE HAPPY HUNTING GROUND OF ALL MINDS THAT HAVE LOST THEIR BALANCE ...
HAHAHA
you slay me!
THANKEW
tee hee
BOOM
and here's art d'ecco — as I was saying, he hasn't a malicious bone in his body
SAY CHEESE
Cheese

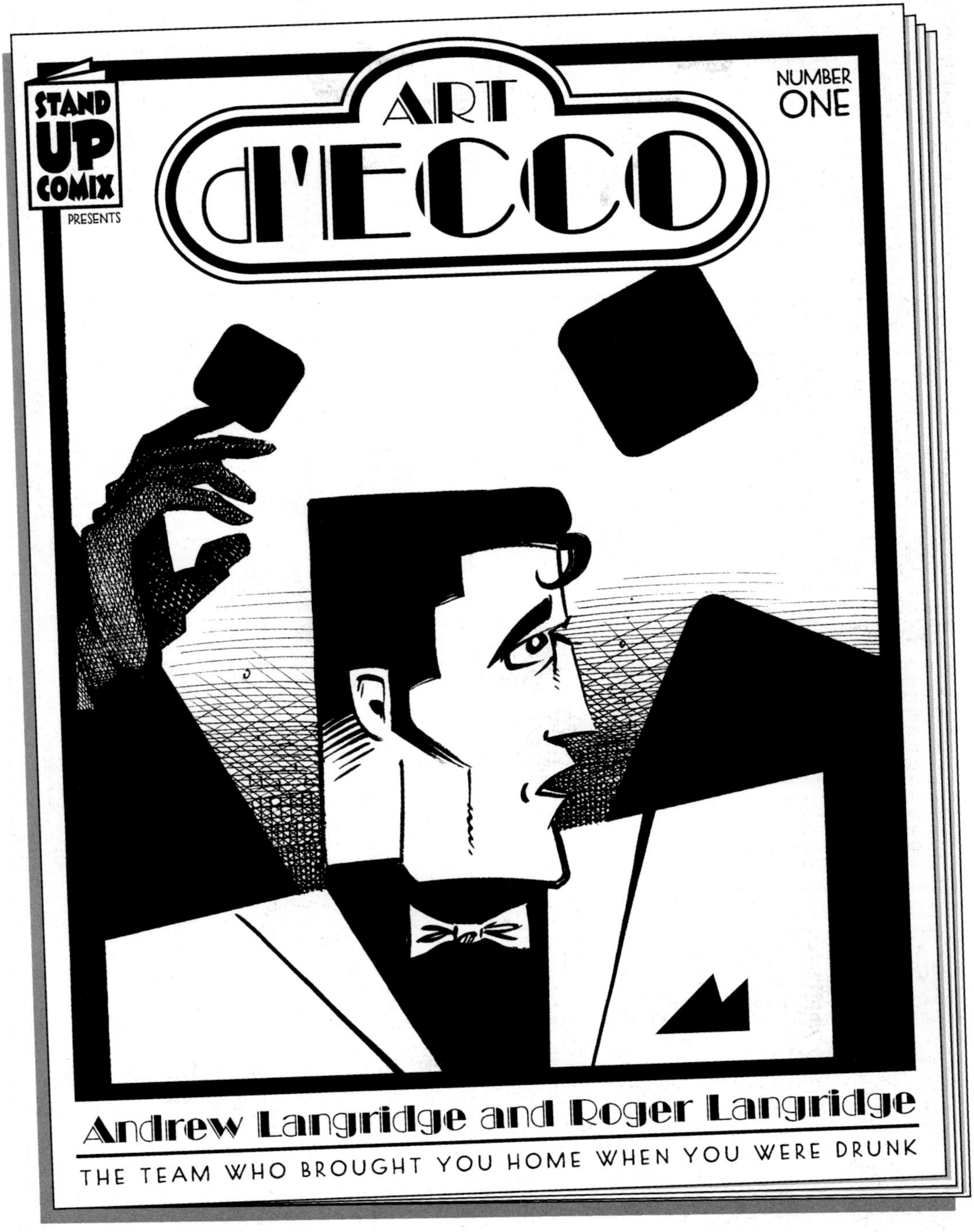
STAND UP COMIX
PRESENTS
ART d'ECCO
NUMBER ONE
Andrew Langridge and Roger Langridge
THE TEAM WHO BROUGHT YOU HOME WHEN YOU WERE DRUNK

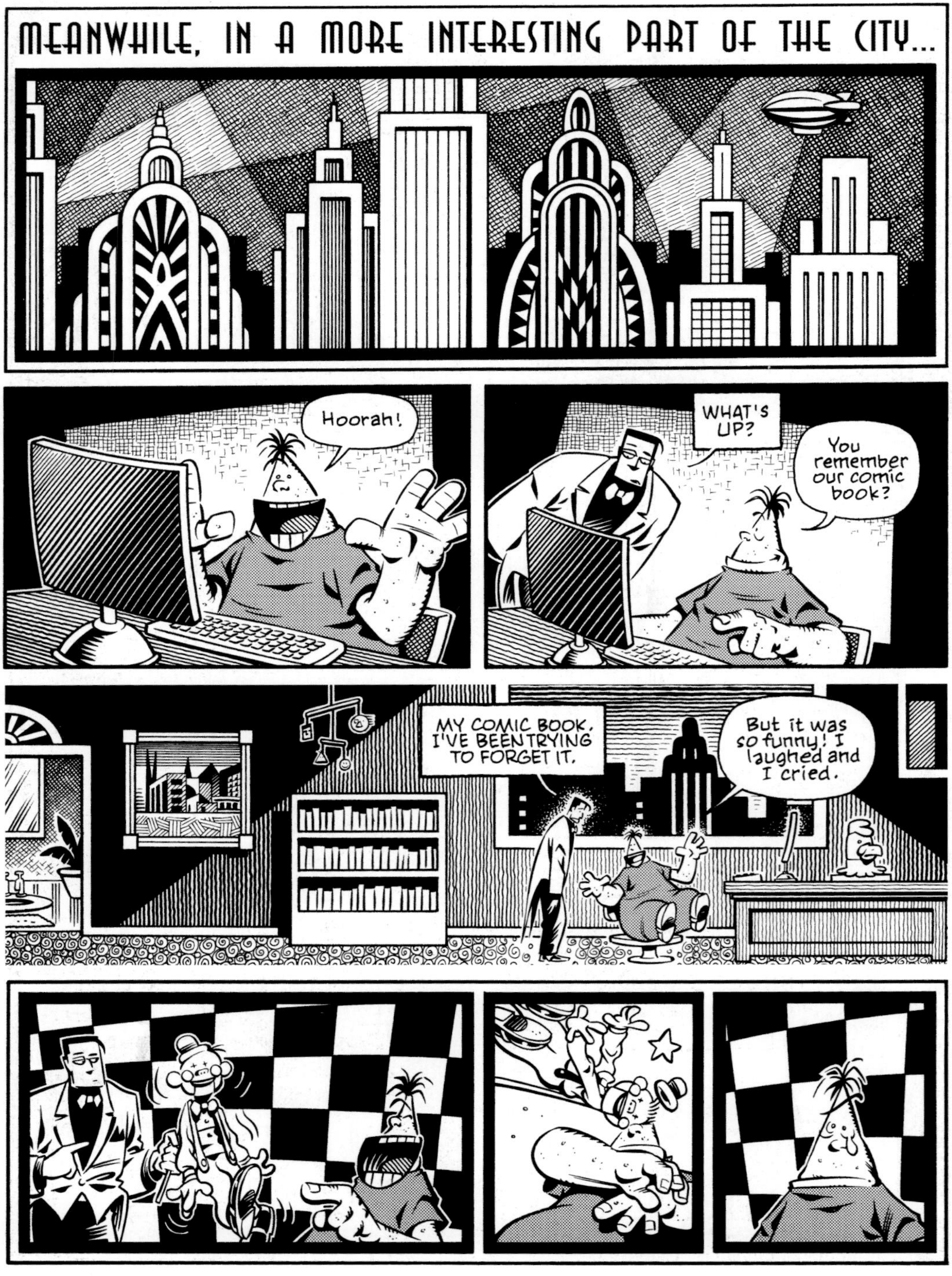
MEANWHILE, IN A MORE INTERESTING PART OF THE CITY...
Hoorah!
WHAT'S UP?
You remember our comic book?
MY COMIC BOOK. I'VE BEEN TRYING TO FORGET IT.
But it was so funny! I laughed and I cried.

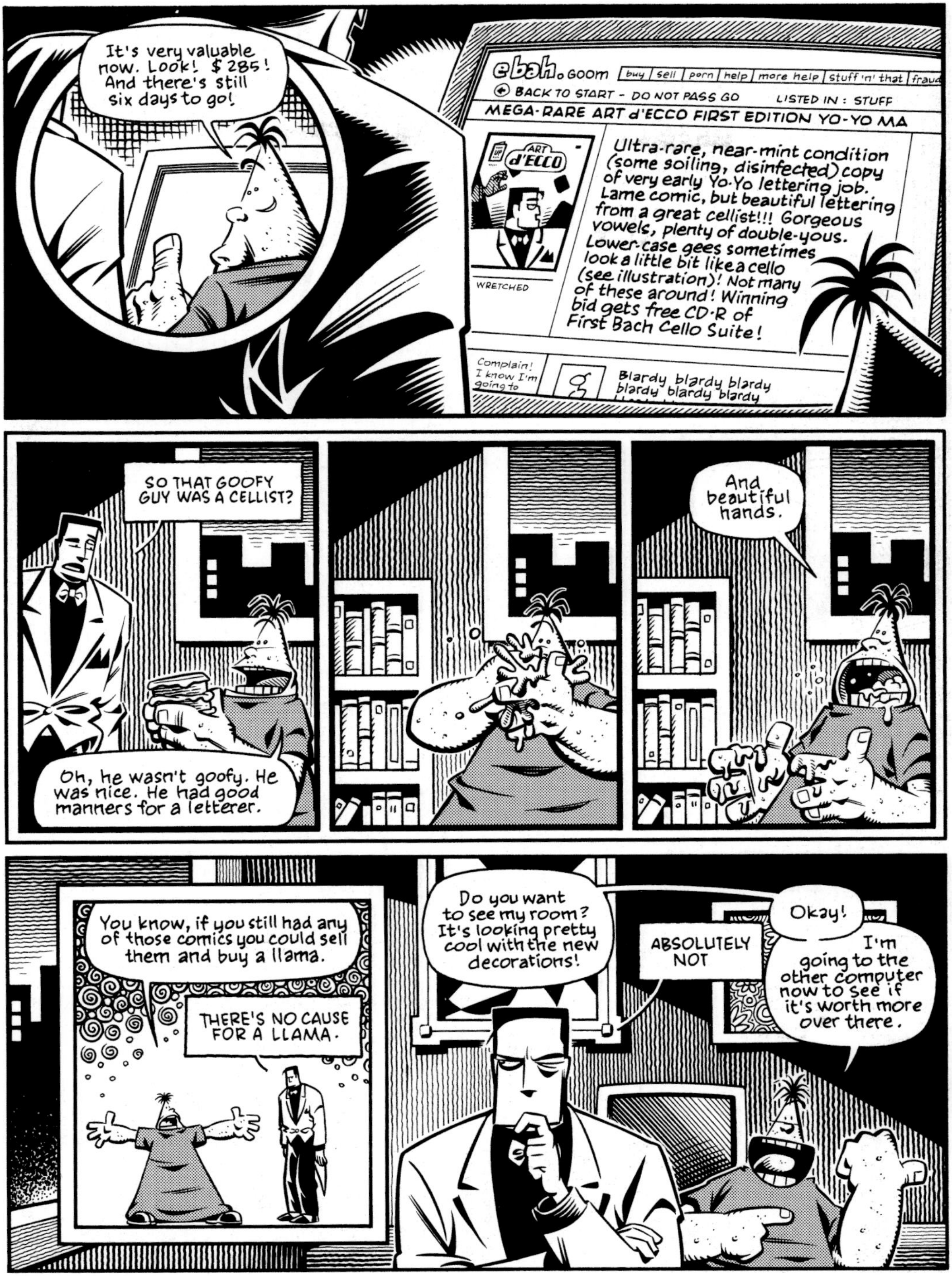

It's very valuable now. Look! $285! And there's still six days to go!
e bah. Goom
buy
sell
porn
help
more help
stuff 'n' that
BACK TO START - DO NOT PASS GO
LISTED IN : STUFF
MEGA-RARE ART d'ECCO FIRST EDITION YO-YO MA
ART d'ECCO
WRETCHED
Ultra-rare, near-mint condition (some soiling, disinfected) copy of very early Yo-Yo lettering job. Lame comic, but beautiful lettering from a great cellist!!! Gorgeous vowels, plenty of double-yous. Lower-case gees sometimes look a little bit like a cello (see illustration)! Not many of these around! Winning bid gets free CD-R of First Bach Cello Suite!
Complain! I know I'm going to
Blardy blardy blardy blardy blardy blardy
SO THAT GOOFY GUY WAS A CELLIST?
Oh, he wasn't goofy. He was nice. He had good manners for a letterer.
And beautiful hands.
You know, if you still had any of those comics you could sell them and buy a llama.
THERE'S NO CAUSE FOR A LLAMA.
Do you want to see my room? It's looking pretty cool with the new decorations!
ABSOLUTELY NOT
Okay!
I'm going to the other computer now to see if it's worth more over there.

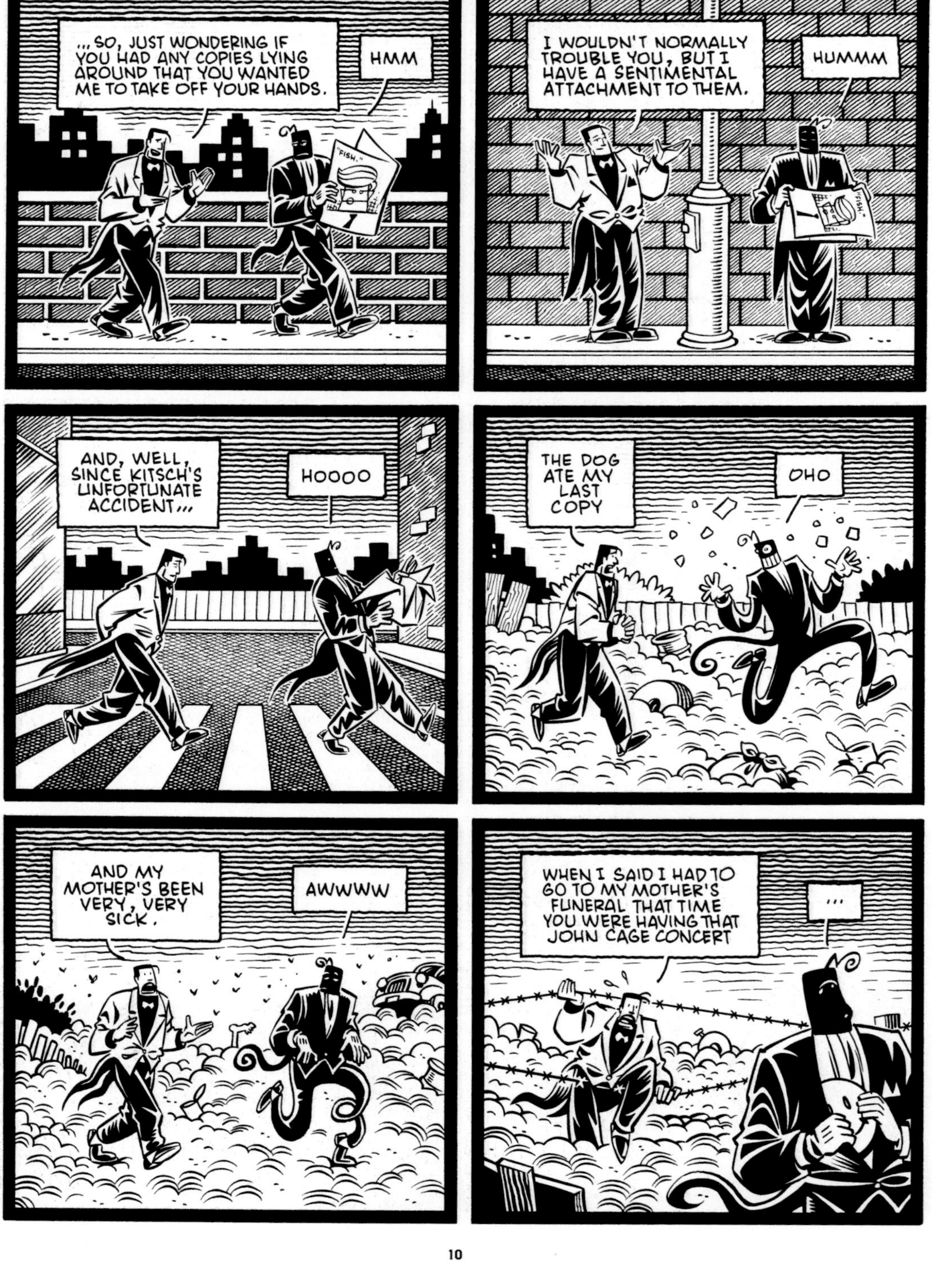

... SO, JUST WONDERING IF YOU HAD ANY COPIES LYING AROUND THAT YOU WANTED ME TO TAKE OFF YOUR HANDS.
HMM
"FISH."
I WOULDN'T NORMALLY TROUBLE YOU, BUT I HAVE A SENTIMENTAL ATTACHMENT TO THEM.
HUMMM
"FISH."
AND, WELL, SINCE KITSCH'S UNFORTUNATE ACCIDENT...
HOOOO
THE DOG ATE MY LAST COPY
OHO
AND MY MOTHER'S BEEN VERY, VERY SICK.
AWWWW
WHEN I SAID I HAD TO GO TO MY MOTHER'S FUNERAL THAT TIME YOU WERE HAVING THAT JOHN CAGE CONCERT
...

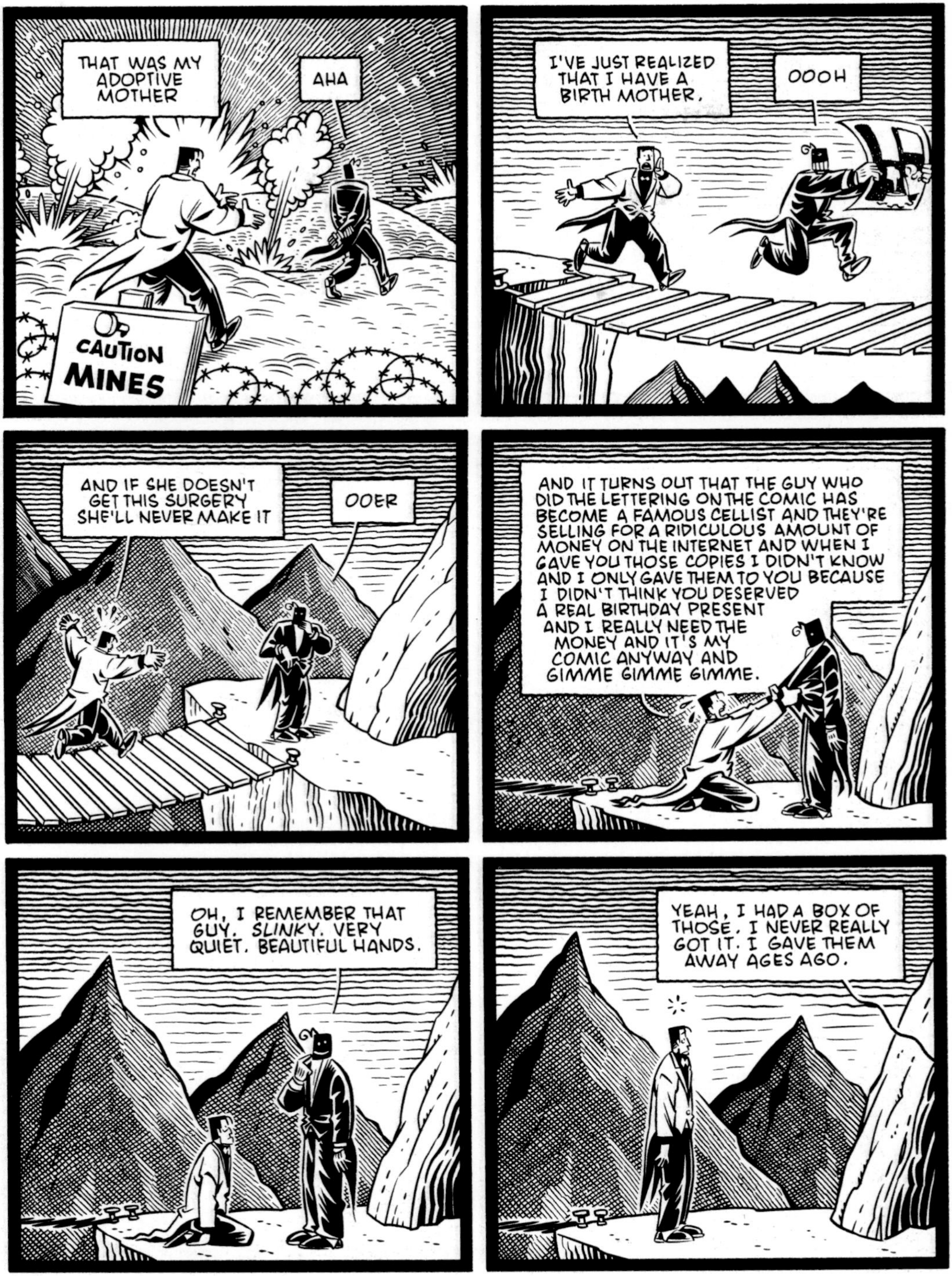
THAT WAS MY ADOPTIVE MOTHER
AHA
CAUTION MINES
I'VE JUST REALIZED THAT I HAVE A BIRTH MOTHER.
OOOH
AND IF SHE DOESN'T GET THIS SURGERY SHE'LL NEVER MAKE IT
OOER
AND IT TURNS OUT THAT THE GUY WHO DID THE LETTERING ON THE COMIC HAS BECOME A FAMOUS CELLIST AND THEY'RE SELLING FOR A RIDICULOUS AMOUNT OF MONEY ON THE INTERNET AND WHEN I GAVE YOU THOSE COPIES I DIDN'T KNOW AND I ONLY GAVE THEM TO YOU BECAUSE I DIDN'T THINK YOU DESERVED A REAL BIRTHDAY PRESENT AND I REALLY NEED THE MONEY AND IT'S MY COMIC ANYWAY AND GIMME GIMME GIMME.
OH, I REMEMBER THAT GUY. SLINKY. VERY QUIET. BEAUTIFUL HANDS.
YEAH, I HAD A BOX OF THOSE. I NEVER REALLY GOT IT. I GAVE THEM AWAY AGES AGO.

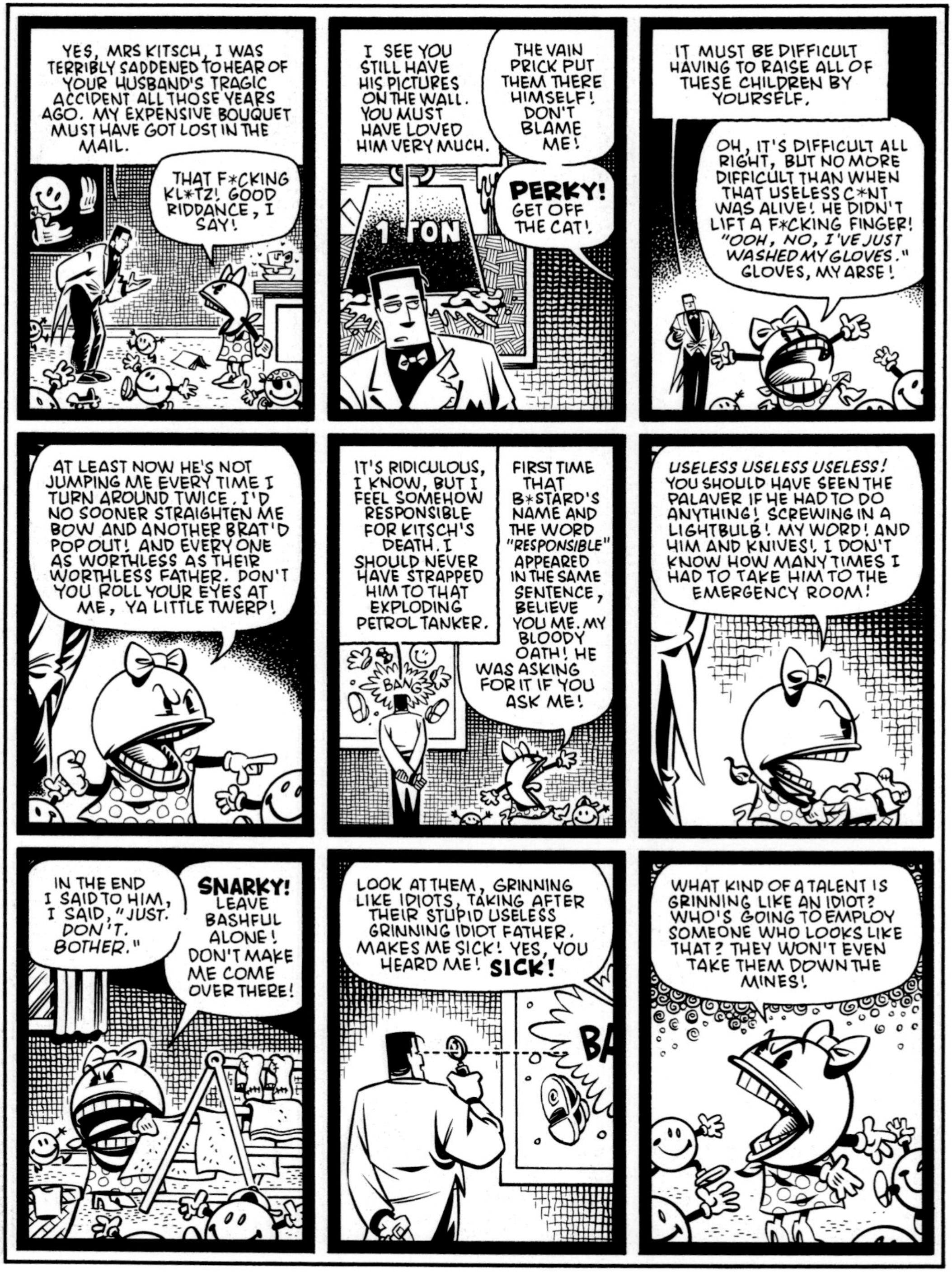

YES, MRS KITSCH, I WAS TERRIBLY SADDENED TO HEAR OF YOUR HUSBAND'S TRAGIC ACCIDENT ALL THOSE YEARS AGO. MY EXPENSIVE BOUQUET MUST HAVE GOT LOST IN THE MAIL.
THAT F*CKING KL*TZ! GOOD RIDDANCE, I SAY!
I SEE YOU STILL HAVE HIS PICTURES ON THE WALL. YOU MUST HAVE LOVED HIM VERY MUCH.
THE VAIN PRICK PUT THEM THERE HIMSELF! DON'T BLAME ME!
1 TON
PERKY! GET OFF THE CAT!
IT MUST BE DIFFICULT HAVING TO RAISE ALL OF THESE CHILDREN BY YOURSELF.
OH, IT'S DIFFICULT ALL RIGHT, BUT NO MORE DIFFICULT THAN WHEN THAT USELESS C*NT WAS ALIVE! HE DIDN'T LIFT A F*CKING FINGER! "OOH, NO, I'VE JUST WASHED MY GLOVES." GLOVES, MY ARSE!
AT LEAST NOW HE'S NOT JUMPING ME EVERY TIME I TURN AROUND TWICE. I'D NO SOONER STRAIGHTEN ME BOW AND ANOTHER BRAT'D POP OUT! AND EVERY ONE AS WORTHLESS AS THEIR WORTHLESS FATHER. DON'T YOU ROLL YOUR EYES AT ME, YA LITTLE TWERP!
IT'S RIDICULOUS, I KNOW, BUT I FEEL SOMEHOW RESPONSIBLE FOR KITSCH'S DEATH. I SHOULD NEVER HAVE STRAPPED HIM TO THAT EXPLODING PETROL TANKER.
FIRST TIME THAT B*STARD'S NAME AND THE WORD "RESPONSIBLE" APPEARED IN THE SAME SENTENCE, BELIEVE YOU ME. MY BLOODY OATH! HE WAS ASKING FOR IT IF YOU ASK ME!
BANG
USELESS USELESS USELESS! YOU SHOULD HAVE SEEN THE PALAVER IF HE HAD TO DO ANYTHING! SCREWING IN A LIGHTBULB! MY WORD! AND HIM AND KNIVES! I DON'T KNOW HOW MANY TIMES I HAD TO TAKE HIM TO THE EMERGENCY ROOM!
IN THE END I SAID TO HIM, I SAID, "JUST. DON'T. BOTHER."
SNARKY! LEAVE BASHFUL ALONE! DON'T MAKE ME COME OVER THERE!
LOOK AT THEM, GRINNING LIKE IDIOTS, TAKING AFTER THEIR STUPID USELESS GRINNING IDIOT FATHER. MAKES ME SICK! YES, YOU HEARD ME! SICK!
WHAT KIND OF A TALENT IS GRINNING LIKE AN IDIOT? WHO'S GOING TO EMPLOY SOMEONE WHO LOOKS LIKE THAT? THEY WON'T EVEN TAKE THEM DOWN THE MINES!

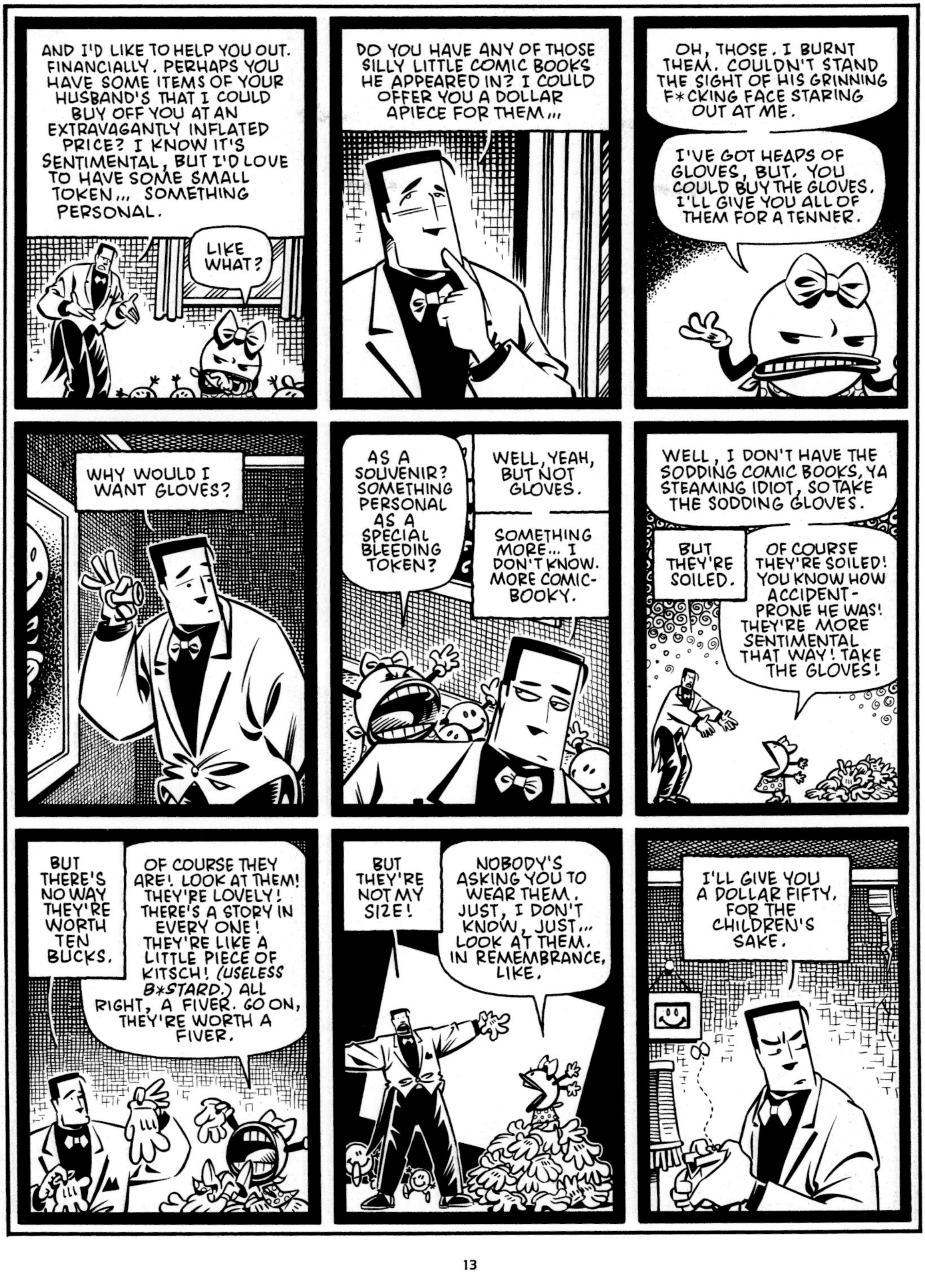

AND I'D LIKE TO HELP YOU OUT. FINANCIALLY. PERHAPS YOU HAVE SOME ITEMS OF YOUR HUSBAND'S THAT I COULD BUY OFF YOU AT AN EXTRAVAGANTLY INFLATED PRICE? I KNOW IT'S SENTIMENTAL, BUT I'D LOVE TO HAVE SOME SMALL TOKEN... SOMETHING PERSONAL.
LIKE WHAT?
DO YOU HAVE ANY OF THOSE SILLY LITTLE COMIC BOOKS HE APPEARED IN? I COULD OFFER YOU A DOLLAR APIECE FOR THEM...
OH, THOSE. I BURNT THEM. COULDN'T STAND THE SIGHT OF HIS GRINNING F*CKING FACE STARING OUT AT ME.
I'VE GOT HEAPS OF GLOVES, BUT. YOU COULD BUY THE GLOVES. I'LL GIVE YOU ALL OF THEM FOR A TENNER.
WHY WOULD I WANT GLOVES?
AS A SOUVENIR? SOMETHING PERSONAL AS A SPECIAL BLEEDING TOKEN?
WELL, YEAH, BUT NOT GLOVES.
SOMETHING MORE... I DON'T KNOW. MORE COMIC-BOOKY.
WELL, I DON'T HAVE THE SODDING COMIC BOOKS, YA STEAMING IDIOT, SO TAKE THE SODDING GLOVES.
BUT THEY'RE SOILED.
OF COURSE THEY'RE SOILED! YOU KNOW HOW ACCIDENT-PRONE HE WAS! THEY'RE MORE SENTIMENTAL THAT WAY! TAKE THE GLOVES!
BUT THERE'S NO WAY THEY'RE WORTH TEN BUCKS.
OF COURSE THEY ARE! LOOK AT THEM! THEY'RE LOVELY! THERE'S A STORY IN EVERY ONE! THEY'RE LIKE A LITTLE PIECE OF KITSCH! (USELESS B*STARD.) ALL RIGHT, A FIVER. GO ON, THEY'RE WORTH A FIVER.
BUT THEY'RE NOT MY SIZE!
NOBODY'S ASKING YOU TO WEAR THEM. JUST, I DON'T KNOW, JUST... LOOK AT THEM. IN REMEMBRANCE, LIKE.
I'LL GIVE YOU A DOLLAR FIFTY, FOR THE CHILDREN'S SAKE.

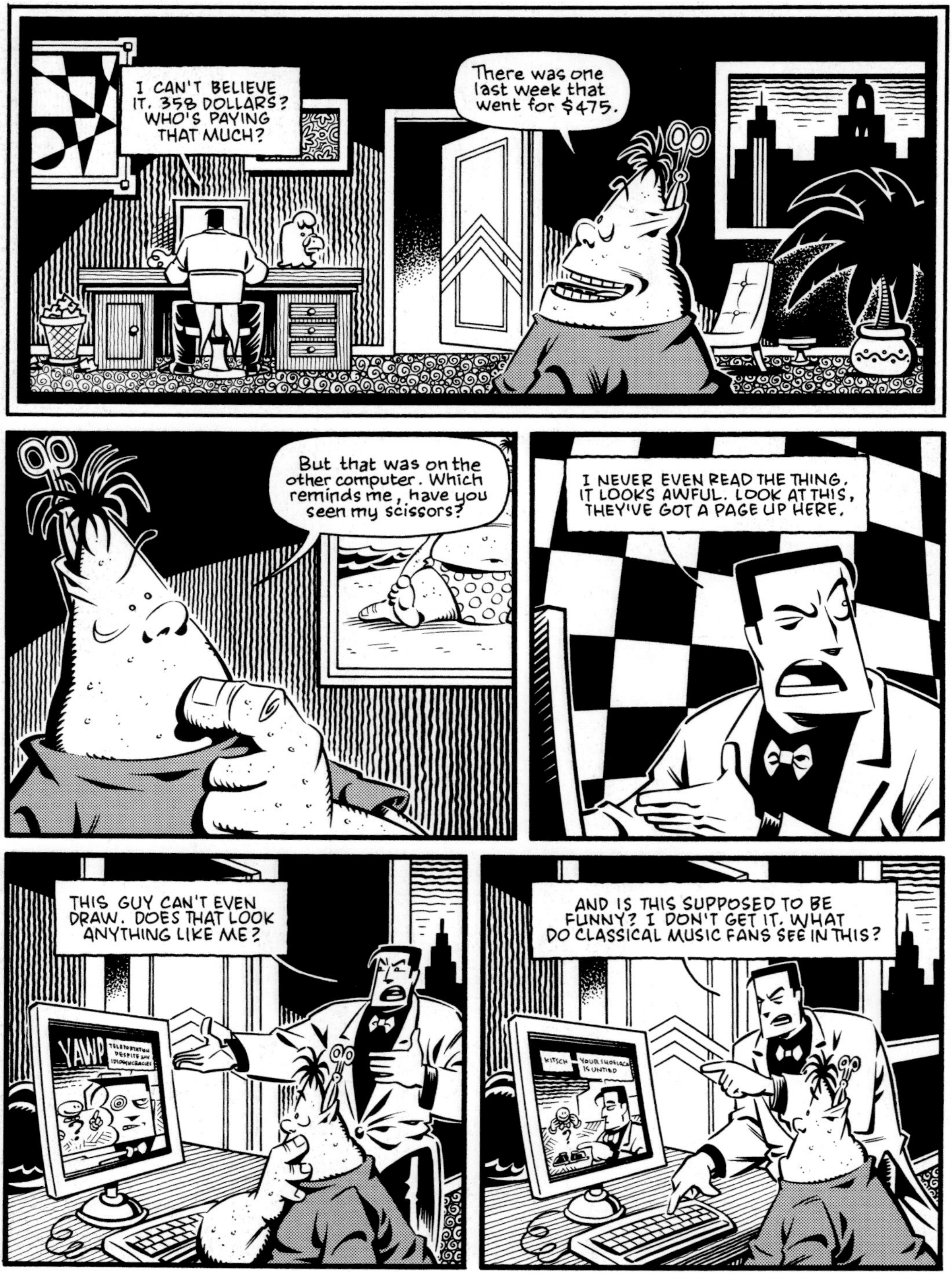
I CAN'T BELIEVE IT. 358 DOLLARS? WHO'S PAYING THAT MUCH?
There was one last week that went for $475.
But that was on the other computer. Which reminds me, have you seen my scissors?
I NEVER EVEN READ THE THING. IT LOOKS AWFUL. LOOK AT THIS, THEY'VE GOT A PAGE UP HERE.
THIS GUY CAN'T EVEN DRAW. DOES THAT LOOK ANYTHING LIKE ME?
YAWP
AND IS THIS SUPPOSED TO BE FUNNY? I DON'T GET IT. WHAT DO CLASSICAL MUSIC FANS SEE IN THIS?
KITSCH

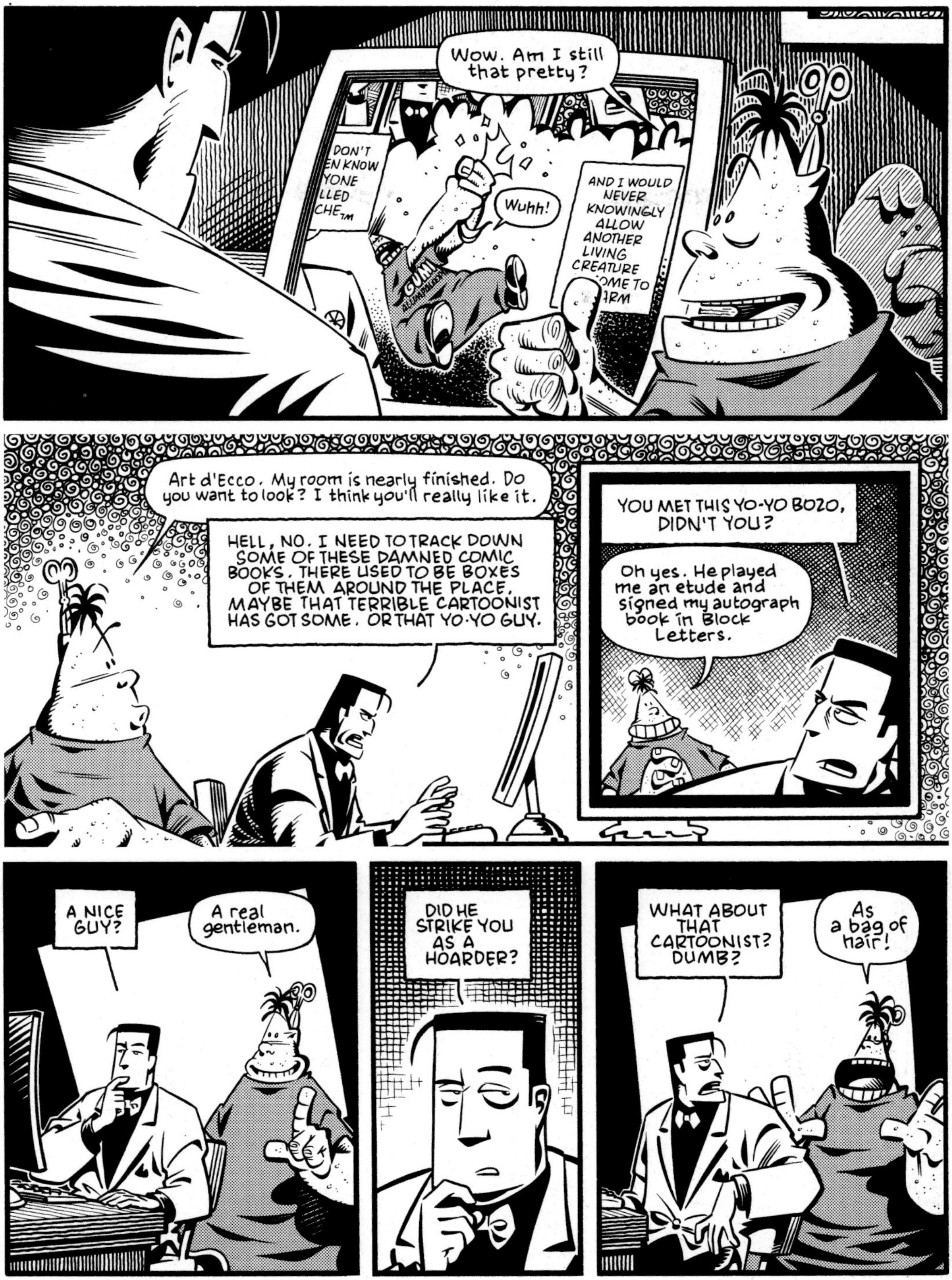
Wow. Am I still that pretty?
DON'T ...EN KNOW ...YONE ...LLED ...CHE TM
Wuhh!
AND I WOULD NEVER KNOWINGLY ALLOW ANOTHER LIVING CREATURE ...OME TO ...ARM
Art d'Ecco. My room is nearly finished. Do you want to look? I think you'll really like it.
HELL, NO. I NEED TO TRACK DOWN SOME OF THESE DAMNED COMIC BOOKS. THERE USED TO BE BOXES OF THEM AROUND THE PLACE. MAYBE THAT TERRIBLE CARTOONIST HAS GOT SOME. OR THAT YO-YO GUY.
YOU MET THIS YO-YO BOZO, DIDN'T YOU?
Oh yes. He played me an etude and signed my autograph book in Block Letters.
A NICE GUY?
A real gentleman.
DID HE STRIKE YOU AS A HOARDER?
WHAT ABOUT THAT CARTOONIST? DUMB?
As a bag of hair!

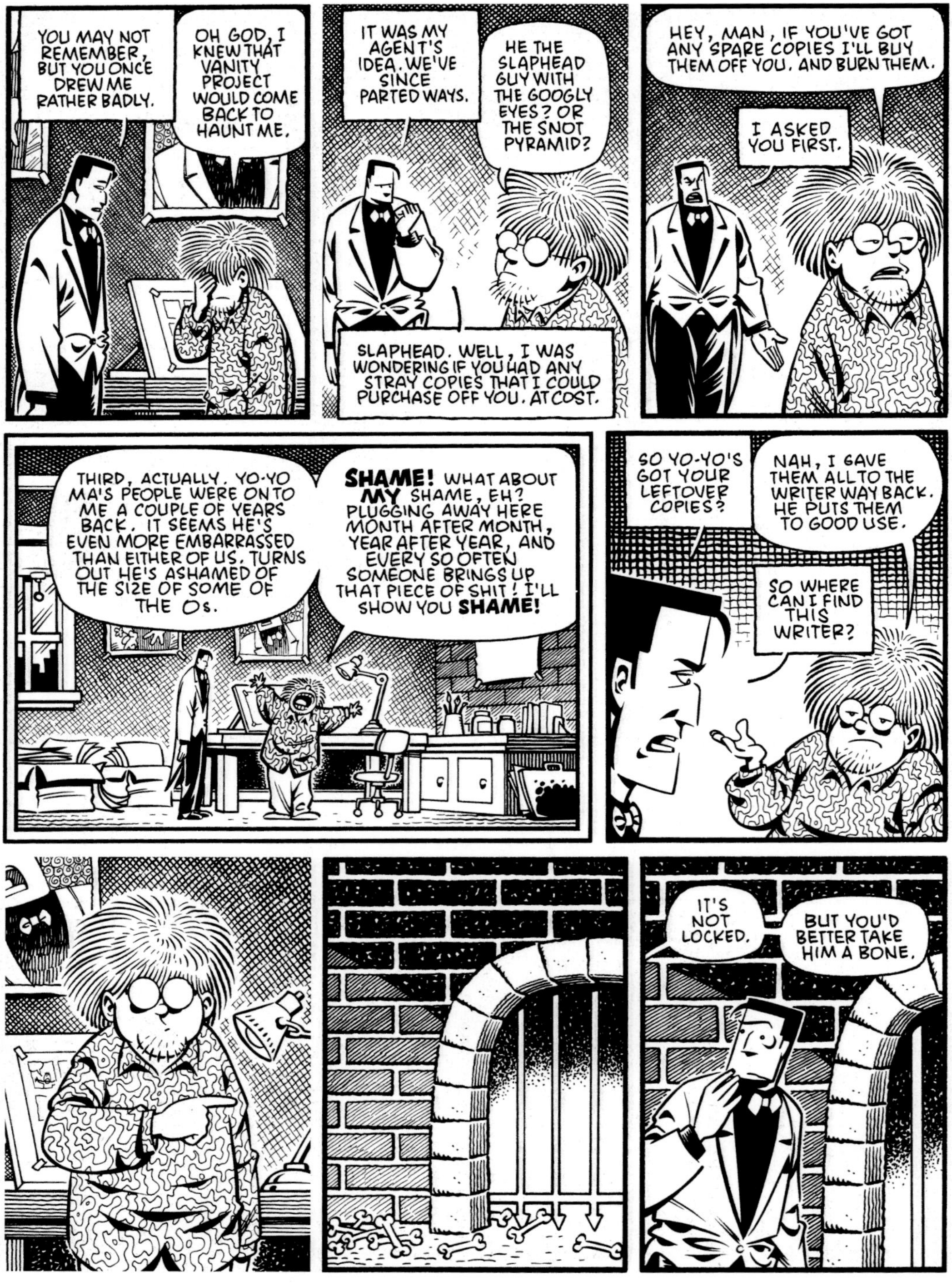
YOU MAY NOT REMEMBER, BUT YOU ONCE DREW ME RATHER BADLY.
OH GOD, I KNEW THAT VANITY PROJECT WOULD COME BACK TO HAUNT ME.
IT WAS MY AGENT'S IDEA. WE'VE SINCE PARTED WAYS.
HE THE SLAPHEAD GUY WITH THE GOOGLY EYES? OR THE SNOT PYRAMID?
SLAPHEAD. WELL, I WAS WONDERING IF YOU HAD ANY STRAY COPIES THAT I COULD PURCHASE OFF YOU. AT COST.
HEY, MAN, IF YOU'VE GOT ANY SPARE COPIES I'LL BUY THEM OFF YOU. AND BURN THEM.
I ASKED YOU FIRST.
THIRD, ACTUALLY. YO-YO MA'S PEOPLE WERE ONTO ME A COUPLE OF YEARS BACK. IT SEEMS HE'S EVEN MORE EMBARRASSED THAN EITHER OF US. TURNS OUT HE'S ASHAMED OF THE SIZE OF SOME OF THE Os.
SHAME! WHAT ABOUT MY SHAME, EH? PLUGGING AWAY HERE MONTH AFTER MONTH, YEAR AFTER YEAR, AND EVERY SO OFTEN SOMEONE BRINGS UP THAT PIECE OF SHIT! I'LL SHOW YOU SHAME!
SO YO-YO'S GOT YOUR LEFTOVER COPIES?
NAH, I GAVE THEM ALL TO THE WRITER WAY BACK. HE PUTS THEM TO GOOD USE.
SO WHERE CAN I FIND THIS WRITER?
IT'S NOT LOCKED.
BUT YOU'D BETTER TAKE HIM A BONE.

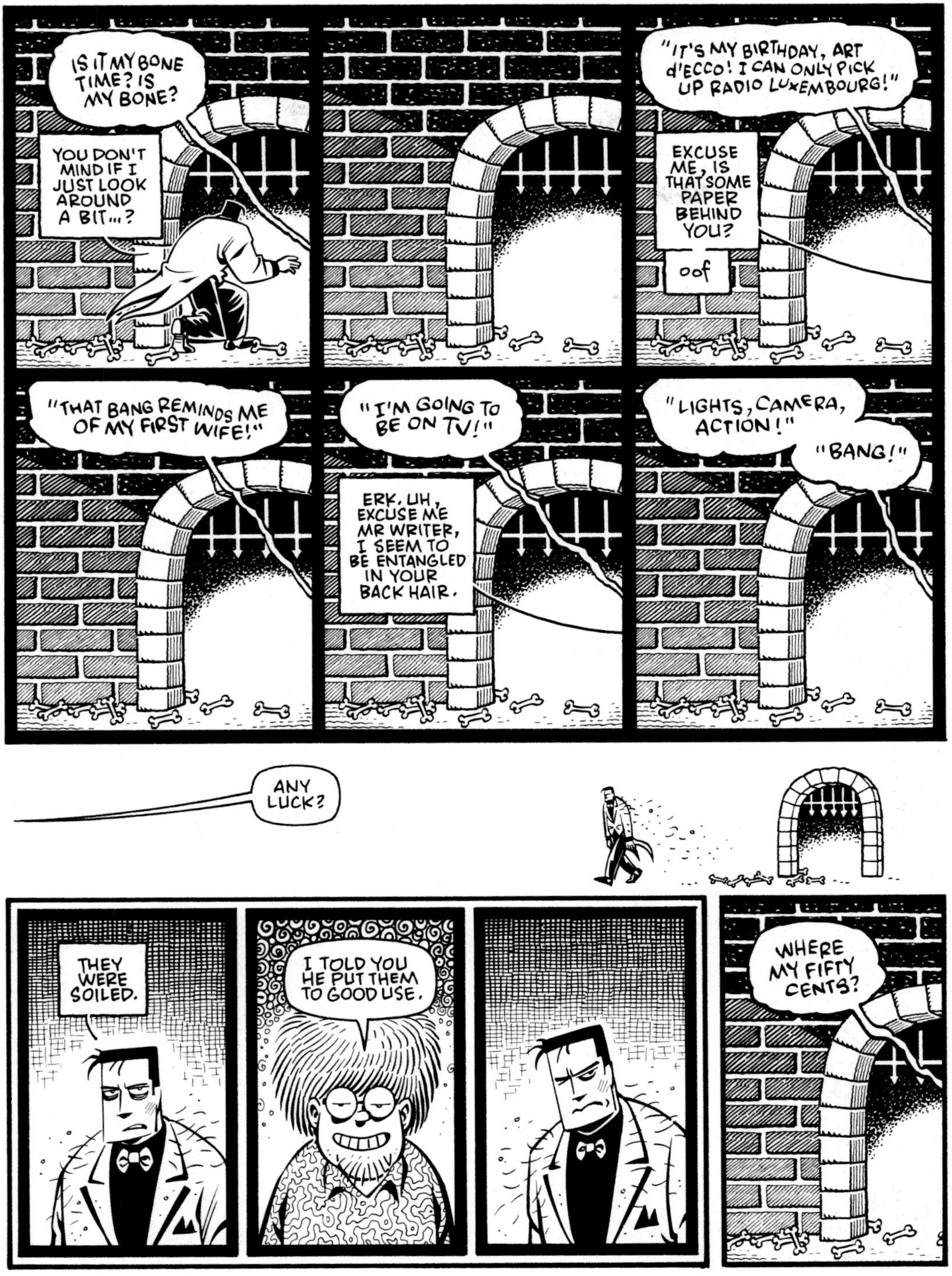
IS IT MY BONE TIME? IS MY BONE?
YOU DON'T MIND IF I JUST LOOK AROUND A BIT...?
"IT'S MY BIRTHDAY, ART d'ECCO! I CAN ONLY PICK UP RADIO LUXEMBOURG!"
EXCUSE ME, IS THAT SOME PAPER BEHIND YOU?
oof
"THAT BANG REMINDS ME OF MY FIRST WIFE!"
"I'M GOING TO BE ON TV!"
ERK, UH, EXCUSE ME MR WRITER, I SEEM TO BE ENTANGLED IN YOUR BACK HAIR.
"LIGHTS, CAMERA, ACTION!"
"BANG!"
ANY LUCK?
THEY WERE SOILED.
I TOLD YOU HE PUT THEM TO GOOD USE.
WHERE MY FIFTY CENTS?

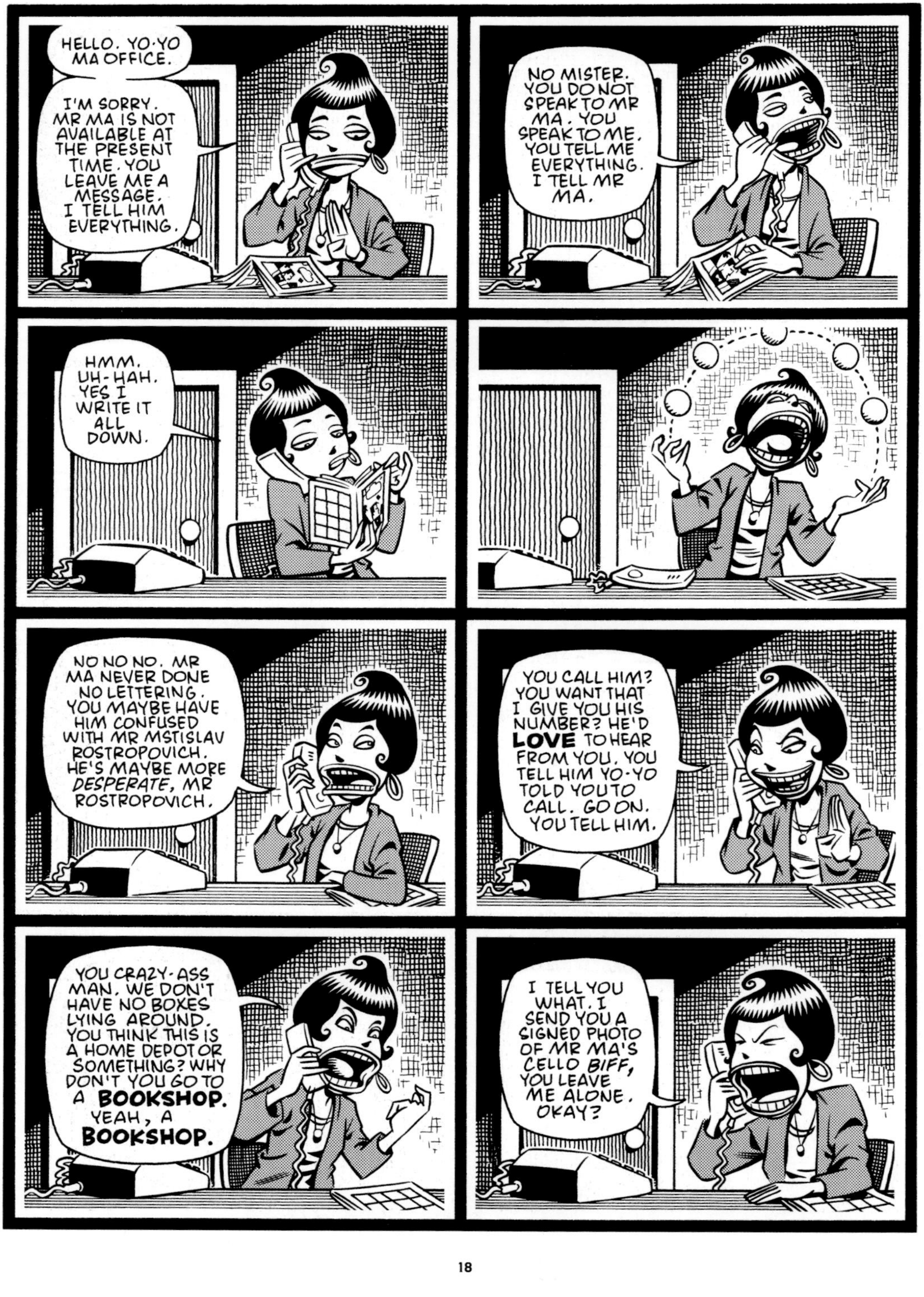

HELLO. YO-YO MA OFFICE.
I'M SORRY. MR MA IS NOT AVAILABLE AT THE PRESENT TIME. YOU LEAVE ME A MESSAGE. I TELL HIM EVERYTHING.
NO MISTER. YOU DO NOT SPEAK TO MR MA. YOU SPEAK TO ME. YOU TELL ME EVERYTHING. I TELL MR MA.
HMM. UH-HAH. YES I WRITE IT ALL DOWN.
NO NO NO. MR MA NEVER DONE NO LETTERING. YOU MAYBE HAVE HIM CONFUSED WITH MR MSTISLAV ROSTROPOVICH. HE'S MAYBE MORE *DESPERATE*, MR ROSTROPOVICH.
YOU CALL HIM? YOU WANT THAT I GIVE YOU HIS NUMBER? HE'D **LOVE** TO HEAR FROM YOU. YOU TELL HIM YO-YO TOLD YOU TO CALL. GO ON. YOU TELL HIM.
YOU CRAZY-ASS MAN. WE DON'T HAVE NO BOXES LYING AROUND. YOU THINK THIS IS A HOME DEPOT OR SOMETHING? WHY DON'T YOU GO TO A **BOOKSHOP.** YEAH, A **BOOKSHOP.**
I TELL YOU WHAT. I SEND YOU A SIGNED PHOTO OF MR MA'S CELLO *BIFF*, YOU LEAVE ME ALONE. OKAY?

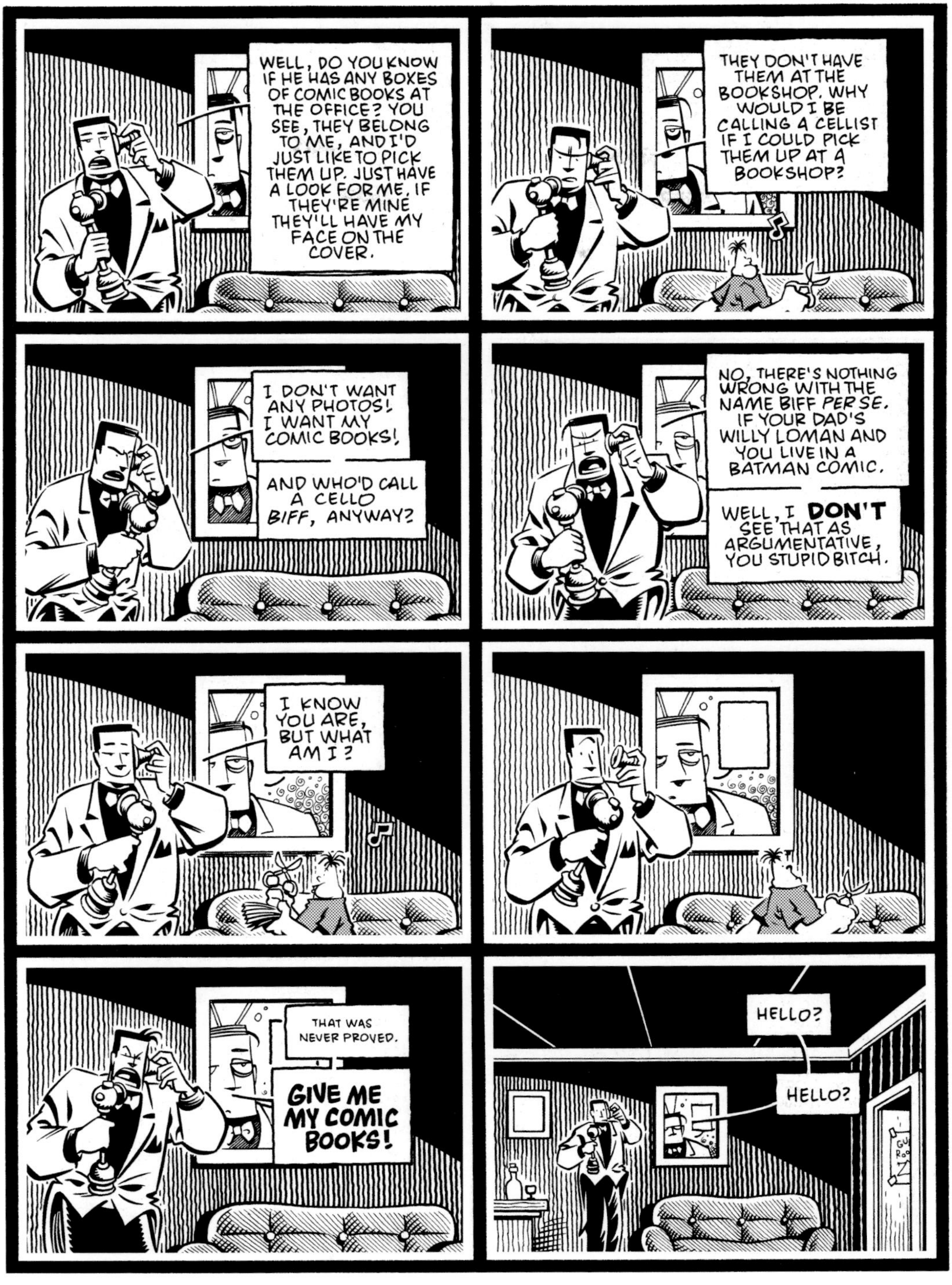
WELL, DO YOU KNOW IF HE HAS ANY BOXES OF COMIC BOOKS AT THE OFFICE? YOU SEE, THEY BELONG TO ME, AND I'D JUST LIKE TO PICK THEM UP. JUST HAVE A LOOK FOR ME, IF THEY'RE MINE THEY'LL HAVE MY FACE ON THE COVER.
THEY DON'T HAVE THEM AT THE BOOKSHOP. WHY WOULD I BE CALLING A CELLIST IF I COULD PICK THEM UP AT A BOOKSHOP?
I DON'T WANT ANY PHOTOS! I WANT MY COMIC BOOKS!
AND WHO'D CALL A CELLO BIFF, ANYWAY?
NO, THERE'S NOTHING WRONG WITH THE NAME BIFF PER SE. IF YOUR DAD'S WILLY LOMAN AND YOU LIVE IN A BATMAN COMIC.
WELL, I DON'T SEE THAT AS ARGUMENTATIVE, YOU STUPID BITCH.
I KNOW YOU ARE, BUT WHAT AM I?
THAT WAS NEVER PROVED.
GIVE ME MY COMIC BOOKS!
HELLO?
HELLO?

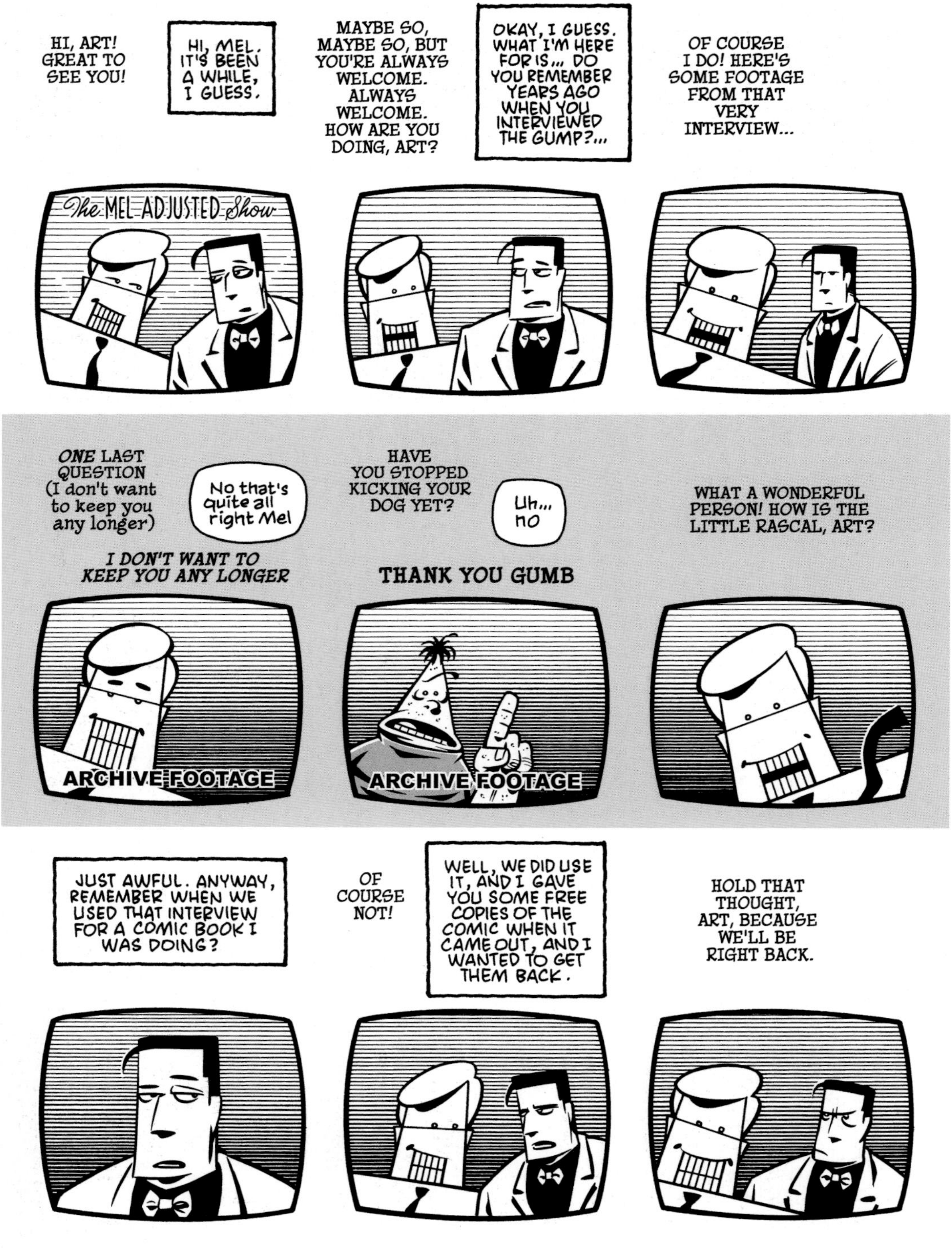
HI, ART! GREAT TO SEE YOU!
HI, MEL. IT'S BEEN A WHILE, I GUESS.
MAYBE SO, MAYBE SO, BUT YOU'RE ALWAYS WELCOME. ALWAYS WELCOME. HOW ARE YOU DOING, ART?
OKAY, I GUESS. WHAT I'M HERE FOR IS... DO YOU REMEMBER YEARS AGO WHEN YOU INTERVIEWED THE GUMP?...
OF COURSE I DO! HERE'S SOME FOOTAGE FROM THAT VERY INTERVIEW...
The MEL ADJUSTED Show
ONE LAST QUESTION (I don't want to keep you any longer)
No that's quite all right Mel
I DON'T WANT TO KEEP YOU ANY LONGER
HAVE YOU STOPPED KICKING YOUR DOG YET?
Uh... no
THANK YOU GUMB
WHAT A WONDERFUL PERSON! HOW IS THE LITTLE RASCAL, ART?
ARCHIVE FOOTAGE
ARCHIVE FOOTAGE
JUST AWFUL. ANYWAY, REMEMBER WHEN WE USED THAT INTERVIEW FOR A COMIC BOOK I WAS DOING?
OF COURSE NOT!
WELL, WE DID USE IT, AND I GAVE YOU SOME FREE COPIES OF THE COMIC WHEN IT CAME OUT, AND I WANTED TO GET THEM BACK.
HOLD THAT THOUGHT, ART, BECAUSE WE'LL BE RIGHT BACK.

WELCOME BACK. I'M TALKING TO ART d'ECCO. FORMER CHILD STAR. HOUSEMATE OF A VERY SPECIAL GUEST FROM YEARS PAST, *THE GUMP*. AND NOW, ART, I HEAR YOU'RE APPEARING IN A COMIC BOOK. WOULD YOU LIKE TO TELL THE STUDIO AUDIENCE SOMETHING ABOUT THAT.

MEL, WE'RE NOT *ON* TELEVISION. THERE IS NO STUDIO AUDIENCE.

SUCH A KIDDER, ART. FOLKS, ISN'T HE A PEACH?

MEL, YOU'RE LIVING UNDER A BRIDGE. NO STUDIO, NO AUDIENCE, NO CAMERA.

LOOK.

SEE?

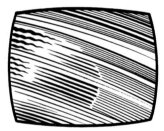

CAN YOU PUT IT BACK THE WAY IT WAS NOW?

SO, HAVE YOU GOT ANY COMICS?

SOLD THEM FOR FOOD

THANK YOU. GOODBYE.

OKAY, FOLKS, LET'S HAVE A BIG HAND FOR MY EXTRA-SPECIAL GUEST, ART d'ECCO!

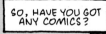
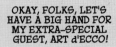

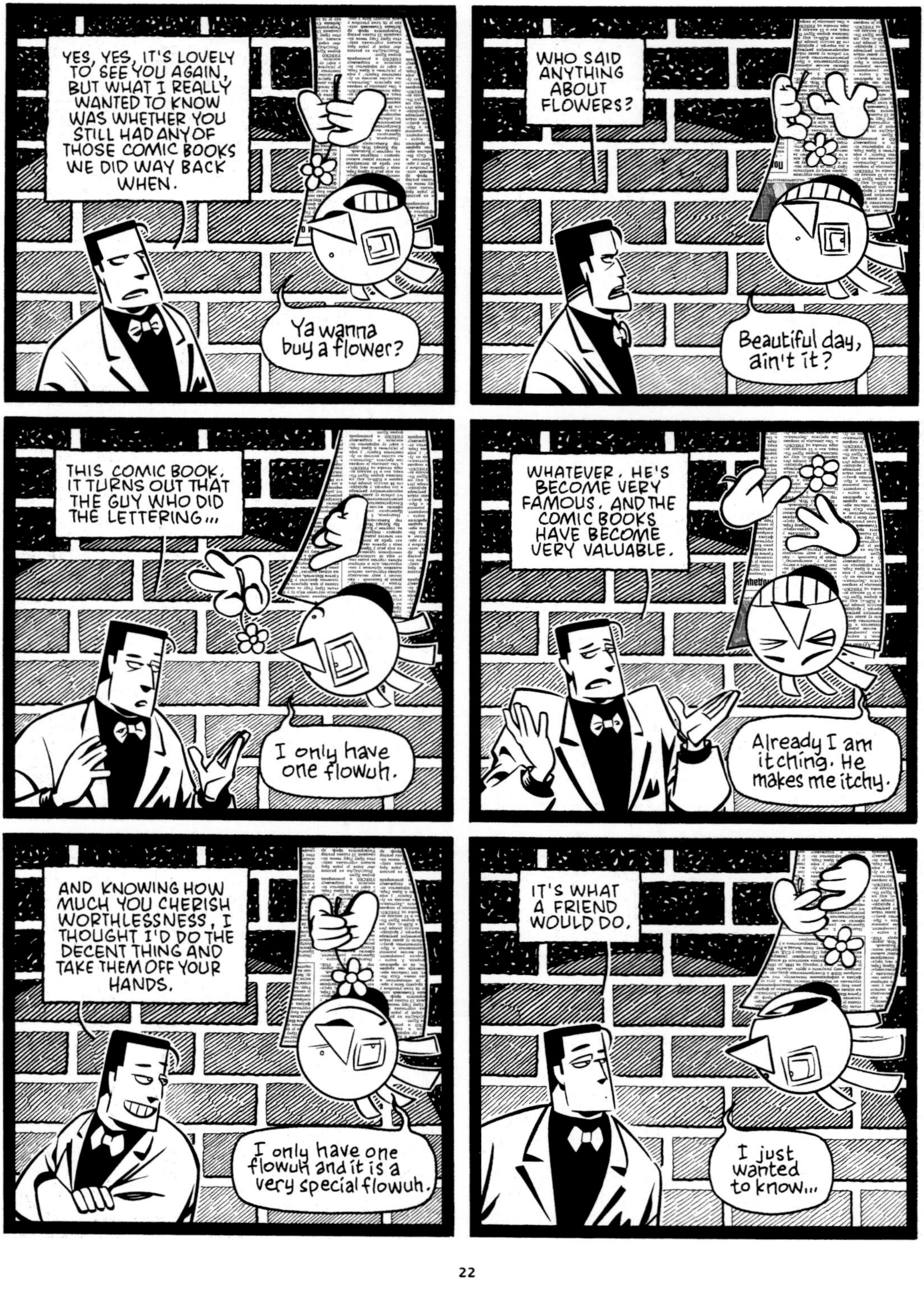
YES, YES, IT'S LOVELY TO SEE YOU AGAIN, BUT WHAT I REALLY WANTED TO KNOW WAS WHETHER YOU STILL HAD ANY OF THOSE COMIC BOOKS WE DID WAY BACK WHEN.
Ya wanna buy a flower?
WHO SAID ANYTHING ABOUT FLOWERS?
Beautiful day, ain't it?
THIS COMIC BOOK, IT TURNS OUT THAT THE GUY WHO DID THE LETTERING...
I only have one flowuh.
WHATEVER. HE'S BECOME VERY FAMOUS. AND THE COMIC BOOKS HAVE BECOME VERY VALUABLE.
Already I am itching. He makes me itchy.
AND KNOWING HOW MUCH YOU CHERISH WORTHLESSNESS, I THOUGHT I'D DO THE DECENT THING AND TAKE THEM OFF YOUR HANDS.
I only have one flowuh and it is a very special flowuh.
IT'S WHAT A FRIEND WOULD DO.
I just wanted to know...

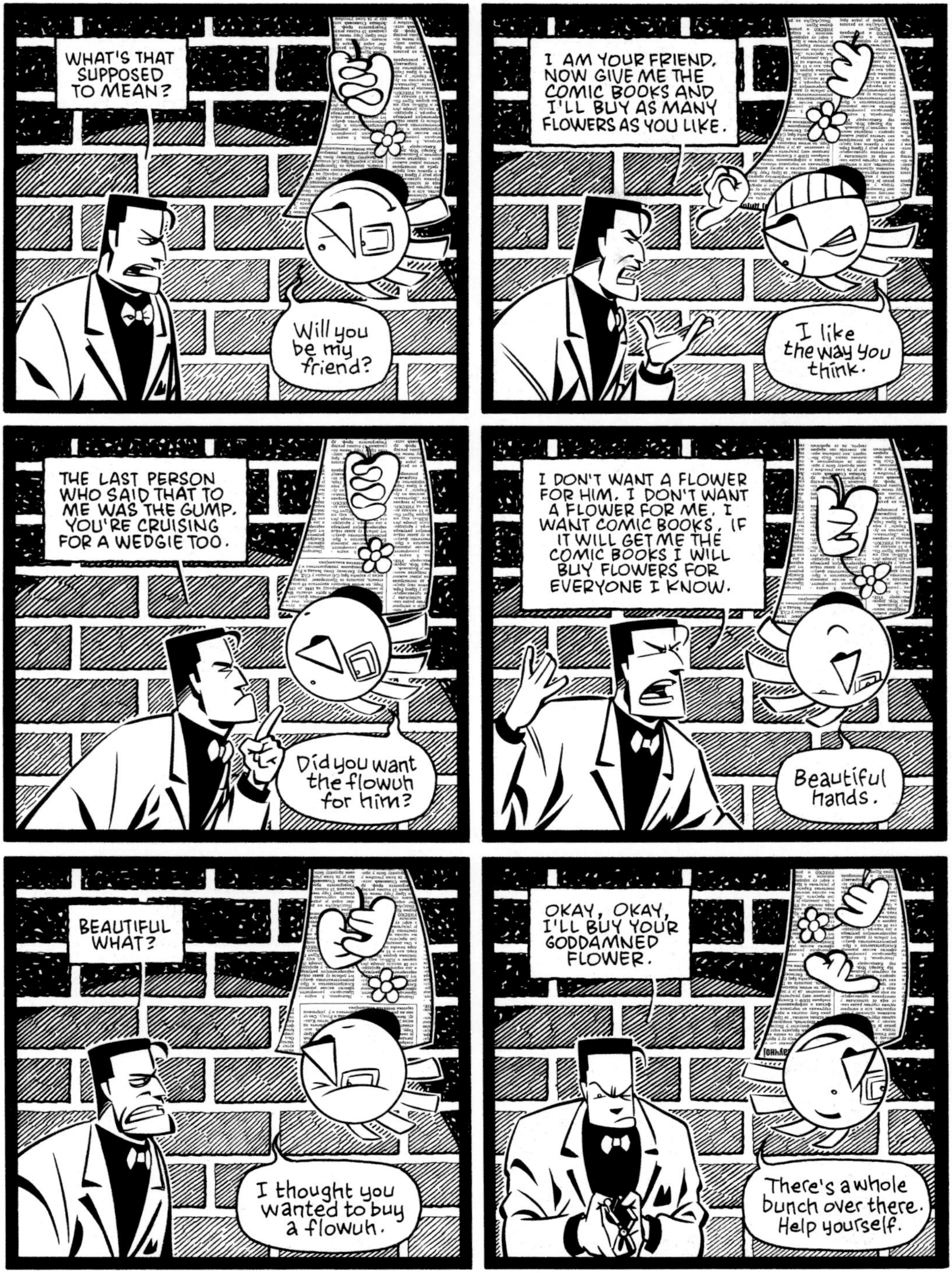
WHAT'S THAT SUPPOSED TO MEAN?
Will you be my friend?
I AM YOUR FRIEND, NOW GIVE ME THE COMIC BOOKS AND I'LL BUY AS MANY FLOWERS AS YOU LIKE.
I like the way you think.
THE LAST PERSON WHO SAID THAT TO ME WAS THE GUMP. YOU'RE CRUISING FOR A WEDGIE TOO.
Did you want the flowuh for him?
I DON'T WANT A FLOWER FOR HIM. I DON'T WANT A FLOWER FOR ME, I WANT COMIC BOOKS, IF IT WILL GET ME THE COMIC BOOKS I WILL BUY FLOWERS FOR EVERYONE I KNOW.
Beautiful hands.
BEAUTIFUL WHAT?
I thought you wanted to buy a flowuh.
OKAY, OKAY, I'LL BUY YOUR GODDAMNED FLOWER.
There's a whole bunch over there. Help yourself.

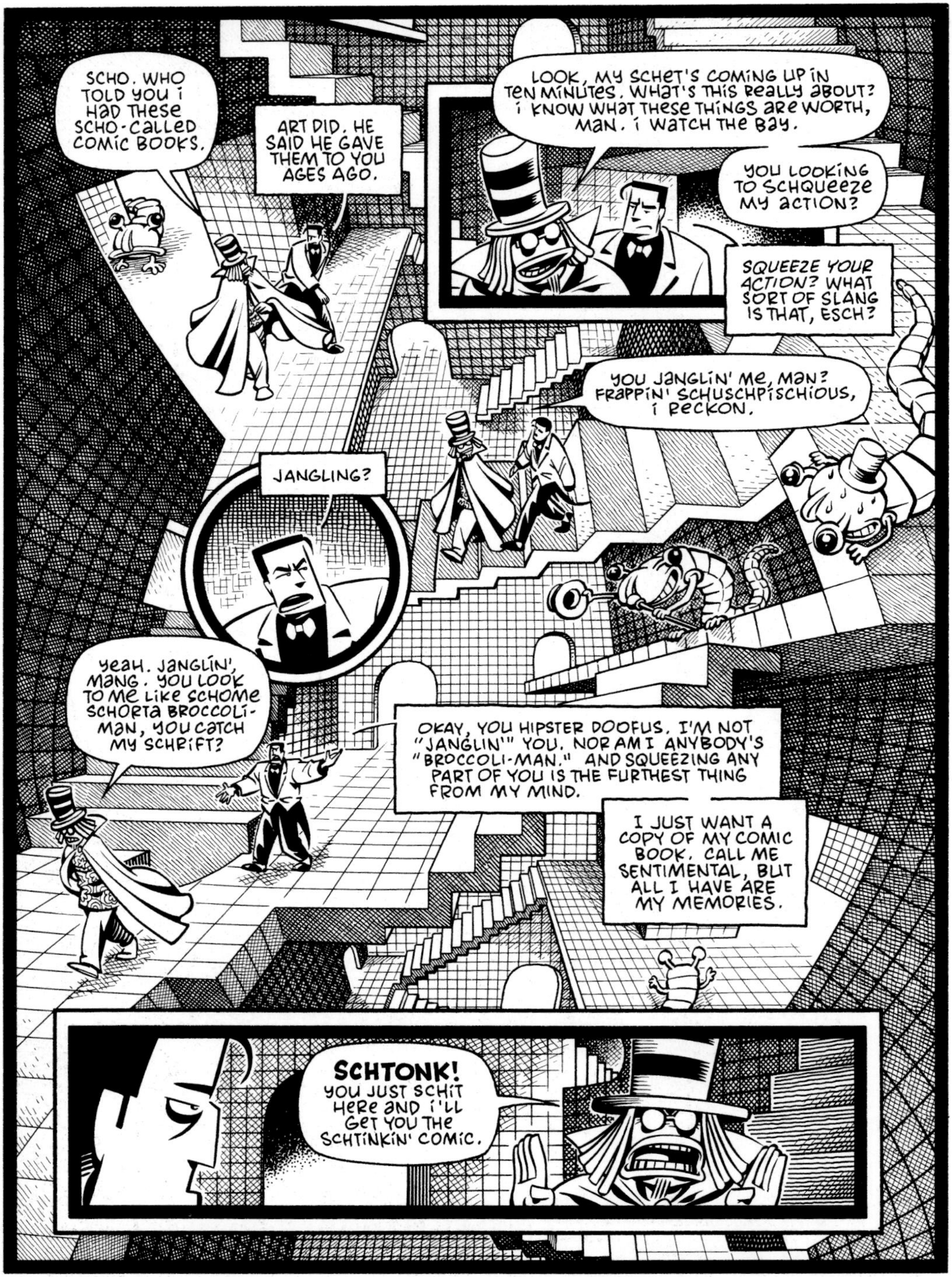
SCHO. WHO TOLD YOU I HAD THESE SCHO-CALLED COMIC BOOKS.
ART DID. HE SAID HE GAVE THEM TO YOU AGES AGO.
LOOK, MY SCHET'S COMING UP IN TEN MINUTES. WHAT'S THIS REALLY ABOUT? I KNOW WHAT THESE THINGS ARE WORTH, MAN. I WATCH THE BAY.
YOU LOOKING TO SCHQUEEZE MY ACTION?
SQUEEZE YOUR ACTION? WHAT SORT OF SLANG IS THAT, ESCH?
YOU JANGLIN' ME, MAN? FRAPPIN' SCHUSCHPISCHIOUS, I RECKON.
JANGLING?
YEAH. JANGLIN', MANG. YOU LOOK TO ME LIKE SCHOME SCHORTA BROCCOLI-MAN, YOU CATCH MY SCHRIFT?
OKAY, YOU HIPSTER DOOFUS, I'M NOT "JANGLIN'" YOU. NOR AM I ANYBODY'S "BROCCOLI-MAN." AND SQUEEZING ANY PART OF YOU IS THE FURTHEST THING FROM MY MIND.
I JUST WANT A COPY OF MY COMIC BOOK. CALL ME SENTIMENTAL, BUT ALL I HAVE ARE MY MEMORIES.
SCHTONK! YOU JUST SCHIT HERE AND I'LL GET YOU THE SCHTINKIN' COMIC.

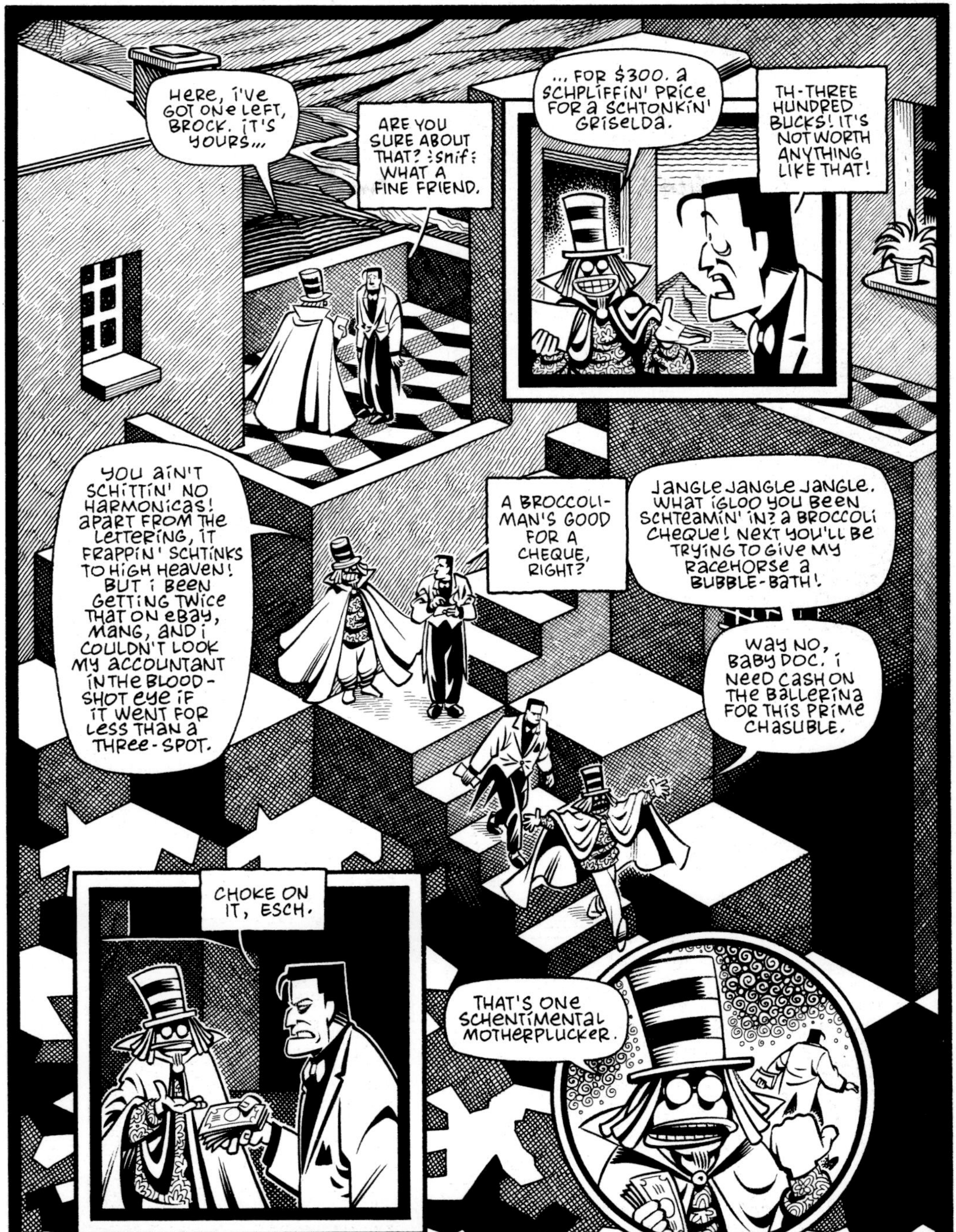
Here, i've got one left, Brock. it's yours...
Are you sure about that? :snif: What a fine friend.
..., for $300. a schpliffin' price for a schtonkin' Griselda.
Th-three hundred bucks! it's not worth anything like that!
You ain't schittin' no harmonicas! apart from the lettering, it frappin' schtinks to high heaven! But i been getting twice that on eBay, mang, and i couldn't look my accountant in the blood-shot eye if it went for less than a three-spot.
A broccoli-man's good for a cheque, right?
Jangle jangle jangle. What igloo you been schteamin' in? a broccoli cheque! Next you'll be trying to give my racehorse a bubble-bath!
Way no, Baby Doc. i need cash on the ballerina for this prime chasuble.
Choke on it, Esch.
That's one schentimental motherplucker.

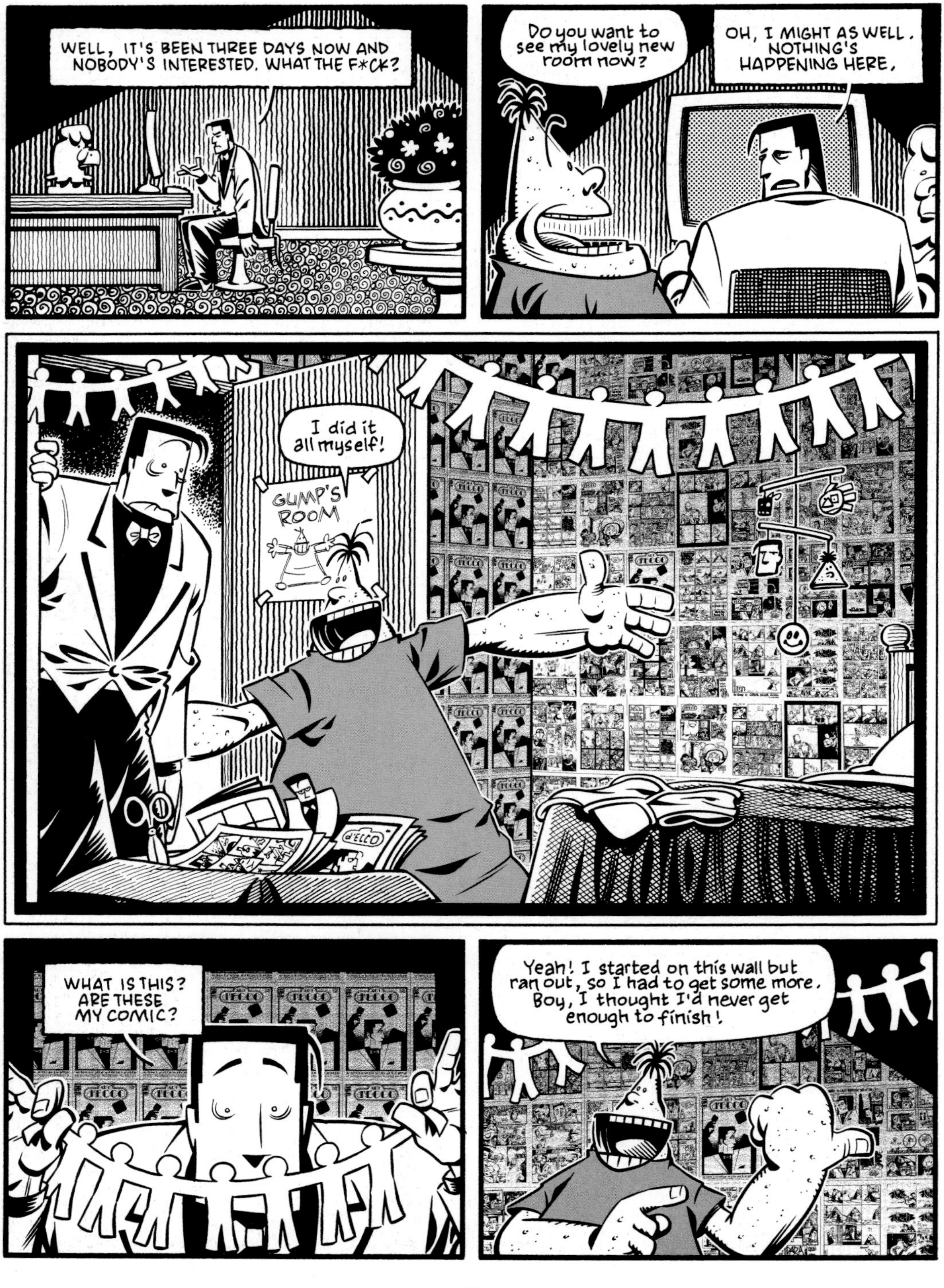
WELL, IT'S BEEN THREE DAYS NOW AND NOBODY'S INTERESTED. WHAT THE F*CK?
Do you want to see my lovely new room now?
OH, I MIGHT AS WELL. NOTHING'S HAPPENING HERE.
I did it all myself!
GUMP'S ROOM
WHAT IS THIS? ARE THESE MY COMIC?
Yeah! I started on this wall but ran out, so I had to get some more. Boy, I thought I'd never get enough to finish!

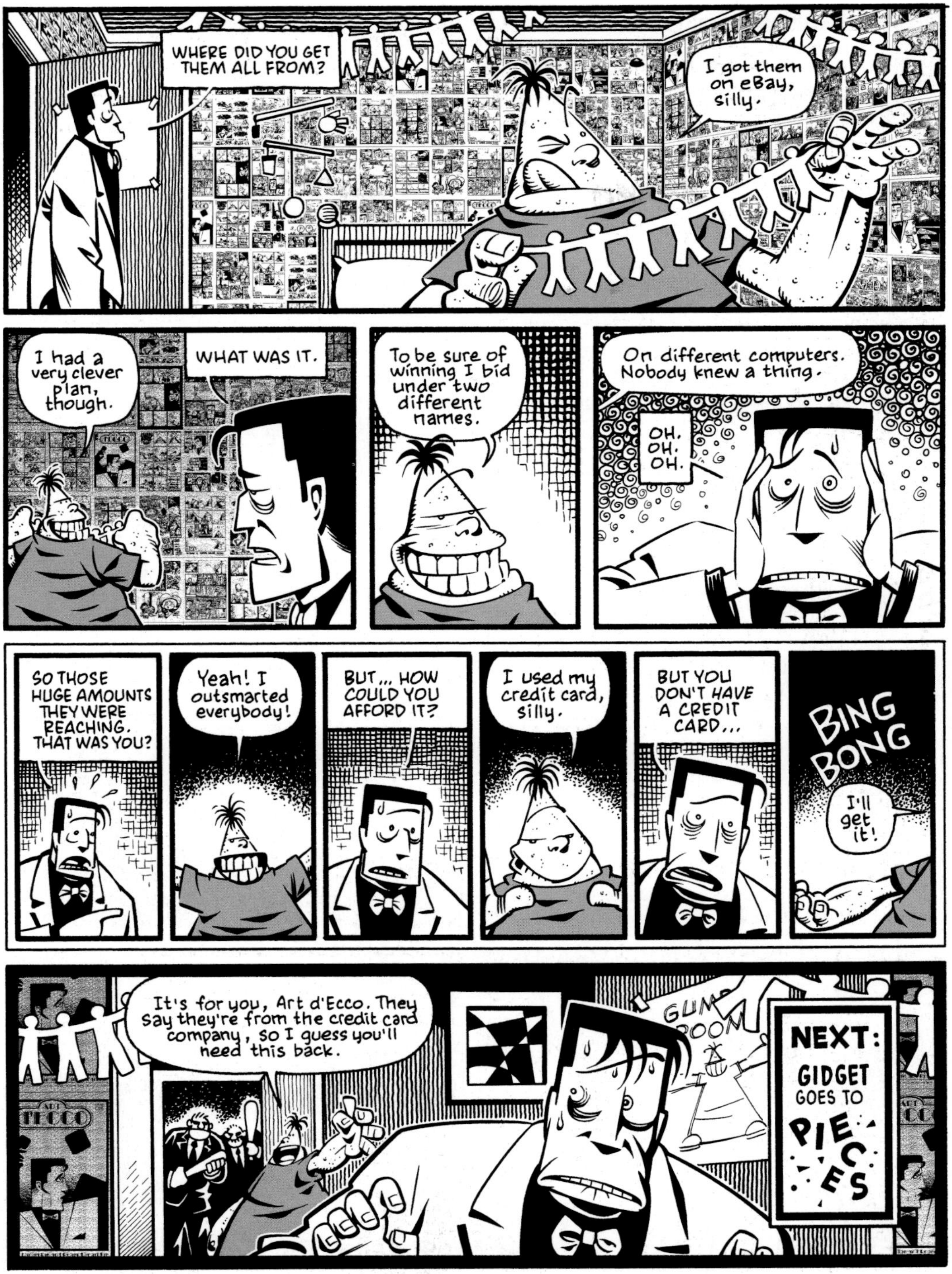
WHERE DID YOU GET THEM ALL FROM?
I got them on eBay, silly.
I had a very clever plan, though.
WHAT WAS IT.
To be sure of winning I bid under two different names.
On different computers. Nobody knew a thing.
OH. OH. OH.
SO THOSE HUGE AMOUNTS THEY WERE REACHING. THAT WAS YOU?
Yeah! I outsmarted everybody!
BUT... HOW COULD YOU AFFORD IT?
I used my credit card, silly.
BUT YOU DON'T HAVE A CREDIT CARD...
BING BONG
I'll get it!
It's for you, Art d'Ecco. They say they're from the credit card company, so I guess you'll need this back.
NEXT: GIDGET GOES TO PIECES

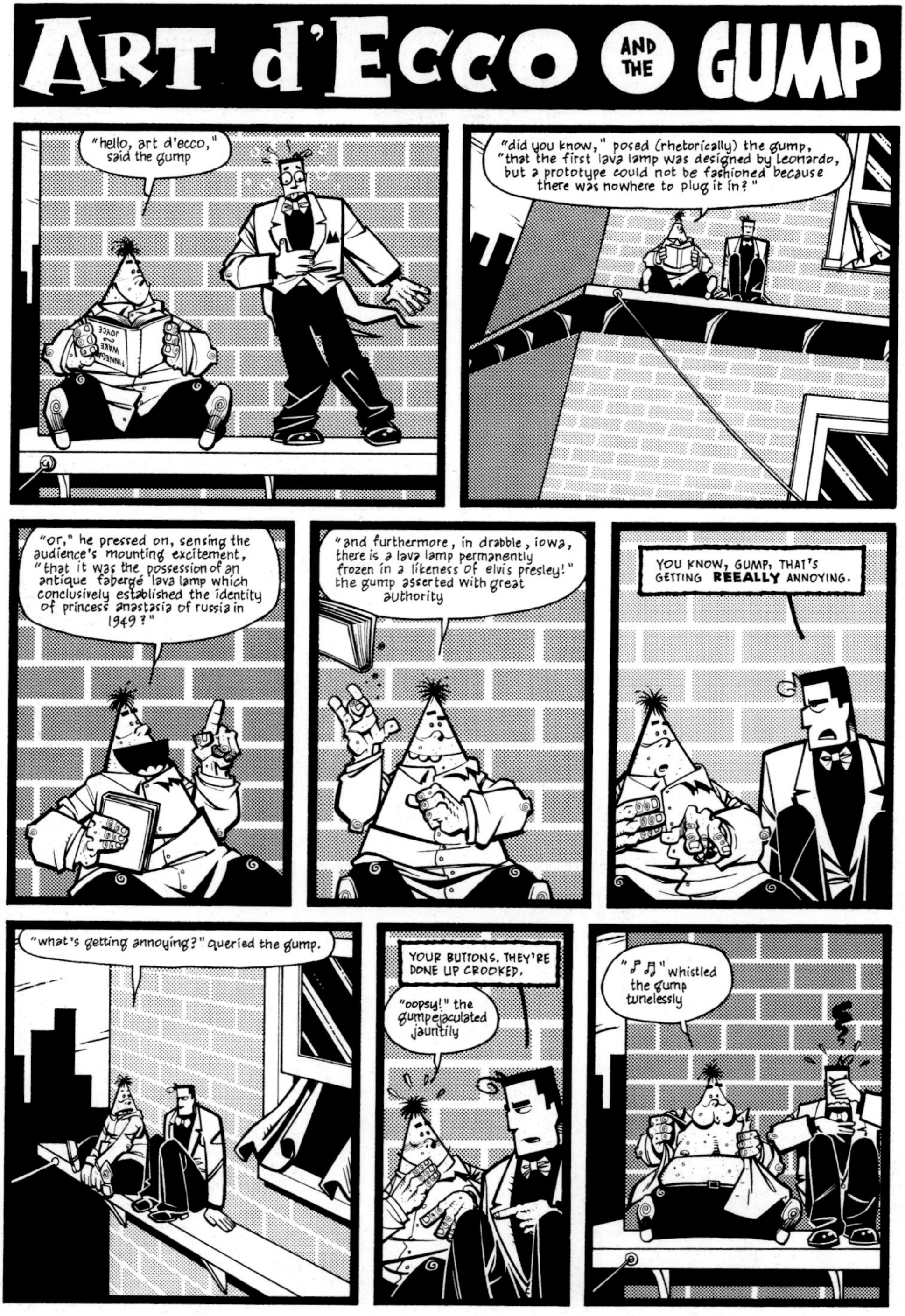
ART d'ECCO AND THE GUMP
"hello, art d'ecco," said the gump
FINNEGANS WAKE ~ JOYCE
"did you know," posed (rhetorically) the gump, "that the first lava lamp was designed by leonardo, but a prototype could not be fashioned because there was nowhere to plug it in?"
"or," he pressed on, sensing the audience's mounting excitement, "that it was the possession of an antique fabergé lava lamp which conclusively established the identity of princess anastasia of russia in 1949?"
"and furthermore, in drabble, iowa, there is a lava lamp permanently frozen in a likeness of elvis presley!" the gump asserted with great authority
YOU KNOW, GUMP, THAT'S GETTING REEALLY ANNOYING.
"what's getting annoying?" queried the gump.
YOUR BUTTONS. THEY'RE DONE UP CROOKED.
"oopsy!" the gump ejaculated jauntily
"♪♫" whistled the gump tunelessly

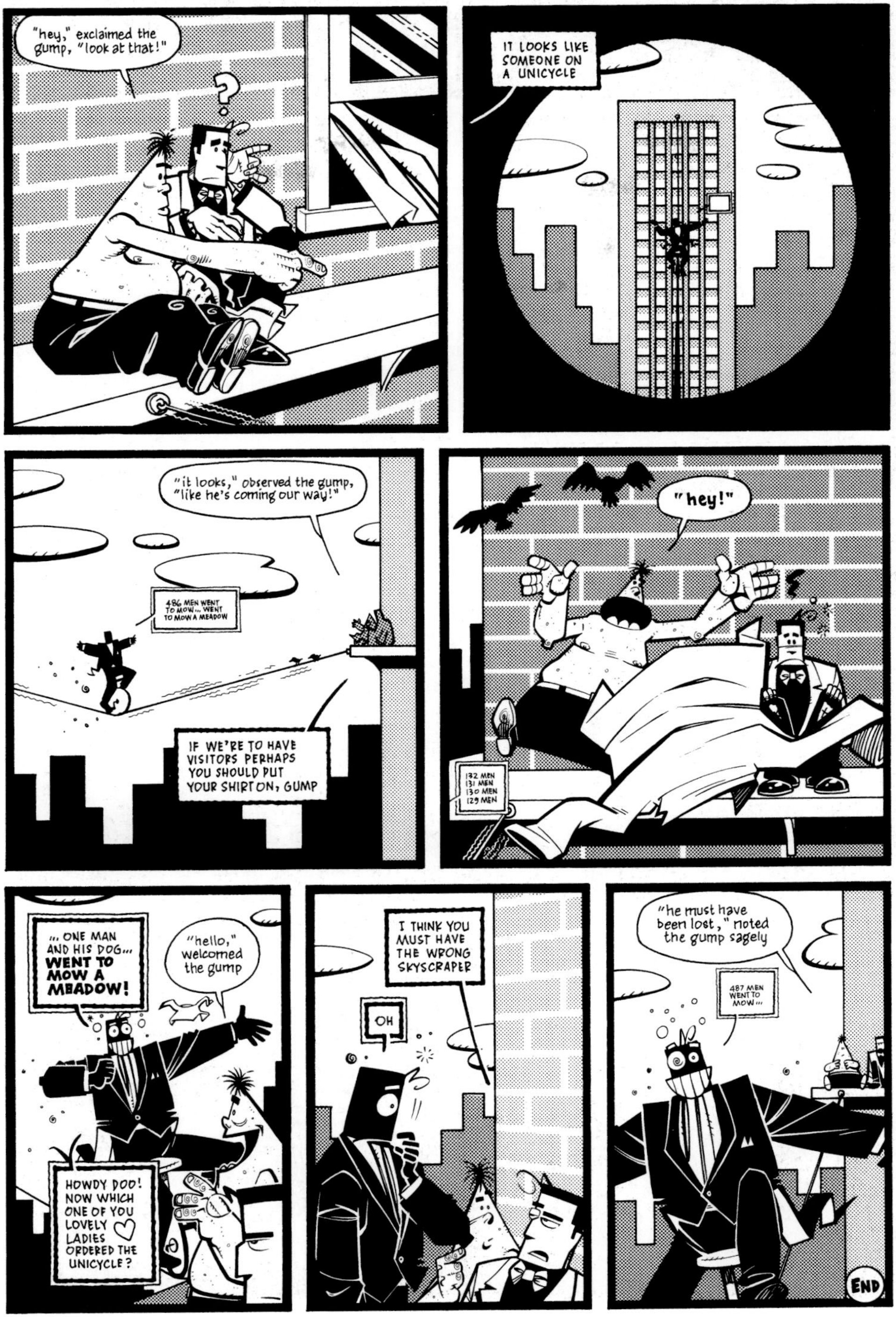
"hey," exclaimed the gump, "look at that!"
?
IT LOOKS LIKE SOMEONE ON A UNICYCLE
"it looks," observed the gump, "like he's coming our way!"
486 MEN WENT TO MOW... WENT TO MOW A MEADOW
IF WE'RE TO HAVE VISITORS PERHAPS YOU SHOULD PUT YOUR SHIRT ON, GUMP
"hey!"
132 MEN 131 MEN 130 MEN 129 MEN
... ONE MAN AND HIS DOG... WENT TO MOW A MEADOW!
"hello," welcomed the gump
HOWDY DOO! NOW WHICH ONE OF YOU LOVELY ♡ LADIES ORDERED THE UNICYCLE?
I THINK YOU MUST HAVE THE WRONG SKYSCRAPER
OH
"he must have been lost," noted the gump sagely
487 MEN WENT TO MOW...
END

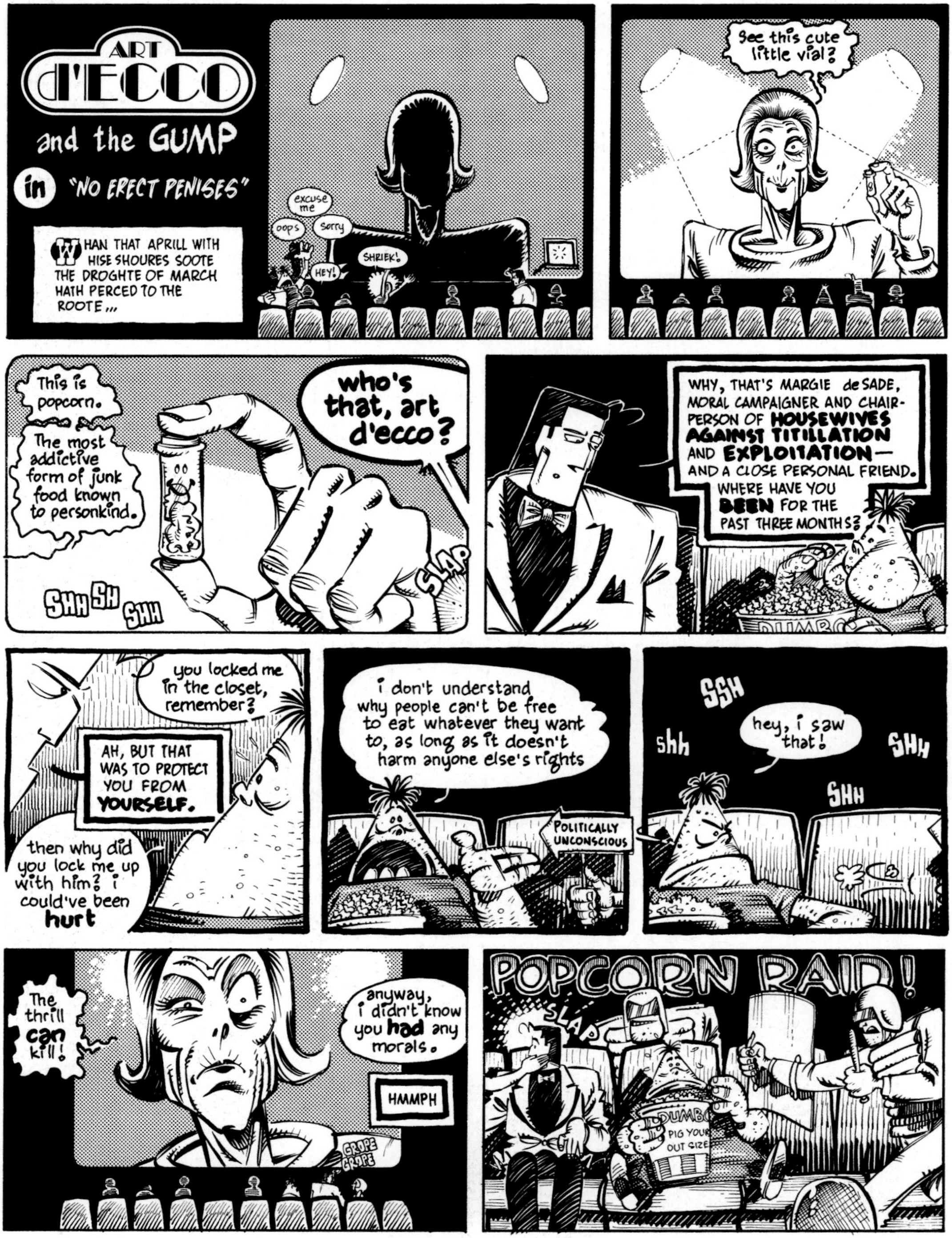
ART d'ECCO
and the GUMP
in "NO ERECT PENISES"
WHAN THAT APRILL WITH HISE SHOURES SOOTE THE DROGHTE OF MARCH HATH PERCED TO THE ROOTE...
excuse me
oops
sorry
SHRIEK!
HEY!
See this cute little vial?
This is popcorn.
The most addictive form of junk food known to personkind.
who's that, art d'ecco?
SLAP
SHH SH SHH
WHY, THAT'S MARGIE de SADE, MORAL CAMPAIGNER AND CHAIRPERSON OF HOUSEWIVES AGAINST TITILLATION AND EXPLOITATION— AND A CLOSE PERSONAL FRIEND.
WHERE HAVE YOU BEEN FOR THE PAST THREE MONTHS?
you locked me in the closet, remember?
AH, BUT THAT WAS TO PROTECT YOU FROM YOURSELF.
then why did you lock me up with him? i could've been hurt
i don't understand why people can't be free to eat whatever they want to, as long as it doesn't harm anyone else's rights
POLITICALLY UNCONSCIOUS
SSH
shh
hey, i saw that!
SHH
SHH
The thrill can kill!
anyway, i didn't know you had any morals.
HMMPH
GROPE GROPE
POPCORN RAID!
SLAP
DUMBO
PIG YOUR OUT SIZE

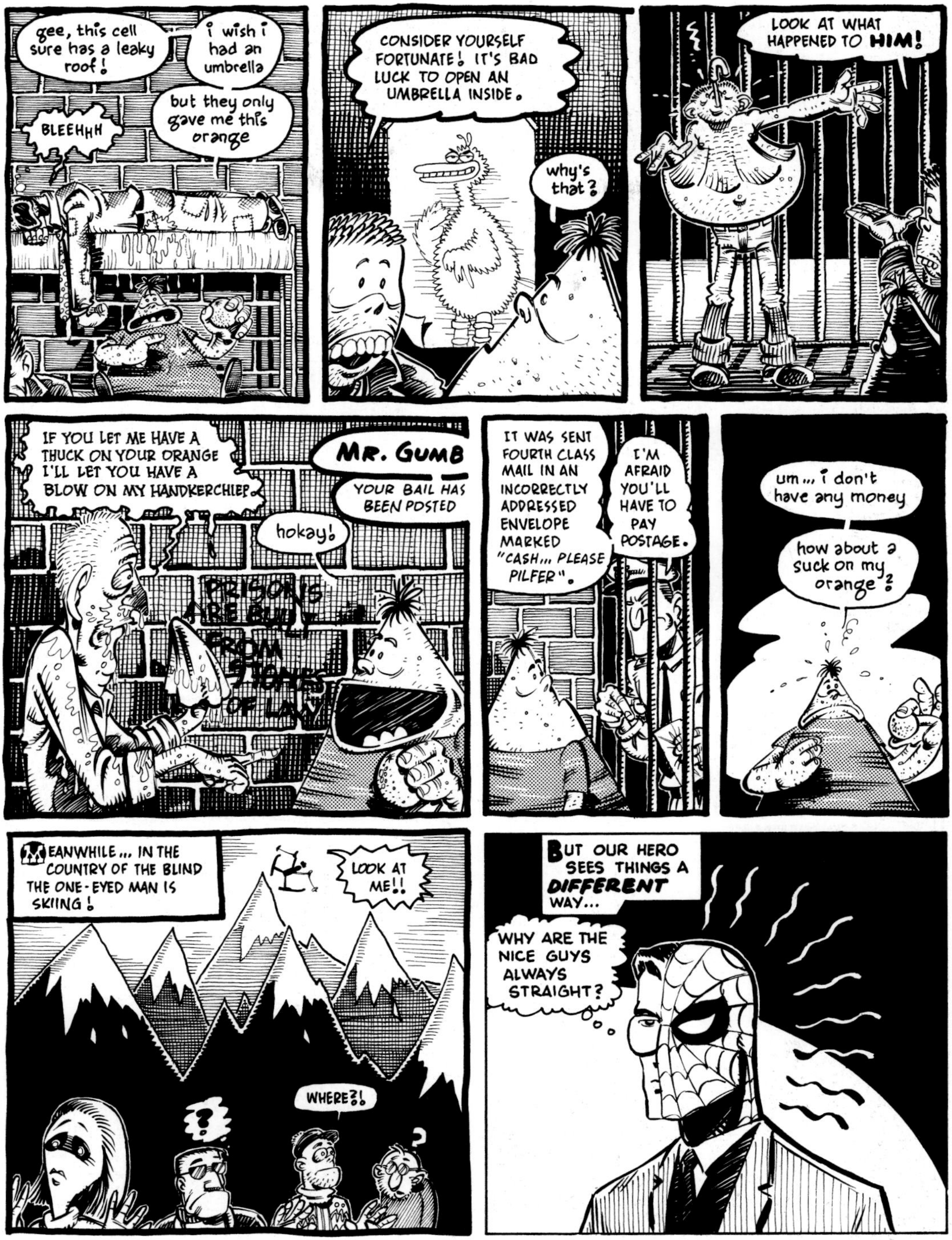
gee, this cell sure has a leaky roof!
i wish i had an umbrella
but they only gave me this orange
BLEEHHH
CONSIDER YOURSELF FORTUNATE! IT'S BAD LUCK TO OPEN AN UMBRELLA INSIDE.
why's that?
LOOK AT WHAT HAPPENED TO HIM!
IF YOU LET ME HAVE A THUCK ON YOUR ORANGE I'LL LET YOU HAVE A BLOW ON MY HANDKERCHIEF.
MR. GUMB
YOUR BAIL HAS BEEN POSTED
hokay!
PRISONS ARE BUILT FROM STONES OF LAW
IT WAS SENT FOURTH CLASS MAIL IN AN INCORRECTLY ADDRESSED ENVELOPE MARKED "CASH... PLEASE PILFER".
I'M AFRAID YOU'LL HAVE TO PAY POSTAGE.
um... i don't have any money
how about a suck on my orange?
MEANWHILE... IN THE COUNTRY OF THE BLIND THE ONE-EYED MAN IS SKIING!
LOOK AT ME!!
WHERE?!
?
?
BUT OUR HERO SEES THINGS A DIFFERENT WAY...
WHY ARE THE NICE GUYS ALWAYS STRAIGHT?

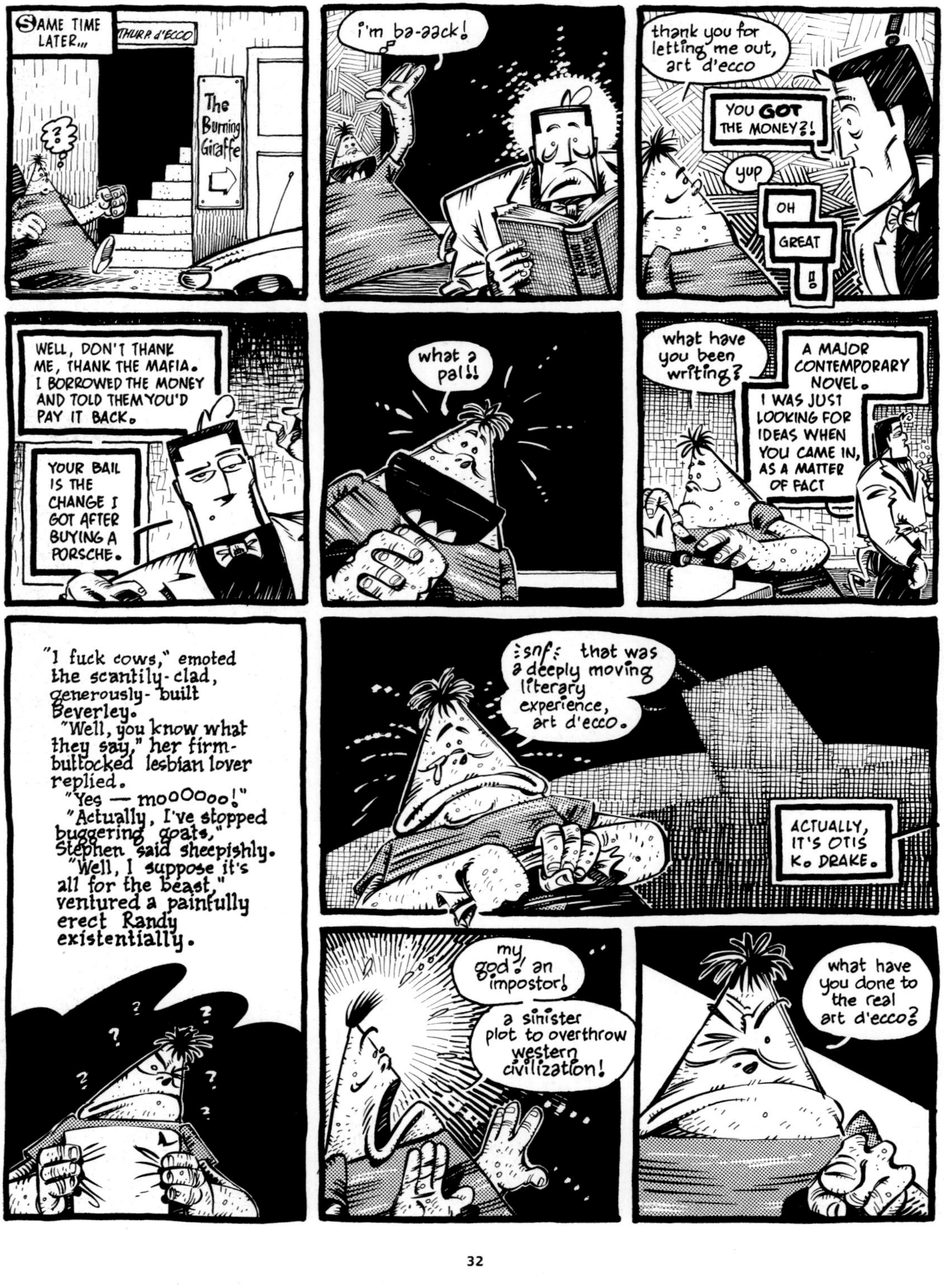
SAME TIME LATER...
THUR P. d'ECCO
The Burning Giraffe
i'm ba-aack!
thank you for letting me out, art d'ecco
YOU GOT THE MONEY?!
yup
OH
GREAT
!!
WELL, DON'T THANK ME, THANK THE MAFIA. I BORROWED THE MONEY AND TOLD THEM YOU'D PAY IT BACK.
YOUR BAIL IS THE CHANGE I GOT AFTER BUYING A PORSCHE.
what a pal!!
what have you been writing?
A MAJOR CONTEMPORARY NOVEL.
I WAS JUST LOOKING FOR IDEAS WHEN YOU CAME IN, AS A MATTER OF FACT
"I fuck cows," emoted the scantily-clad, generously-built Beverley.
"Well, you know what they say," her firm-buttocked lesbian lover replied.
"Yes — mooOOoo!"
"Actually, I've stopped buggering goats," Stephen said sheepishly.
"Well, I suppose it's all for the beast," ventured a painfully erect Randy existentially.
snf that was a deeply moving literary experience, art d'ecco.
ACTUALLY, IT'S OTIS K. DRAKE.
my god! an impostor!
a sinister plot to overthrow western civilization!
what have you done to the real art d'ecco?

HE WENT MAD AND I SHOT HIM. :sigh:

I'M THE REAL ART d'ECCO

OTIS K. DRAKE IS A **PEN NAME.**

i understand— my pen has a name too!

i call it 'home sweet home'

NO, NO! I'M ART d'ECCO **AND** OTIS K. DRAKE!

are you sure you're not... schizophrenic?

ꓤOSES AꓤE ꓤED

violetꙅ Aꓤe bluE

I'M A ꙅCHIZOPHRENIC

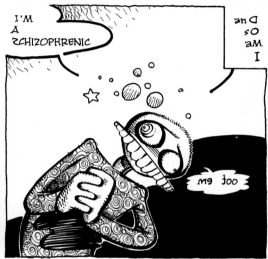

anꓷ ꙅO MA I

me too

actually, that's not strictly true. schizophrenics don't have split personalities

THANK YOU, I'LL BEAR THAT IN MIND

HA! I kneW thaT!

go rupture yourself, capitalist lackey

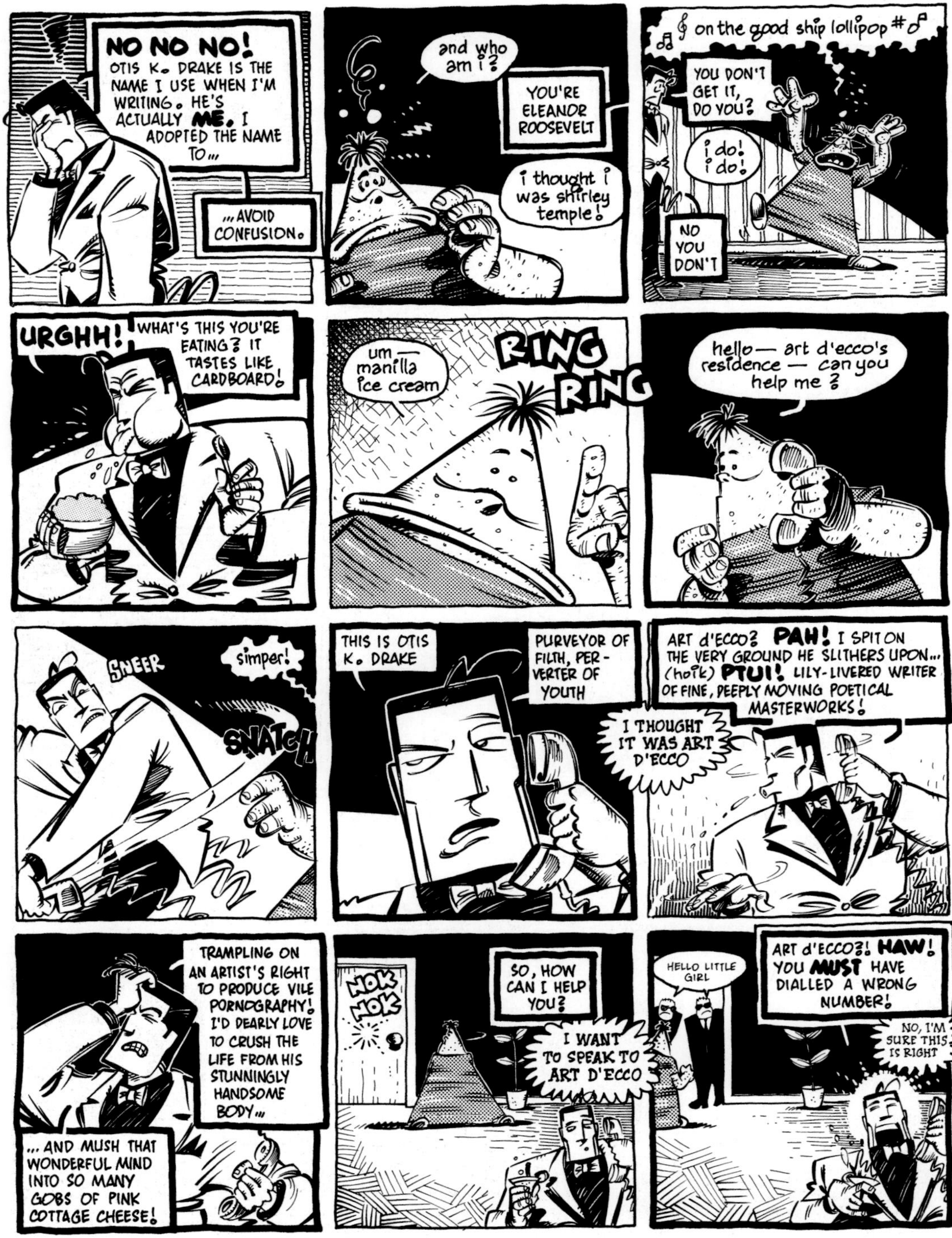

NO NO NO! OTIS K. DRAKE IS THE NAME I USE WHEN I'M WRITING. HE'S ACTUALLY ME. I ADOPTED THE NAME TO...
...AVOID CONFUSION.
and who am i?
YOU'RE ELEANOR ROOSEVELT
i thought i was shirley temple!
on the good ship lollipop
YOU DON'T GET IT, DO YOU?
i do! i do!
NO YOU DON'T
URGHH!
WHAT'S THIS YOU'RE EATING? IT TASTES LIKE CARDBOARD!
um — manilla ice cream
RING RING
hello — art d'ecco's residence — can you help me?
SNEER
simper!
SNATCH
THIS IS OTIS K. DRAKE
PURVEYOR OF FILTH, PERVERTER OF YOUTH
ART d'ECCO? PAH! I SPIT ON THE VERY GROUND HE SLITHERS UPON... (hoik) PTUI! LILY-LIVERED WRITER OF FINE, DEEPLY MOVING POETICAL MASTERWORKS!
I THOUGHT IT WAS ART D'ECCO
TRAMPLING ON AN ARTIST'S RIGHT TO PRODUCE VILE PORNOGRAPHY! I'D DEARLY LOVE TO CRUSH THE LIFE FROM HIS STUNNINGLY HANDSOME BODY...
...AND MUSH THAT WONDERFUL MIND INTO SO MANY GOBS OF PINK COTTAGE CHEESE!
NOK NOK
SO, HOW CAN I HELP YOU?
I WANT TO SPEAK TO ART D'ECCO
HELLO LITTLE GIRL
ART d'ECCO?! HAW! YOU MUST HAVE DIALLED A WRONG NUMBER!
NO, I'M SURE THIS IS RIGHT

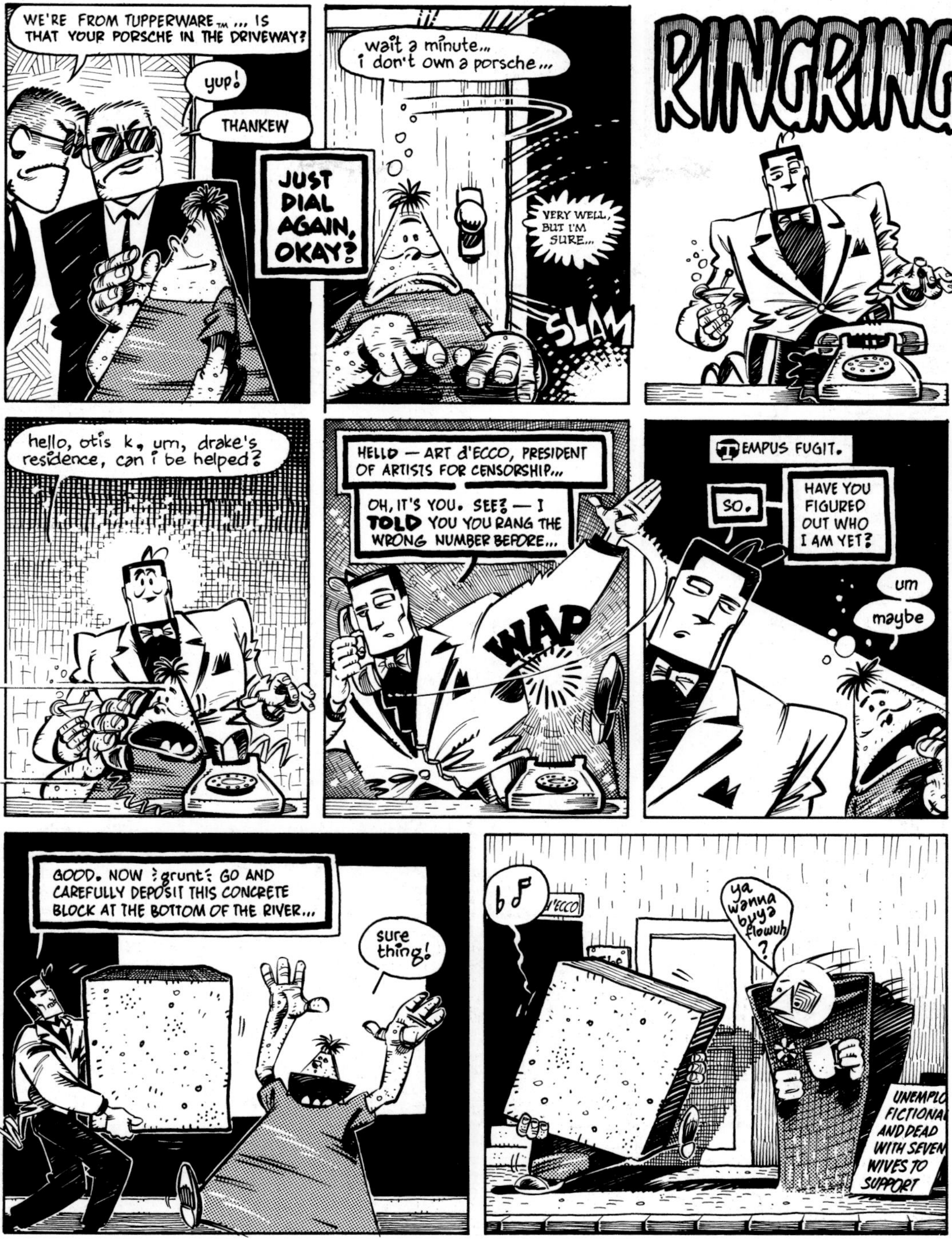
WE'RE FROM TUPPERWARE TM ... IS THAT YOUR PORSCHE IN THE DRIVEWAY?
yup!
THANKEW
JUST DIAL AGAIN, OKAY?
wait a minute... i don't own a porsche...
VERY WELL, BUT I'M SURE...
SLAM
RINGRING
hello, otis k, um, drake's residence, can i be helped?
HELLO — ART d'ECCO, PRESIDENT OF ARTISTS FOR CENSORSHIP...
OH, IT'S YOU. SEE? — I TOLD YOU YOU RANG THE WRONG NUMBER BEFORE...
WAP
TEMPUS FUGIT.
SO.
HAVE YOU FIGURED OUT WHO I AM YET?
um
maybe
GOOD. NOW ;grunt; GO AND CAREFULLY DEPOSIT THIS CONCRETE BLOCK AT THE BOTTOM OF THE RIVER...
sure thing!
D'ECCO
ya wanna buy ya flowuh?
UNEMPLO FICTIONAL AND DEAD WITH SEVEN WIVES TO SUPPORT

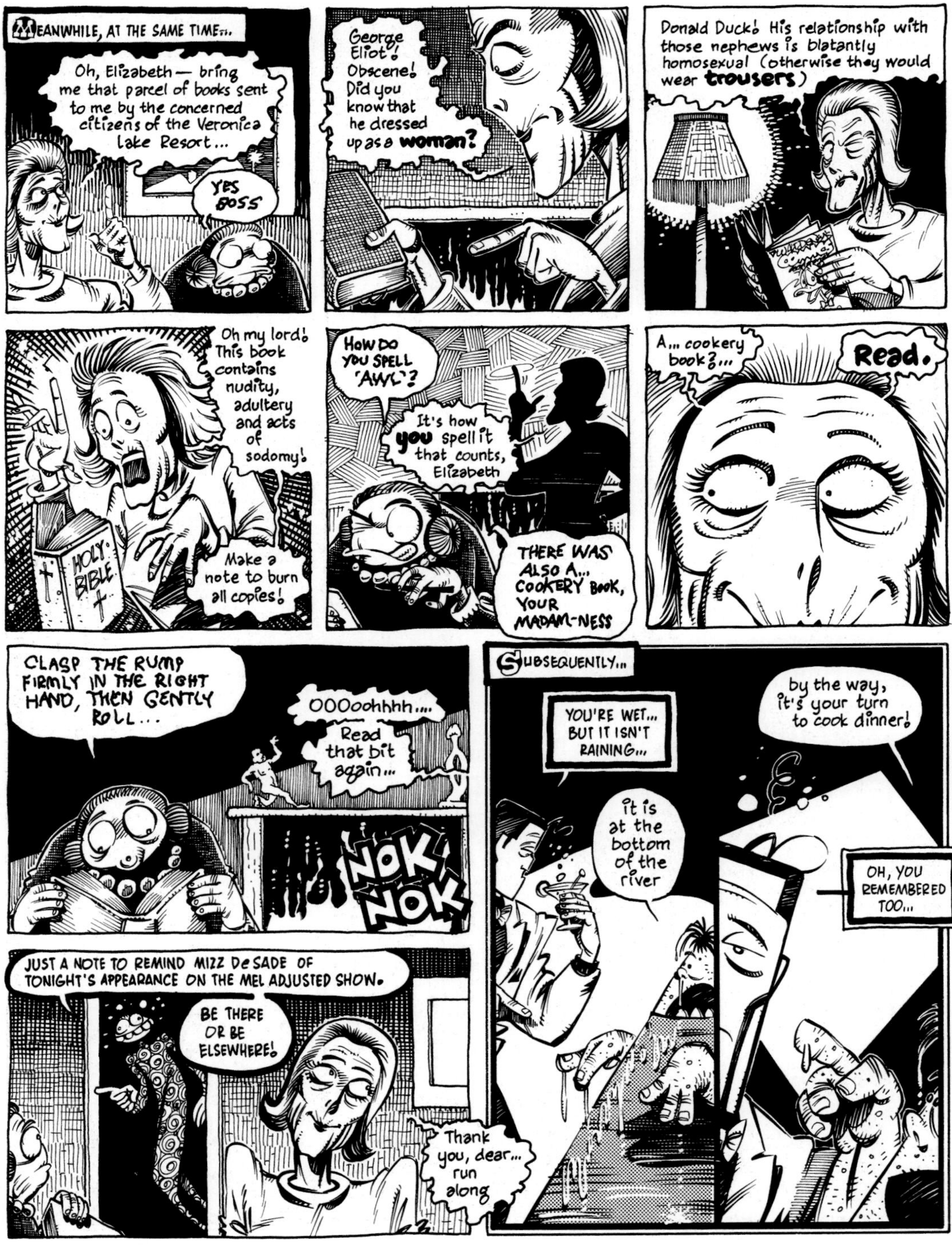

MEANWHILE, AT THE SAME TIME...
Oh, Elizabeth — bring me that parcel of books sent to me by the concerned citizens of the Veronica Lake Resort...
YES BOSS
George Eliot! Obscene! Did you know that he dressed up as a woman?
Donald Duck! His relationship with those nephews is blatantly homosexual (otherwise they would wear trousers)
Oh my lord! This book contains nudity, adultery and acts of sodomy!
HOLY BIBLE
Make a note to burn all copies!
HOW DO YOU SPELL 'AWL'?
It's how you spell it that counts, Elizabeth
THERE WAS ALSO A... COOKERY BOOK, YOUR MADAM-NESS
A... cookery book?...
Read.
CLASP THE RUMP FIRMLY IN THE RIGHT HAND, THEN GENTLY ROLL...
OOOoohhhh....
Read that bit again...
NOK NOK
JUST A NOTE TO REMIND MIZZ DE SADE OF TONIGHT'S APPEARANCE ON THE MEL ADJUSTED SHOW.
BE THERE OR BE ELSEWHERE!
Thank you, dear... run along
SUBSEQUENTLY...
YOU'RE WET... BUT IT ISN'T RAINING...
it is at the bottom of the river
by the way, it's your turn to cook dinner!
OH, YOU REMEMBERED TOO...

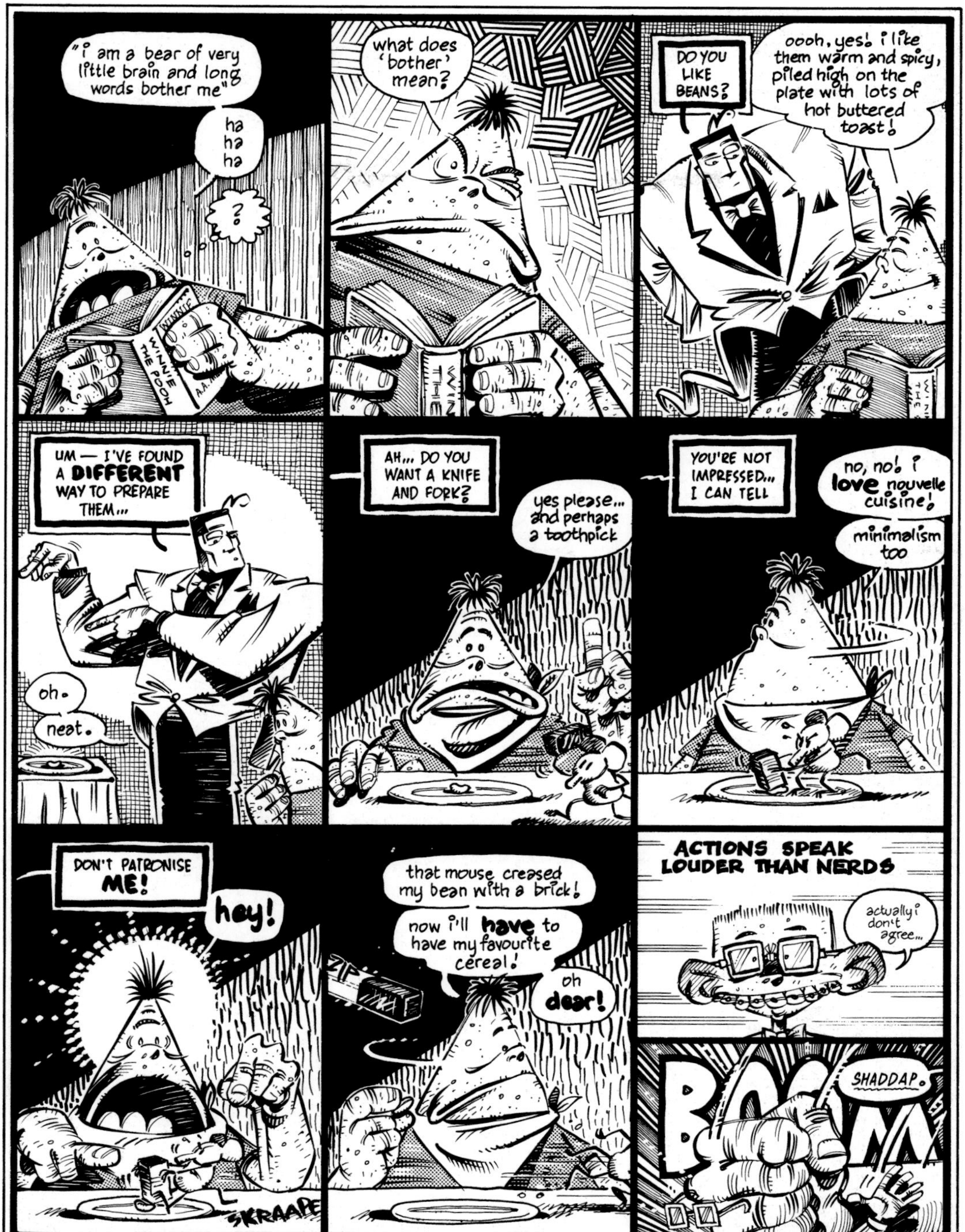
"i am a bear of very little brain and long words bother me"
ha ha ha
?
what does 'bother' mean?
WINNIE THE POOH
DO YOU LIKE BEANS?
oooh, yes! i like them warm and spicy, piled high on the plate with lots of hot buttered toast!
UM — I'VE FOUND A DIFFERENT WAY TO PREPARE THEM...
oh.
neat.
AH... DO YOU WANT A KNIFE AND FORK?
yes please... and perhaps a toothpick
YOU'RE NOT IMPRESSED... I CAN TELL
no, no! i love nouvelle cuisine!
minimalism too
DON'T PATRONISE ME!
hey!
SKRAAPE
that mouse creased my bean with a brick!
now i'll have to have my favourite cereal!
ZIP
oh dear!
ACTIONS SPEAK LOUDER THAN NERDS
actually i don't agree...
SHADDAP.

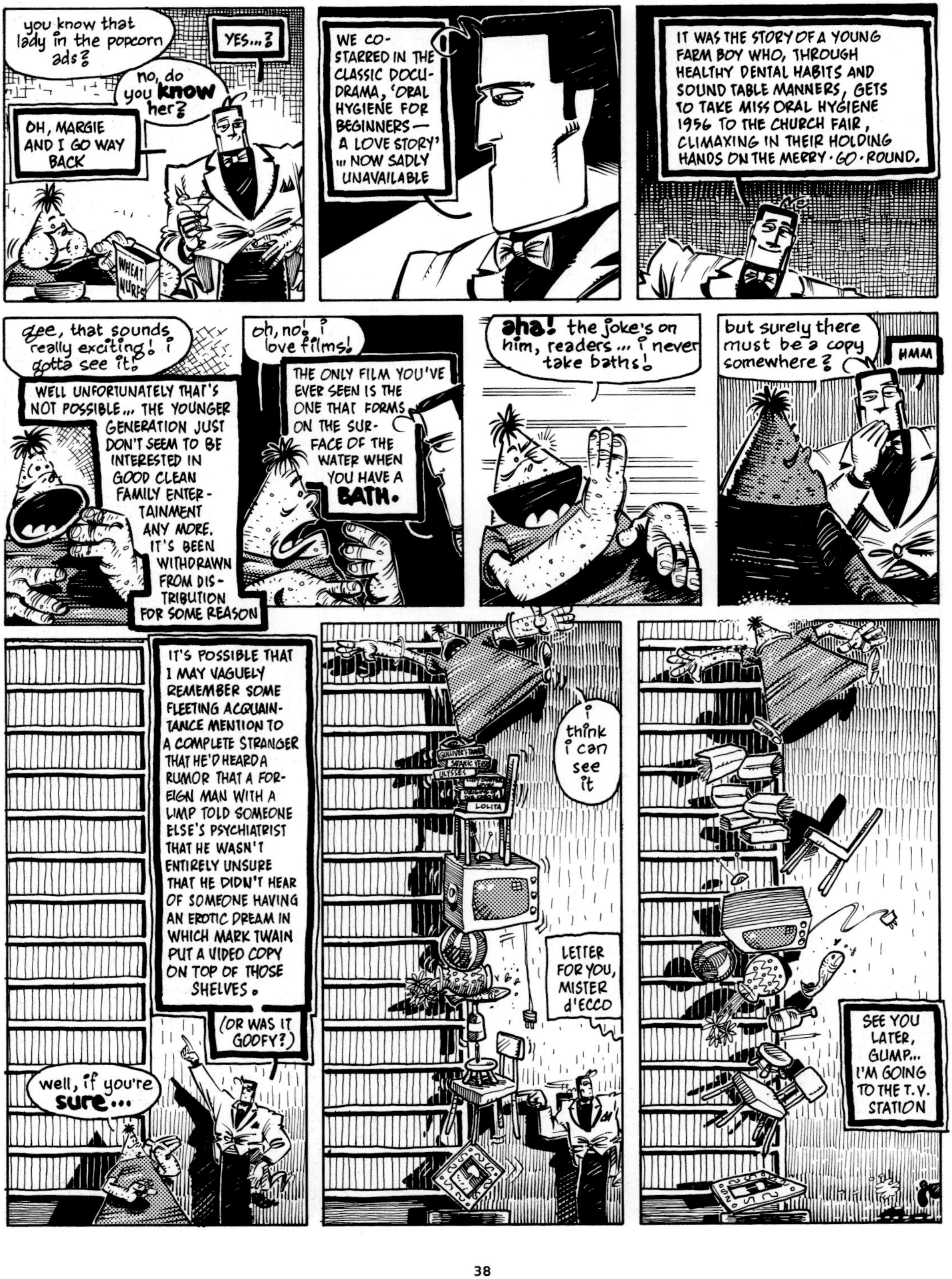
you know that lady in the popcorn ads?
YES...?
no, do you know her?
OH, MARGIE AND I GO WAY BACK
WHEAT NURFS
WE CO-STARRED IN THE CLASSIC DOCU-DRAMA, 'ORAL HYGIENE FOR BEGINNERS — A LOVE STORY' ... NOW SADLY UNAVAILABLE
IT WAS THE STORY OF A YOUNG FARM BOY WHO, THROUGH HEALTHY DENTAL HABITS AND SOUND TABLE MANNERS, GETS TO TAKE MISS ORAL HYGIENE 1956 TO THE CHURCH FAIR, CLIMAXING IN THEIR HOLDING HANDS ON THE MERRY-GO-ROUND.
gee, that sounds really exciting! i gotta see it!
WELL UNFORTUNATELY THAT'S NOT POSSIBLE... THE YOUNGER GENERATION JUST DON'T SEEM TO BE INTERESTED IN GOOD CLEAN FAMILY ENTERTAINMENT ANY MORE. IT'S BEEN WITHDRAWN FROM DISTRIBUTION FOR SOME REASON
oh, no! i love films!
THE ONLY FILM YOU'VE EVER SEEN IS THE ONE THAT FORMS ON THE SURFACE OF THE WATER WHEN YOU HAVE A BATH.
aha! the joke's on him, readers ... i never take baths!
but surely there must be a copy somewhere?
HMM
IT'S POSSIBLE THAT I MAY VAGUELY REMEMBER SOME FLEETING ACQUAINTANCE MENTION TO A COMPLETE STRANGER THAT HE'D HEARD A RUMOR THAT A FOREIGN MAN WITH A LIMP TOLD SOMEONE ELSE'S PSYCHIATRIST THAT HE WASN'T ENTIRELY UNSURE THAT HE DIDN'T HEAR OF SOMEONE HAVING AN EROTIC DREAM IN WHICH MARK TWAIN PUT A VIDEO COPY ON TOP OF THOSE SHELVES.
(OR WAS IT GOOFY?)
well, if you're sure...
i think i can see it
ULYSSES
LOLITA
LETTER FOR YOU, MISTER d'ECCO
SEE YOU LATER, GUMP... I'M GOING TO THE T.V. STATION

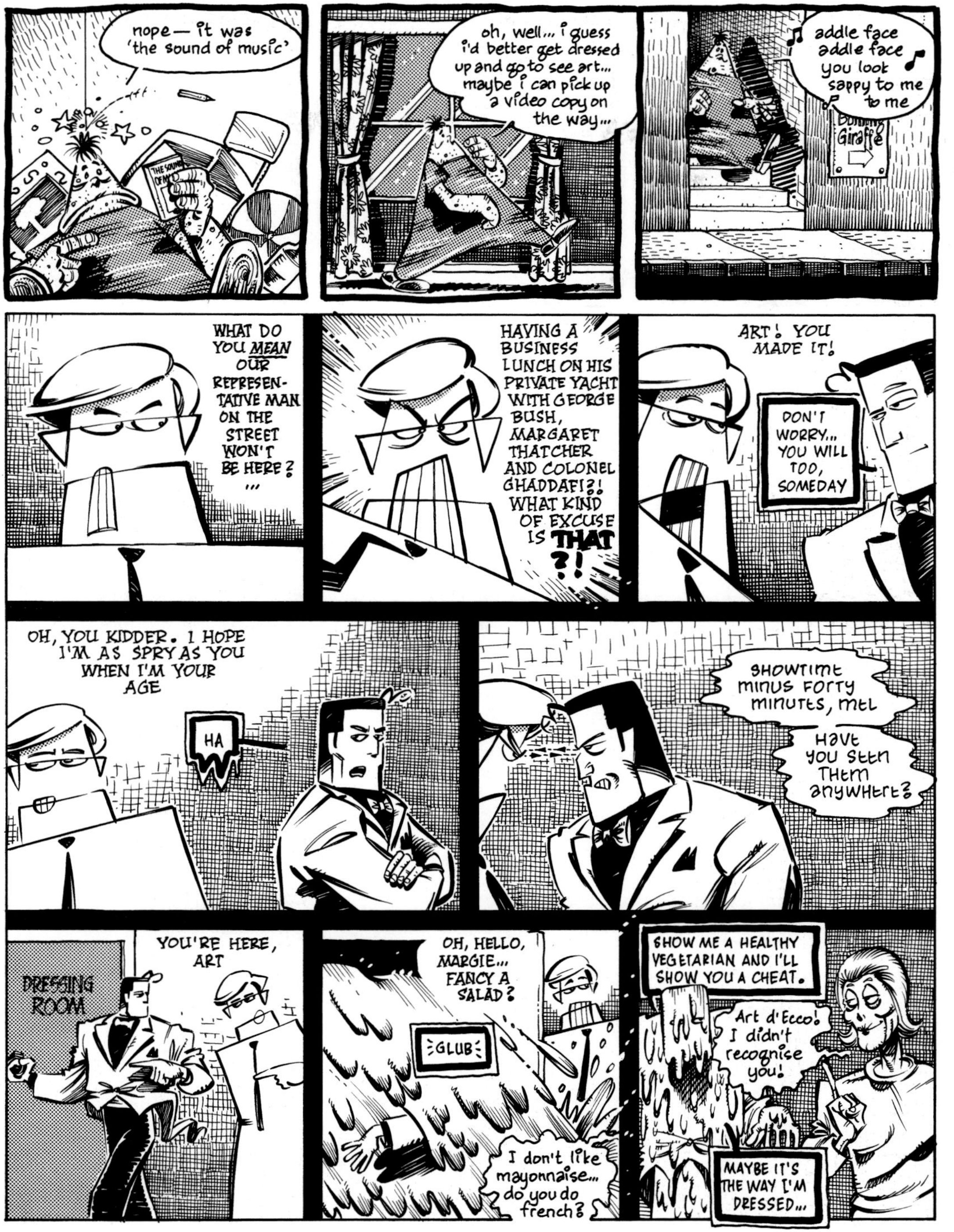

nope — it was 'the sound of music'
THE SOUND OF MU
oh, well... i guess i'd better get dressed up and go to see art... maybe i can pick up a video copy on the way...
addle face addle face you look sappy to me to me
Burning Giraffe
WHAT DO YOU MEAN OUR REPRESENTATIVE MAN ON THE STREET WON'T BE HERE?...
HAVING A BUSINESS LUNCH ON HIS PRIVATE YACHT WITH GEORGE BUSH, MARGARET THATCHER AND COLONEL GHADDAFI?! WHAT KIND OF EXCUSE IS THAT?!
ART! YOU MADE IT!
DON'T WORRY... YOU WILL TOO, SOMEDAY
OH, YOU KIDDER. I HOPE I'M AS SPRY AS YOU WHEN I'M YOUR AGE
HA
SHOWTIME MINUS FORTY MINUTES, MEL
HAVE YOU SEEN THEM ANYWHERE?
DRESSING ROOM
YOU'RE HERE, ART
OH, HELLO, MARGIE... FANCY A SALAD?
GLUB
I don't like mayonnaise... do you do french?
SHOW ME A HEALTHY VEGETARIAN AND I'LL SHOW YOU A CHEAT.
Art d'Ecco! I didn't recognise you!
MAYBE IT'S THE WAY I'M DRESSED...

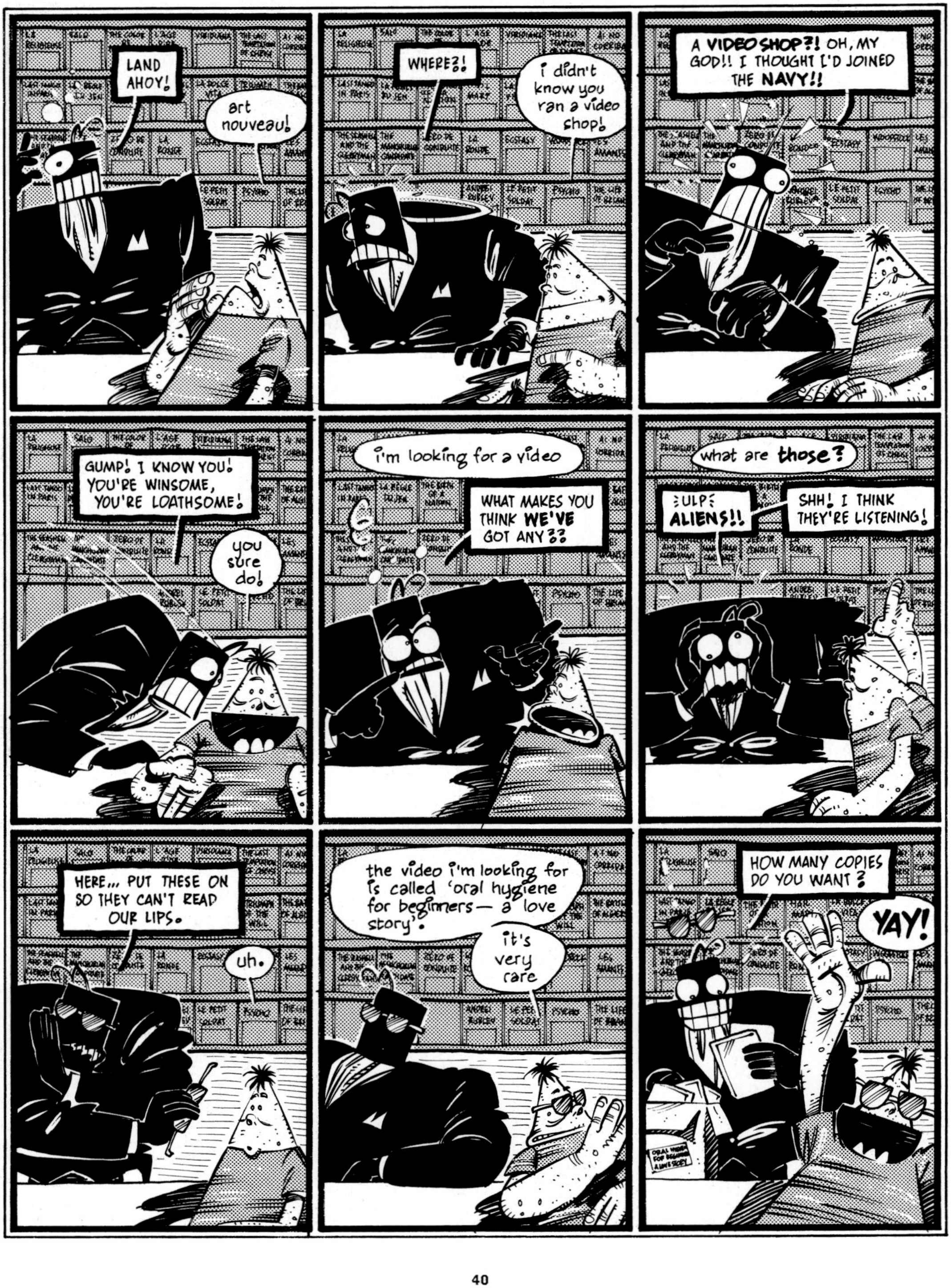
LAND AHOY!
art nouveau!
WHERE?!
i didn't know you ran a video shop!
A VIDEO SHOP?! OH, MY GOD!! I THOUGHT I'D JOINED THE NAVY!!
GUMP! I KNOW YOU! YOU'RE WINSOME, YOU'RE LOATHSOME!
you sure do!
i'm looking for a video
WHAT MAKES YOU THINK WE'VE GOT ANY??
what are those?
ULP! ALIENS!!
SHH! I THINK THEY'RE LISTENING!
HERE... PUT THESE ON SO THEY CAN'T READ OUR LIPS.
uh.
the video i'm looking for is called 'oral hygiene for beginners— a love story'.
it's very rare
HOW MANY COPIES DO YOU WANT?
YAY!

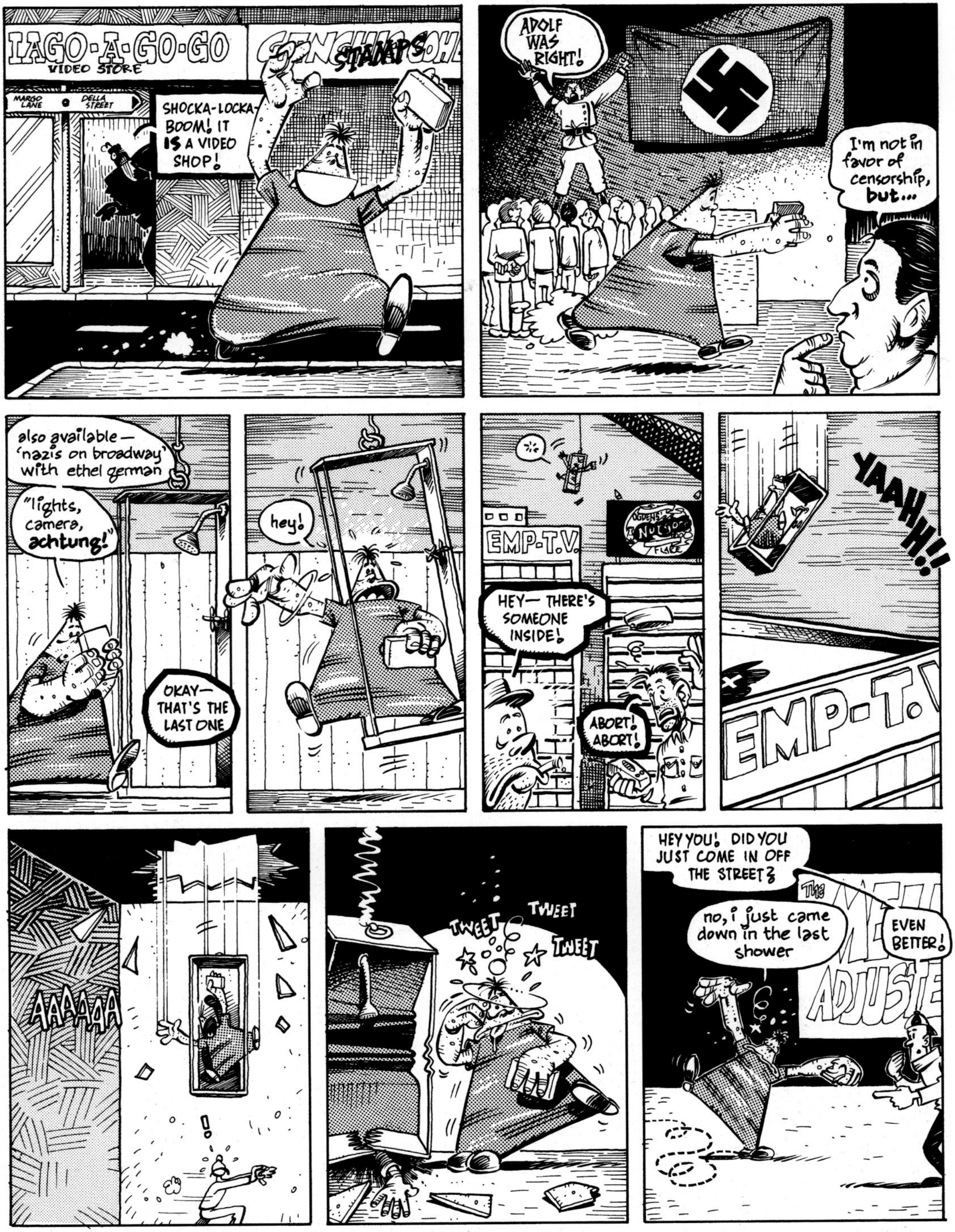
IAGO-A-GO-GO
VIDEO STORE
MARGO LANE
DELLA STREET
STAAMPS
SHOCKA-LOCKA-BOOM! IT IS A VIDEO SHOP!
ADOLF WAS RIGHT!
I'm not in favor of censorship, but...
also available— 'nazis on broadway' with ethel german
"lights, camera, achtung!"
OKAY— THAT'S THE LAST ONE
hey!
EMP-T.V.
HEY— THERE'S SOMEONE INSIDE!
ABORT! ABORT!
YAAHHH!!
EMP-T.V.
AAAAAA
!
TWEET
TWEET
TWEET
HEY YOU! DID YOU JUST COME IN OFF THE STREET?
no, i just came down in the last shower
EVEN BETTER!
ADJUSTE

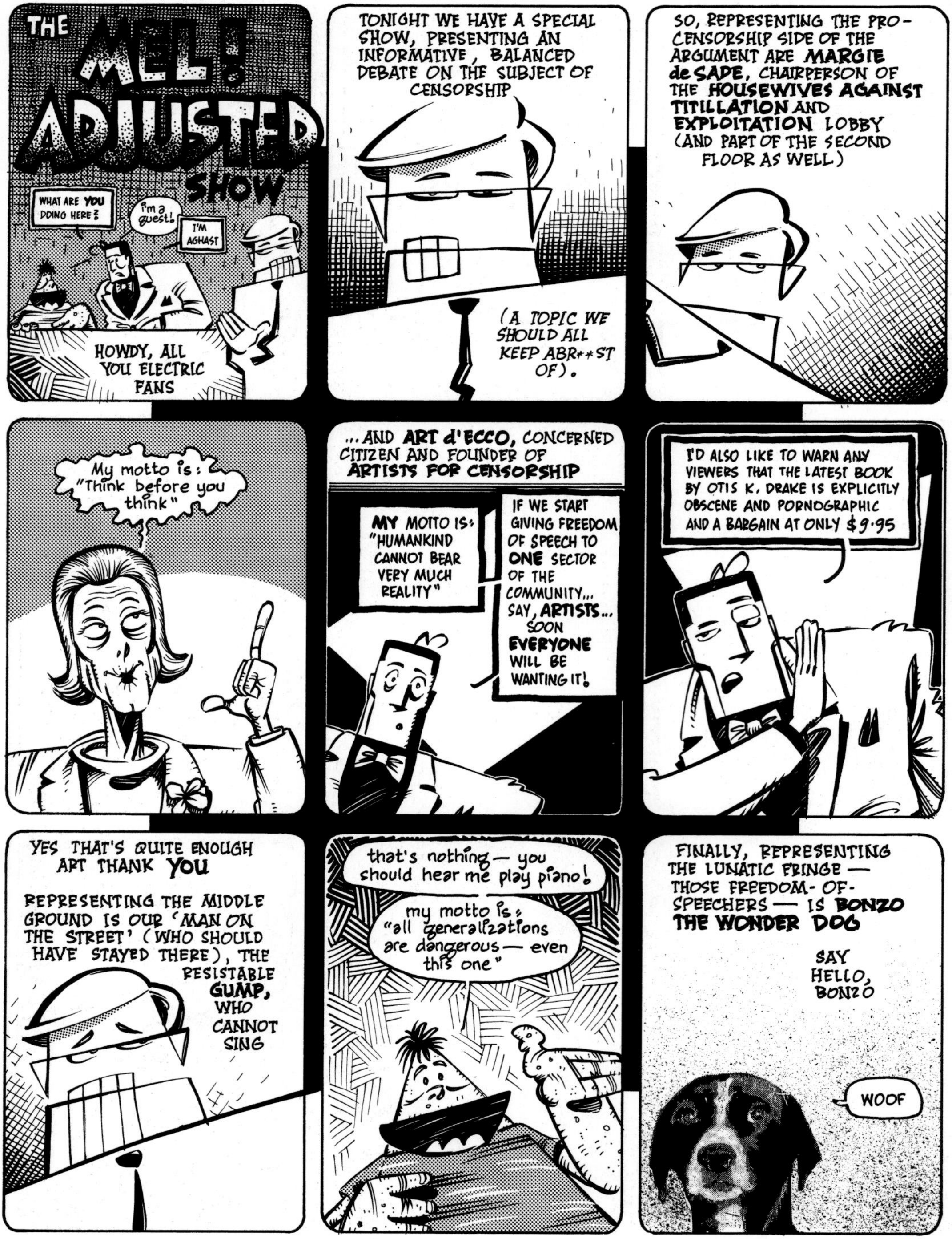

THE MEL! ADJUSTED SHOW
WHAT ARE YOU DOING HERE?
I'm a guest!
I'M AGHAST
HOWDY, ALL YOU ELECTRIC FANS
TONIGHT WE HAVE A SPECIAL SHOW, PRESENTING AN INFORMATIVE, BALANCED DEBATE ON THE SUBJECT OF CENSORSHIP
(A TOPIC WE SHOULD ALL KEEP ABR**ST OF).
SO, REPRESENTING THE PRO-CENSORSHIP SIDE OF THE ARGUMENT ARE MARGIE de SADE, CHAIRPERSON OF THE HOUSEWIVES AGAINST TITILLATION AND EXPLOITATION LOBBY (AND PART OF THE SECOND FLOOR AS WELL)
My motto is: "Think before you think"
...AND ART d'ECCO, CONCERNED CITIZEN AND FOUNDER OF ARTISTS FOR CENSORSHIP
MY MOTTO IS: "HUMANKIND CANNOT BEAR VERY MUCH REALITY"
IF WE START GIVING FREEDOM OF SPEECH TO ONE SECTOR OF THE COMMUNITY... SAY, ARTISTS... SOON EVERYONE WILL BE WANTING IT!
I'D ALSO LIKE TO WARN ANY VIEWERS THAT THE LATEST BOOK BY OTIS K. DRAKE IS EXPLICITLY OBSCENE AND PORNOGRAPHIC AND A BARGAIN AT ONLY $9.95
YES THAT'S QUITE ENOUGH ART THANK YOU
REPRESENTING THE MIDDLE GROUND IS OUR 'MAN ON THE STREET' (WHO SHOULD HAVE STAYED THERE), THE RESISTABLE GUMP, WHO CANNOT SING
that's nothing — you should hear me play piano!
my motto is: "all generalizations are dangerous — even this one"
FINALLY, REPRESENTING THE LUNATIC FRINGE — THOSE FREEDOM-OF-SPEECHERS — IS BONZO THE WONDER DOG
SAY HELLO, BONZO
WOOF

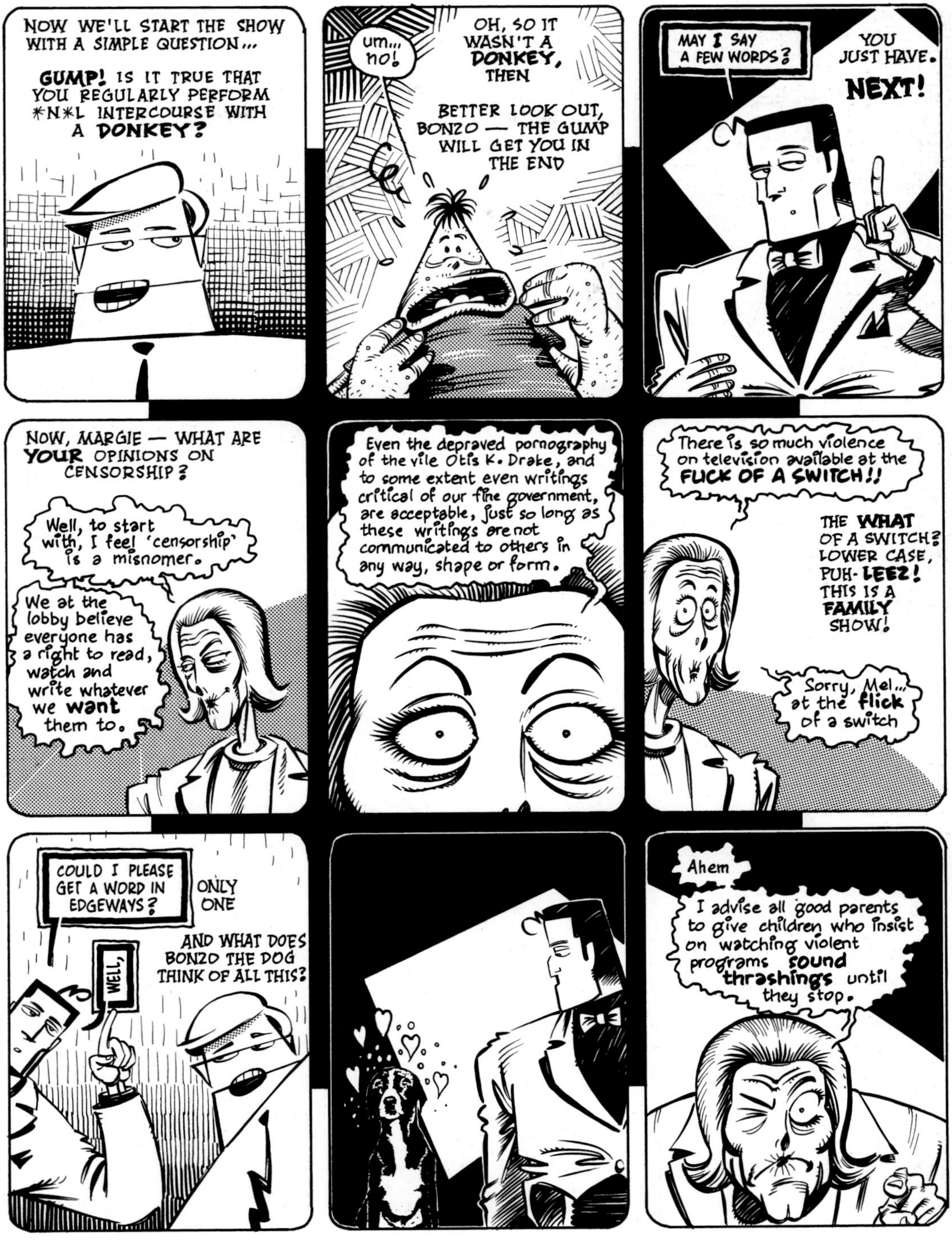

NOW WE'LL START THE SHOW WITH A SIMPLE QUESTION...
GUMP! IS IT TRUE THAT YOU REGULARLY PERFORM *N*L INTERCOURSE WITH A DONKEY?
um... no!
OH, SO IT WASN'T A DONKEY, THEN
BETTER LOOK OUT, BONZO — THE GUMP WILL GET YOU IN THE END
MAY I SAY A FEW WORDS?
YOU JUST HAVE.
NEXT!
NOW, MARGIE — WHAT ARE YOUR OPINIONS ON CENSORSHIP?
Well, to start with, I feel 'censorship' is a misnomer.
We at the lobby believe everyone has a right to read, watch and write whatever we want them to.
Even the depraved pornography of the vile Otis K. Drake, and to some extent even writings critical of our fine government, are acceptable, just so long as these writings are not communicated to others in any way, shape or form.
There is so much violence on television available at the FLICK OF A SWITCH!!
THE WHAT OF A SWITCH? LOWER CASE, PUH-LEEZ! THIS IS A FAMILY SHOW!
Sorry, Mel... at the flick of a switch
COULD I PLEASE GET A WORD IN EDGEWAYS?
ONLY ONE
WELL,
AND WHAT DOES BONZO THE DOG THINK OF ALL THIS?
Ahem
I advise all good parents to give children who insist on watching violent programs sound thrashings until they stop.

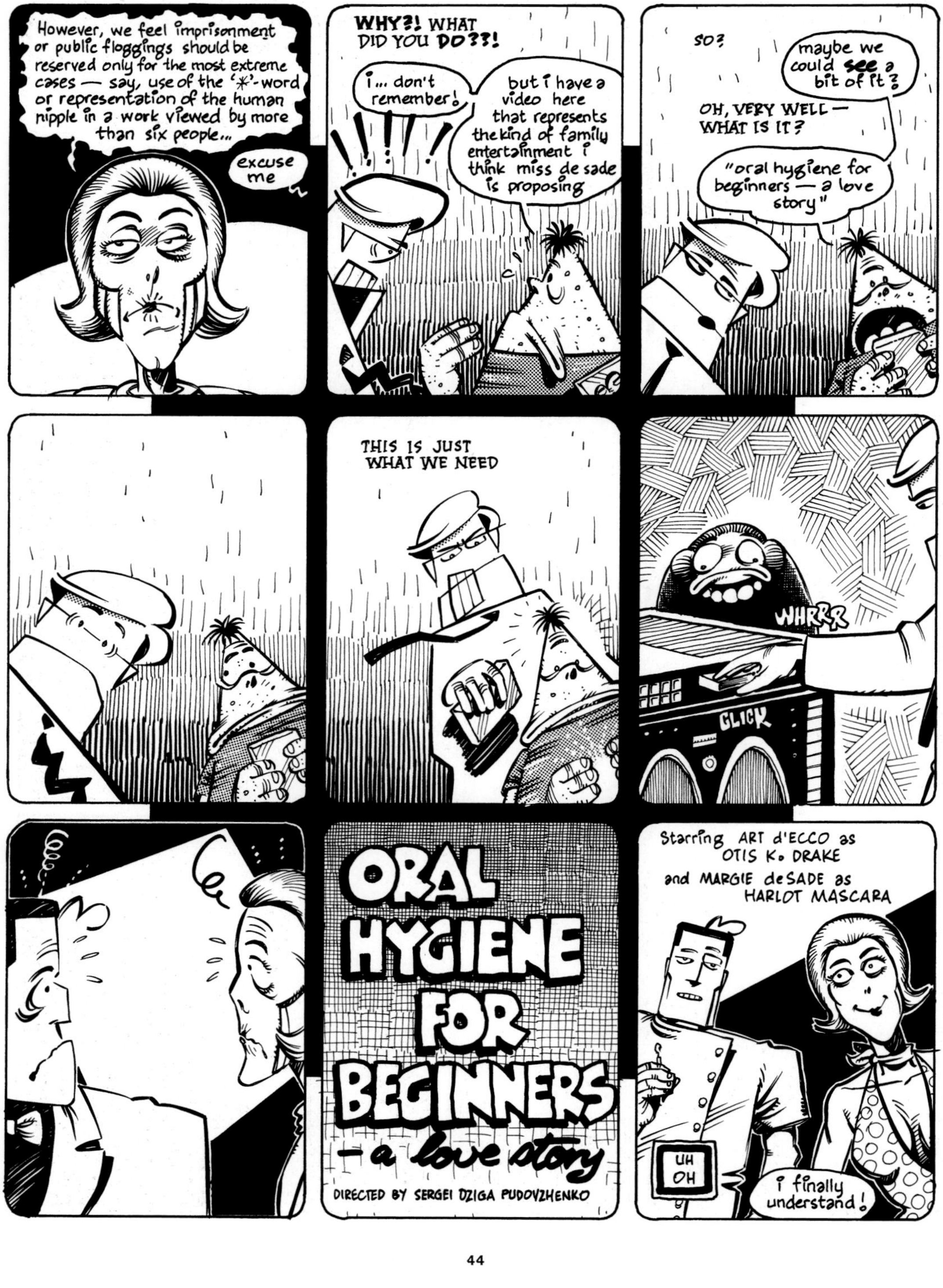
However, we feel imprisonment or public floggings should be reserved only for the most extreme cases — say, use of the '*'-word or representation of the human nipple in a work viewed by more than six people...
excuse me
WHY?! WHAT DID YOU DO??!
i... don't remember!
but i have a video here that represents the kind of family entertainment i think miss de sade is proposing
SO?
maybe we could see a bit of it?
OH, VERY WELL — WHAT IS IT?
"oral hygiene for beginners — a love story"
THIS IS JUST WHAT WE NEED
WHRRR
CLICK
ORAL HYGIENE FOR BEGINNERS
— a love story
DIRECTED BY SERGEI DZIGA PUDOVZHENKO
Starring ART d'ECCO as OTIS K. DRAKE
and MARGIE deSADE as HARLOT MASCARA
UH OH
i finally understand!

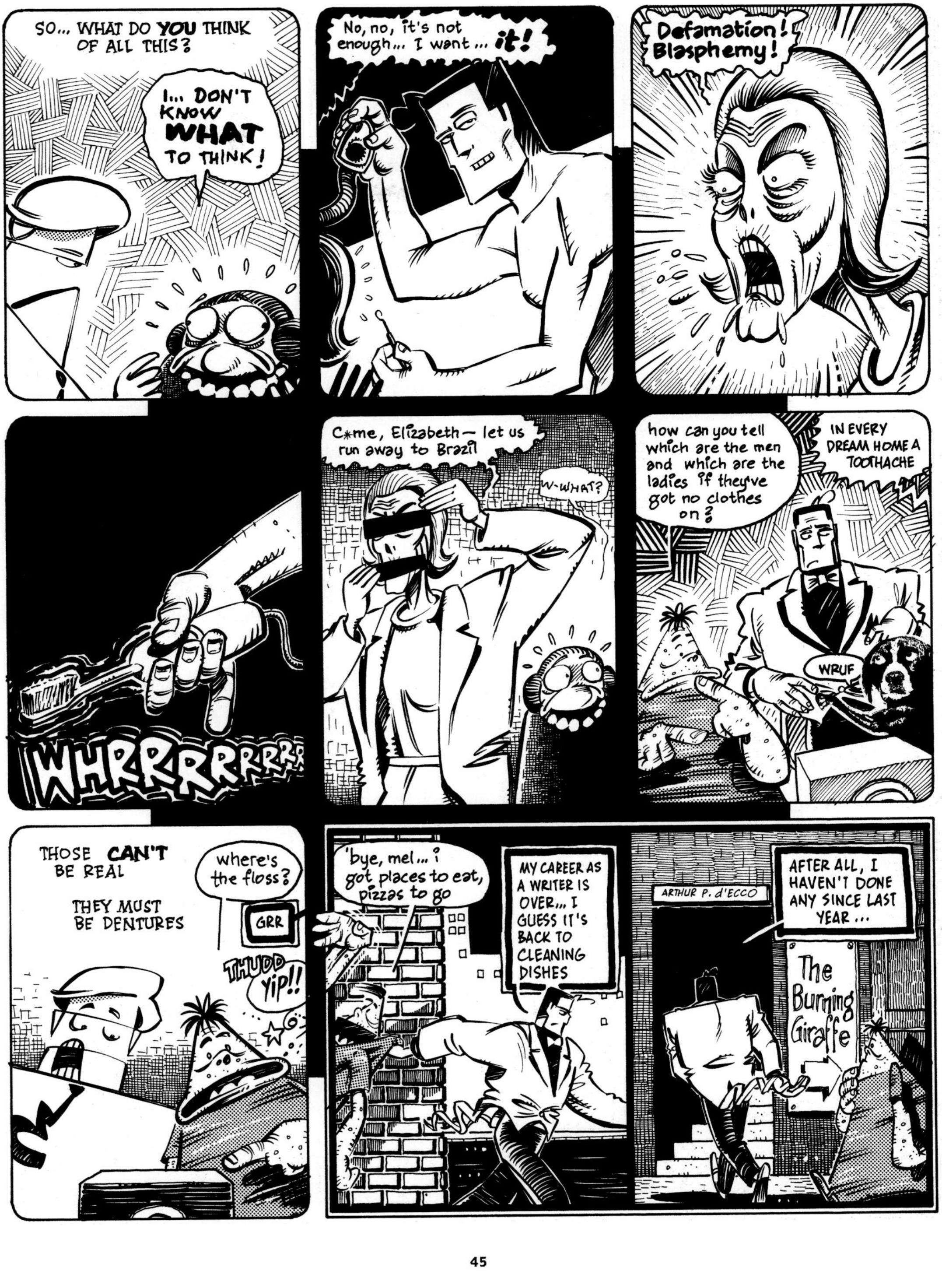
SO... WHAT DO YOU THINK OF ALL THIS?
I... DON'T KNOW WHAT TO THINK!
No, no, it's not enough... I want... it!
Defamation! Blasphemy!
WHRRRRRRR
C*me, Elizabeth — let us run away to Brazil
W-WHAT?
how can you tell which are the men and which are the ladies if they've got no clothes on?
IN EVERY DREAM HOME A TOOTHACHE
WRUF
THOSE CAN'T BE REAL
THEY MUST BE DENTURES
where's the floss?
GRR
THUDD
YIP!!
'bye, mel... i got places to eat, pizzas to go
MY CAREER AS A WRITER IS OVER... I GUESS IT'S BACK TO CLEANING DISHES
ARTHUR P. d'ECCO
AFTER ALL, I HAVEN'T DONE ANY SINCE LAST YEAR...
The Burning Giraffe

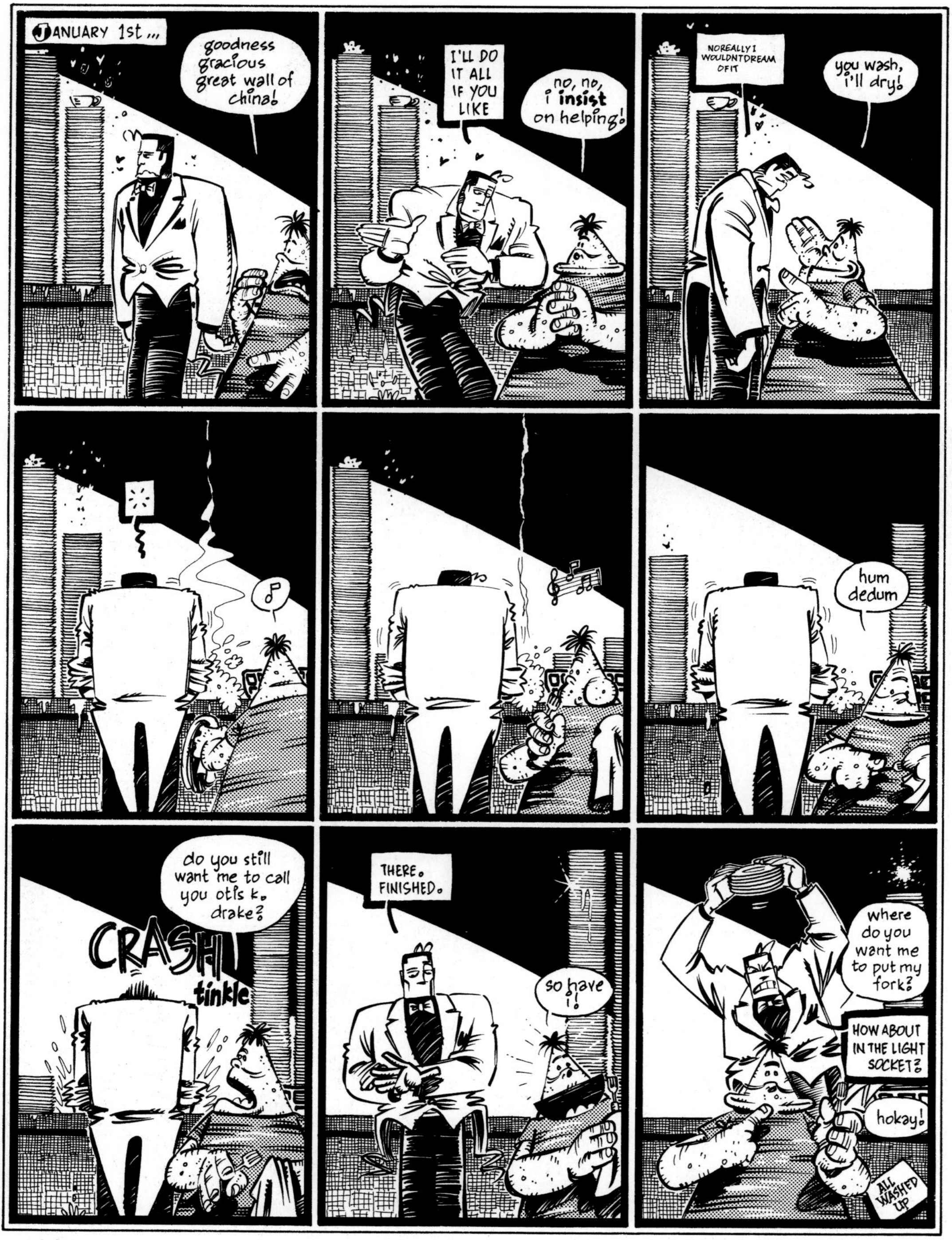
JANUARY 1st ...
goodness gracious great wall of china!
I'LL DO IT ALL IF YOU LIKE
no, no, i insist on helping!
NOREALLYI WOULDNTDREAM OFIT
you wash, i'll dry!
hum dedum
do you still want me to call you otis k. drake?
CRASH!
tinkle
THERE. FINISHED.
so have i!
where do you want me to put my fork?
HOW ABOUT IN THE LIGHT SOCKET?
hokay!
ALL WASHED UP

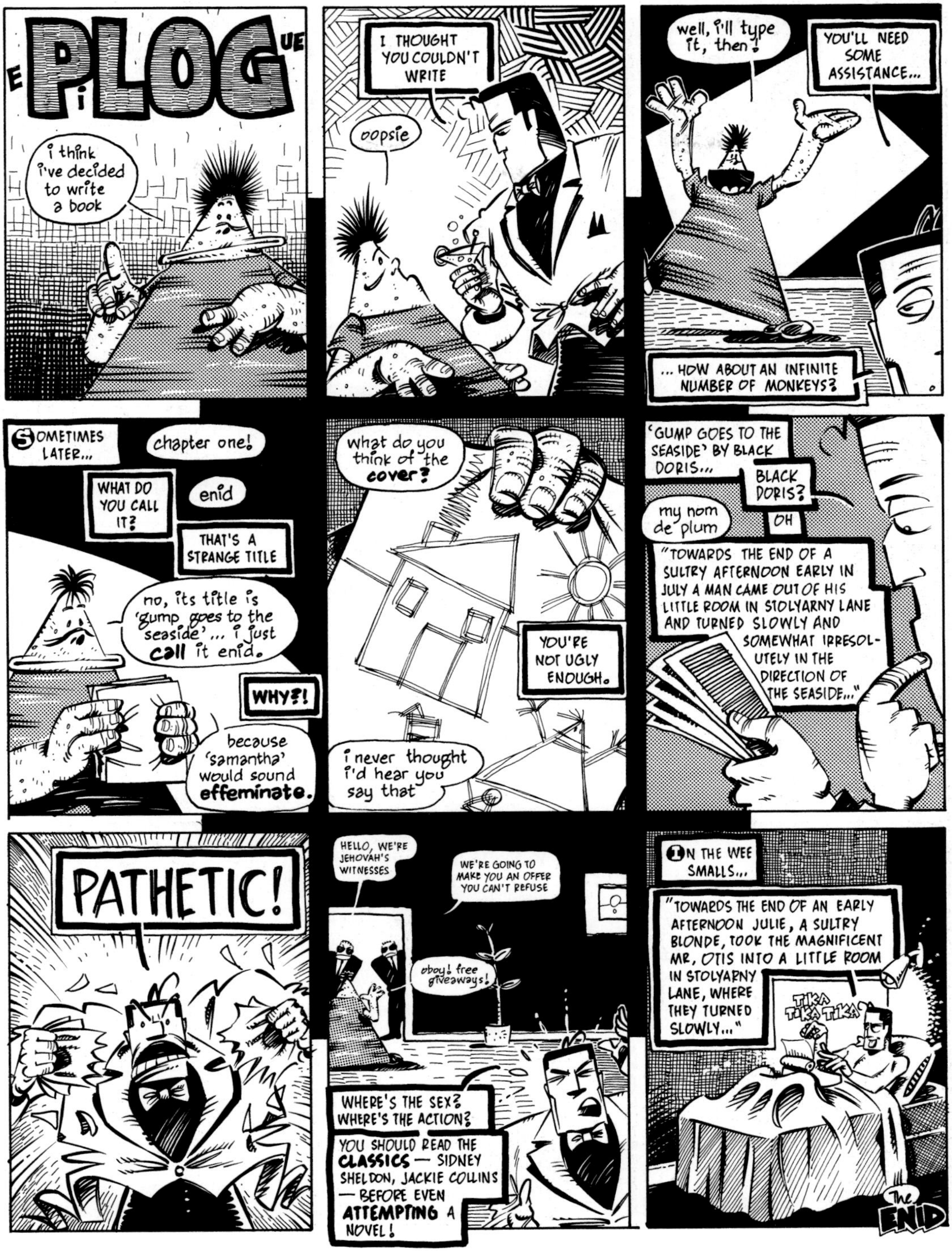
EPiLOGUE
i think i've decided to write a book
I THOUGHT YOU COULDN'T WRITE
oopsie
well, i'll type it, then!
YOU'LL NEED SOME ASSISTANCE...
... HOW ABOUT AN INFINITE NUMBER OF MONKEYS?
SOMETIMES LATER...
chapter one!
WHAT DO YOU CALL IT?
enid
THAT'S A STRANGE TITLE
no, its title is 'gump goes to the seaside'... i just call it enid.
WHY?!
because 'samantha' would sound effeminate.
what do you think of the cover?
YOU'RE NOT UGLY ENOUGH.
i never thought i'd hear you say that
'GUMP GOES TO THE SEASIDE' BY BLACK DORIS...
BLACK DORIS?
my nom de plum
OH
"TOWARDS THE END OF A SULTRY AFTERNOON EARLY IN JULY A MAN CAME OUT OF HIS LITTLE ROOM IN STOLYARNY LANE AND TURNED SLOWLY AND SOMEWHAT IRRESOLUTELY IN THE DIRECTION OF THE SEASIDE..."
PATHETIC!
HELLO, WE'RE JEHOVAH'S WITNESSES
WE'RE GOING TO MAKE YOU AN OFFER YOU CAN'T REFUSE
oboy! free giveaways!
WHERE'S THE SEX? WHERE'S THE ACTION?
YOU SHOULD READ THE CLASSICS — SIDNEY SHELDON, JACKIE COLLINS — BEFORE EVEN ATTEMPTING A NOVEL!
IN THE WEE SMALLS...
"TOWARDS THE END OF AN EARLY AFTERNOON JULIE, A SULTRY BLONDE, TOOK THE MAGNIFICENT MR. OTIS INTO A LITTLE ROOM IN STOLYARNY LANE, WHERE THEY TURNED SLOWLY..."
TIKA TIKA TIKA
The ENID

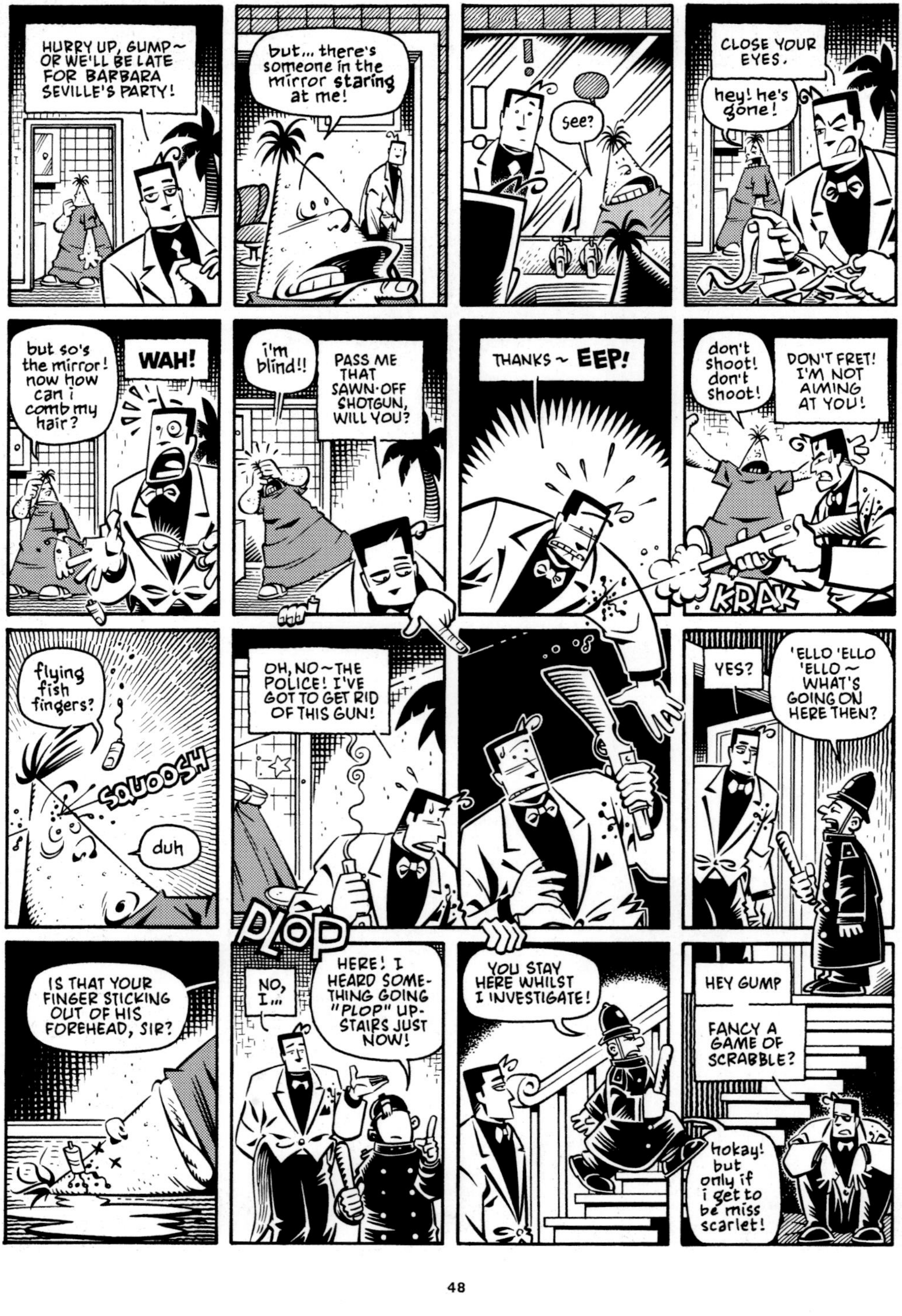
HURRY UP, GUMP ~ OR WE'LL BE LATE FOR BARBARA SEVILLE'S PARTY!
but... there's someone in the mirror staring at me!
!
see?
CLOSE YOUR EYES.
hey! he's gone!
but so's the mirror! now how can i comb my hair?
WAH!
i'm blind!!
PASS ME THAT SAWN-OFF SHOTGUN, WILL YOU?
THANKS ~ EEP!
don't shoot! don't shoot!
DON'T FRET! I'M NOT AIMING AT YOU!
KRAK
flying fish fingers?
SQUOOSH
duh
OH, NO ~ THE POLICE! I'VE GOT TO GET RID OF THIS GUN!
PLOP
YES?
'ELLO 'ELLO 'ELLO ~ WHAT'S GOING ON HERE THEN?
IS THAT YOUR FINGER STICKING OUT OF HIS FOREHEAD, SIR?
NO, I...
HERE! I HEARD SOMETHING GOING "PLOP" UPSTAIRS JUST NOW!
YOU STAY HERE WHILST I INVESTIGATE!
HEY GUMP
FANCY A GAME OF SCRABBLE?
hokay! but only if i get to be miss scarlet!

The Gump's "Funny" Papers

Book Review

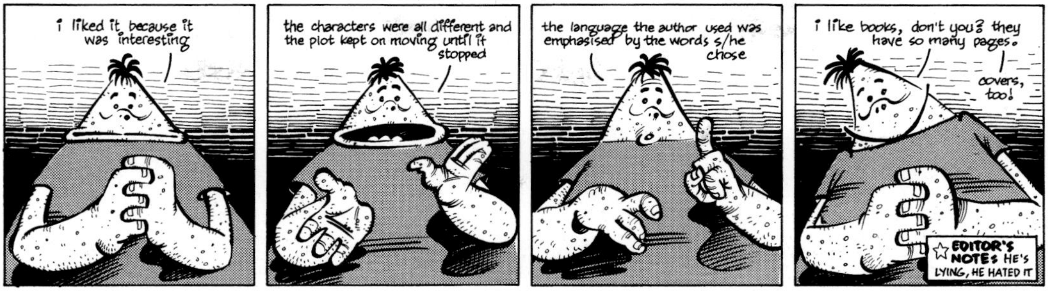

i liked it because it was interesting
the characters were all different and the plot kept on moving until it stopped
the language the author used was emphasised by the words s/he chose
i like books, don't you? they have so many pages.
covers, too!
EDITOR'S NOTE: HE'S LYING, HE HATED IT

Hairway to Neville

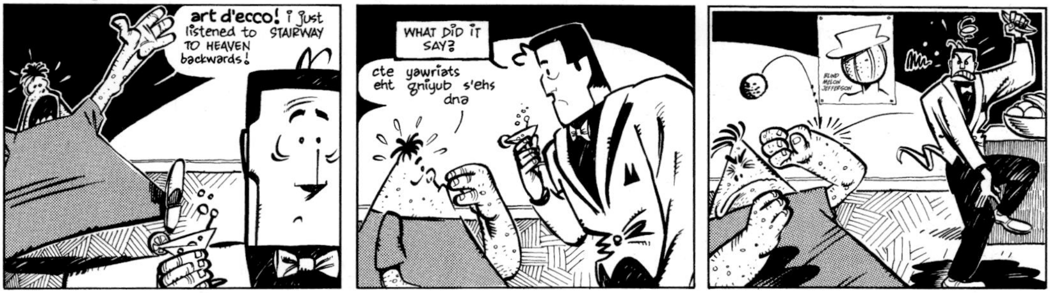

art d'ecco! i just listened to STAIRWAY TO HEAVEN backwards!
WHAT DID IT SAY?
cte yawriats eht gniyub s'ehs dna
BLIND MELON JEFFERSON

New Musical Egg & Cress

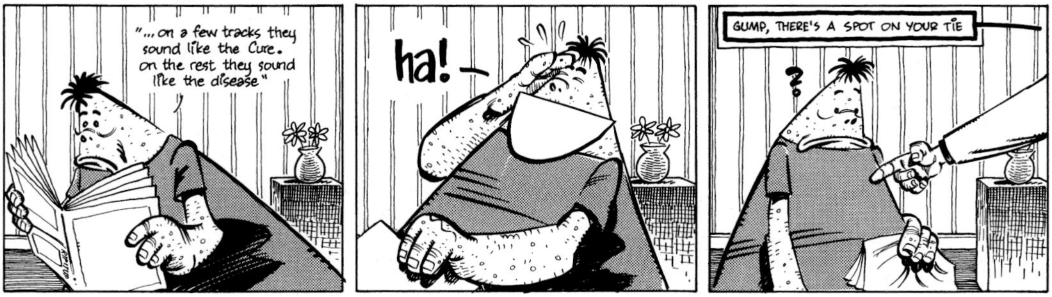

"...on a few tracks they sound like the Cure. on the rest they sound like the disease"
ha!
GUMP, THERE'S A SPOT ON YOUR TIE

The Gump in Concert

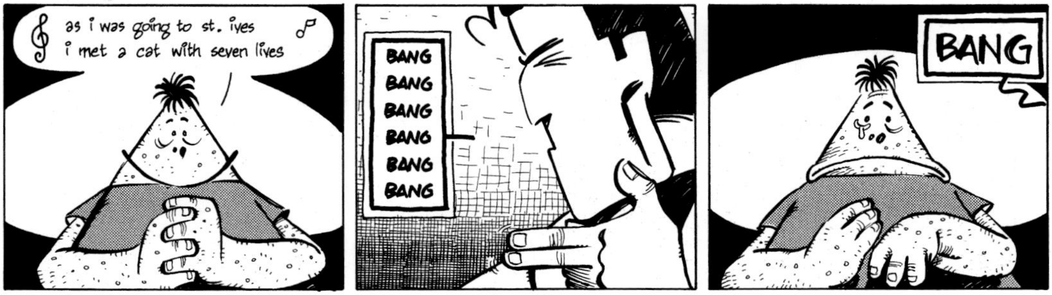

as i was going to st. ives
i met a cat with seven lives
BANG
BANG
BANG
BANG
BANG
BANG
BANG

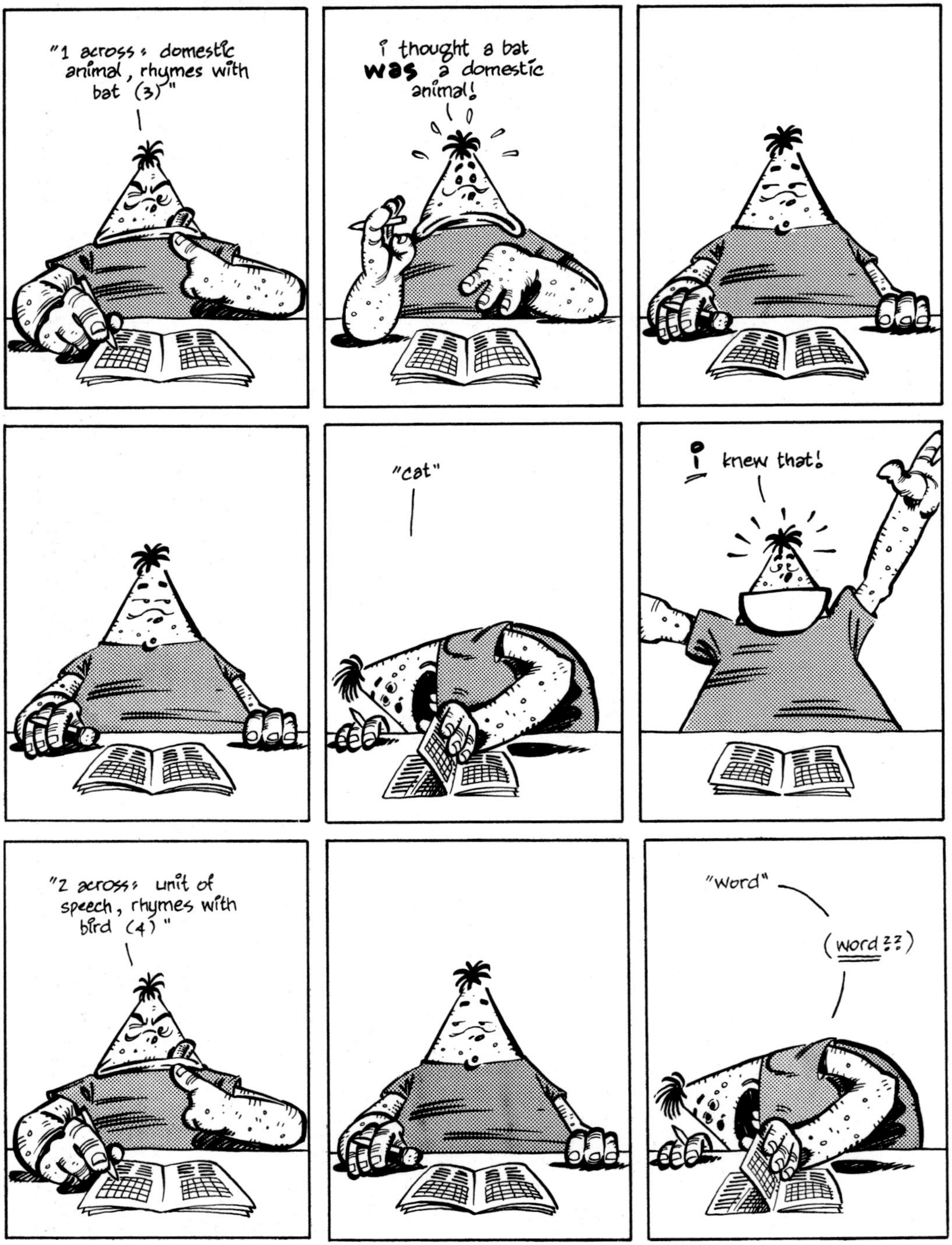
"1 across: domestic animal, rhymes with bat (3)"
i thought a bat **was** a domestic animal!
"cat"
i knew that!
"2 across: unit of speech, rhymes with bird (4)"
"word"
(word??)

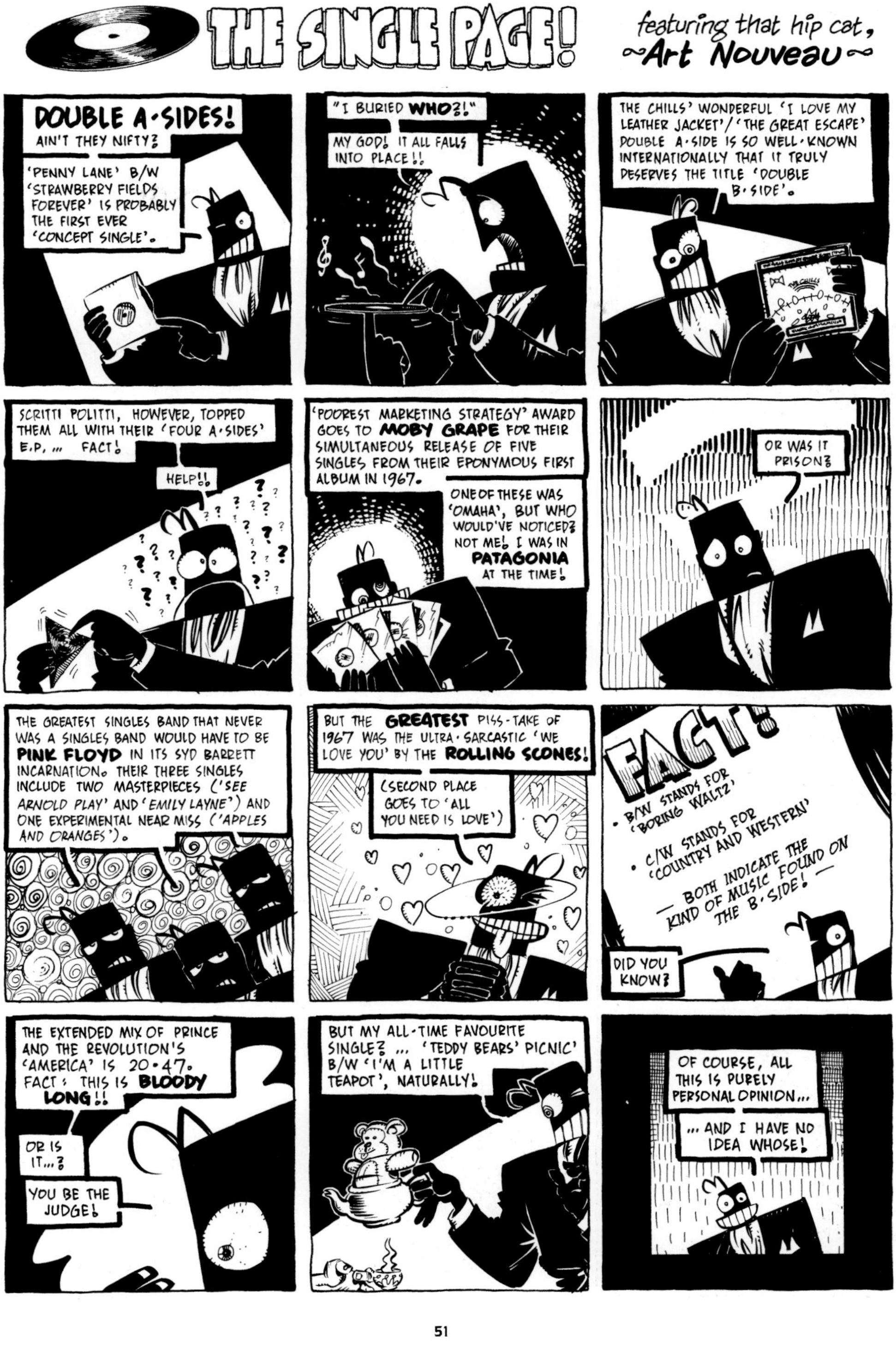
THE SINGLE PAGE!
featuring that hip cat, ~Art Nouveau~
DOUBLE A-SIDES! AIN'T THEY NIFTY?
'PENNY LANE' B/W 'STRAWBERRY FIELDS FOREVER' IS PROBABLY THE FIRST EVER 'CONCEPT SINGLE'.
"I BURIED WHO?!"
MY GOD! IT ALL FALLS INTO PLACE!!
THE CHILLS' WONDERFUL 'I LOVE MY LEATHER JACKET'/'THE GREAT ESCAPE' DOUBLE A-SIDE IS SO WELL-KNOWN INTERNATIONALLY THAT IT TRULY DESERVES THE TITLE 'DOUBLE B-SIDE'.
SCRITTI POLITTI, HOWEVER, TOPPED THEM ALL WITH THEIR 'FOUR A-SIDES' E.P. ... FACT!
HELP!!
'POOREST MARKETING STRATEGY' AWARD GOES TO MOBY GRAPE FOR THEIR SIMULTANEOUS RELEASE OF FIVE SINGLES FROM THEIR EPONYMOUS FIRST ALBUM IN 1967.
ONE OF THESE WAS 'OMAHA', BUT WHO WOULD'VE NOTICED? NOT ME! I WAS IN PATAGONIA AT THE TIME!
OR WAS IT PRISON?
THE GREATEST SINGLES BAND THAT NEVER WAS A SINGLES BAND WOULD HAVE TO BE PINK FLOYD IN ITS SYD BARRETT INCARNATION. THEIR THREE SINGLES INCLUDE TWO MASTERPIECES ('SEE ARNOLD PLAY' AND 'EMILY LAYNE') AND ONE EXPERIMENTAL NEAR MISS ('APPLES AND ORANGES').
BUT THE GREATEST PISS-TAKE OF 1967 WAS THE ULTRA-SARCASTIC 'WE LOVE YOU' BY THE ROLLING SCONES!
(SECOND PLACE GOES TO 'ALL YOU NEED IS LOVE')
FACT!
• B/W STANDS FOR 'BORING WALTZ'
• C/W STANDS FOR 'COUNTRY AND WESTERN'
— BOTH INDICATE THE KIND OF MUSIC FOUND ON THE B-SIDE! —
DID YOU KNOW?
THE EXTENDED MIX OF PRINCE AND THE REVOLUTION'S 'AMERICA' IS 20-47. FACT: THIS IS BLOODY LONG!!
OR IS IT...?
YOU BE THE JUDGE!
BUT MY ALL-TIME FAVOURITE SINGLE? ... 'TEDDY BEARS' PICNIC' B/W 'I'M A LITTLE TEAPOT', NATURALLY!
OF COURSE, ALL THIS IS PURELY PERSONAL OPINION...
... AND I HAVE NO IDEA WHOSE!

AN ART D'ECCO ADVENTURE

LA TRAHISON DES IMAGES

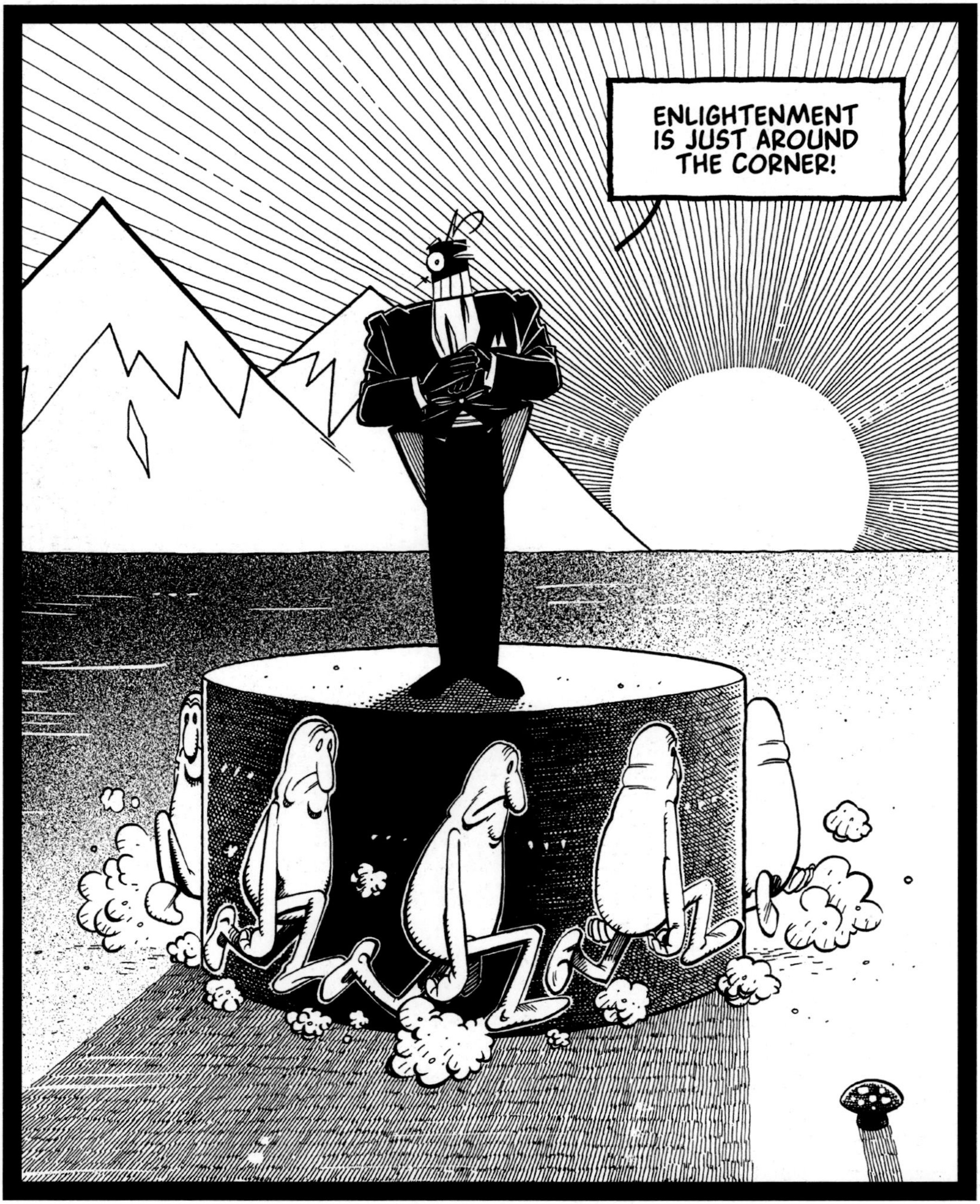
ENLIGHTENMENT IS JUST AROUND THE CORNER!

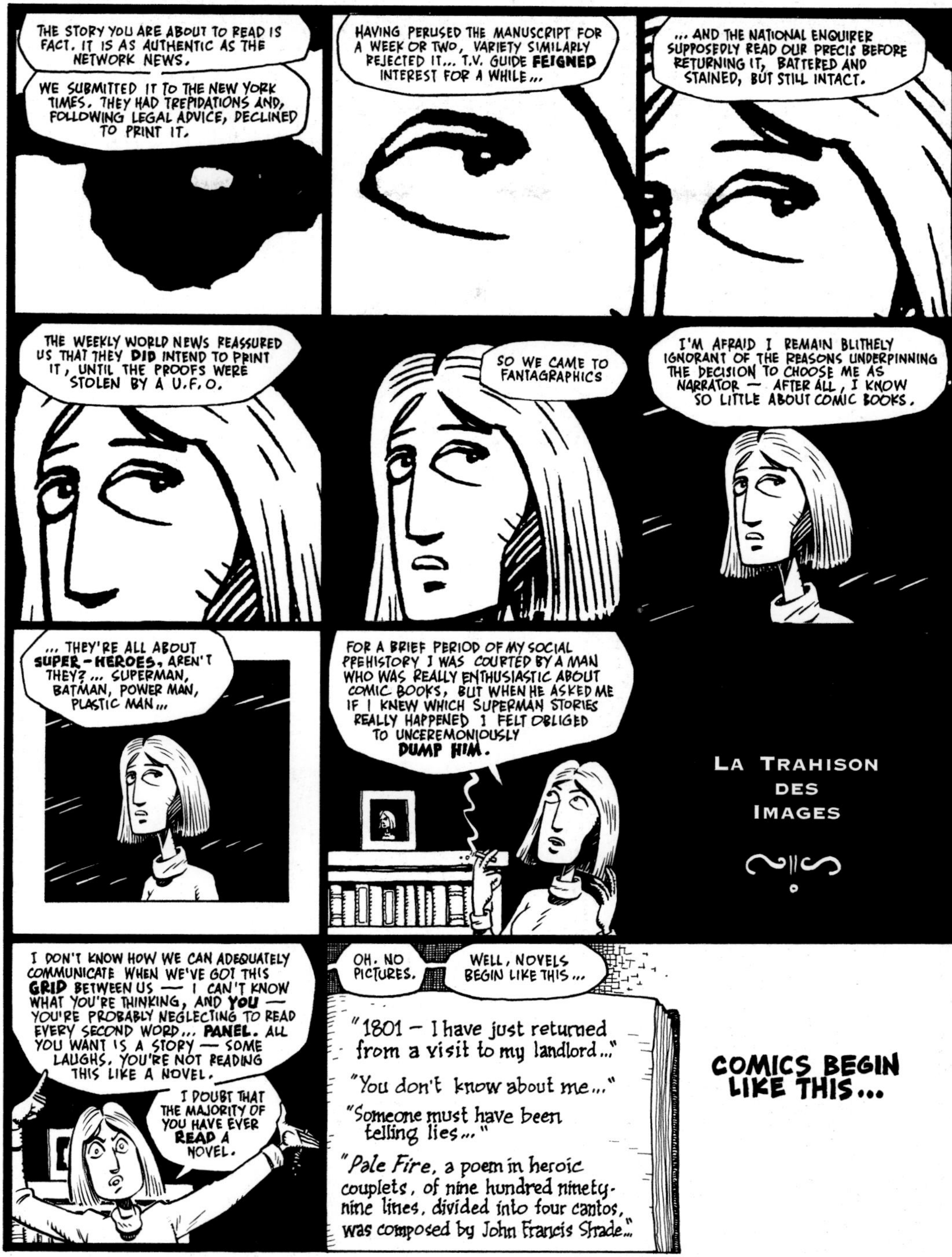

THE STORY YOU ARE ABOUT TO READ IS FACT. IT IS AS AUTHENTIC AS THE NETWORK NEWS.
WE SUBMITTED IT TO THE NEW YORK TIMES. THEY HAD TREPIDATIONS AND, FOLLOWING LEGAL ADVICE, DECLINED TO PRINT IT.
HAVING PERUSED THE MANUSCRIPT FOR A WEEK OR TWO, VARIETY SIMILARLY REJECTED IT... T.V. GUIDE FEIGNED INTEREST FOR A WHILE...
... AND THE NATIONAL ENQUIRER SUPPOSEDLY READ OUR PRECIS BEFORE RETURNING IT, BATTERED AND STAINED, BUT STILL INTACT.
THE WEEKLY WORLD NEWS REASSURED US THAT THEY DID INTEND TO PRINT IT, UNTIL THE PROOFS WERE STOLEN BY A U.F.O.
SO WE CAME TO FANTAGRAPHICS
I'M AFRAID I REMAIN BLITHELY IGNORANT OF THE REASONS UNDERPINNING THE DECISION TO CHOOSE ME AS NARRATOR — AFTER ALL, I KNOW SO LITTLE ABOUT COMIC BOOKS.
... THEY'RE ALL ABOUT SUPER-HEROES, AREN'T THEY? ... SUPERMAN, BATMAN, POWER MAN, PLASTIC MAN...
FOR A BRIEF PERIOD OF MY SOCIAL PREHISTORY I WAS COURTED BY A MAN WHO WAS REALLY ENTHUSIASTIC ABOUT COMIC BOOKS, BUT WHEN HE ASKED ME IF I KNEW WHICH SUPERMAN STORIES REALLY HAPPENED I FELT OBLIGED TO UNCEREMONIOUSLY DUMP HIM.
LA TRAHISON DES IMAGES
I DON'T KNOW HOW WE CAN ADEQUATELY COMMUNICATE WHEN WE'VE GOT THIS GRID BETWEEN US — I CAN'T KNOW WHAT YOU'RE THINKING, AND YOU — YOU'RE PROBABLY NEGLECTING TO READ EVERY SECOND WORD... PANEL. ALL YOU WANT IS A STORY — SOME LAUGHS. YOU'RE NOT READING THIS LIKE A NOVEL.
I DOUBT THAT THE MAJORITY OF YOU HAVE EVER READ A NOVEL.
OH. NO PICTURES.
WELL, NOVELS BEGIN LIKE THIS...
"1801 — I have just returned from a visit to my landlord..."
"You don't know about me..."
"Someone must have been telling lies..."
"Pale Fire, a poem in heroic couplets, of nine hundred ninety-nine lines, divided into four cantos, was composed by John Francis Shade..."
COMICS BEGIN LIKE THIS...

FUCK ME DAYS, I'M OFF TO WORK ON MY OPERA

don't forget the lunch i made for you

HOW COULD I ,... IT'S VASELINE AND MARMITE AGAIN

o! what can i do, alone in this big empty house all day?

TRY POURING WATER INTO A **SPOON**.

hokay!

now what do i do, art d'ecco?

art d'ecco?

mayhaps i need a job too...

oh boysenberry!

LIKE ANIMALS?

i love animals — they taste so good!

hello um

any training?

does potty training count?

oh, okay!

HELLO, IT'S ONLY ME. SO — ONCE UPON A TIME DOT DOT DOT ,... NOW, FOR YOUR EDIFICATION, A FLASHBACK TO THE GUMP'S POTTY TRAINING (YES, IT'S THAT KIND OF STORY) ...

hooplah!

i gotta job! i gotta dance!

i'm ... putting on my top hat ... tying up my white rat ... stepping on his tail!

LIKE ANIMALS? We are looking for people who are like animals' and don't mind being prodded, poked or even lightly maimed. Persons with no living relatives preferred. Please contact: SHENANDALU COSMETICS

PIANO LOOKING FOR WOMAN WITH CARVED LEGS

54

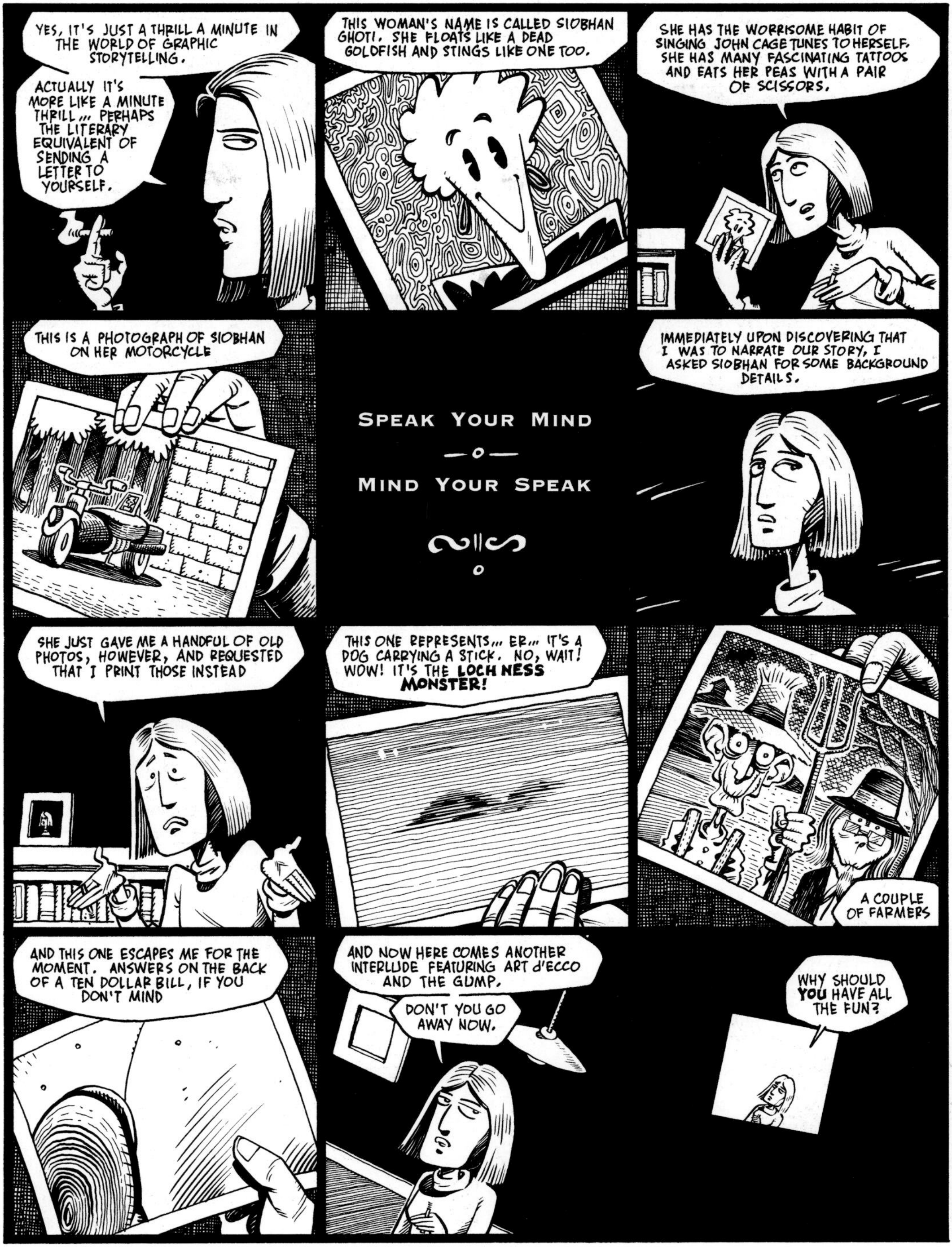

YES, IT'S JUST A THRILL A MINUTE IN THE WORLD OF GRAPHIC STORYTELLING.
ACTUALLY IT'S MORE LIKE A MINUTE THRILL... PERHAPS THE LITERARY EQUIVALENT OF SENDING A LETTER TO YOURSELF.
THIS WOMAN'S NAME IS CALLED SIOBHAN GHOTI. SHE FLOATS LIKE A DEAD GOLDFISH AND STINGS LIKE ONE TOO.
SHE HAS THE WORRISOME HABIT OF SINGING JOHN CAGE TUNES TO HERSELF. SHE HAS MANY FASCINATING TATTOOS AND EATS HER PEAS WITH A PAIR OF SCISSORS.
THIS IS A PHOTOGRAPH OF SIOBHAN ON HER MOTORCYCLE
SPEAK YOUR MIND
MIND YOUR SPEAK
IMMEDIATELY UPON DISCOVERING THAT I WAS TO NARRATE OUR STORY, I ASKED SIOBHAN FOR SOME BACKGROUND DETAILS.
SHE JUST GAVE ME A HANDFUL OF OLD PHOTOS, HOWEVER, AND REQUESTED THAT I PRINT THOSE INSTEAD
THIS ONE REPRESENTS... ER... IT'S A DOG CARRYING A STICK. NO, WAIT! WOW! IT'S THE LOCH NESS MONSTER!
A COUPLE OF FARMERS
AND THIS ONE ESCAPES ME FOR THE MOMENT. ANSWERS ON THE BACK OF A TEN DOLLAR BILL, IF YOU DON'T MIND
AND NOW HERE COMES ANOTHER INTERLUDE FEATURING ART d'ECCO AND THE GUMP.
DON'T YOU GO AWAY NOW.
WHY SHOULD YOU HAVE ALL THE FUN?

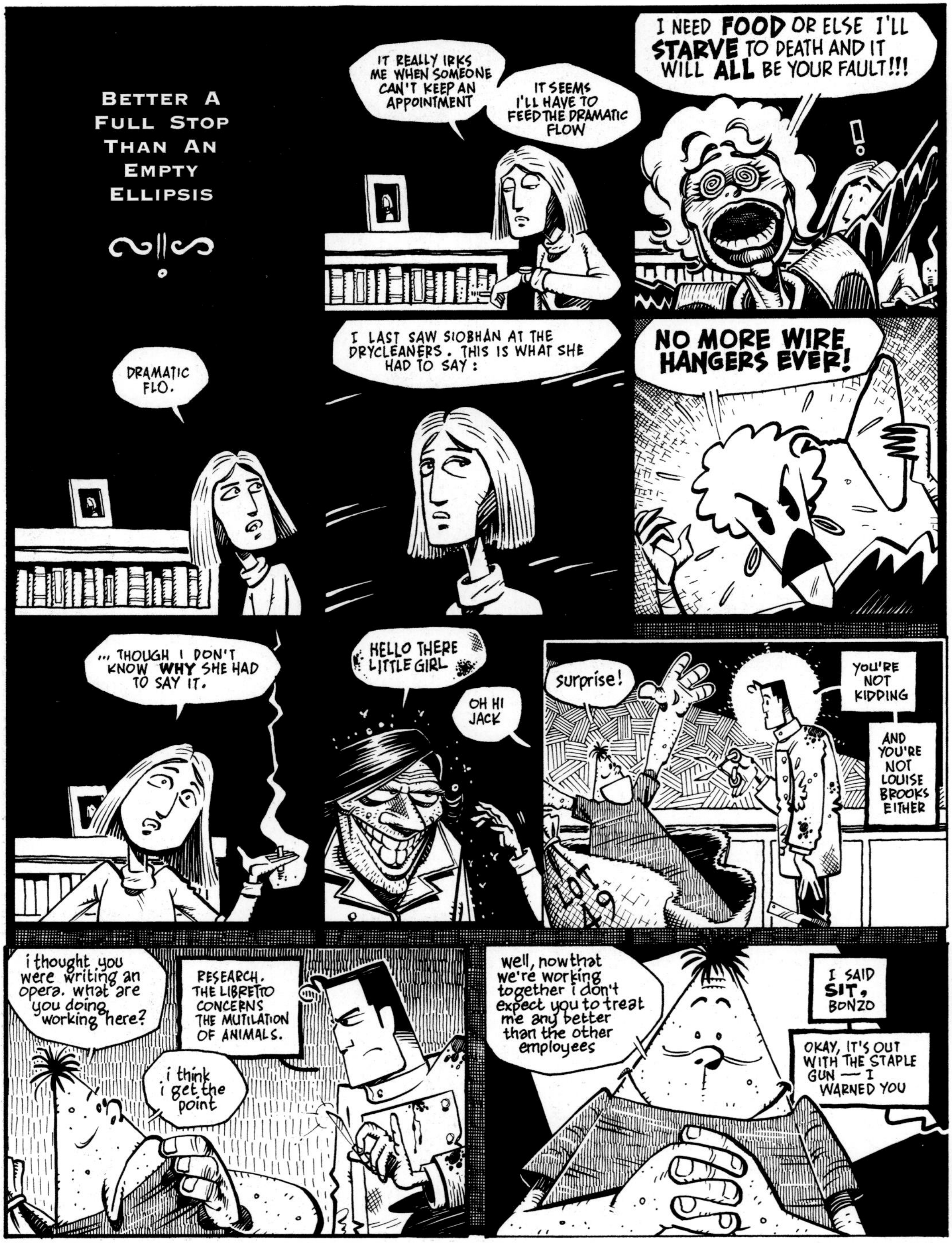

Better A Full Stop Than An Empty Ellipsis
IT REALLY IRKS ME WHEN SOMEONE CAN'T KEEP AN APPOINTMENT
IT SEEMS I'LL HAVE TO FEED THE DRAMATIC FLOW
I NEED FOOD OR ELSE I'LL STARVE TO DEATH AND IT WILL ALL BE YOUR FAULT!!!
!
DRAMATIC FLO.
I LAST SAW SIOBHAN AT THE DRYCLEANERS. THIS IS WHAT SHE HAD TO SAY:
NO MORE WIRE HANGERS EVER!
... THOUGH I DON'T KNOW WHY SHE HAD TO SAY IT.
HELLO THERE LITTLE GIRL
OH HI JACK
surprise!
YOU'RE NOT KIDDING
AND YOU'RE NOT LOUISE BROOKS EITHER
i thought you were writing an opera. what are you doing working here?
RESEARCH. THE LIBRETTO CONCERNS THE MUTILATION OF ANIMALS.
i think i get the point
well, now that we're working together i don't expect you to treat me any better than the other employees
I SAID SIT, BONZO
OKAY, IT'S OUT WITH THE STAPLE GUN — I WARNED YOU

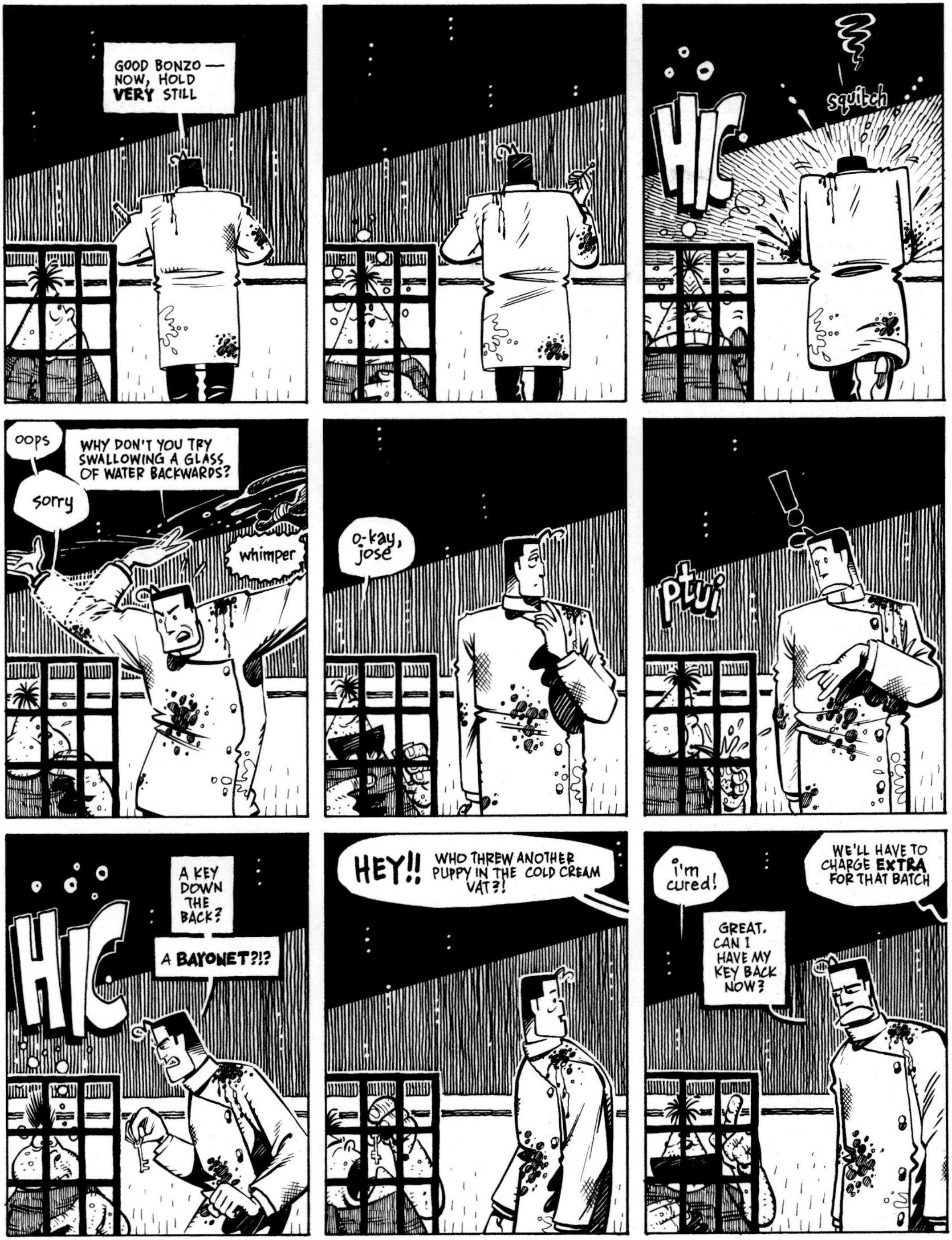
GOOD BONZO — NOW, HOLD VERY STILL
HIC
squitch
oops
WHY DON'T YOU TRY SWALLOWING A GLASS OF WATER BACKWARDS?
sorry
whimper
o-kay, josé
!
ptui
HIC
A KEY DOWN THE BACK?
A BAYONET?!?
HEY!! WHO THREW ANOTHER PUPPY IN THE COLD CREAM VAT?!
i'm cured!
WE'LL HAVE TO CHARGE EXTRA FOR THAT BATCH
GREAT. CAN I HAVE MY KEY BACK NOW?

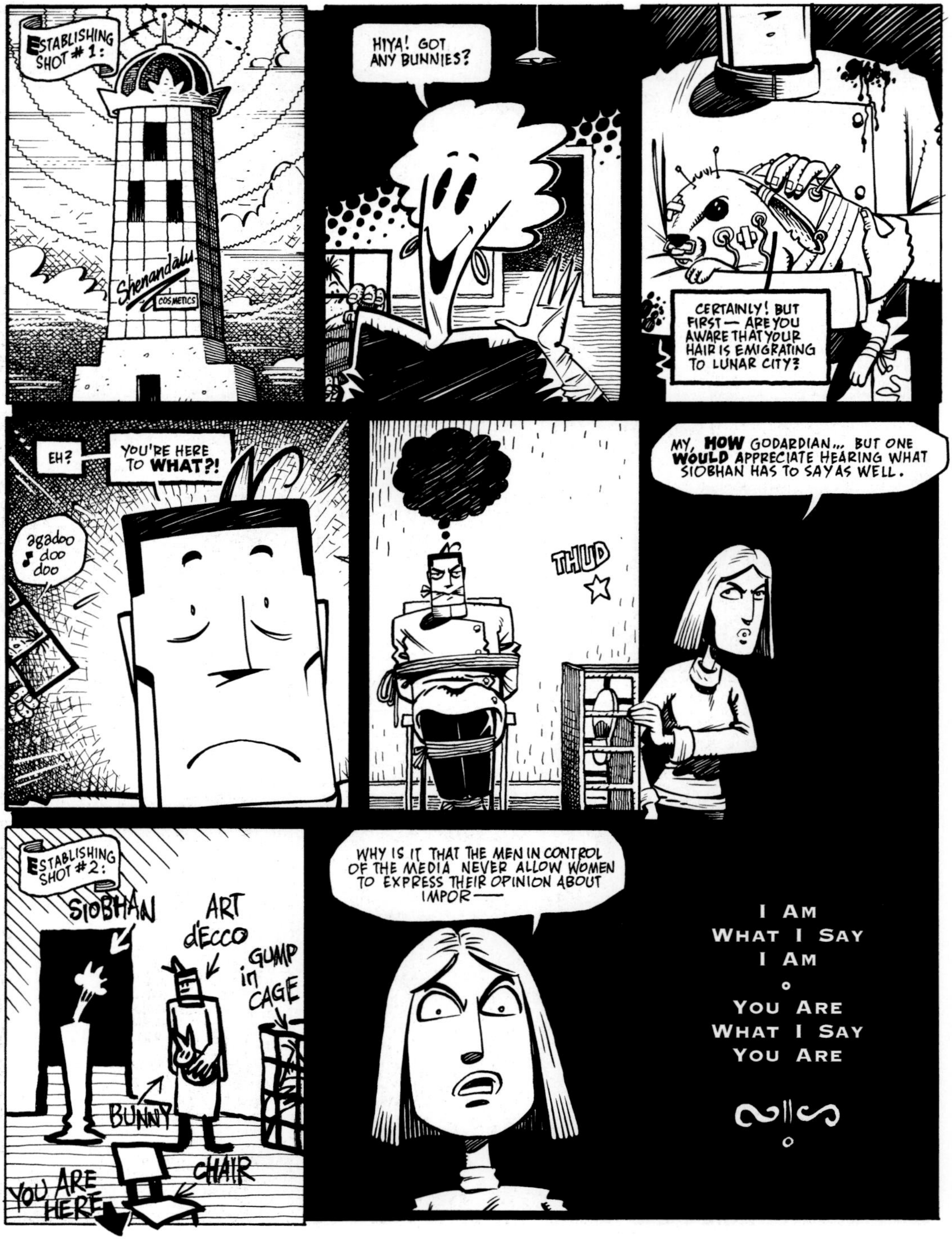
ESTABLISHING SHOT # 1:
Shenandalu
COSMETICS
HIYA! GOT ANY BUNNIES?
CERTAINLY! BUT FIRST— ARE YOU AWARE THAT YOUR HAIR IS EMIGRATING TO LUNAR CITY?
EH?
YOU'RE HERE TO WHAT?!
agadoo doo doo
THUD
MY, HOW GODARDIAN... BUT ONE WOULD APPRECIATE HEARING WHAT SIOBHAN HAS TO SAY AS WELL.
ESTABLISHING SHOT # 2:
SIOBHAN
ART d'ECCO
GUMP in CAGE
BUNNY
CHAIR
YOU ARE HERE
WHY IS IT THAT THE MEN IN CONTROL OF THE MEDIA NEVER ALLOW WOMEN TO EXPRESS THEIR OPINION ABOUT IMPOR—
I AM
WHAT I SAY
I AM
YOU ARE
WHAT I SAY
YOU ARE

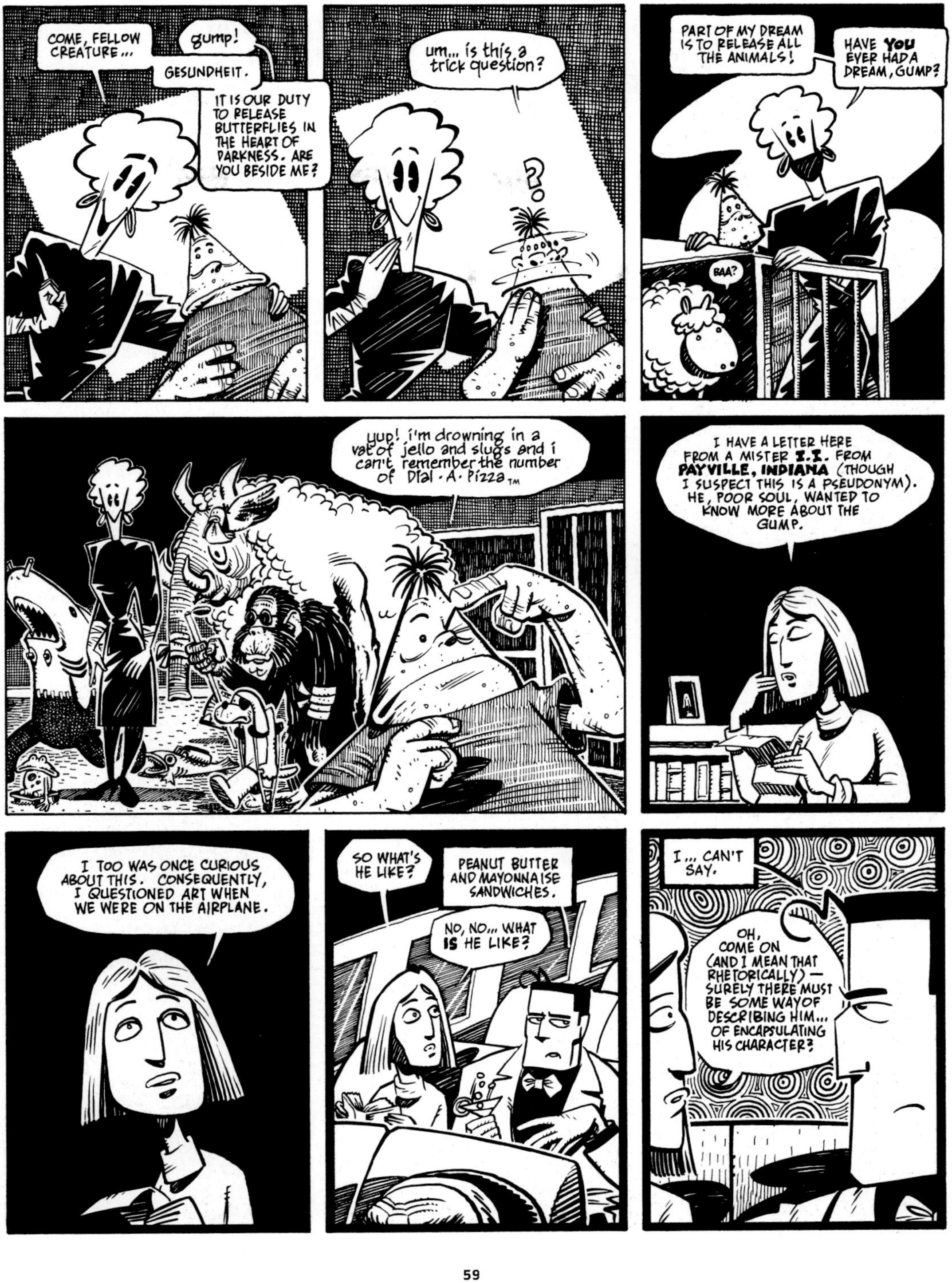
COME, FELLOW CREATURE...
gump!
GESUNDHEIT.
IT IS OUR DUTY TO RELEASE BUTTERFLIES IN THE HEART OF DARKNESS. ARE YOU BESIDE ME?
um... is this a trick question?
?
PART OF MY DREAM IS TO RELEASE ALL THE ANIMALS!
HAVE YOU EVER HAD A DREAM, GUMP?
BAA?
yup! i'm drowning in a vat of jello and slugs and i can't remember the number of Dial-A-Pizza TM
I HAVE A LETTER HERE FROM A MISTER I.I. FROM PAYVILLE, INDIANA (THOUGH I SUSPECT THIS IS A PSEUDONYM). HE, POOR SOUL, WANTED TO KNOW MORE ABOUT THE GUMP.
I TOO WAS ONCE CURIOUS ABOUT THIS. CONSEQUENTLY, I QUESTIONED ART WHEN WE WERE ON THE AIRPLANE.
SO WHAT'S HE LIKE?
PEANUT BUTTER AND MAYONNAISE SANDWICHES.
NO, NO... WHAT IS HE LIKE?
I... CAN'T SAY.
OH, COME ON (AND I MEAN THAT RHETORICALLY)— SURELY THERE MUST BE SOME WAY OF DESCRIBING HIM... OF ENCAPSULATING HIS CHARACTER?

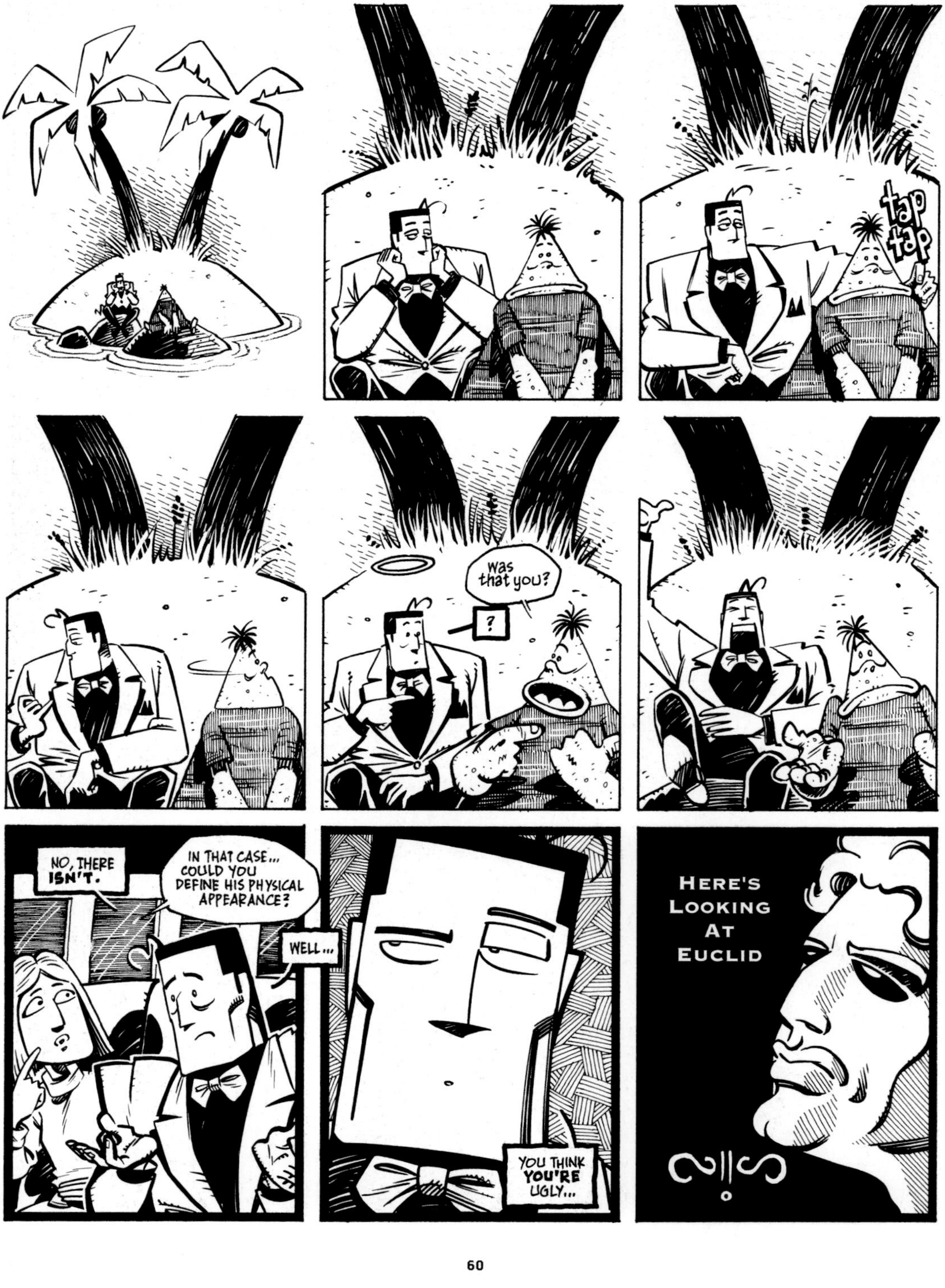
tap tap
was that you?
?
NO, THERE ISN'T.
IN THAT CASE... COULD YOU DEFINE HIS PHYSICAL APPEARANCE?
WELL...
YOU THINK YOU'RE UGLY...
HERE'S LOOKING AT EUCLID

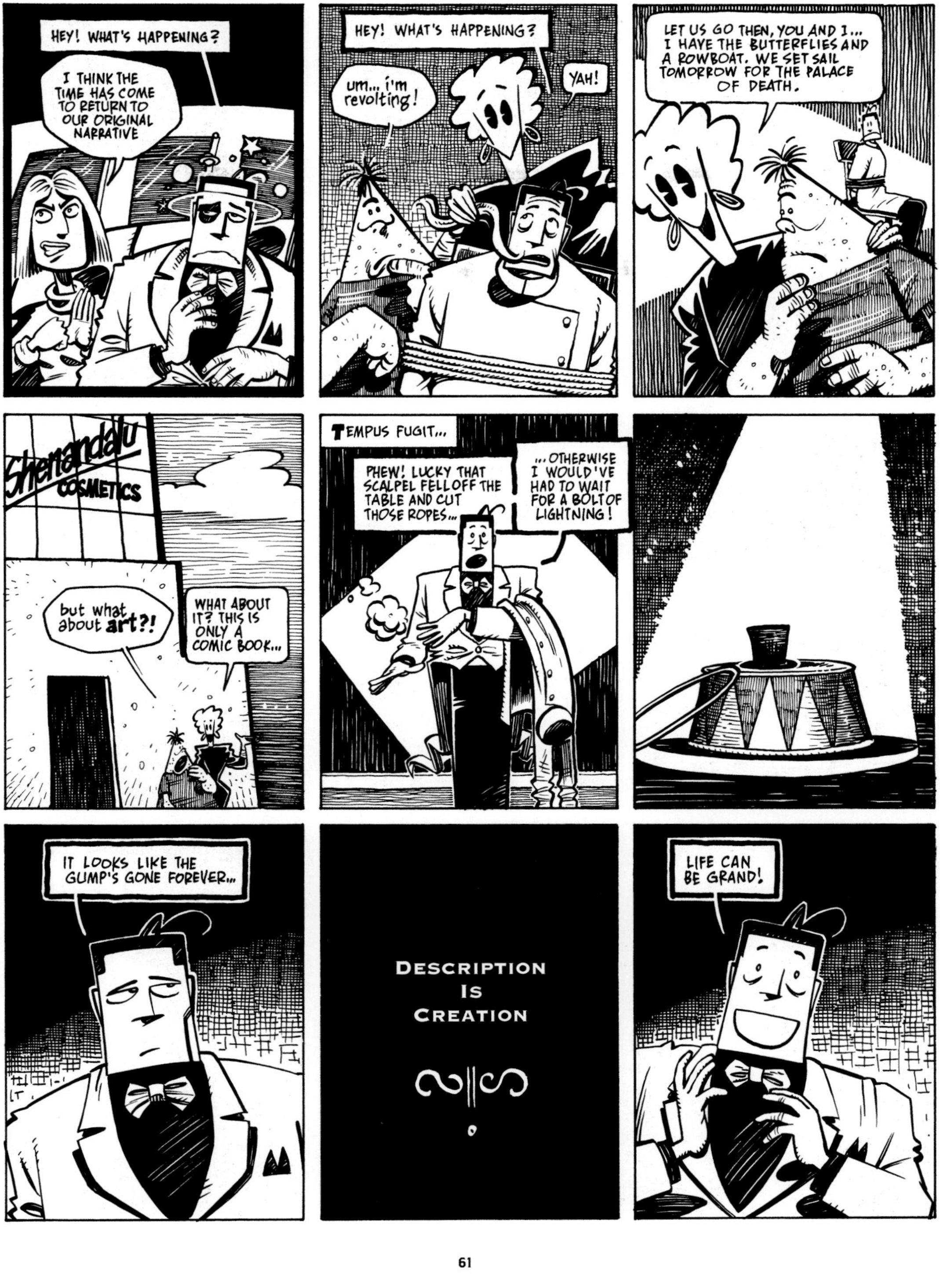
HEY! WHAT'S HAPPENING?
I THINK THE TIME HAS COME TO RETURN TO OUR ORIGINAL NARRATIVE
HEY! WHAT'S HAPPENING?
um... i'm revolting!
YAH!
LET US GO THEN, YOU AND I... I HAVE THE BUTTERFLIES AND A ROWBOAT. WE SET SAIL TOMORROW FOR THE PALACE OF DEATH.
Shenandalu COSMETICS
but what about art?!
WHAT ABOUT IT? THIS IS ONLY A COMIC BOOK...
TEMPUS FUGIT...
PHEW! LUCKY THAT SCALPEL FELL OFF THE TABLE AND CUT THOSE ROPES...
...OTHERWISE I WOULD'VE HAD TO WAIT FOR A BOLT OF LIGHTNING!
IT LOOKS LIKE THE GUMP'S GONE FOREVER...
DESCRIPTION IS CREATION
LIFE CAN BE GRAND!

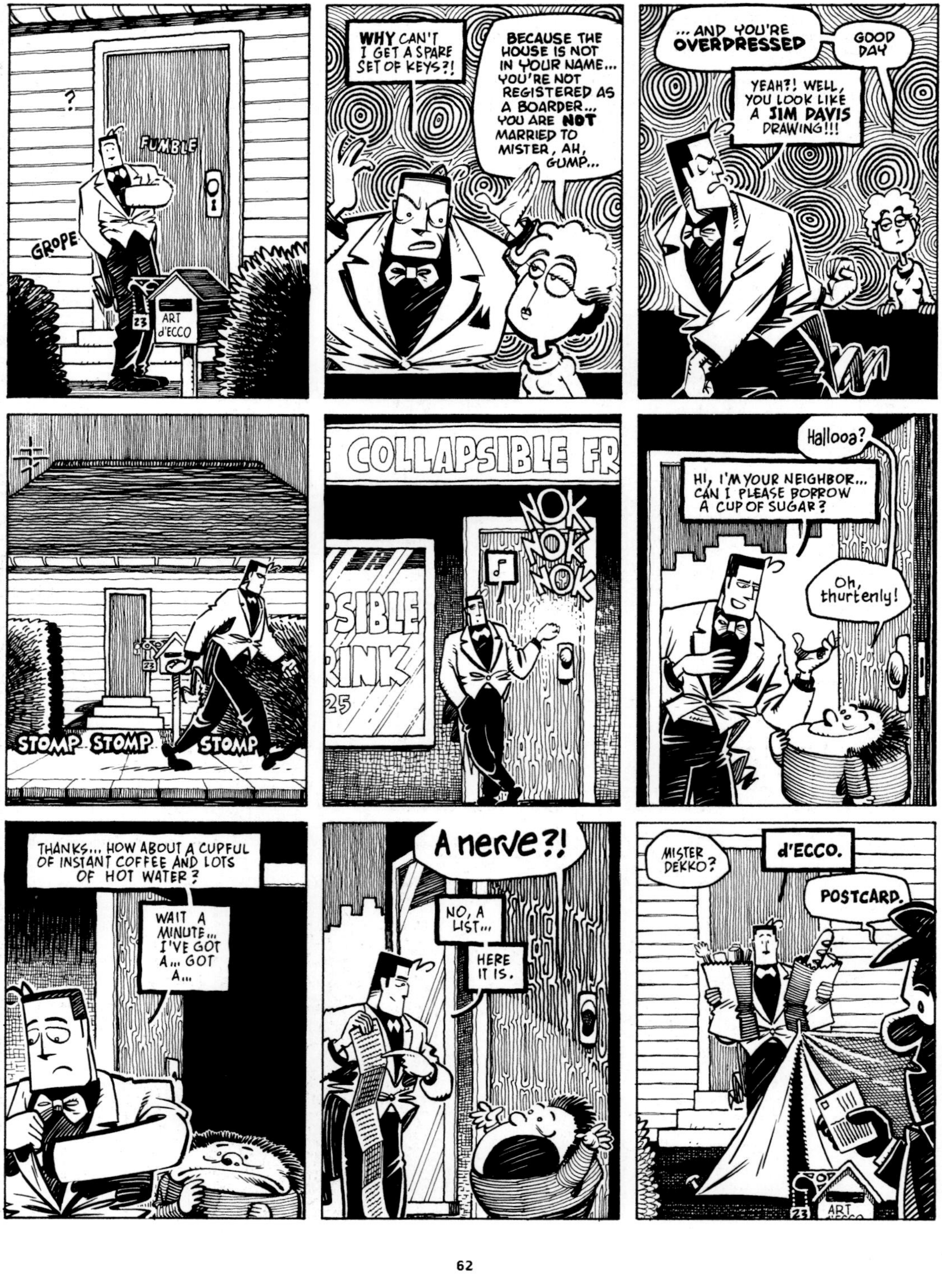
?
FUMBLE
GROPE
23
ART d'ECCO
WHY CAN'T I GET A SPARE SET OF KEYS?!
BECAUSE THE HOUSE IS NOT IN YOUR NAME... YOU'RE NOT REGISTERED AS A BOARDER... YOU ARE NOT MARRIED TO MISTER, AH, GUMP...
... AND YOU'RE OVERDRESSED
GOOD DAY
YEAH?! WELL, YOU LOOK LIKE A JIM DAVIS DRAWING!!!
STOMP STOMP STOMP
COLLAPSIBLE FR
NOK NOK NOK
PSIBLE RINK
25
Hallooa?
HI, I'M YOUR NEIGHBOR... CAN I PLEASE BORROW A CUP OF SUGAR?
Oh, thurtenly!
THANKS... HOW ABOUT A CUPFUL OF INSTANT COFFEE AND LOTS OF HOT WATER?
WAIT A MINUTE... I'VE GOT A... GOT A...
A nerve?!
NO, A LIST...
HERE IT IS.
MISTER DEKKO?
d'ECCO.
POSTCARD.
23
ART

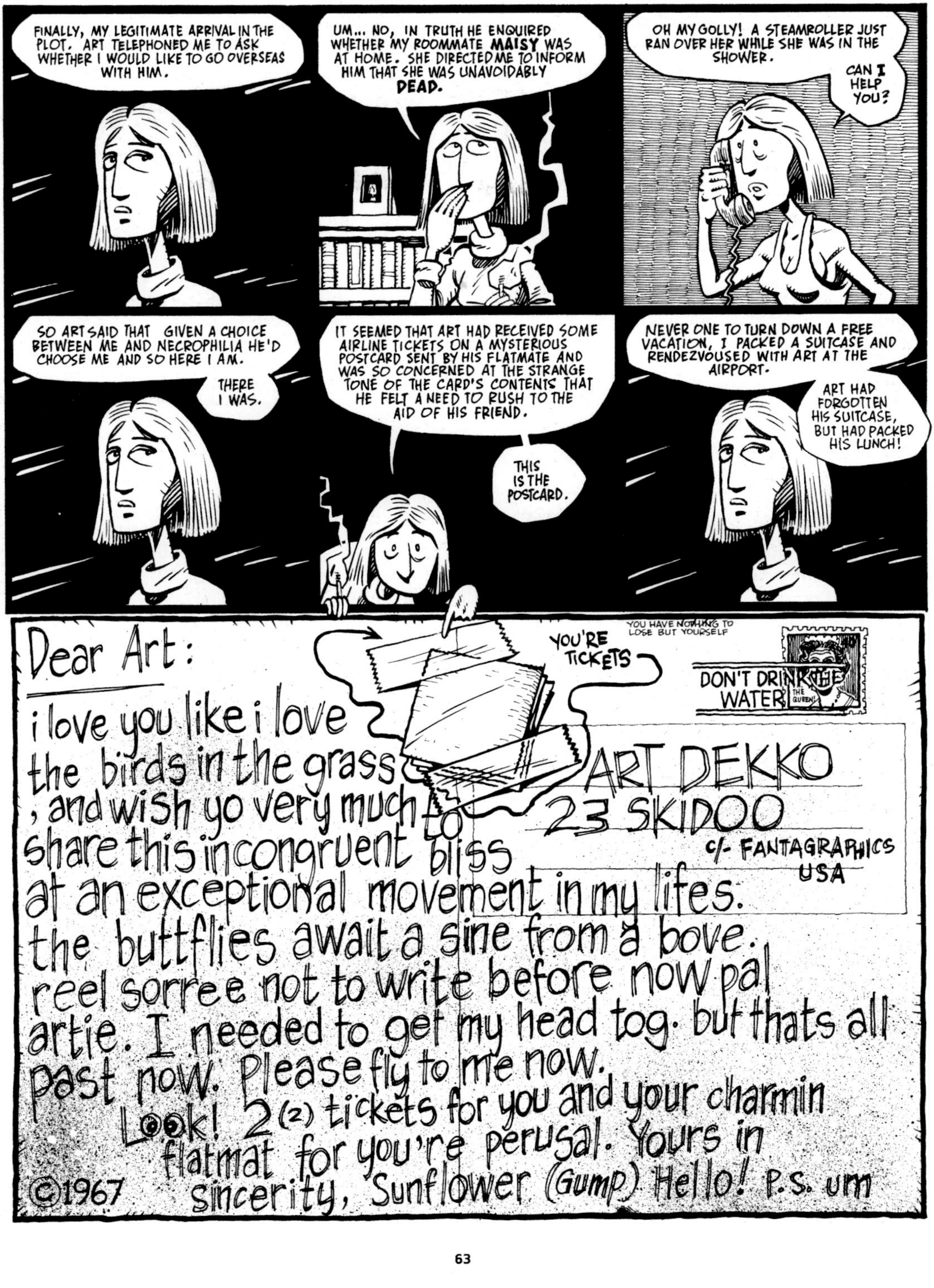

FINALLY, MY LEGITIMATE ARRIVAL IN THE PLOT. ART TELEPHONED ME TO ASK WHETHER I WOULD LIKE TO GO OVERSEAS WITH HIM.
UM... NO, IN TRUTH HE ENQUIRED WHETHER MY ROOMMATE MAISY WAS AT HOME. SHE DIRECTED ME TO INFORM HIM THAT SHE WAS UNAVOIDABLY DEAD.
OH MY GOLLY! A STEAMROLLER JUST RAN OVER HER WHILE SHE WAS IN THE SHOWER.
CAN I HELP YOU?
SO ART SAID THAT GIVEN A CHOICE BETWEEN ME AND NECROPHILIA HE'D CHOOSE ME AND SO HERE I AM.
THERE I WAS.
IT SEEMED THAT ART HAD RECEIVED SOME AIRLINE TICKETS ON A MYSTERIOUS POSTCARD SENT BY HIS FLATMATE AND WAS SO CONCERNED AT THE STRANGE TONE OF THE CARD'S CONTENTS THAT HE FELT A NEED TO RUSH TO THE AID OF HIS FRIEND.
THIS IS THE POSTCARD.
NEVER ONE TO TURN DOWN A FREE VACATION, I PACKED A SUITCASE AND RENDEZVOUSED WITH ART AT THE AIRPORT.
ART HAD FORGOTTEN HIS SUITCASE, BUT HAD PACKED HIS LUNCH!
Dear Art:
YOU'RE TICKETS
YOU HAVE NOTHING TO LOSE BUT YOURSELF
DON'T DRINK THE WATER
THE QUEEN!
ART DEKKO
23 SKIDOO
c/- FANTAGRAPHICS
USA
i love you like i love the birds in the grass, and wish yo very much to share this incongruent bliss at an exceptional movement in my lifes. the buttflies await a sine from a bove. reel sorree not to write before now pal artie. I needed to get my head tog. but thats all past now. Please fly to me now.
Look! 2 (2) tickets for you and your charmin flatmat for you're perusal. Yours in sincerity, Sunflower (Gump) Hello! P.S. um
©1967

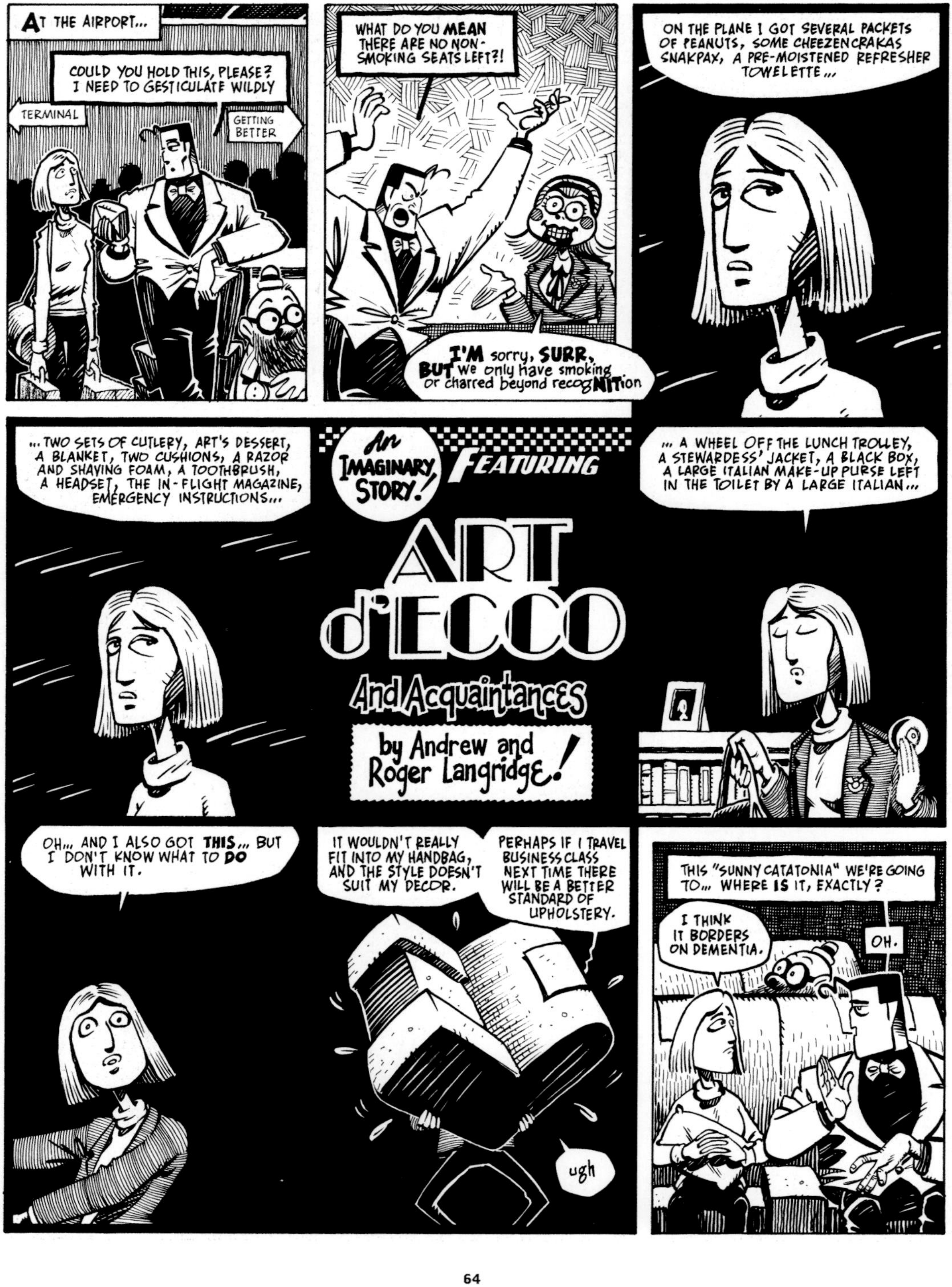
AT THE AIRPORT...
COULD YOU HOLD THIS, PLEASE? I NEED TO GESTICULATE WILDLY
TERMINAL
GETTING BETTER
WHAT DO YOU MEAN THERE ARE NO NON-SMOKING SEATS LEFT?!
I'M sorry, SURR, BUT we only have smoking or charred beyond recogNITion
ON THE PLANE I GOT SEVERAL PACKETS OF PEANUTS, SOME CHEEZENCRAKAS SNAKPAX, A PRE-MOISTENED REFRESHER TOWELETTE...
...TWO SETS OF CUTLERY, ART'S DESSERT, A BLANKET, TWO CUSHIONS, A RAZOR AND SHAVING FOAM, A TOOTHBRUSH, A HEADSET, THE IN-FLIGHT MAGAZINE, EMERGENCY INSTRUCTIONS...
An IMAGINARY STORY!
FEATURING
ART d'ECCO
And Acquaintances
by Andrew and Roger Langridge!
... A WHEEL OFF THE LUNCH TROLLEY, A STEWARDESS' JACKET, A BLACK BOX, A LARGE ITALIAN MAKE-UP PURSE LEFT IN THE TOILET BY A LARGE ITALIAN...
OH... AND I ALSO GOT THIS... BUT I DON'T KNOW WHAT TO DO WITH IT.
IT WOULDN'T REALLY FIT INTO MY HANDBAG, AND THE STYLE DOESN'T SUIT MY DECOR.
PERHAPS IF I TRAVEL BUSINESS CLASS NEXT TIME THERE WILL BE A BETTER STANDARD OF UPHOLSTERY.
ugh
THIS "SUNNY CATATONIA" WE'RE GOING TO... WHERE IS IT, EXACTLY?
I THINK IT BORDERS ON DEMENTIA.
OH.

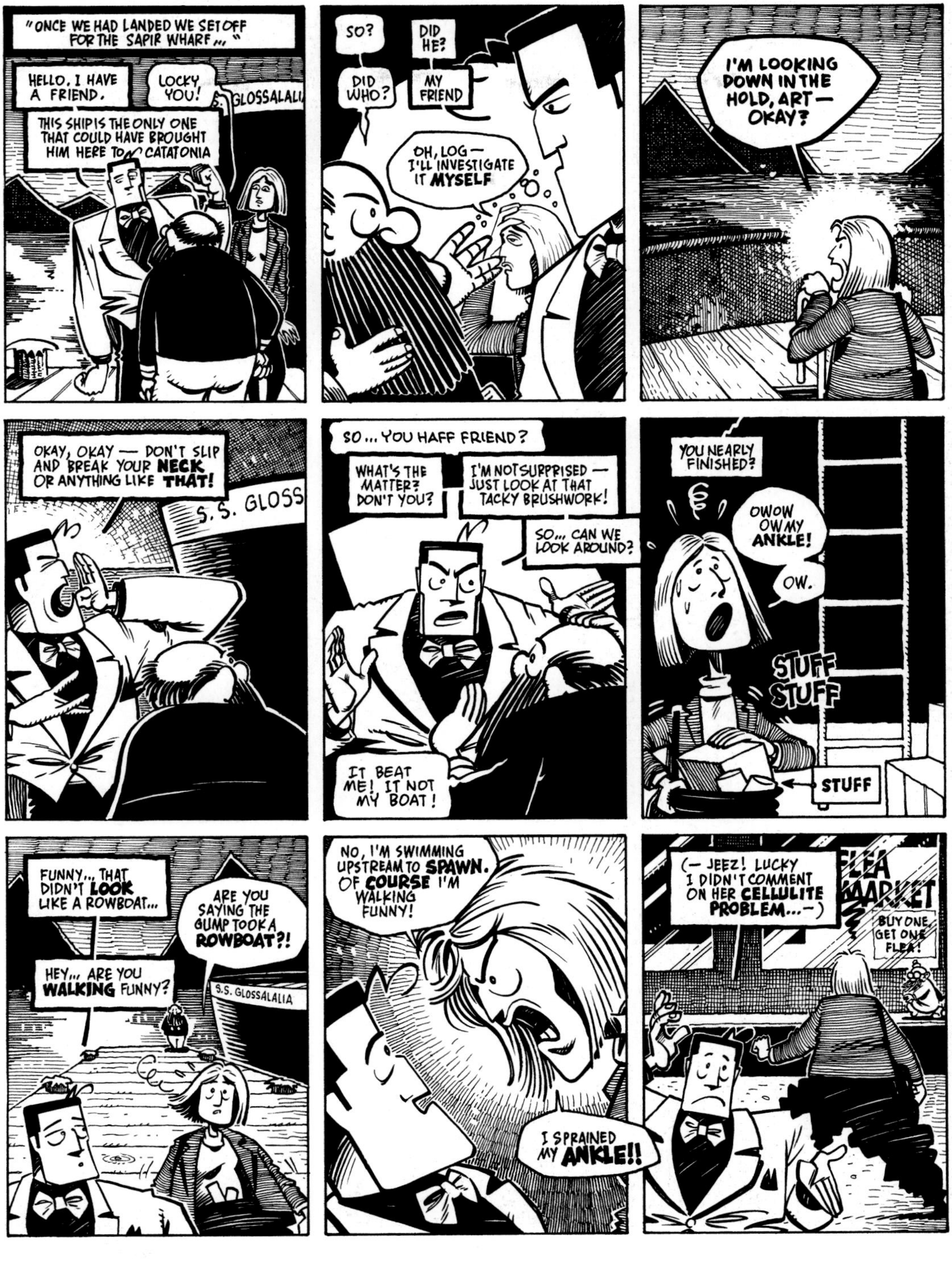
"ONCE WE HAD LANDED WE SET OFF FOR THE SAPIR WHARF..."
HELLO. I HAVE A FRIEND.
LOCKY YOU!
GLOSSALALI
THIS SHIP IS THE ONLY ONE THAT COULD HAVE BROUGHT HIM HERE TO CATATONIA
SO?
DID WHO?
DID HE?
MY FRIEND
OH, LOG — I'LL INVESTIGATE IT **MYSELF**
I'M LOOKING DOWN IN THE HOLD, ART — OKAY?
OKAY, OKAY — DON'T SLIP AND BREAK YOUR **NECK** OR ANYTHING LIKE **THAT!**
S.S. GLOSS
SO... YOU HAFF FRIEND?
WHAT'S THE MATTER? DON'T YOU?
I'M NOT SURPRISED — JUST LOOK AT THAT TACKY BRUSHWORK!
SO... CAN WE LOOK AROUND?
IT BEAT ME! IT NOT MY BOAT!
YOU NEARLY FINISHED?
OWOW OW MY **ANKLE!**
OW.
STUFF STUFF
STUFF
FUNNY... THAT DIDN'T **LOOK** LIKE A ROWBOAT...
ARE YOU SAYING THE GUMP TOOK A **ROWBOAT?!**
HEY... ARE YOU **WALKING** FUNNY?
S.S. GLOSSALALIA
NO, I'M SWIMMING UPSTREAM TO **SPAWN.** OF **COURSE** I'M WALKING FUNNY!
I SPRAINED MY **ANKLE!!**
(— JEEZ! LUCKY I DIDN'T COMMENT ON HER **CELLULITE PROBLEM...** —)
FLEA MARKET
BUY ONE, GET ONE FLEA!

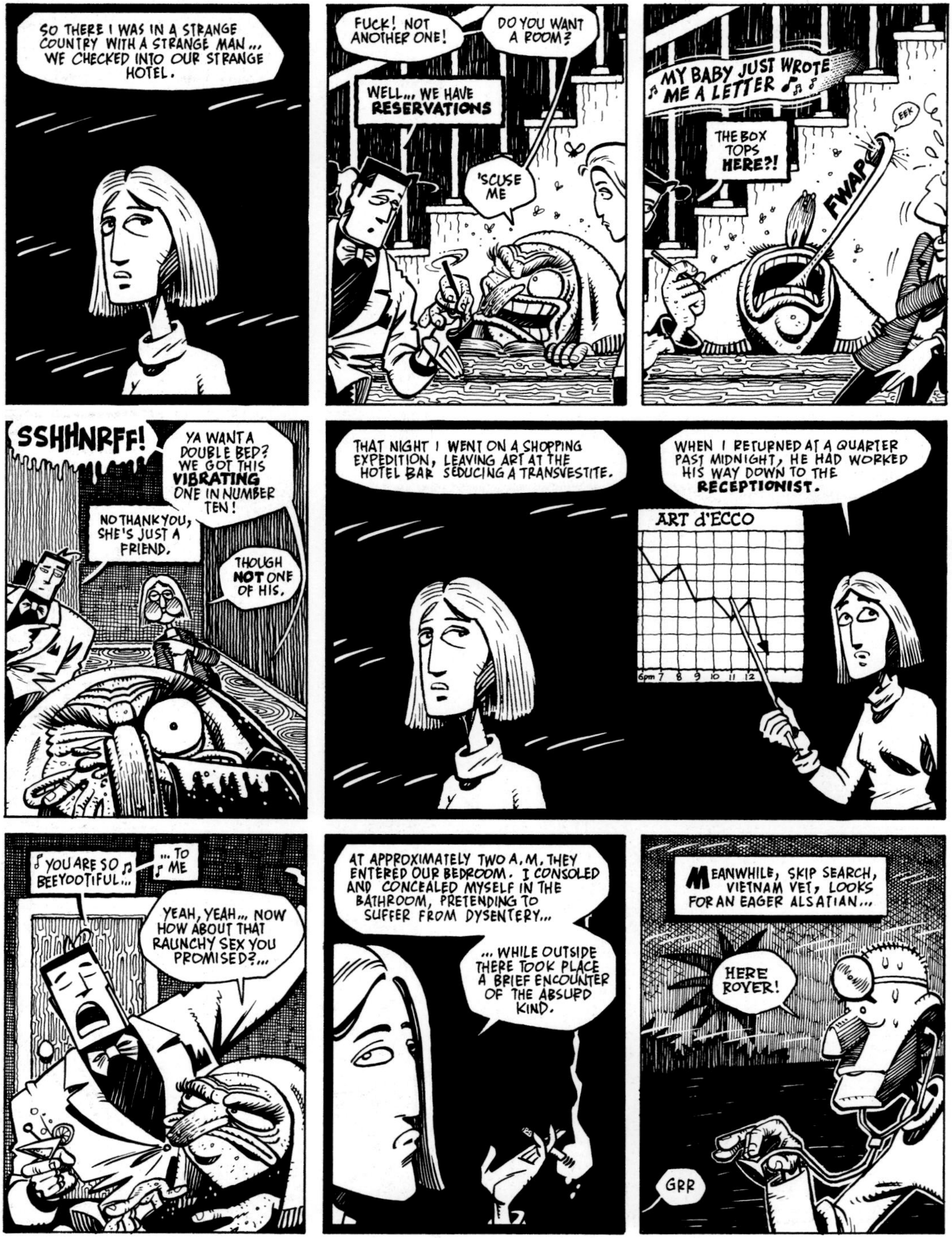

SO THERE I WAS IN A STRANGE COUNTRY WITH A STRANGE MAN... WE CHECKED INTO OUR STRANGE HOTEL.
FUCK! NOT ANOTHER ONE!
DO YOU WANT A ROOM?
WELL... WE HAVE RESERVATIONS
'SCUSE ME
♪ MY BABY JUST WROTE ME A LETTER ♪
THE BOX TOPS HERE?!
EEK
FWAP
SSHHNRFF!
YA WANT A DOUBLE BED? WE GOT THIS VIBRATING ONE IN NUMBER TEN!
NO THANK YOU, SHE'S JUST A FRIEND.
THOUGH NOT ONE OF HIS.
THAT NIGHT I WENT ON A SHOPPING EXPEDITION, LEAVING ART AT THE HOTEL BAR SEDUCING A TRANSVESTITE.
WHEN I RETURNED AT A QUARTER PAST MIDNIGHT, HE HAD WORKED HIS WAY DOWN TO THE RECEPTIONIST.
ART d'ECCO
6pm 7 8 9 10 11 12
♪ YOU ARE SO BEEYOOTIFUL... ♪
... TO ME ♪
YEAH, YEAH... NOW HOW ABOUT THAT RAUNCHY SEX YOU PROMISED?...
AT APPROXIMATELY TWO A.M. THEY ENTERED OUR BEDROOM. I CONSOLED AND CONCEALED MYSELF IN THE BATHROOM, PRETENDING TO SUFFER FROM DYSENTERY...
... WHILE OUTSIDE THERE TOOK PLACE A BRIEF ENCOUNTER OF THE ABSURD KIND.
MEANWHILE, SKIP SEARCH, VIETNAM VET, LOOKS FOR AN EAGER ALSATIAN...
HERE ROVER!
GRR

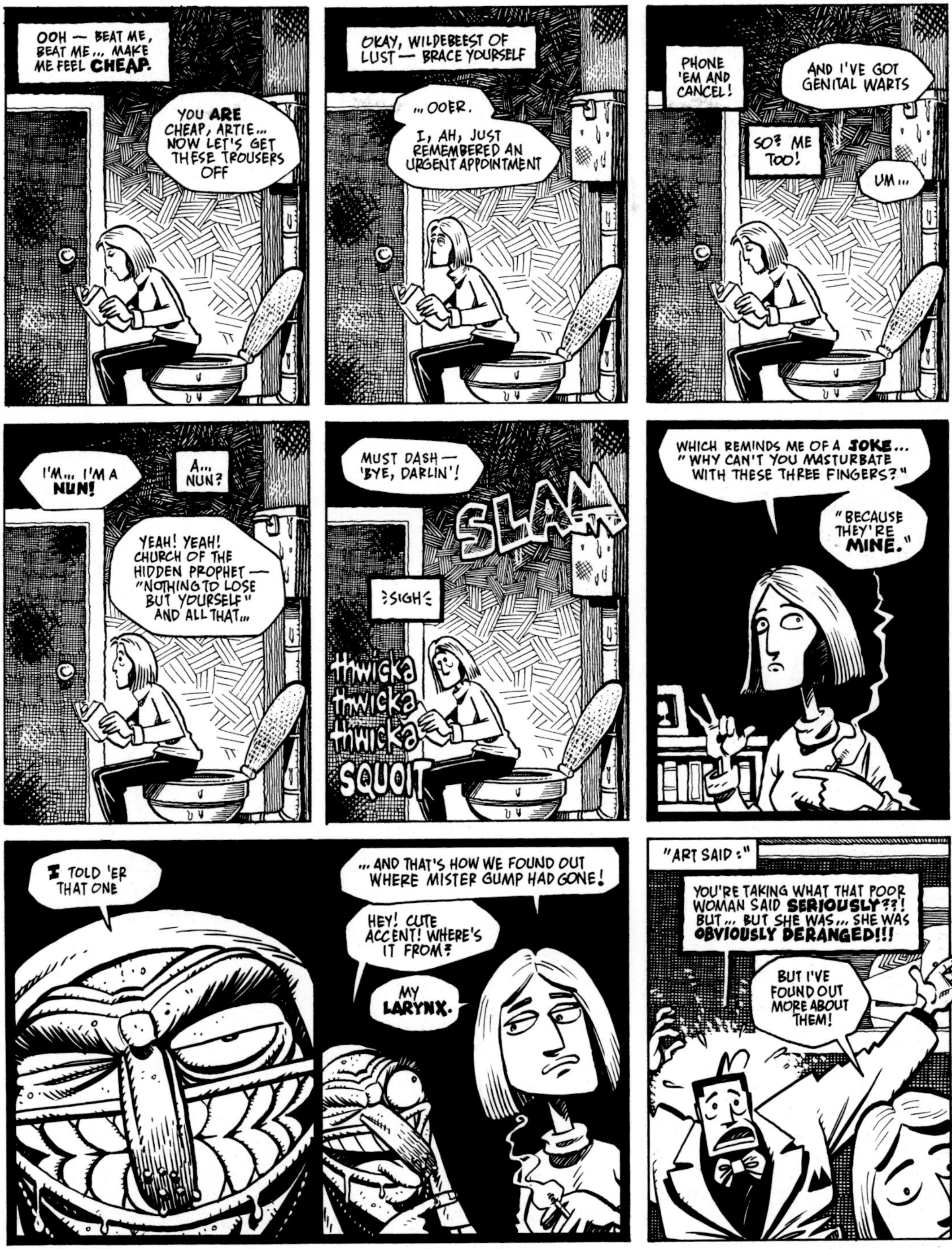

OOH — BEAT ME, BEAT ME... MAKE ME FEEL CHEAP.
YOU ARE CHEAP, ARTIE... NOW LET'S GET THESE TROUSERS OFF
OKAY, WILDEBEEST OF LUST — BRACE YOURSELF
...OOER.
I, AH, JUST REMEMBERED AN URGENT APPOINTMENT
PHONE 'EM AND CANCEL!
AND I'VE GOT GENITAL WARTS
SO? ME TOO!
UM...
I'M... I'M A NUN!
A... NUN?
YEAH! YEAH! CHURCH OF THE HIDDEN PROPHET — "NOTHING TO LOSE BUT YOURSELF" AND ALL THAT...
MUST DASH — 'BYE, DARLIN'!
SLAM
SIGH
thwicka thwicka thwicka
SQUOIT
WHICH REMINDS ME OF A JOKE... "WHY CAN'T YOU MASTURBATE WITH THESE THREE FINGERS?"
"BECAUSE THEY'RE MINE."
I TOLD 'ER THAT ONE
...AND THAT'S HOW WE FOUND OUT WHERE MISTER GUMP HAD GONE!
HEY! CUTE ACCENT! WHERE'S IT FROM?
MY LARYNX.
"ART SAID:"
YOU'RE TAKING WHAT THAT POOR WOMAN SAID SERIOUSLY??! BUT... BUT SHE WAS... SHE WAS OBVIOUSLY DERANGED!!!
BUT I'VE FOUND OUT MORE ABOUT THEM!

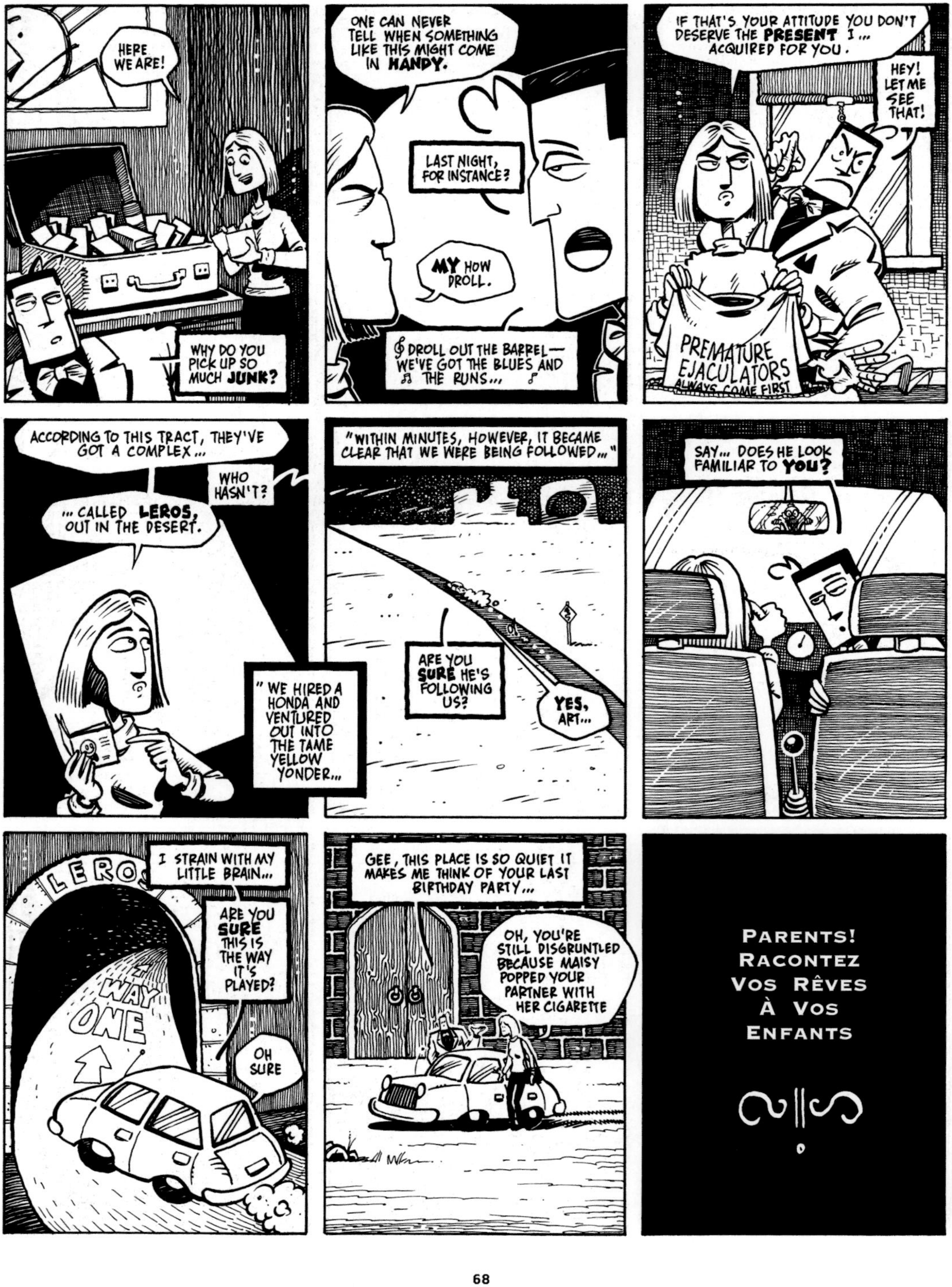

HERE WE ARE!
WHY DO YOU PICK UP SO MUCH JUNK?
ONE CAN NEVER TELL WHEN SOMETHING LIKE THIS MIGHT COME IN HANDY.
LAST NIGHT, FOR INSTANCE?
MY HOW DROLL.
DROLL OUT THE BARREL— WE'VE GOT THE BLUES AND THE RUNS...
IF THAT'S YOUR ATTITUDE YOU DON'T DESERVE THE PRESENT I... ACQUIRED FOR YOU.
HEY! LET ME SEE THAT!
PREMATURE EJACULATORS ALWAYS COME FIRST
ACCORDING TO THIS TRACT, THEY'VE GOT A COMPLEX...
WHO HASN'T?
...CALLED LEROS, OUT IN THE DESERT.
" WE HIRED A HONDA AND VENTURED OUT INTO THE TAME YELLOW YONDER...
"WITHIN MINUTES, HOWEVER, IT BECAME CLEAR THAT WE WERE BEING FOLLOWED..."
ARE YOU SURE HE'S FOLLOWING US?
YES, ART...
SAY... DOES HE LOOK FAMILIAR TO YOU?
LEROS
I STRAIN WITH MY LITTLE BRAIN...
ARE YOU SURE THIS IS THE WAY IT'S PLAYED?
WAY ONE
OH SURE
GEE, THIS PLACE IS SO QUIET IT MAKES ME THINK OF YOUR LAST BIRTHDAY PARTY...
OH, YOU'RE STILL DISGRUNTLED BECAUSE MAISY POPPED YOUR PARTNER WITH HER CIGARETTE
PARENTS! RACONTEZ VOS RÊVES À VOS ENFANTS

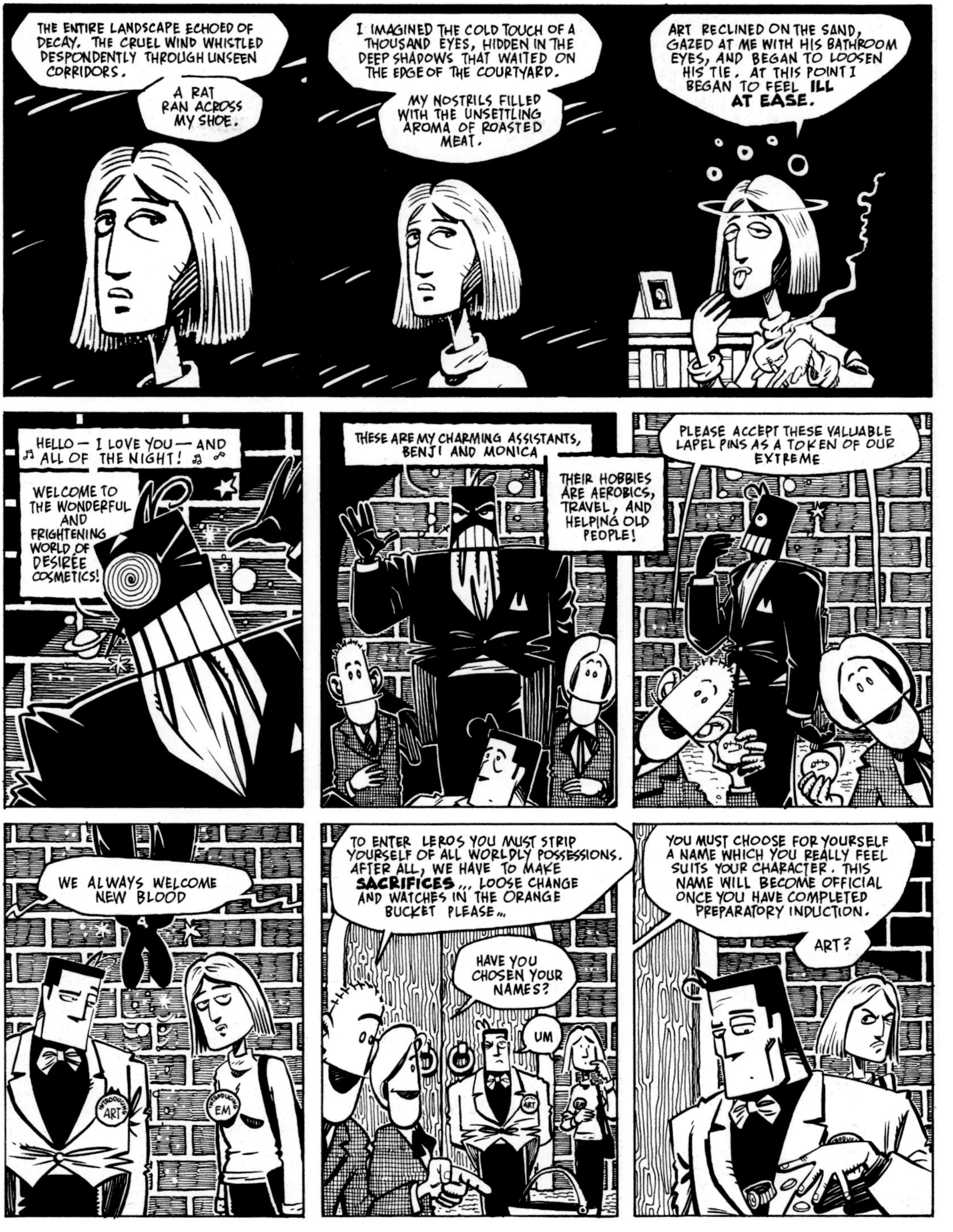

THE ENTIRE LANDSCAPE ECHOED OF DECAY. THE CRUEL WIND WHISTLED DESPONDENTLY THROUGH UNSEEN CORRIDORS.
A RAT RAN ACROSS MY SHOE.
I IMAGINED THE COLD TOUCH OF A THOUSAND EYES, HIDDEN IN THE DEEP SHADOWS THAT WAITED ON THE EDGE OF THE COURTYARD.
MY NOSTRILS FILLED WITH THE UNSETTLING AROMA OF ROASTED MEAT.
ART RECLINED ON THE SAND, GAZED AT ME WITH HIS BATHROOM EYES, AND BEGAN TO LOOSEN HIS TIE. AT THIS POINT I BEGAN TO FEEL **ILL AT EASE.**
♫ HELLO — I LOVE YOU — AND ALL OF THE NIGHT! ♫
WELCOME TO THE WONDERFUL AND FRIGHTENING WORLD OF DESIRÉE COSMETICS!
THESE ARE MY CHARMING ASSISTANTS, BENJI AND MONICA
THEIR HOBBIES ARE AEROBICS, TRAVEL, AND HELPING OLD PEOPLE!
PLEASE ACCEPT THESE VALUABLE LAPEL PINS AS A TOKEN OF OUR EXTREME
WE ALWAYS WELCOME NEW BLOOD
INTRODUCING ART
INTRODUCING EM
TO ENTER LEROS YOU MUST STRIP YOURSELF OF ALL WORLDLY POSSESSIONS. AFTER ALL, WE HAVE TO MAKE **SACRIFICES**... LOOSE CHANGE AND WATCHES IN THE ORANGE BUCKET PLEASE...
HAVE YOU CHOSEN YOUR NAMES?
UM
YOU MUST CHOOSE FOR YOURSELF A NAME WHICH YOU REALLY FEEL SUITS YOUR CHARACTER. THIS NAME WILL BECOME OFFICIAL ONCE YOU HAVE COMPLETED PREPARATORY INDUCTION.
ART?

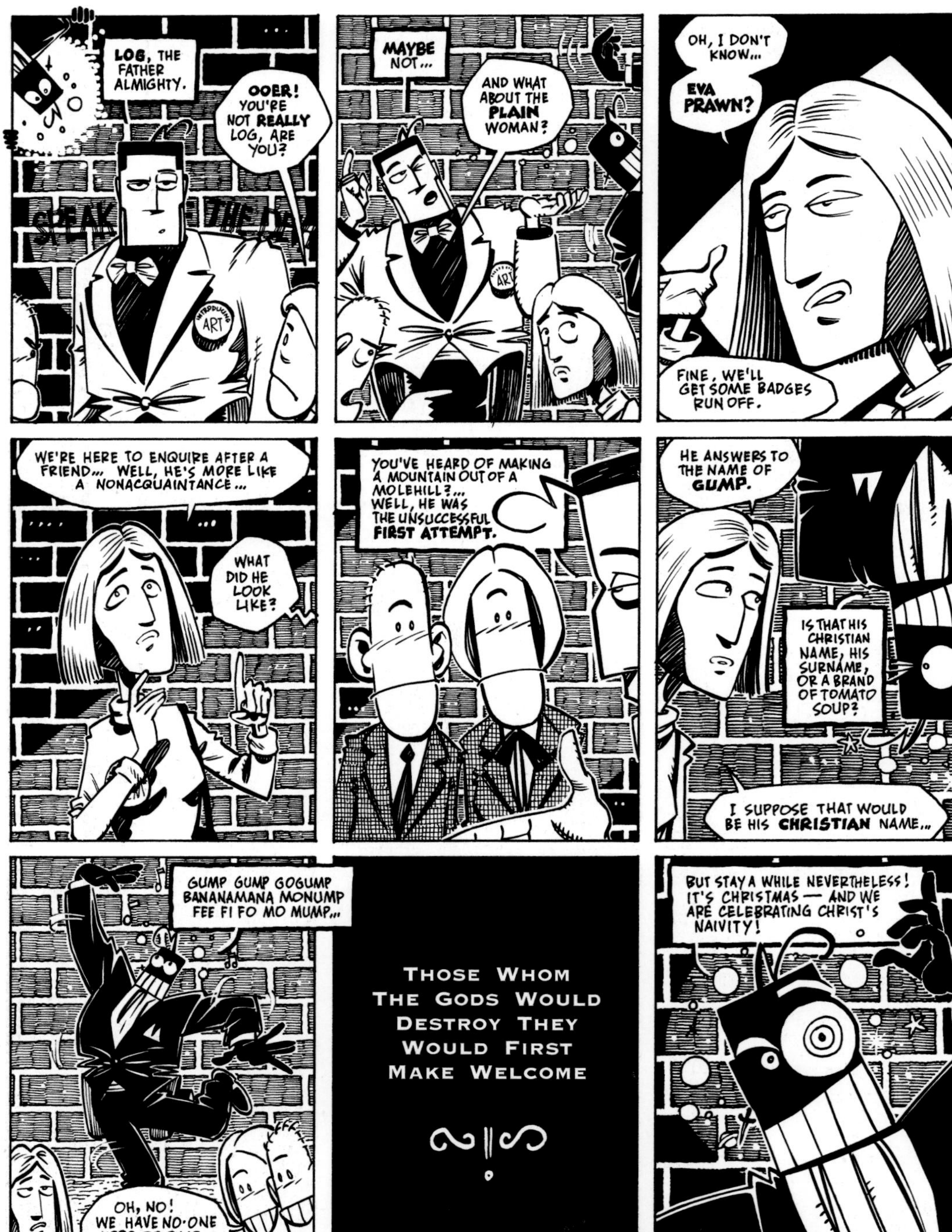
LOG, THE FATHER ALMIGHTY.
OOER! YOU'RE NOT REALLY LOG, ARE YOU?
SPEAK
MAYBE NOT...
AND WHAT ABOUT THE PLAIN WOMAN?
OH, I DON'T KNOW...
EVA PRAWN?
FINE, WE'LL GET SOME BADGES RUN OFF.
WE'RE HERE TO ENQUIRE AFTER A FRIEND... WELL, HE'S MORE LIKE A NONACQUAINTANCE...
WHAT DID HE LOOK LIKE?
YOU'VE HEARD OF MAKING A MOUNTAIN OUT OF A MOLEHILL?... WELL, HE WAS THE UNSUCCESSFUL FIRST ATTEMPT.
HE ANSWERS TO THE NAME OF GUMP.
IS THAT HIS CHRISTIAN NAME, HIS SURNAME, OR A BRAND OF TOMATO SOUP?
I SUPPOSE THAT WOULD BE HIS CHRISTIAN NAME...
GUMP GUMP GOGUMP BANANAMANA MONUMP FEE FI FO MO MUMP...
OH, NO! WE HAVE NO-ONE HERE OF THAT NAME!
THOSE WHOM THE GODS WOULD DESTROY THEY WOULD FIRST MAKE WELCOME
BUT STAY A WHILE NEVERTHELESS! IT'S CHRISTMAS — AND WE ARE CELEBRATING CHRIST'S NAIVITY!

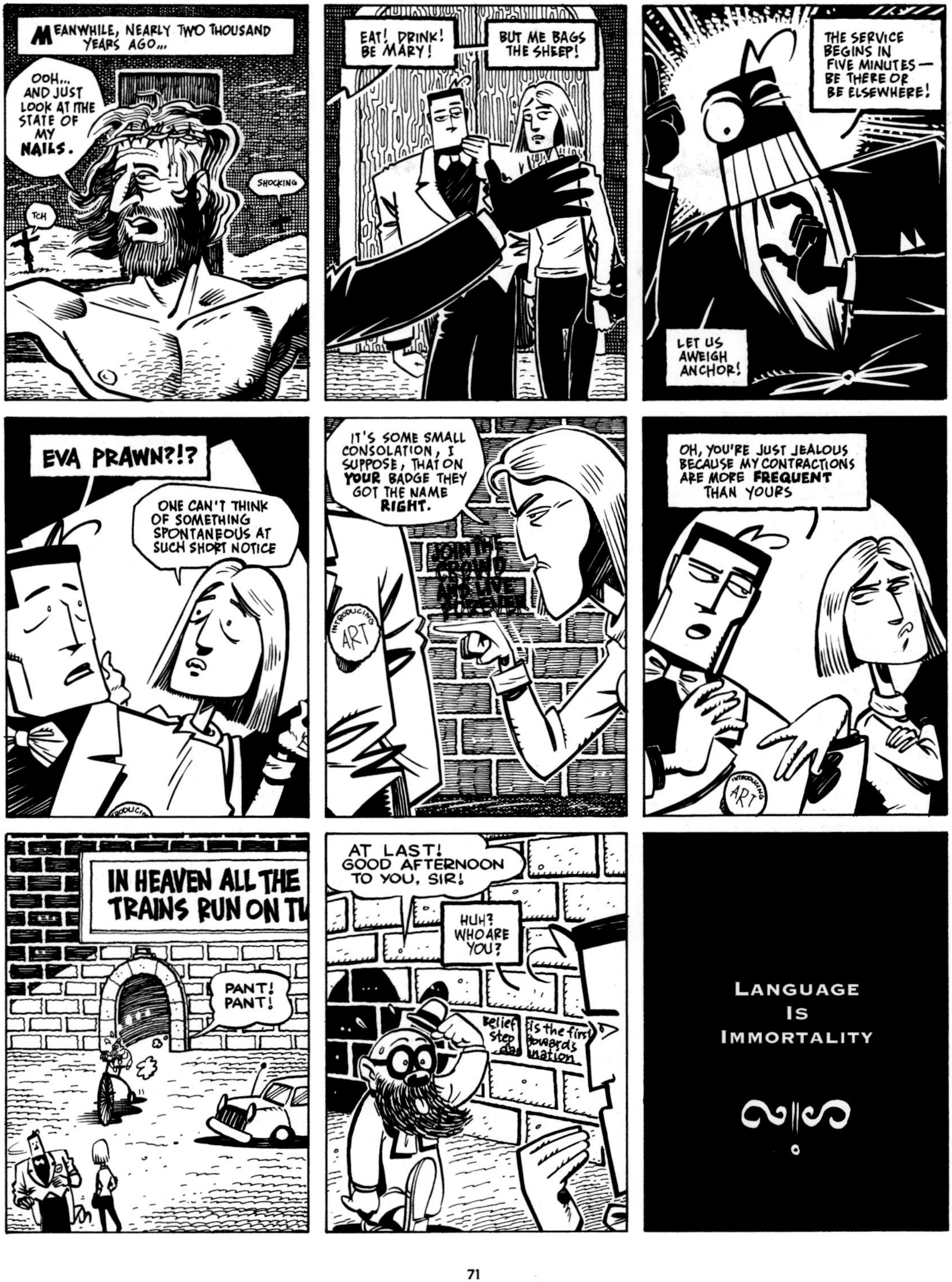
MEANWHILE, NEARLY TWO THOUSAND YEARS AGO...
OOH... AND JUST LOOK AT THE STATE OF MY NAILS.
SHOCKING
TCH
EAT! DRINK! BE MARY!
BUT ME BAGS THE SHEEP!
THE SERVICE BEGINS IN FIVE MINUTES— BE THERE OR BE ELSEWHERE!
LET US AWEIGH ANCHOR!
EVA PRAWN?!?
ONE CAN'T THINK OF SOMETHING SPONTANEOUS AT SUCH SHORT NOTICE
IT'S SOME SMALL CONSOLATION, I SUPPOSE, THAT ON YOUR BADGE THEY GOT THE NAME RIGHT.
INTRODUCING ART
OH, YOU'RE JUST JEALOUS BECAUSE MY CONTRACTIONS ARE MORE FREQUENT THAN YOURS
INTRODUCING ART
IN HEAVEN ALL THE TRAINS RUN ON T
PANT! PANT!
AT LAST! GOOD AFTERNOON TO YOU, SIR!
HUH? WHO ARE YOU?
LANGUAGE IS IMMORTALITY

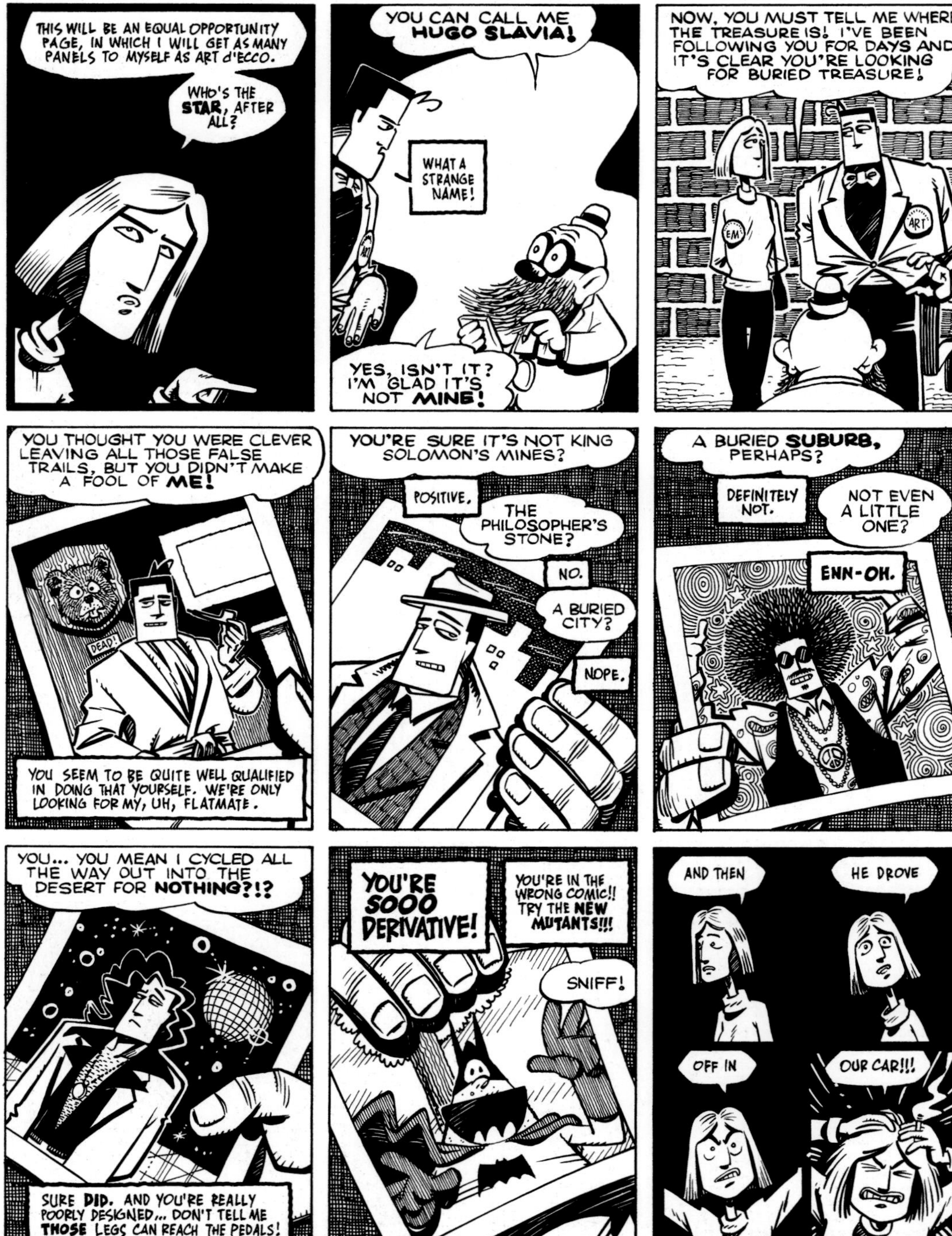
THIS WILL BE AN EQUAL OPPORTUNITY PAGE, IN WHICH I WILL GET AS MANY PANELS TO MYSELF AS ART d'ECCO.
WHO'S THE STAR, AFTER ALL?
YOU CAN CALL ME HUGO SLAVIA!
WHAT A STRANGE NAME!
YES, ISN'T IT? I'M GLAD IT'S NOT MINE!
NOW, YOU MUST TELL ME WHERE THE TREASURE IS! I'VE BEEN FOLLOWING YOU FOR DAYS AND IT'S CLEAR YOU'RE LOOKING FOR BURIED TREASURE!
EM
ART
YOU THOUGHT YOU WERE CLEVER LEAVING ALL THOSE FALSE TRAILS, BUT YOU DIDN'T MAKE A FOOL OF ME!
DEAD!
YOU SEEM TO BE QUITE WELL QUALIFIED IN DOING THAT YOURSELF. WE'RE ONLY LOOKING FOR MY, UH, FLATMATE.
YOU'RE SURE IT'S NOT KING SOLOMON'S MINES?
POSITIVE.
THE PHILOSOPHER'S STONE?
NO.
A BURIED CITY?
NOPE.
A BURIED SUBURB, PERHAPS?
DEFINITELY NOT.
NOT EVEN A LITTLE ONE?
ENN-OH.
YOU... YOU MEAN I CYCLED ALL THE WAY OUT INTO THE DESERT FOR NOTHING?!?
SURE DID. AND YOU'RE REALLY POORLY DESIGNED... DON'T TELL ME THOSE LEGS CAN REACH THE PEDALS!
YOU'RE SOOO DERIVATIVE!
YOU'RE IN THE WRONG COMIC!! TRY THE NEW MUTANTS!!!
SNIFF!
AND THEN
HE DROVE
OFF IN
OUR CAR!!!

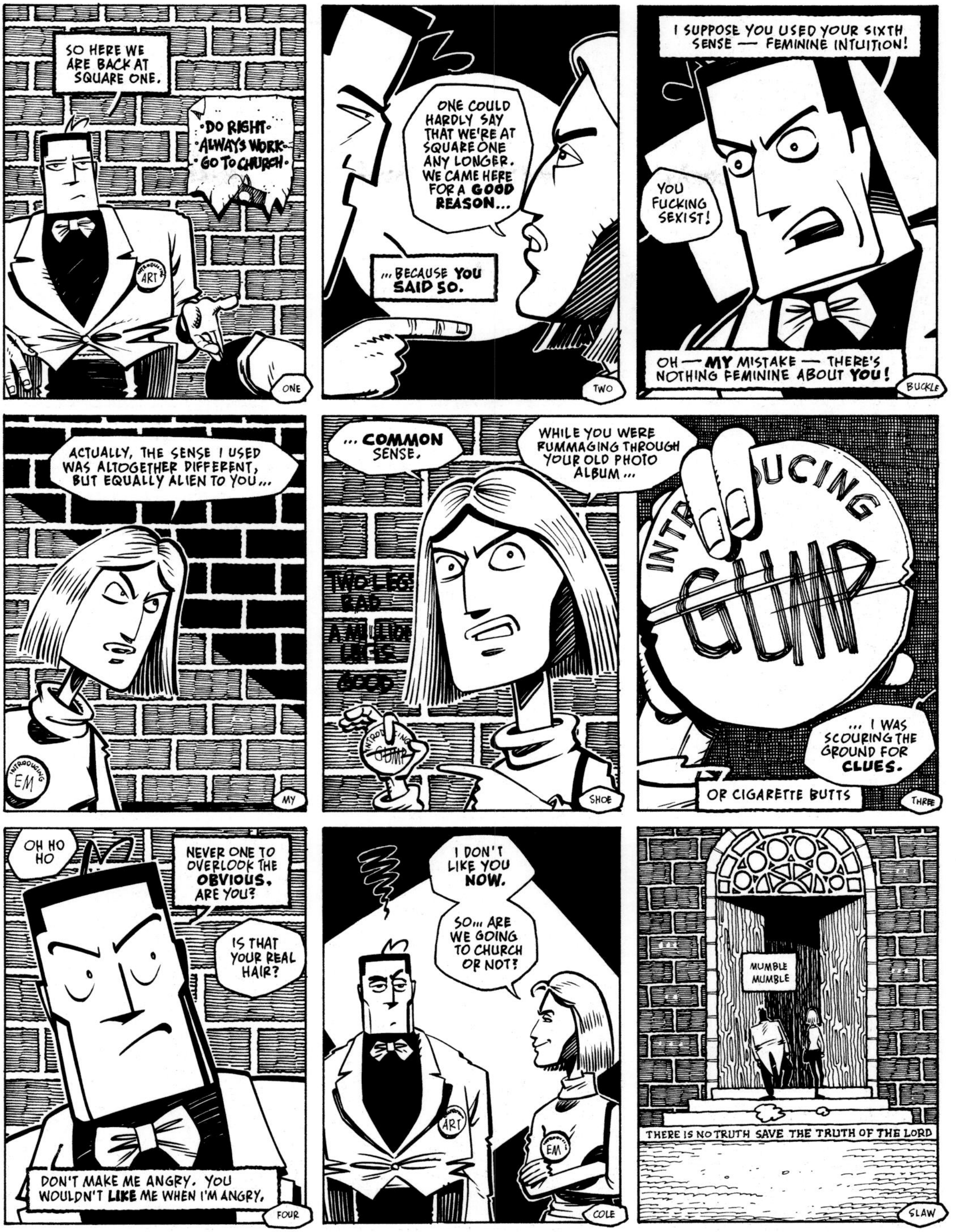
SO HERE WE ARE BACK AT SQUARE ONE.
•DO RIGHT• •ALWAYS WORK• •GO TO CHURCH•
ART
ONE
ONE COULD HARDLY SAY THAT WE'RE AT SQUARE ONE ANY LONGER. WE CAME HERE FOR A GOOD REASON...
...BECAUSE YOU SAID SO.
TWO
I SUPPOSE YOU USED YOUR SIXTH SENSE — FEMININE INTUITION!
YOU FUCKING SEXIST!
OH — MY MISTAKE — THERE'S NOTHING FEMININE ABOUT YOU!
BUCKLE
ACTUALLY, THE SENSE I USED WAS ALTOGETHER DIFFERENT, BUT EQUALLY ALIEN TO YOU...
INTRODUCING EM
MY
...COMMON SENSE.
WHILE YOU WERE RUMMAGING THROUGH YOUR OLD PHOTO ALBUM...
SHOE
INTRODUCING GUMP
... I WAS SCOURING THE GROUND FOR CLUES.
OR CIGARETTE BUTTS
THREE
OH HO HO
NEVER ONE TO OVERLOOK THE OBVIOUS. ARE YOU?
IS THAT YOUR REAL HAIR?
DON'T MAKE ME ANGRY. YOU WOULDN'T LIKE ME WHEN I'M ANGRY.
FOUR
I DON'T LIKE YOU NOW.
SO... ARE WE GOING TO CHURCH OR NOT?
ART
EM
COLE
MUMBLE MUMBLE
THERE IS NO TRUTH SAVE THE TRUTH OF THE LORD
SLAW

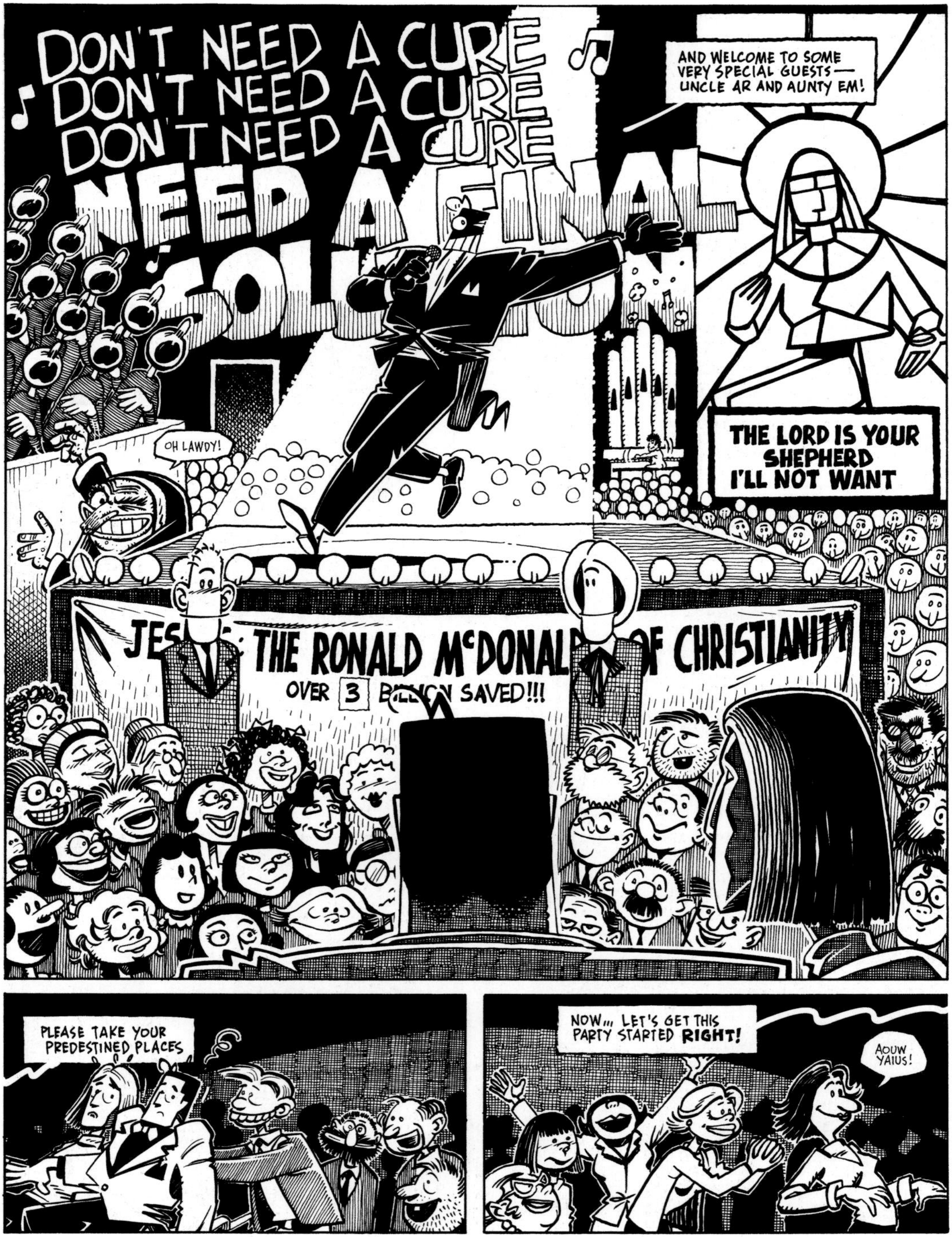

DON'T NEED A CURE
DON'T NEED A CURE
DON'T NEED A CURE
NEED A FINAL
AND WELCOME TO SOME VERY SPECIAL GUESTS— UNCLE AR AND AUNTY EM!
THE LORD IS YOUR SHEPHERD I'LL NOT WANT
OH LAWDY!
THE RONALD McDONAL
OF CHRISTIANITY
OVER 3
SAVED!!!
PLEASE TAKE YOUR PREDESTINED PLACES
NOW... LET'S GET THIS PARTY STARTED RIGHT!
AOUW YAIUS!

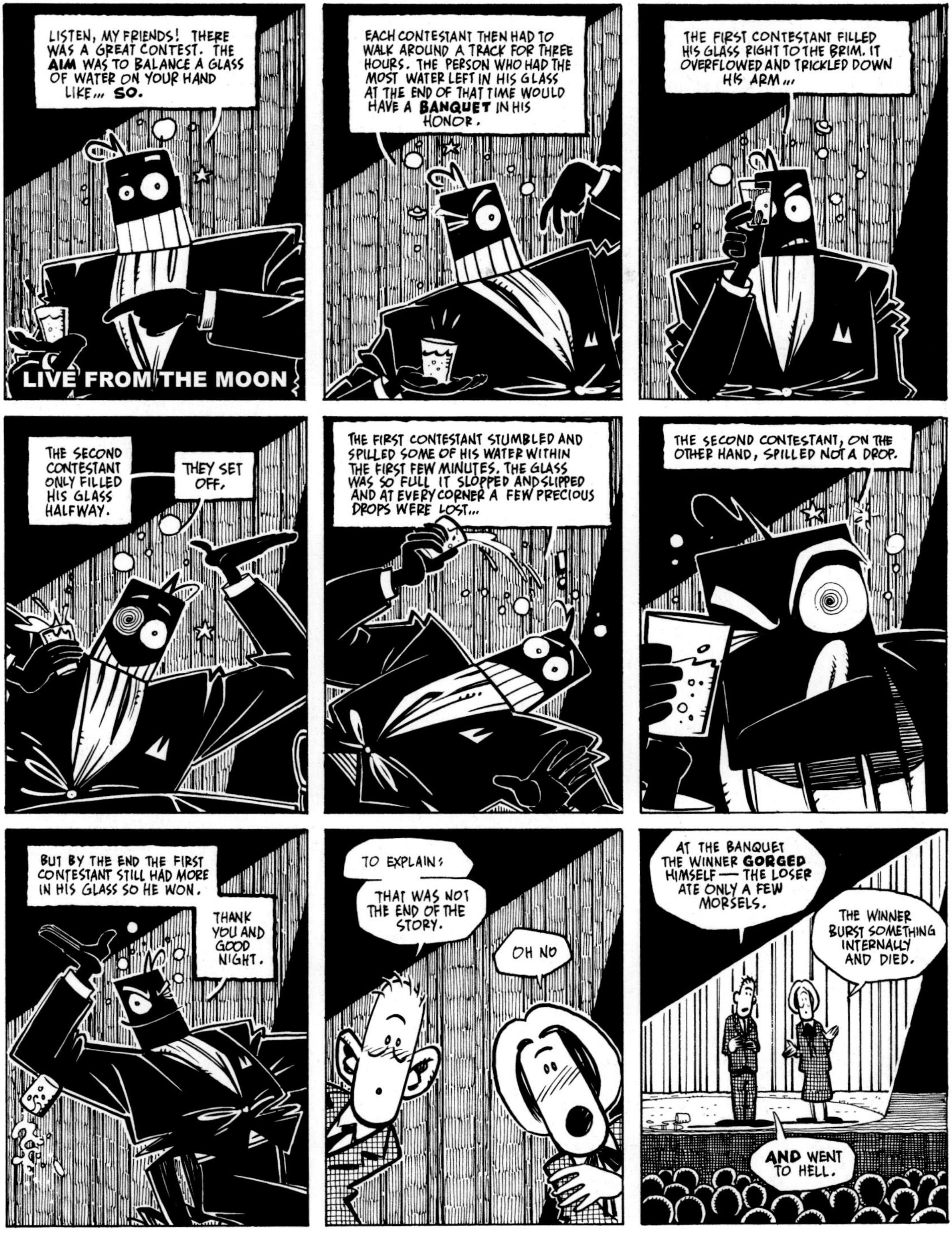
LISTEN, MY FRIENDS! THERE WAS A GREAT CONTEST. THE AIM WAS TO BALANCE A GLASS OF WATER ON YOUR HAND LIKE... SO.
LIVE FROM THE MOON
EACH CONTESTANT THEN HAD TO WALK AROUND A TRACK FOR THREE HOURS. THE PERSON WHO HAD THE MOST WATER LEFT IN HIS GLASS AT THE END OF THAT TIME WOULD HAVE A BANQUET IN HIS HONOR.
THE FIRST CONTESTANT FILLED HIS GLASS RIGHT TO THE BRIM. IT OVERFLOWED AND TRICKLED DOWN HIS ARM...
THE SECOND CONTESTANT ONLY FILLED HIS GLASS HALFWAY.
THEY SET OFF.
THE FIRST CONTESTANT STUMBLED AND SPILLED SOME OF HIS WATER WITHIN THE FIRST FEW MINUTES. THE GLASS WAS SO FULL IT SLOPPED AND SLIPPED AND AT EVERY CORNER A FEW PRECIOUS DROPS WERE LOST...
THE SECOND CONTESTANT, ON THE OTHER HAND, SPILLED NOT A DROP.
BUT BY THE END THE FIRST CONTESTANT STILL HAD MORE IN HIS GLASS SO HE WON.
THANK YOU AND GOOD NIGHT.
TO EXPLAIN:
THAT WAS NOT THE END OF THE STORY.
OH NO
AT THE BANQUET THE WINNER GORGED HIMSELF — THE LOSER ATE ONLY A FEW MORSELS.
THE WINNER BURST SOMETHING INTERNALLY AND DIED.
AND WENT TO HELL.

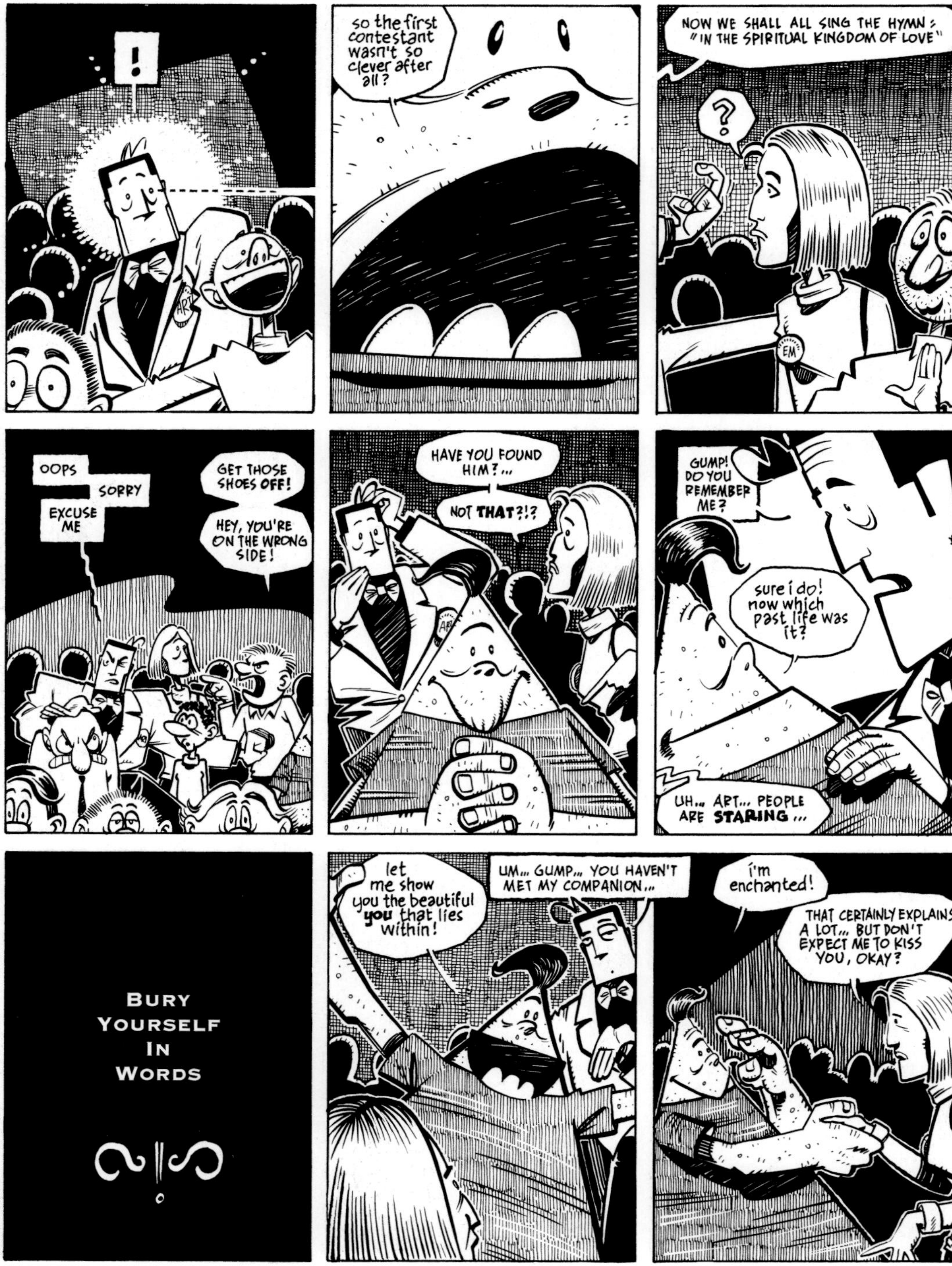
!
so the first contestant wasn't so clever after all?
NOW WE SHALL ALL SING THE HYMN: "IN THE SPIRITUAL KINGDOM OF LOVE"
?
OOPS
SORRY
EXCUSE ME
GET THOSE SHOES OFF!
HEY, YOU'RE ON THE WRONG SIDE!
HAVE YOU FOUND HIM?...
NOT THAT?!?
GUMP! DO YOU REMEMBER ME?
sure i do! now which past life was it?
UH... ART... PEOPLE ARE STARING...
BURY YOURSELF IN WORDS
let me show you the beautiful you that lies within!
UM... GUMP... YOU HAVEN'T MET MY COMPANION...
i'm enchanted!
THAT CERTAINLY EXPLAINS A LOT... BUT DON'T EXPECT ME TO KISS YOU, OKAY?

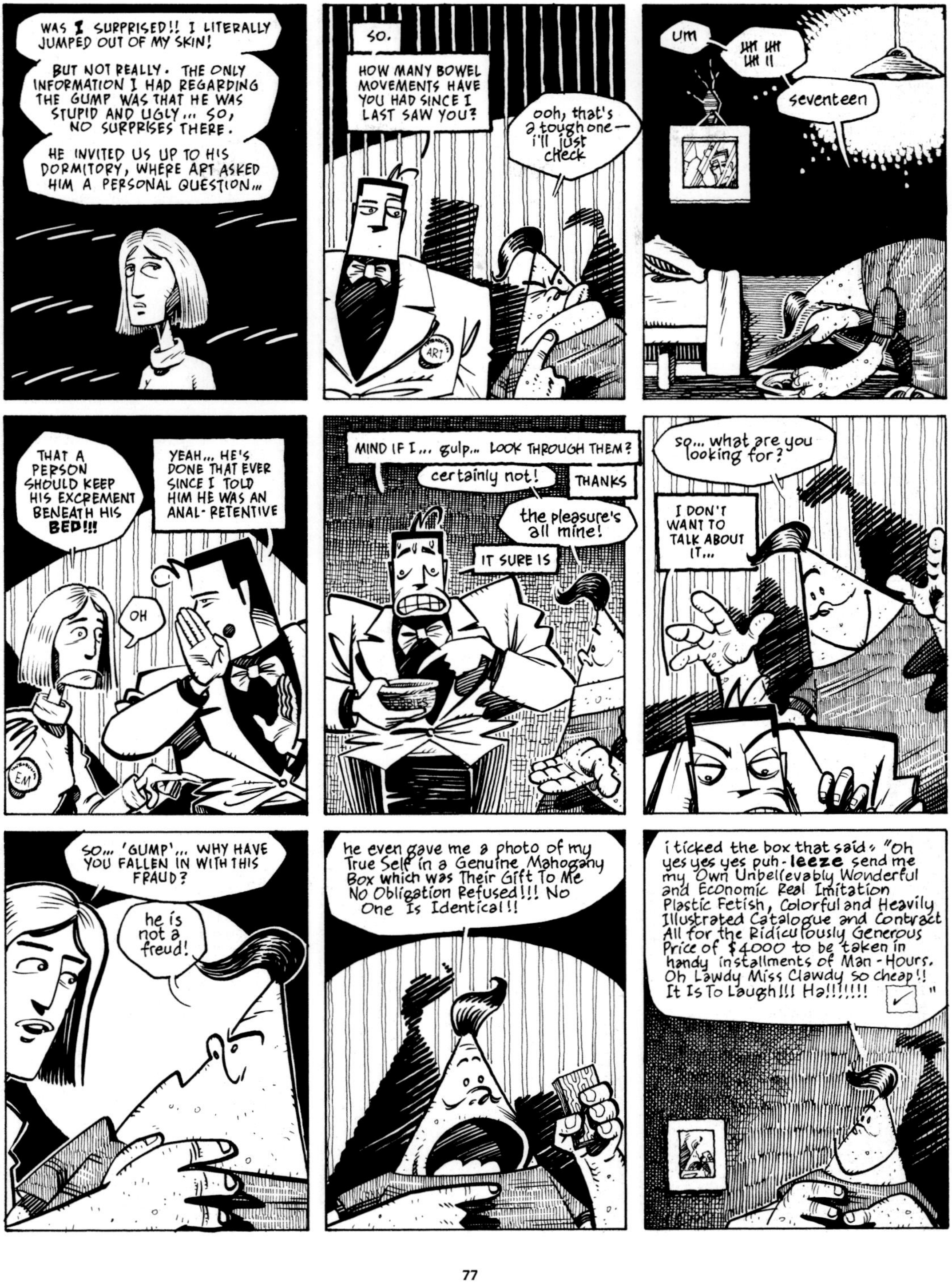
WAS I SURPRISED!! I LITERALLY JUMPED OUT OF MY SKIN!
BUT NOT REALLY. THE ONLY INFORMATION I HAD REGARDING THE GUMP WAS THAT HE WAS STUPID AND UGLY... SO, NO SURPRISES THERE.
HE INVITED US UP TO HIS DORMITORY, WHERE ART ASKED HIM A PERSONAL QUESTION...
SO.
HOW MANY BOWEL MOVEMENTS HAVE YOU HAD SINCE I LAST SAW YOU?
ooh, that's a tough one — i'll just check
ART
um
seventeen
THAT A PERSON SHOULD KEEP HIS EXCREMENT BENEATH HIS BED!!!
YEAH... HE'S DONE THAT EVER SINCE I TOLD HIM HE WAS AN ANAL-RETENTIVE
OH
EM
MIND IF I... gulp... LOOK THROUGH THEM?
certainly not!
THANKS
the pleasure's all mine!
IT SURE IS
so... what are you looking for?
I DON'T WANT TO TALK ABOUT IT...
SO... 'GUMP'... WHY HAVE YOU FALLEN IN WITH THIS FRAUD?
he is not a freud!
he even gave me a photo of my True Self in a Genuine Mahogany Box which was Their Gift To Me No Obligation Refused!!! No One Is Identical!!
i ticked the box that said: "Oh yes yes yes puh-leeze send me my Own Unbelievably Wonderful and Economic Real Imitation Plastic Fetish, Colorful and Heavily Illustrated Catalogue and Contract All for the Ridiculously Generous Price of $4000 to be taken in handy installments of Man-Hours. Oh Lawdy Miss Clawdy so cheap!! It Is To Laugh!!! Ha!!!!!!! ✓ "

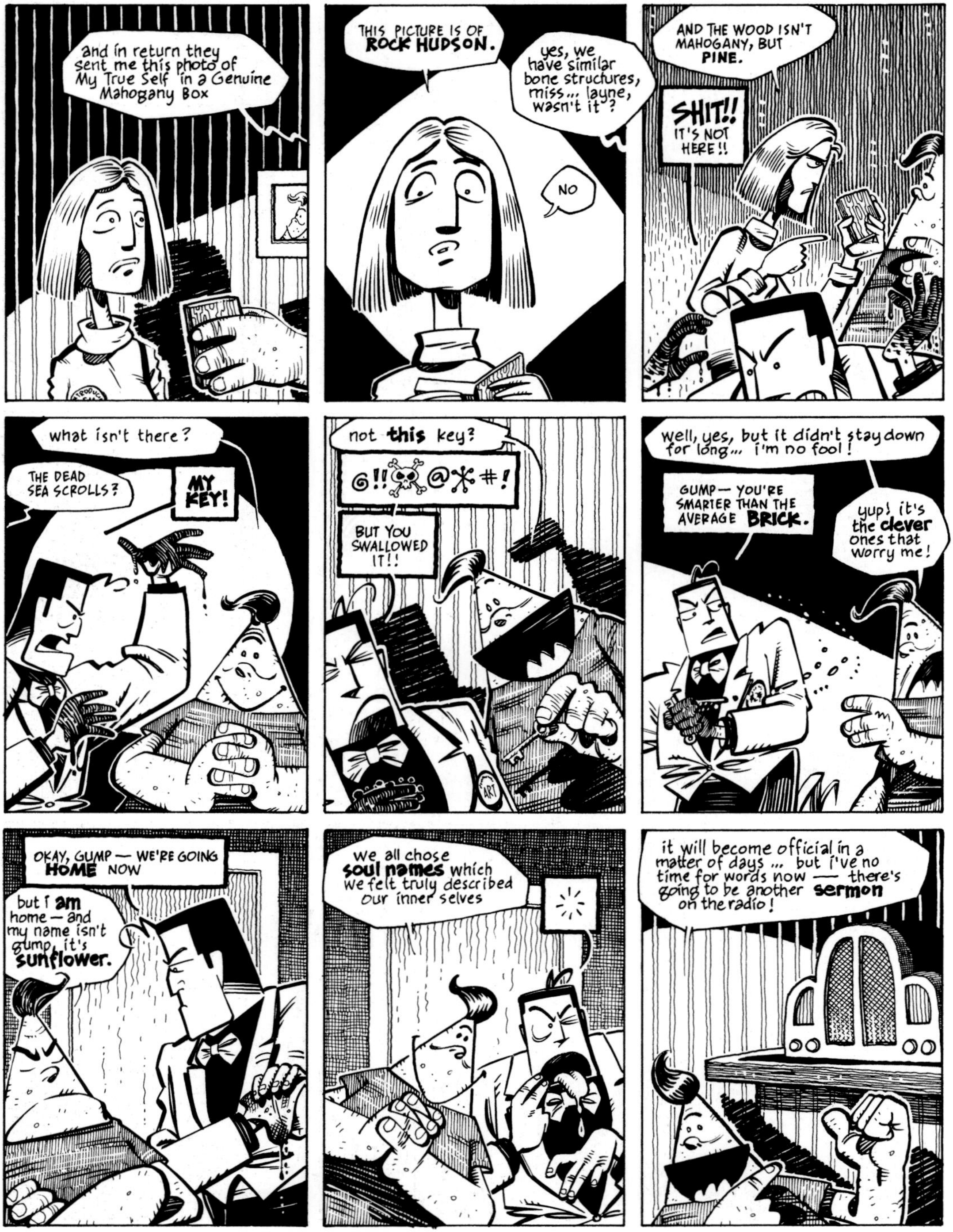

and in return they sent me this photo of My True Self in a Genuine Mahogany Box
THIS PICTURE IS OF ROCK HUDSON.
yes, we have similar bone structures, miss... layne, wasn't it?
NO
AND THE WOOD ISN'T MAHOGANY, BUT PINE.
SHIT!! IT'S NOT HERE!!
what isn't there?
THE DEAD SEA SCROLLS?
MY KEY!
not this key?
@!!☠@✱#!
BUT YOU SWALLOWED IT!!
well, yes, but it didn't stay down for long... i'm no fool!
GUMP— YOU'RE SMARTER THAN THE AVERAGE BRICK.
yup! it's the clever ones that worry me!
OKAY, GUMP — WE'RE GOING HOME NOW
but I am home — and my name isn't gump, it's sunflower.
we all chose soul names which we felt truly described our inner selves
it will become official in a matter of days ... but i've no time for words now — there's going to be another sermon on the radio!

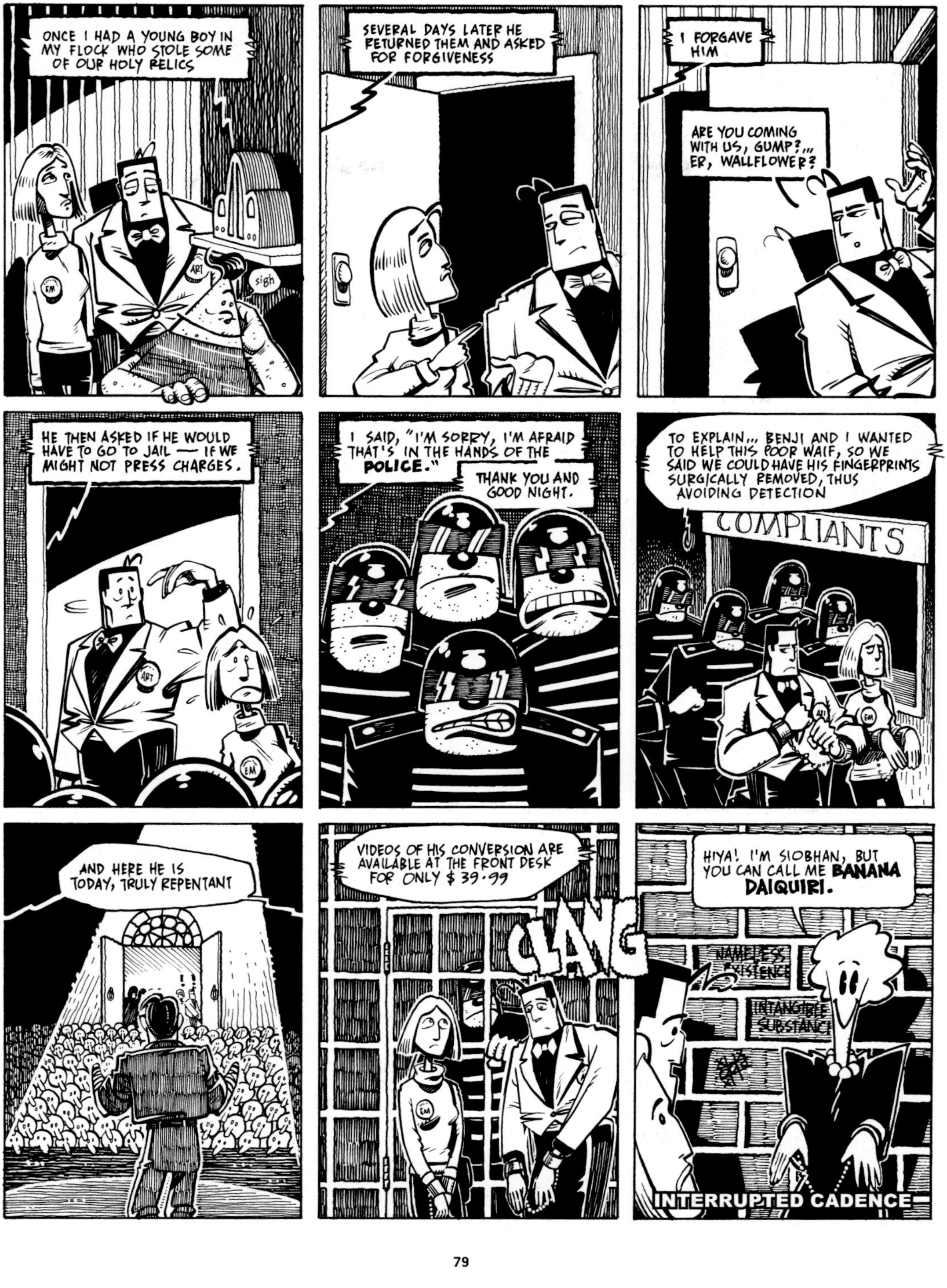
ONCE I HAD A YOUNG BOY IN MY FLOCK WHO STOLE SOME OF OUR HOLY RELICS
ART
EM
sigh
SEVERAL DAYS LATER HE RETURNED THEM AND ASKED FOR FORGIVENESS
I FORGAVE HIM
ARE YOU COMING WITH US, GUMP?... ER, WALLFLOWER?
HE THEN ASKED IF HE WOULD HAVE TO GO TO JAIL — IF WE MIGHT NOT PRESS CHARGES.
ART
EM
I SAID, "I'M SORRY, I'M AFRAID THAT'S IN THE HANDS OF THE **POLICE**."
THANK YOU AND GOOD NIGHT.
TO EXPLAIN... BENJI AND I WANTED TO HELP THIS POOR WAIF, SO WE SAID WE COULD HAVE HIS FINGERPRINTS SURGICALLY REMOVED, THUS AVOIDING DETECTION
COMPLIANTS
AND HERE HE IS TODAY, TRULY REPENTANT
VIDEOS OF HIS CONVERSION ARE AVAILABLE AT THE FRONT DESK FOR ONLY $ 39·99
CLANG
HIYA! I'M SIOBHAN, BUT YOU CAN CALL ME **BANANA DAIQUIRI**.
NAMELESS EXISTENCE
INTANGIBLE SUBSTANCE
INTERRUPTED CADENCE

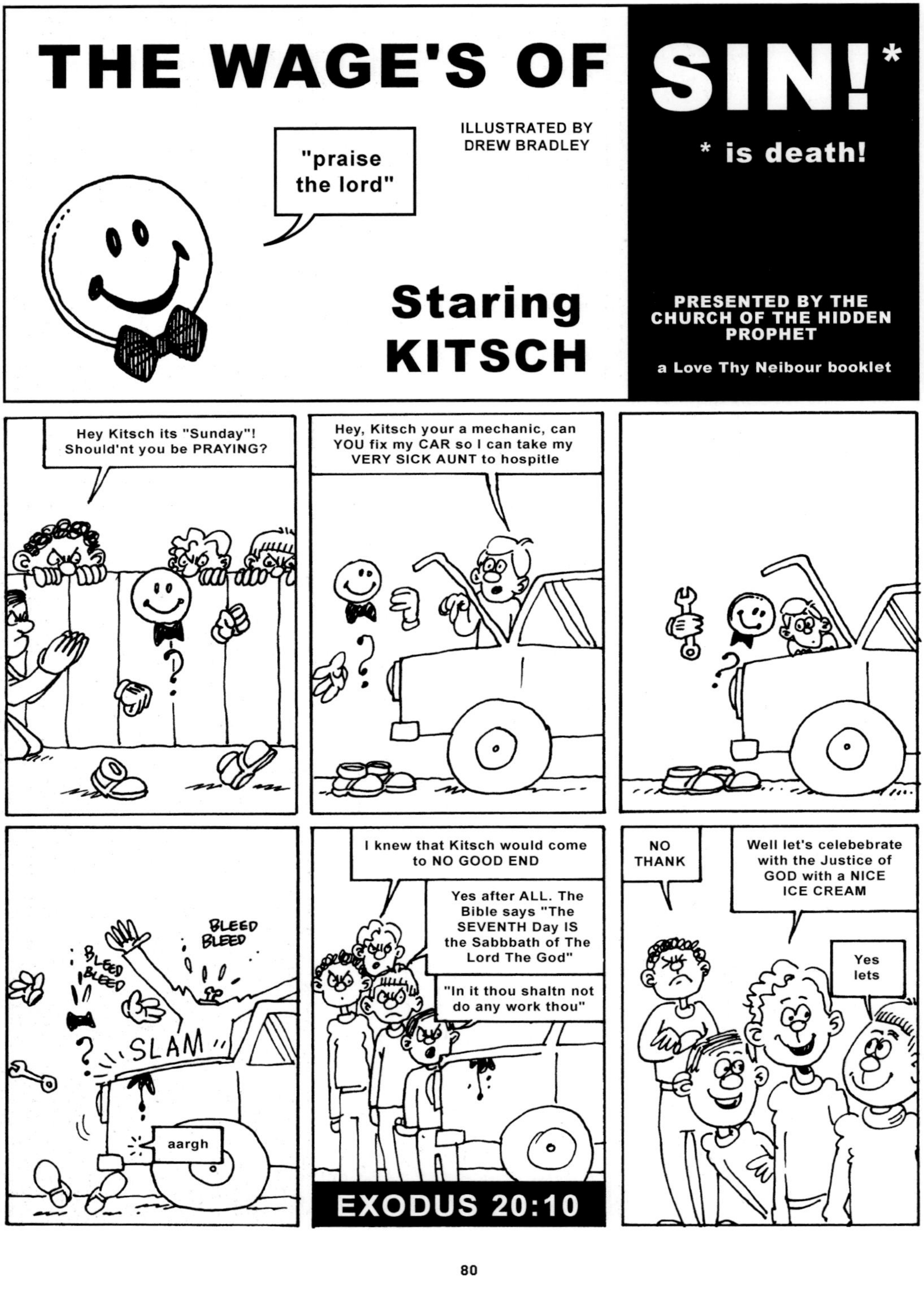

THE WAGE'S OF SIN!*
ILLUSTRATED BY DREW BRADLEY
"praise the lord"
* is death!
Staring KITSCH
PRESENTED BY THE CHURCH OF THE HIDDEN PROPHET
a Love Thy Neibour booklet
Hey Kitsch its "Sunday"! Should'nt you be PRAYING?
Hey, Kitsch your a mechanic, can YOU fix my CAR so I can take my VERY SICK AUNT to hospitle
BLEED BLEED
BLEED BLEED
SLAM
aargh
I knew that Kitsch would come to NO GOOD END
Yes after ALL. The Bible says "The SEVENTH Day IS the Sabbbath of The Lord The God"
"In it thou shaltn not do any work thou"
EXODUS 20:10
NO THANK
Well let's celebebrate with the Justice of GOD with a NICE ICE CREAM
Yes lets

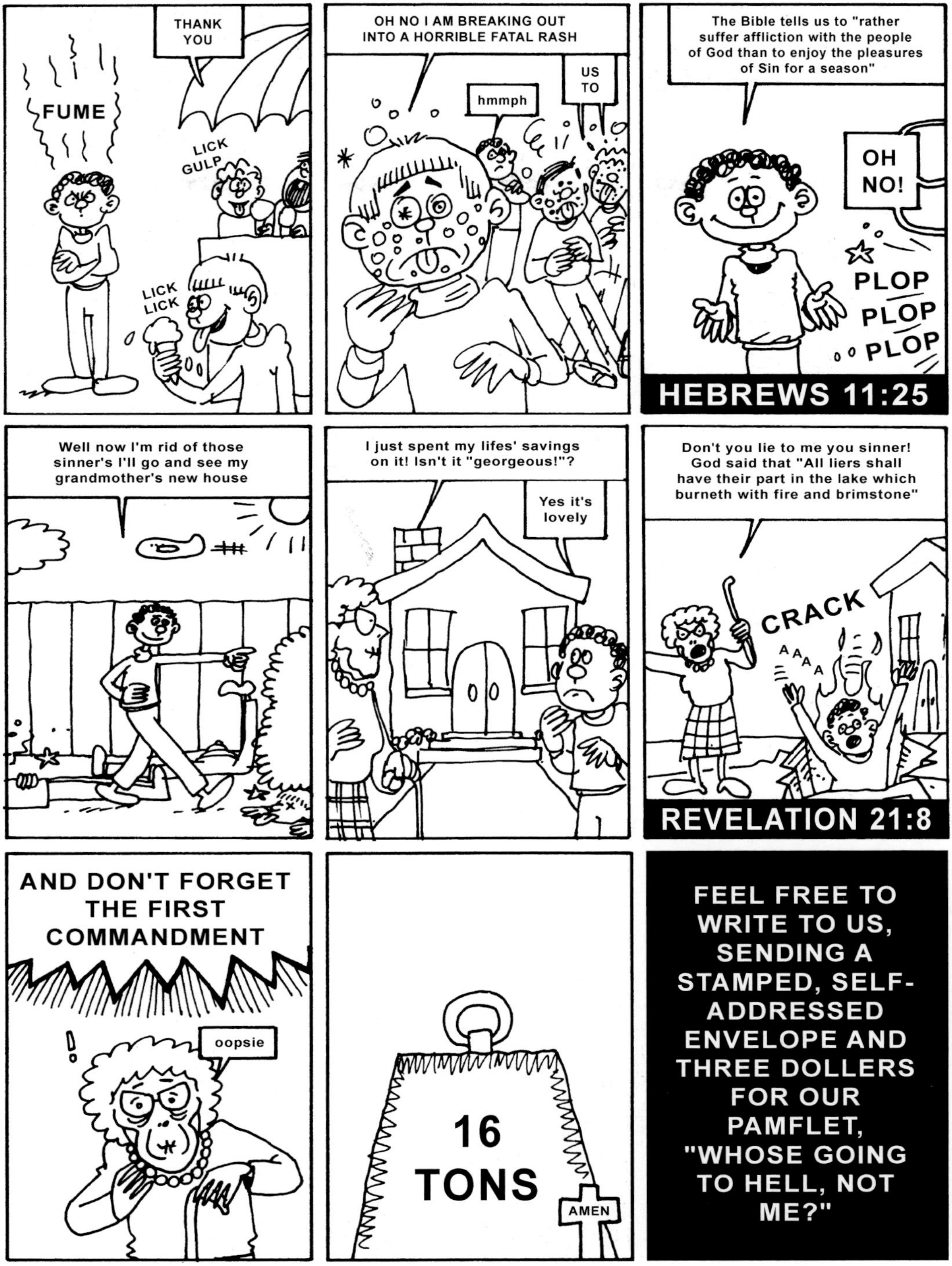

THANK YOU
FUME
LICK GULP
LICK LICK
OH NO I AM BREAKING OUT INTO A HORRIBLE FATAL RASH
hmmph
US TO
The Bible tells us to "rather suffer affliction with the people of God than to enjoy the pleasures of Sin for a season"
OH NO!
PLOP
PLOP
PLOP
HEBREWS 11:25
Well now I'm rid of those sinner's I'll go and see my grandmother's new house
I just spent my lifes' savings on it! Isn't it "georgeous!"?
Yes it's lovely
Don't you lie to me you sinner! God said that "All liers shall have their part in the lake which burneth with fire and brimstone"
CRACK
AAAA
REVELATION 21:8
AND DON'T FORGET THE FIRST COMMANDMENT
oopsie
16 TONS
AMEN
FEEL FREE TO WRITE TO US, SENDING A STAMPED, SELF-ADDRESSED ENVELOPE AND THREE DOLLERS FOR OUR PAMFLET, "WHOSE GOING TO HELL, NOT ME?"

STATE OF THE ART

AND SO WE MERRILY DEPARTED, BOUND FOR SUNNY CATATONIA, IN OUR ENDEAVOR TO LOCATE THE CUSTODIAN OF ART'S HOUSEKEYS, A CERTAIN MISTER **GUMP.**

"DUE TO A FREAK ENCOUNTER, WE FOUND A CLUE TO HIS WHEREABOUTS... THAT BEING THE SETTLEMENT OF **LEROS,** MECCA-SUBSTITUTE FOR THE **CHURCH OF THE HIDDEN PROPHET.**"

"AND THERE, LIKE A VISION FROM A RAREBIT-INDUCED DREAM, HE APPEARED... ACCOMPANIED BY HIS CURIOUS FRIEND."

hallooo!!!

OH FUCK IT. IF YOU HAD BEEN GENUINELY INTERESTED YOU WOULDN'T HAVE WAITED UNTIL AFTER THE INTERMISSION TO JOIN US.

THESE 'WORDS' SIMPLY ARE NOT SUFFICIENT.

C'EST AUSSI LA TRAHISON DU LANGAGE

CONVERSE

OBSERVE OBVERSE

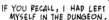

IF YOU RECALL, I HAD LEFT MYSELF IN THE DUNGEON.

Psst — girlie — wanna make a movie?

WHO ARE YOU?

SPECIAL DELIVERY? SURE, I'LL SIGN

I'm the Bergman of Alcatraz!

pinch

YEEP!

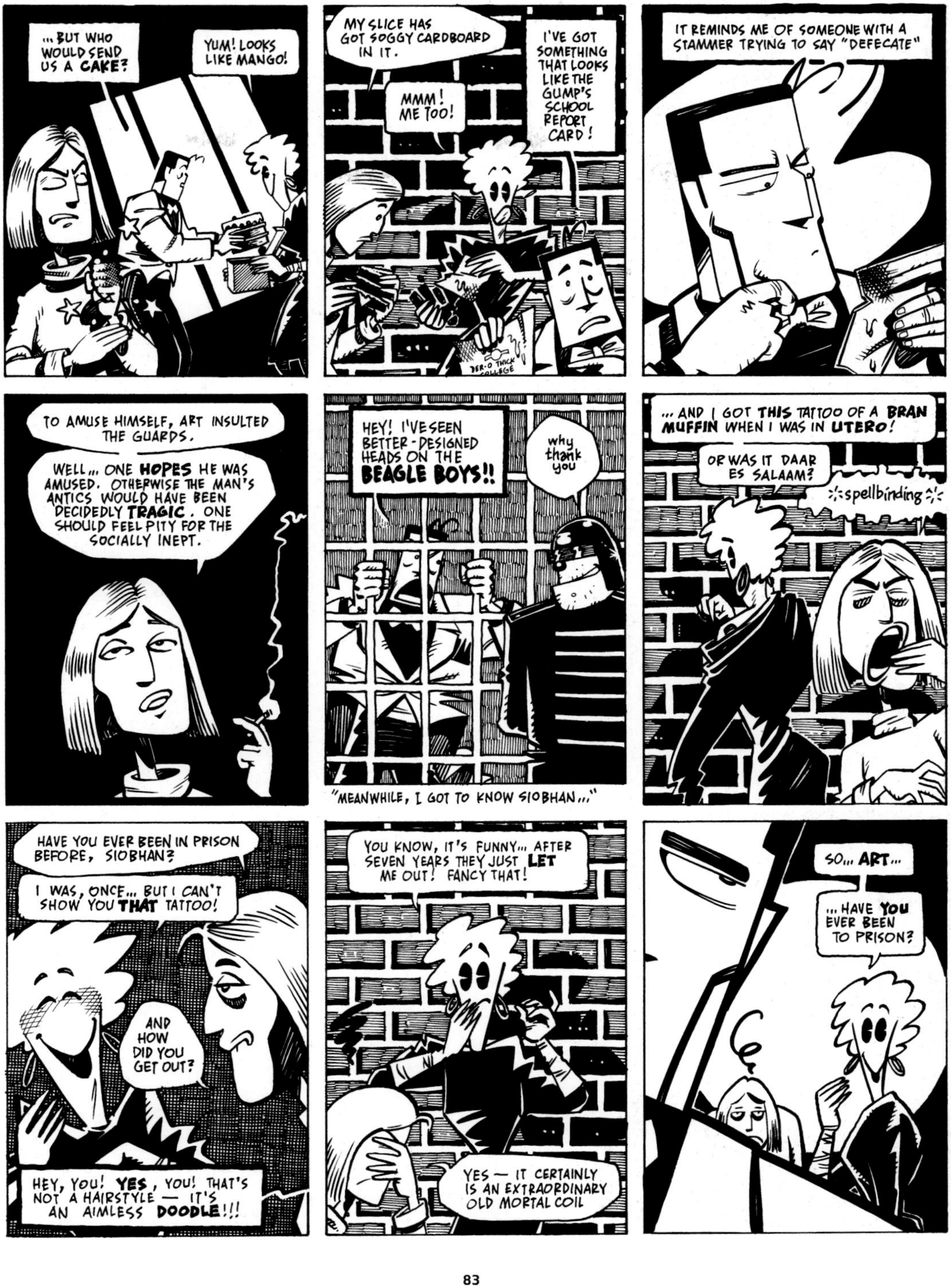

...BUT WHO WOULD SEND US A CAKE?
YUM! LOOKS LIKE MANGO!
MY SLICE HAS GOT SOGGY CARDBOARD IN IT.
MMM! ME TOO!
I'VE GOT SOMETHING THAT LOOKS LIKE THE GUMP'S SCHOOL REPORT CARD!
IT REMINDS ME OF SOMEONE WITH A STAMMER TRYING TO SAY "DEFECATE"
TO AMUSE HIMSELF, ART INSULTED THE GUARDS.
WELL... ONE HOPES HE WAS AMUSED. OTHERWISE THE MAN'S ANTICS WOULD HAVE BEEN DECIDEDLY TRAGIC. ONE SHOULD FEEL PITY FOR THE SOCIALLY INEPT.
HEY! I'VE SEEN BETTER-DESIGNED HEADS ON THE BEAGLE BOYS!!
why thank you
"MEANWHILE, I GOT TO KNOW SIOBHAN..."
...AND I GOT THIS TATTOO OF A BRAN MUFFIN WHEN I WAS IN UTERO!
OR WAS IT DAAR ES SALAAM?
spellbinding
HAVE YOU EVER BEEN IN PRISON BEFORE, SIOBHAN?
I WAS, ONCE... BUT I CAN'T SHOW YOU THAT TATTOO!
AND HOW DID YOU GET OUT?
HEY, YOU! YES, YOU! THAT'S NOT A HAIRSTYLE — IT'S AN AIMLESS DOODLE!!!
YOU KNOW, IT'S FUNNY... AFTER SEVEN YEARS THEY JUST LET ME OUT! FANCY THAT!
YES — IT CERTAINLY IS AN EXTRAORDINARY OLD MORTAL COIL
SO... ART...
...HAVE YOU EVER BEEN TO PRISON?

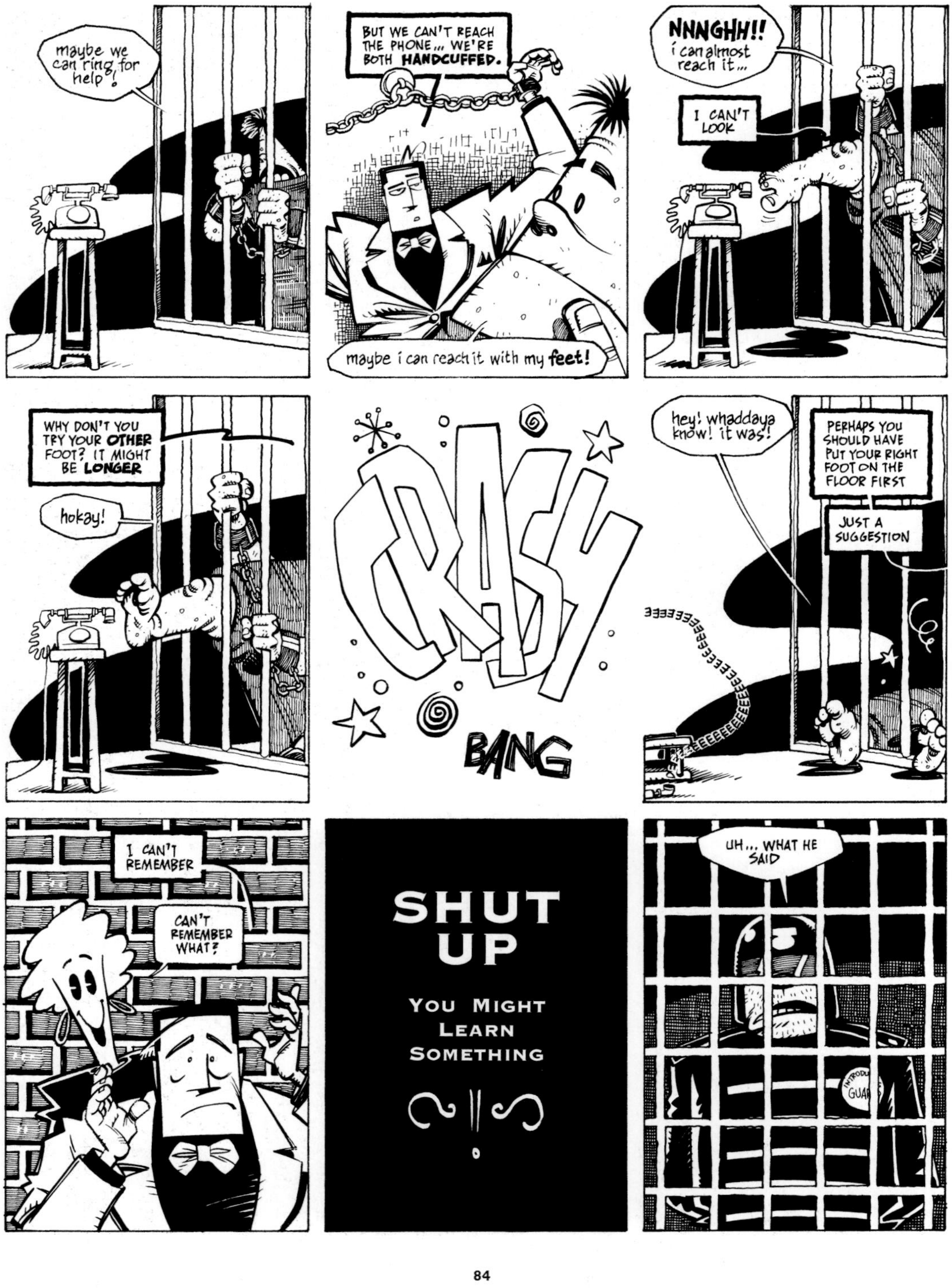
maybe we can ring for help?
BUT WE CAN'T REACH THE PHONE... WE'RE BOTH HANDCUFFED.
maybe i can reach it with my feet!
NNNGHH!! i can almost reach it...
I CAN'T LOOK
WHY DON'T YOU TRY YOUR OTHER FOOT? IT MIGHT BE LONGER
hokay!
CRASH
BANG
hey! whaddaya know! it was!
PERHAPS YOU SHOULD HAVE PUT YOUR RIGHT FOOT ON THE FLOOR FIRST
JUST A SUGGESTION
EEEEEEEEEEEEEEEEEEEEEEEEEEEEEEEEEE
I CAN'T REMEMBER
CAN'T REMEMBER WHAT?
SHUT UP
YOU MIGHT LEARN SOMETHING
UH... WHAT HE SAID

THE HOLY MAN, HAVING DIED, FOUND HIMSELF AT THE GATES OF HEAVEN.

HE TOLD SAINT PETER THAT HE HAD SPREAD THE WORD OF LOG

AND LOOKED AFTER THE FAITHFUL

HE DEMANDED TO BE LET IN.

LOG HEARD THE COMMOTION (HE HAS SUPER-HEARING) AND WENT TO THE GATES

UPON SEEING THE HOLY MAN, HE EXCLAIMED, "YOU!"

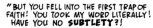

"BUT YOU FELL INTO THE FIRST TRAP OF FAITH! YOU TOOK MY WORD LITERALLY! HAVE YOU NO **SUBTLETY**?!

"BY YOUR NARROWNESS OF MIND YOU TURNED ALL THESE PEOPLE AGAINST ME!"

AND BEHIND LOG APPEARED WOMEN AND MEN FROM ALL WALKS OF LIFE AND OF EVERY HUE ....

AND THE GATES OF HEAVEN WERE FOREVER CLOSED TO THE HOLY MAN

IT'S GOT A BEAT AND YOU CAN DANCE TO IT!

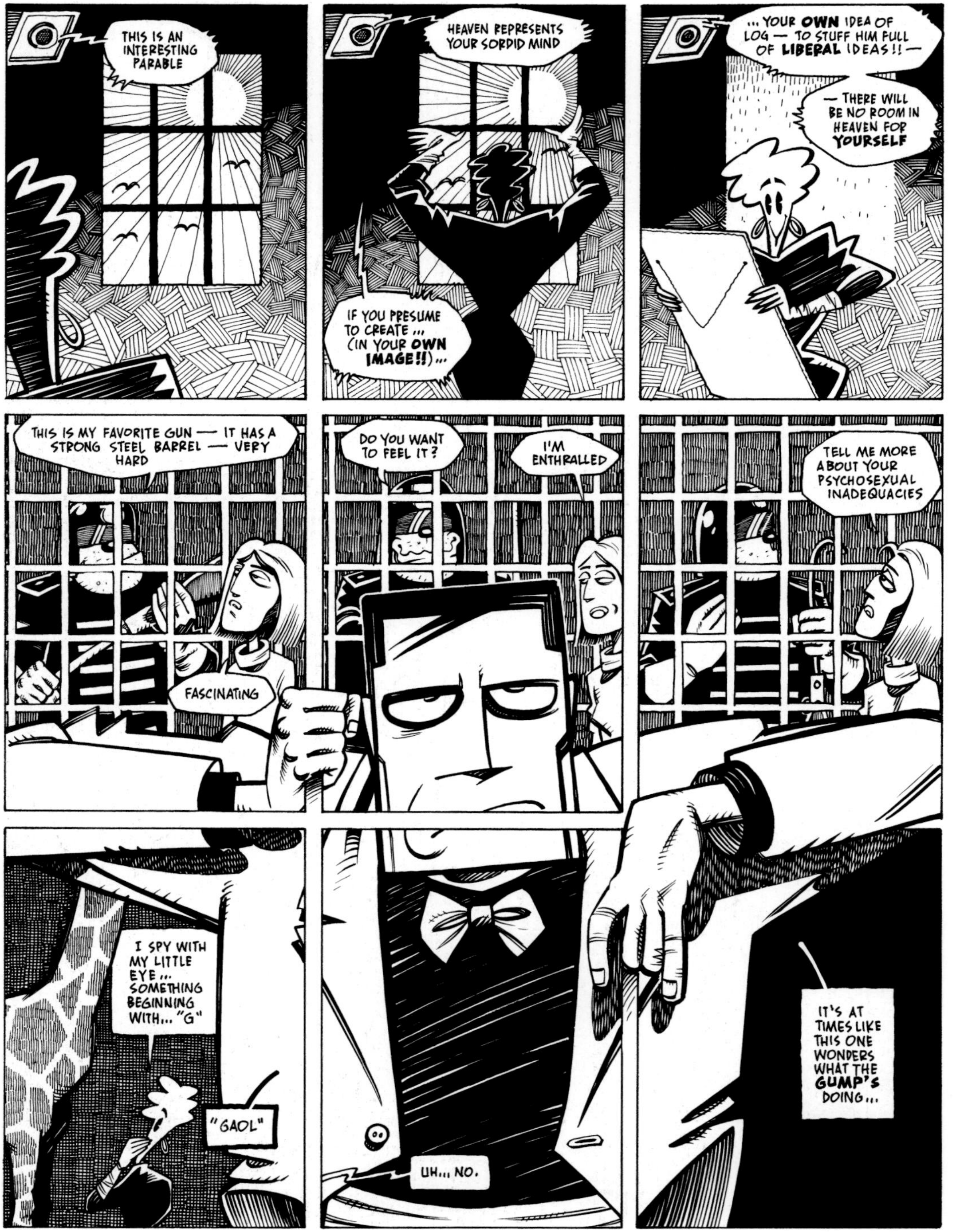
THIS IS AN INTERESTING PARABLE
HEAVEN REPRESENTS YOUR SORDID MIND
IF YOU PRESUME TO CREATE ... (IN YOUR OWN IMAGE!!) ...
... YOUR OWN IDEA OF LOG — TO STUFF HIM FULL OF LIBERAL IDEAS!! —
— THERE WILL BE NO ROOM IN HEAVEN FOR YOURSELF
THIS IS MY FAVORITE GUN — IT HAS A STRONG STEEL BARREL — VERY HARD
FASCINATING
DO YOU WANT TO FEEL IT?
I'M ENTHRALLED
TELL ME MORE ABOUT YOUR PSYCHOSEXUAL INADEQUACIES
I SPY WITH MY LITTLE EYE ... SOMETHING BEGINNING WITH ... "G"
"GAOL"
UH ... NO.
IT'S AT TIMES LIKE THIS ONE WONDERS WHAT THE GUMP'S DOING ...

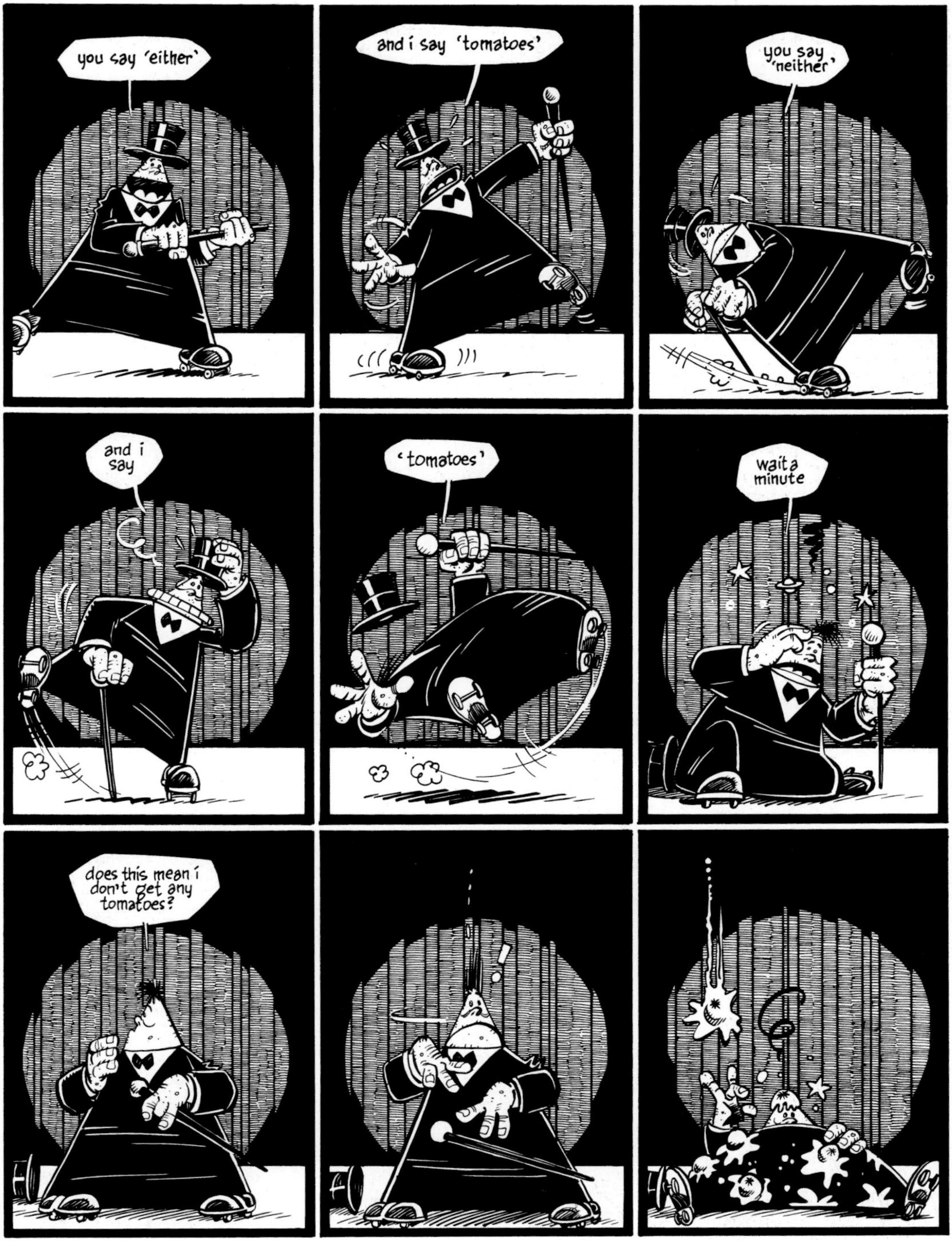
you say 'either'
and i say 'tomatoes'
you say 'neither'
and i say
'tomatoes'
wait a minute
does this mean i don't get any tomatoes?
!

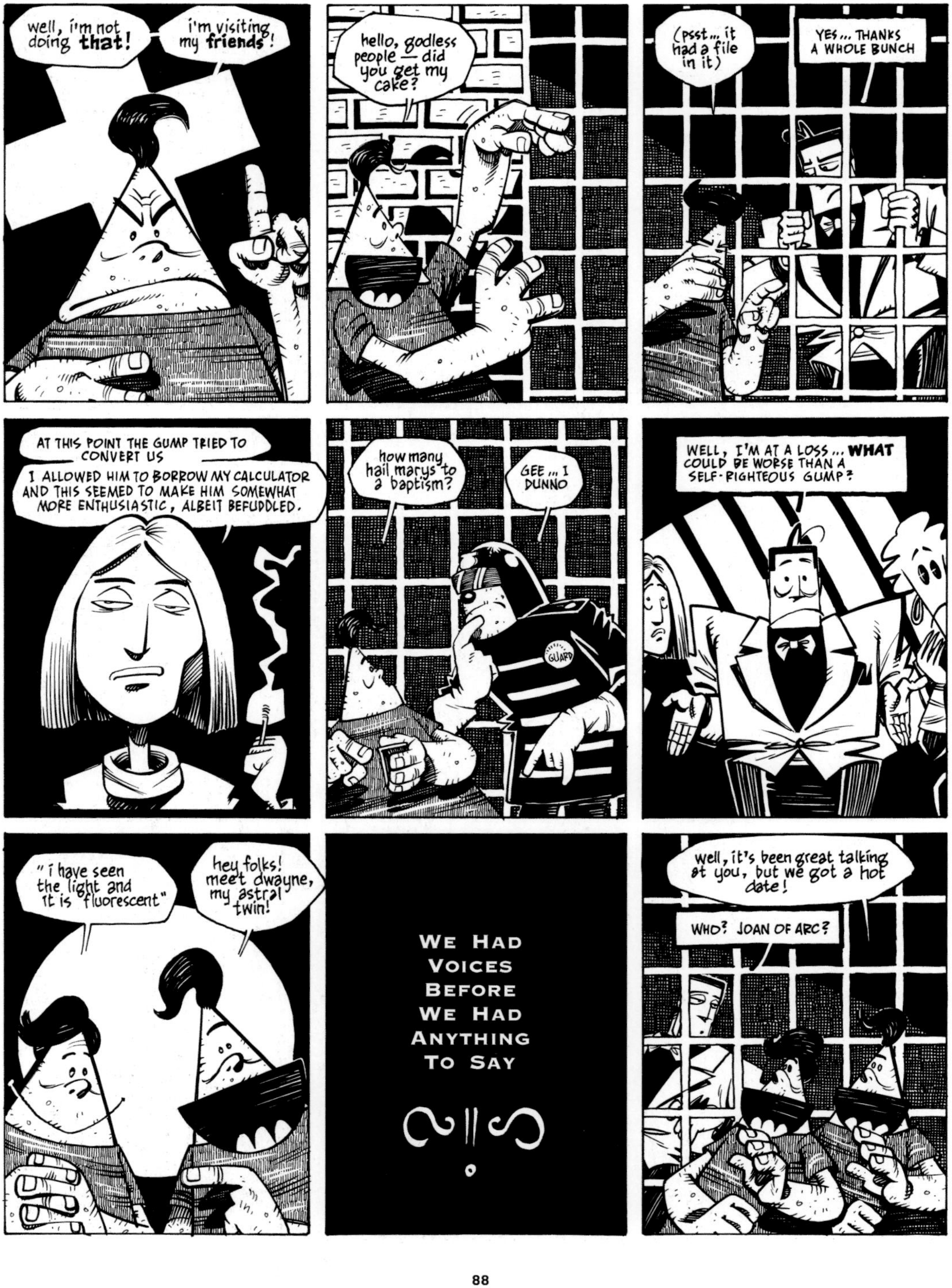

well, i'm not doing **that**!
i'm visiting my **friends**!
hello, godless people — did you get my cake?
(psst... it had a file in it)
YES... THANKS A WHOLE BUNCH
AT THIS POINT THE GUMP TRIED TO CONVERT US
I ALLOWED HIM TO BORROW MY CALCULATOR AND THIS SEEMED TO MAKE HIM SOMEWHAT MORE ENTHUSIASTIC, ALBEIT BEFUDDLED.
how many hail marys to a baptism?
GEE... I DUNNO
GUARD
WELL, I'M AT A LOSS... **WHAT** COULD BE WORSE THAN A SELF-RIGHTEOUS GUMP?
"i have seen the light and it is fluorescent"
hey folks! meet dwayne, my astral twin!
WE HAD VOICES BEFORE WE HAD ANYTHING TO SAY
well, it's been great talking at you, but we got a hot date!
WHO? JOAN OF ARC?

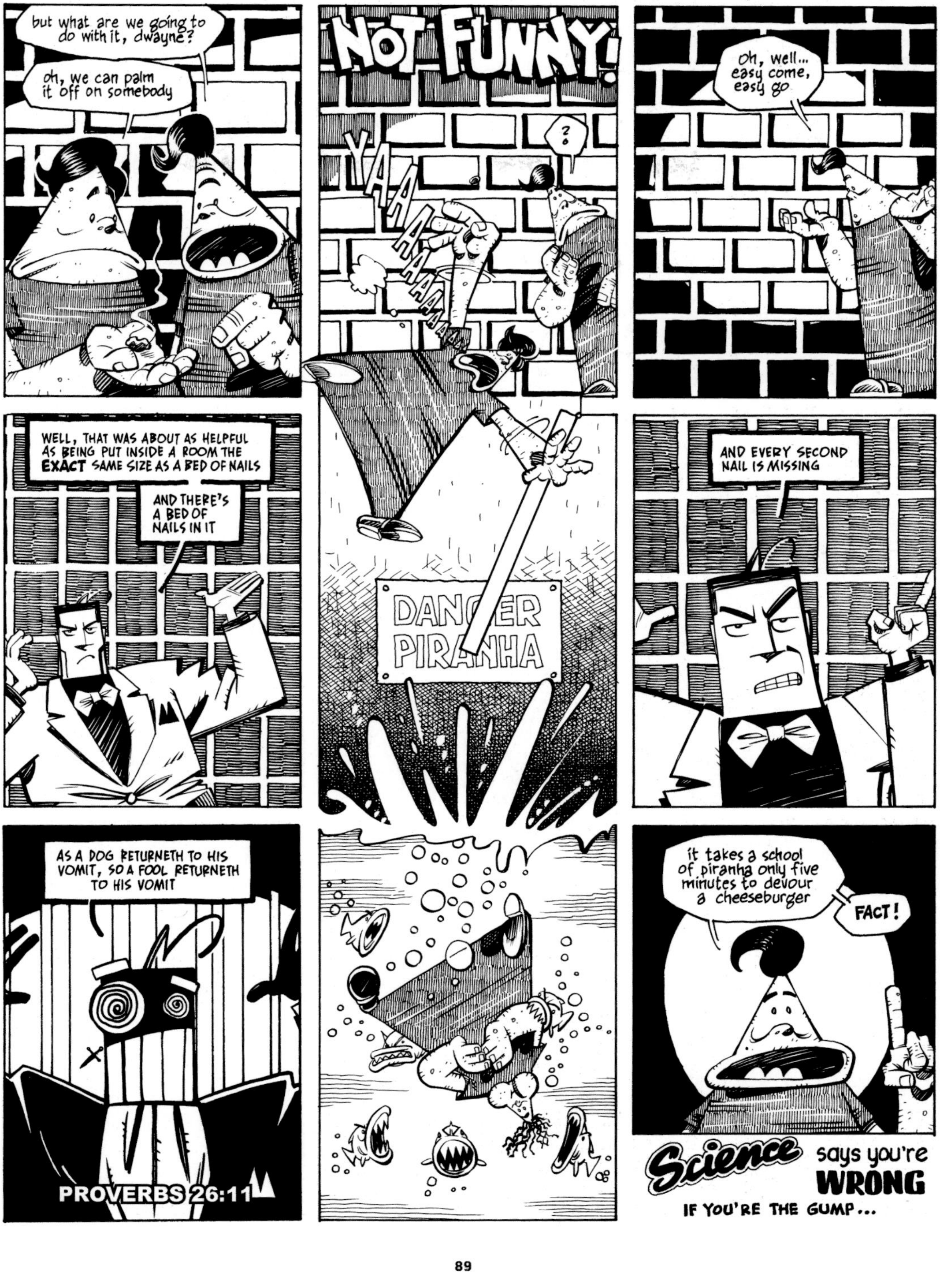

but what are we going to do with it, dwayne?
oh, we can palm it off on somebody
NOT FUNNY!
?
YAAAAAAAAAA
oh, well... easy come, easy go
WELL, THAT WAS ABOUT AS HELPFUL AS BEING PUT INSIDE A ROOM THE EXACT SAME SIZE AS A BED OF NAILS
AND THERE'S A BED OF NAILS IN IT
DANGER PIRANHA
AND EVERY SECOND NAIL IS MISSING
AS A DOG RETURNETH TO HIS VOMIT, SO A FOOL RETURNETH TO HIS VOMIT
PROVERBS 26:11
it takes a school of piranha only five minutes to devour a cheeseburger
FACT!
Science says you're WRONG
IF YOU'RE THE GUMP...

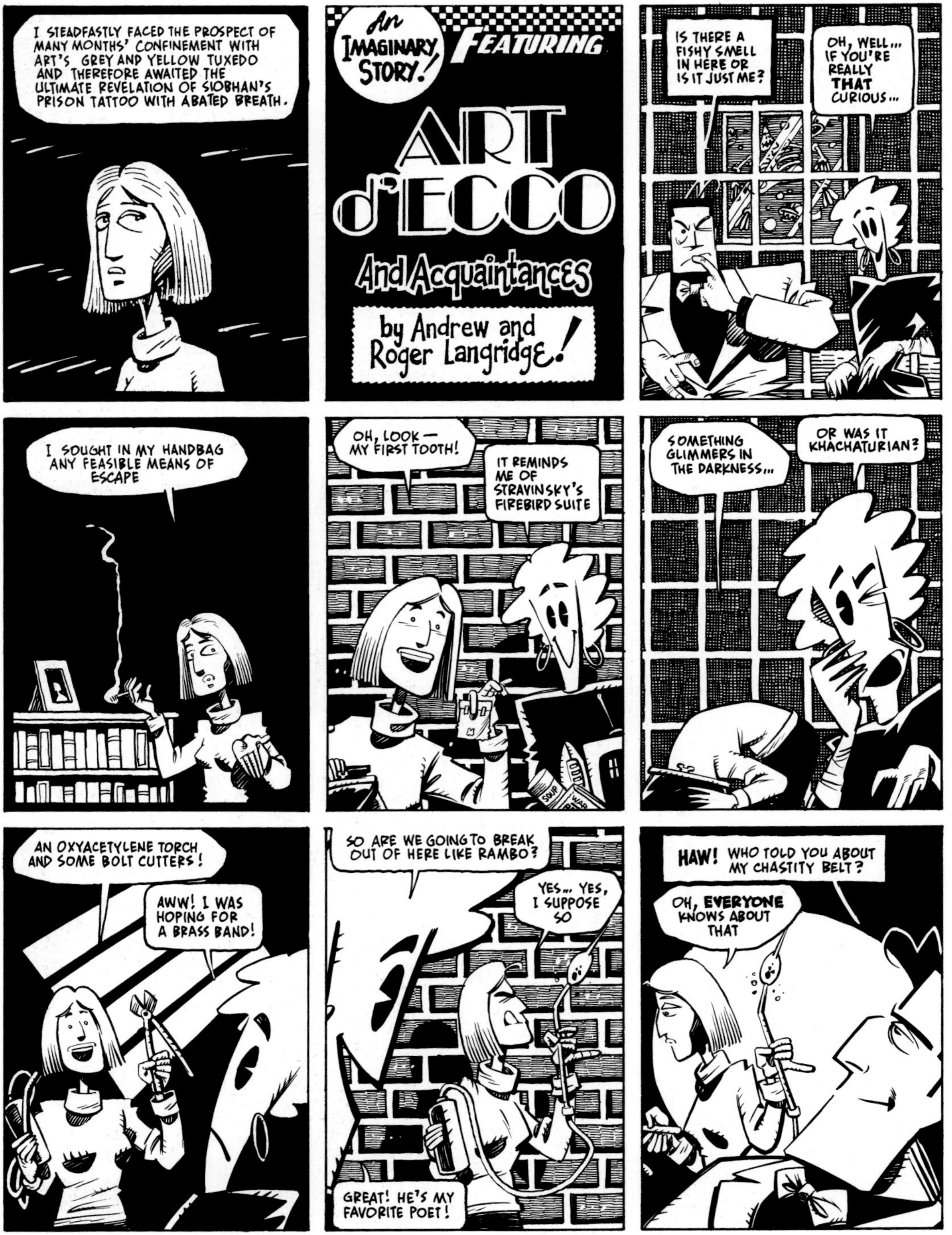
I STEADFASTLY FACED THE PROSPECT OF MANY MONTHS' CONFINEMENT WITH ART'S GREY AND YELLOW TUXEDO AND THEREFORE AWAITED THE ULTIMATE REVELATION OF SIOBHAN'S PRISON TATTOO WITH ABATED BREATH.
An IMAGINARY STORY! FEATURING
ART d'ECCO
And Acquaintances
by Andrew and Roger Langridge!
IS THERE A FISHY SMELL IN HERE OR IS IT JUST ME?
OH, WELL... IF YOU'RE REALLY THAT CURIOUS...
I SOUGHT IN MY HANDBAG ANY FEASIBLE MEANS OF ESCAPE
OH, LOOK — MY FIRST TOOTH!
IT REMINDS ME OF STRAVINSKY'S FIREBIRD SUITE
SOMETHING GLIMMERS IN THE DARKNESS...
OR WAS IT KHACHATURIAN?
AN OXYACETYLENE TORCH AND SOME BOLT CUTTERS!
AWW! I WAS HOPING FOR A BRASS BAND!
SO ARE WE GOING TO BREAK OUT OF HERE LIKE RAMBO?
YES... YES, I SUPPOSE SO
GREAT! HE'S MY FAVORITE POET!
HAW! WHO TOLD YOU ABOUT MY CHASTITY BELT?
OH, EVERYONE KNOWS ABOUT THAT

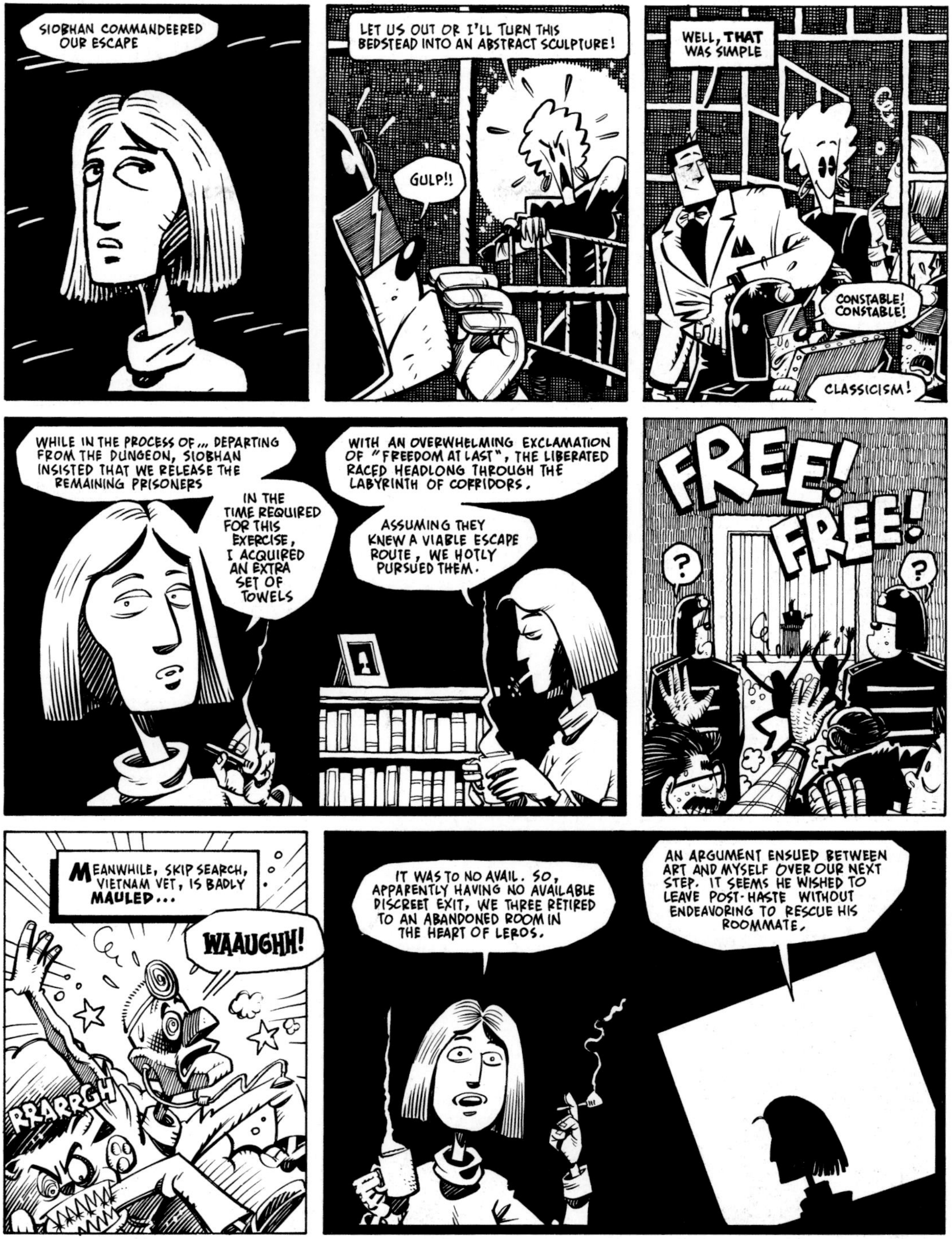
SIOBHAN COMMANDEERED OUR ESCAPE
LET US OUT OR I'LL TURN THIS BEDSTEAD INTO AN ABSTRACT SCULPTURE!
GULP!!
WELL, THAT WAS SIMPLE
CONSTABLE! CONSTABLE!
CLASSICISM!
WHILE IN THE PROCESS OF... DEPARTING FROM THE DUNGEON, SIOBHAN INSISTED THAT WE RELEASE THE REMAINING PRISONERS
IN THE TIME REQUIRED FOR THIS EXERCISE, I ACQUIRED AN EXTRA SET OF TOWELS
WITH AN OVERWHELMING EXCLAMATION OF "FREEDOM AT LAST", THE LIBERATED RACED HEADLONG THROUGH THE LABYRINTH OF CORRIDORS.
ASSUMING THEY KNEW A VIABLE ESCAPE ROUTE, WE HOTLY PURSUED THEM.
FREE! FREE!
?
?
MEANWHILE, SKIP SEARCH, VIETNAM VET, IS BADLY MAULED...
WAAUGHH!
RRARRGH
IT WAS TO NO AVAIL. SO, APPARENTLY HAVING NO AVAILABLE DISCREET EXIT, WE THREE RETIRED TO AN ABANDONED ROOM IN THE HEART OF LEROS.
AN ARGUMENT ENSUED BETWEEN ART AND MYSELF OVER OUR NEXT STEP. IT SEEMS HE WISHED TO LEAVE POST-HASTE WITHOUT ENDEAVORING TO RESCUE HIS ROOMMATE.

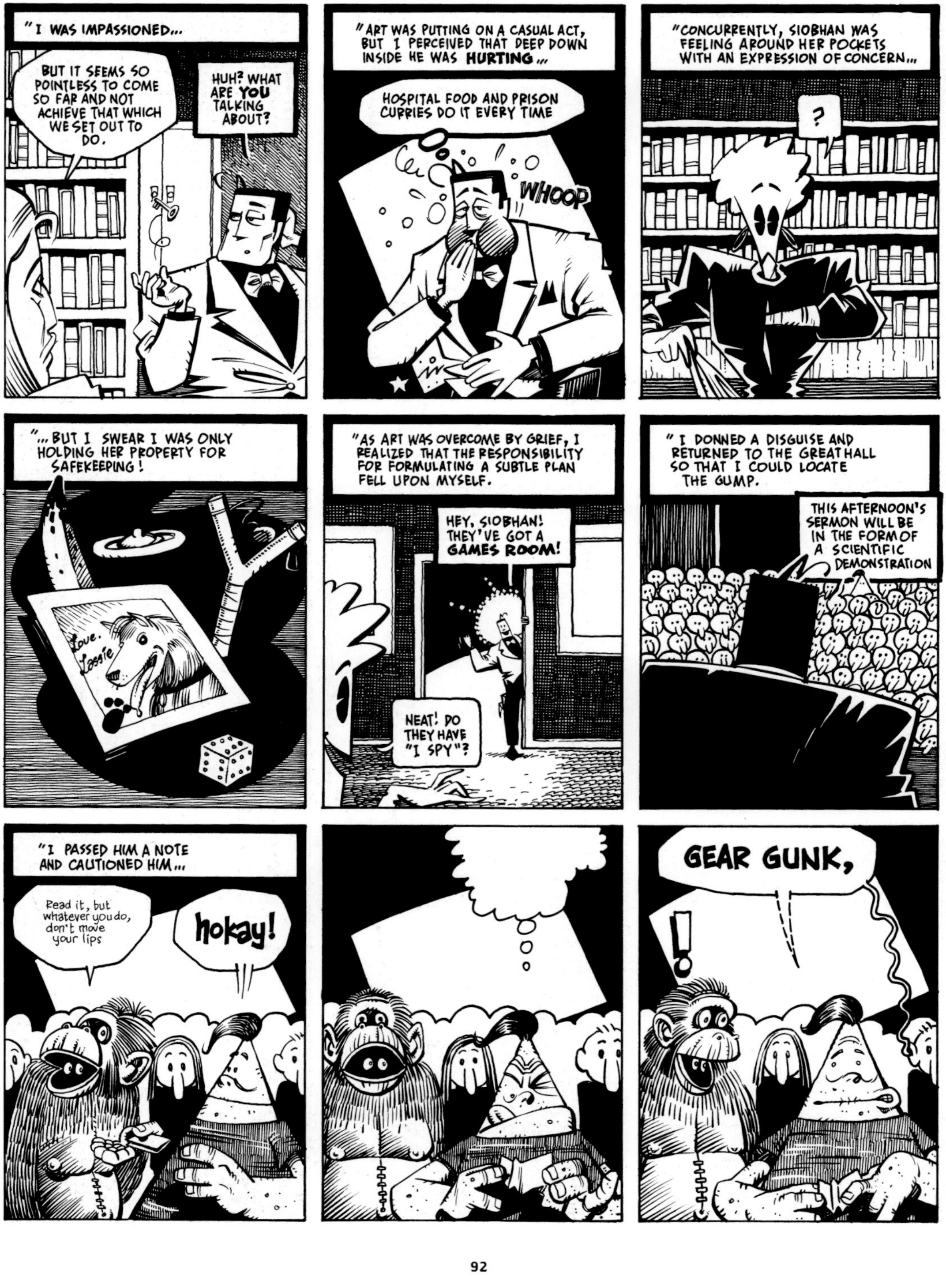
"I WAS IMPASSIONED...
BUT IT SEEMS SO POINTLESS TO COME SO FAR AND NOT ACHIEVE THAT WHICH WE SET OUT TO DO.
HUH? WHAT ARE YOU TALKING ABOUT?
"ART WAS PUTTING ON A CASUAL ACT, BUT I PERCEIVED THAT DEEP DOWN INSIDE HE WAS HURTING...
HOSPITAL FOOD AND PRISON CURRIES DO IT EVERY TIME
WHOOP
"CONCURRENTLY, SIOBHAN WAS FEELING AROUND HER POCKETS WITH AN EXPRESSION OF CONCERN...
?
"... BUT I SWEAR I WAS ONLY HOLDING HER PROPERTY FOR SAFEKEEPING!
Love. Lassie
"AS ART WAS OVERCOME BY GRIEF, I REALIZED THAT THE RESPONSIBILITY FOR FORMULATING A SUBTLE PLAN FELL UPON MYSELF.
HEY, SIOBHAN! THEY'VE GOT A GAMES ROOM!
NEAT! DO THEY HAVE "I SPY"?
"I DONNED A DISGUISE AND RETURNED TO THE GREAT HALL SO THAT I COULD LOCATE THE GUMP.
THIS AFTERNOON'S SERMON WILL BE IN THE FORM OF A SCIENTIFIC DEMONSTRATION
"I PASSED HIM A NOTE AND CAUTIONED HIM...
Read it, but whatever you do, don't move your lips
hokay!
GEAR GUNK,
!

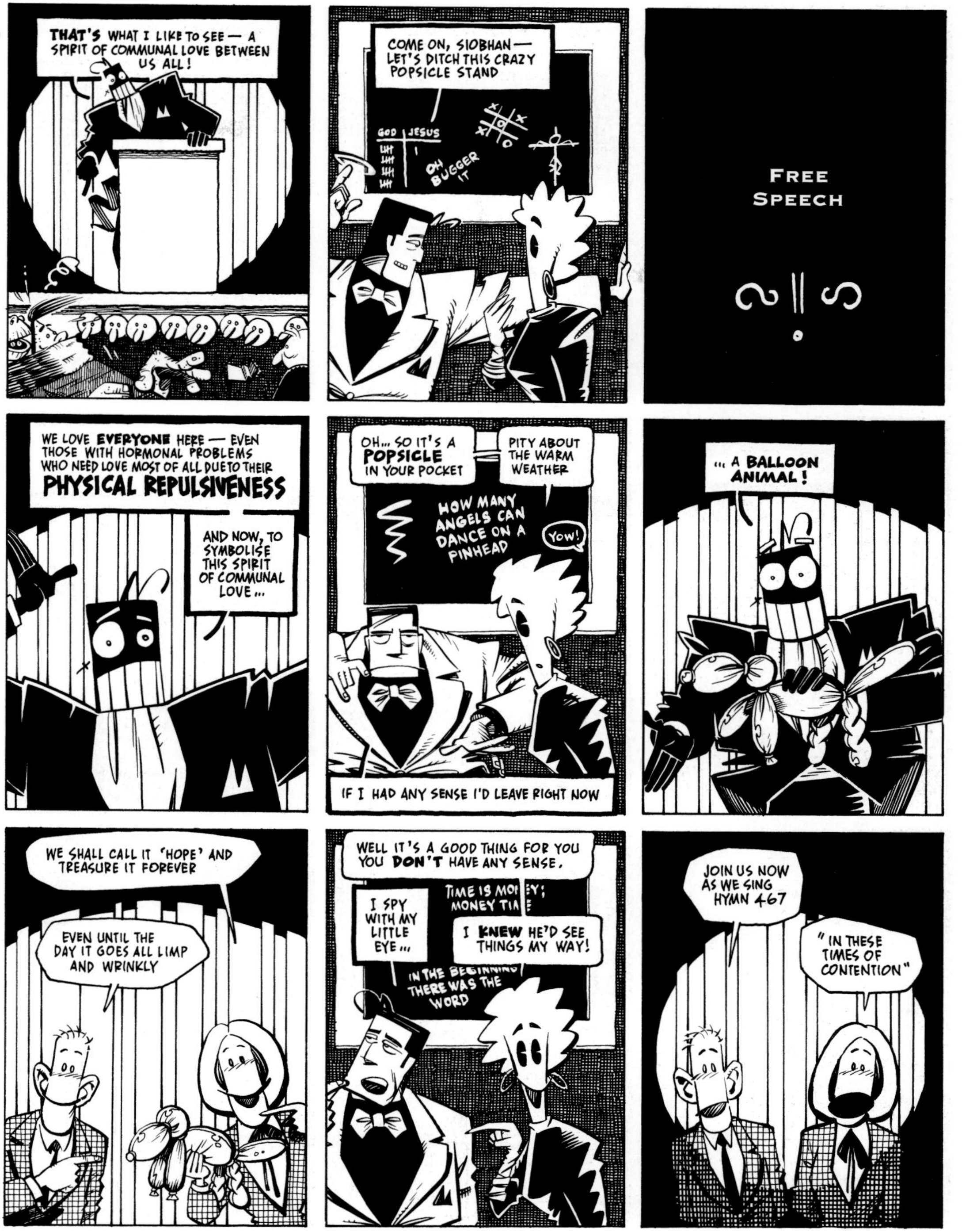
THAT'S WHAT I LIKE TO SEE — A SPIRIT OF COMMUNAL LOVE BETWEEN US ALL!
COME ON, SIOBHAN — LET'S DITCH THIS CRAZY POPSICLE STAND
GOD JESUS
OH BUGGER IT
FREE SPEECH
WE LOVE EVERYONE HERE — EVEN THOSE WITH HORMONAL PROBLEMS WHO NEED LOVE MOST OF ALL DUE TO THEIR PHYSICAL REPULSIVENESS
AND NOW, TO SYMBOLISE THIS SPIRIT OF COMMUNAL LOVE...
OH... SO IT'S A POPSICLE IN YOUR POCKET
PITY ABOUT THE WARM WEATHER
HOW MANY ANGELS CAN DANCE ON A PINHEAD
YOW!
IF I HAD ANY SENSE I'D LEAVE RIGHT NOW
... A BALLOON ANIMAL!
WE SHALL CALL IT 'HOPE' AND TREASURE IT FOREVER
EVEN UNTIL THE DAY IT GOES ALL LIMP AND WRINKLY
WELL IT'S A GOOD THING FOR YOU YOU DON'T HAVE ANY SENSE.
I SPY WITH MY LITTLE EYE...
I KNEW HE'D SEE THINGS MY WAY!
IN THE BEGINNING THERE WAS THE WORD
JOIN US NOW AS WE SING HYMN 467
"IN THESE TIMES OF CONTENTION"

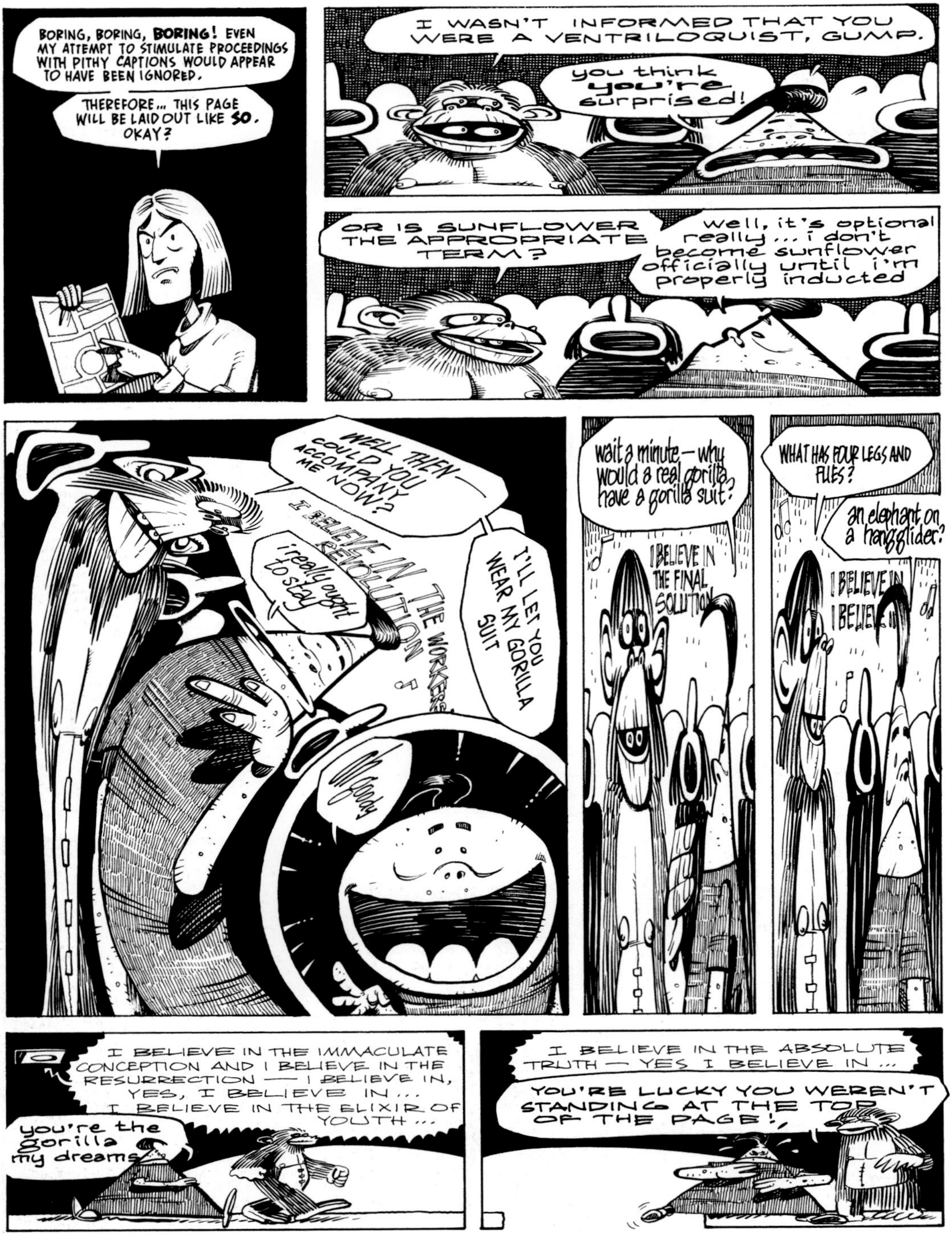

BORING, BORING, BORING! EVEN MY ATTEMPT TO STIMULATE PROCEEDINGS WITH PITHY CAPTIONS WOULD APPEAR TO HAVE BEEN IGNORED.
THEREFORE... THIS PAGE WILL BE LAID OUT LIKE SO. OKAY?
I WASN'T INFORMED THAT YOU WERE A VENTRILOQUIST, GUMP.
you think you're surprised!
OR IS SUNFLOWER THE APPROPRIATE TERM?
well, it's optional really... i don't become sunflower officially until i'm properly inducted
WELL THEN — COULD YOU ACCOMPANY ME NOW?
I BELIEVE IN THE REVOLUTION
i really ought to stay
THE WORKERS
I'LL LET YOU WEAR MY GORILLA SUIT
wait a minute — why would a real gorilla have a gorilla suit?
I BELIEVE IN THE FINAL SOLUTION
WHAT HAS FOUR LEGS AND FLIES?
an elephant on a hangglider?
I BELIEVE IN I BELIEVE IN
I BELIEVE IN THE IMMACULATE CONCEPTION AND I BELIEVE IN THE RESURRECTION — I BELIEVE IN, YES, I BELIEVE IN... I BELIEVE IN THE ELIXIR OF YOUTH...
you're the gorilla my dreams
I BELIEVE IN THE ABSOLUTE TRUTH — YES I BELIEVE IN...
YOU'RE LUCKY YOU WEREN'T STANDING AT THE TOP OF THE PAGE!

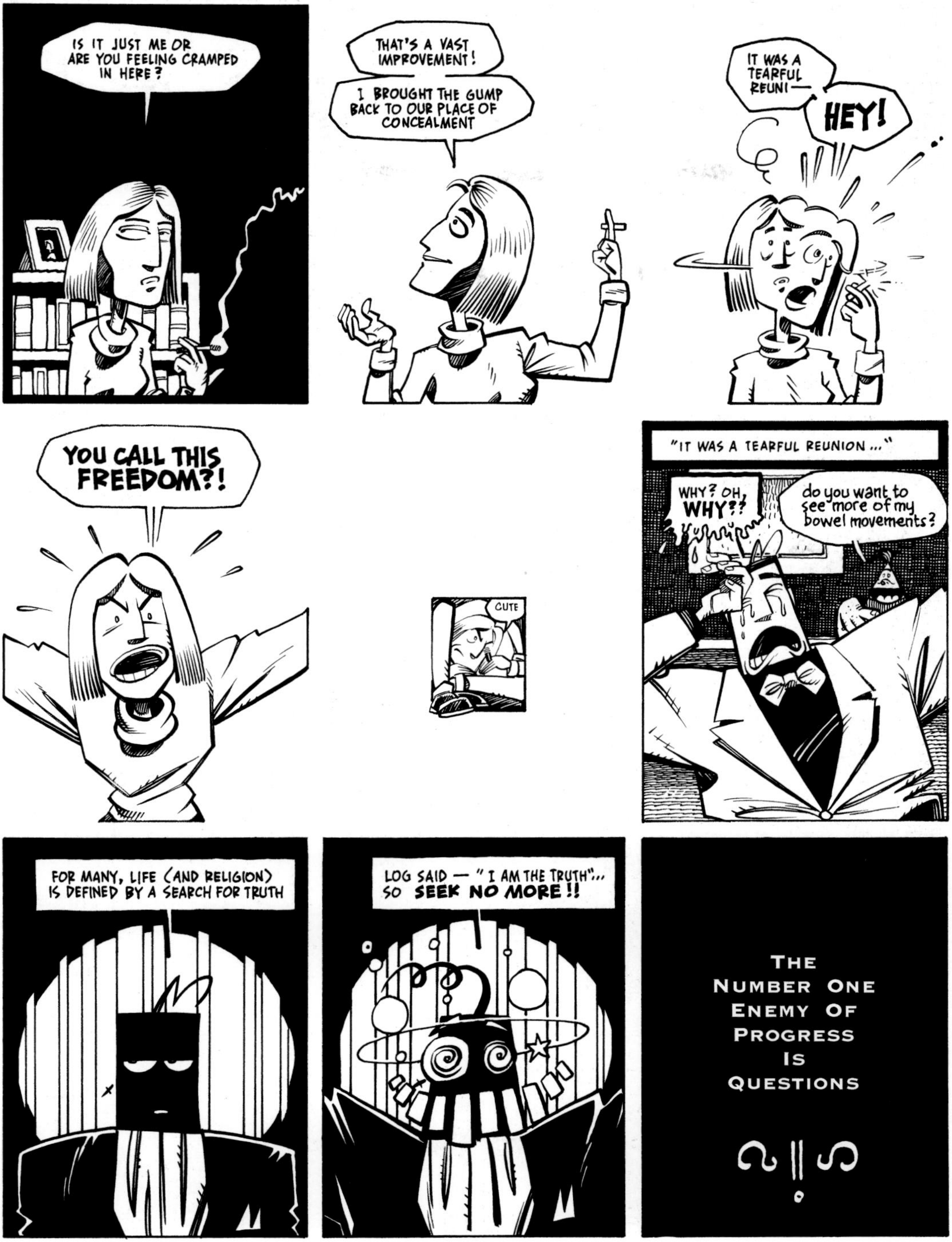

IS IT JUST ME OR ARE YOU FEELING CRAMPED IN HERE?
THAT'S A VAST IMPROVEMENT!
I BROUGHT THE GUMP BACK TO OUR PLACE OF CONCEALMENT
IT WAS A TEARFUL REUNI—
HEY!
YOU CALL THIS FREEDOM?!
CUTE
"IT WAS A TEARFUL REUNION..."
WHY? OH, WHY??
do you want to see more of my bowel movements?
FOR MANY, LIFE (AND RELIGION) IS DEFINED BY A SEARCH FOR TRUTH
LOG SAID — "I AM THE TRUTH"... SO SEEK NO MORE!!
THE NUMBER ONE ENEMY OF PROGRESS IS QUESTIONS

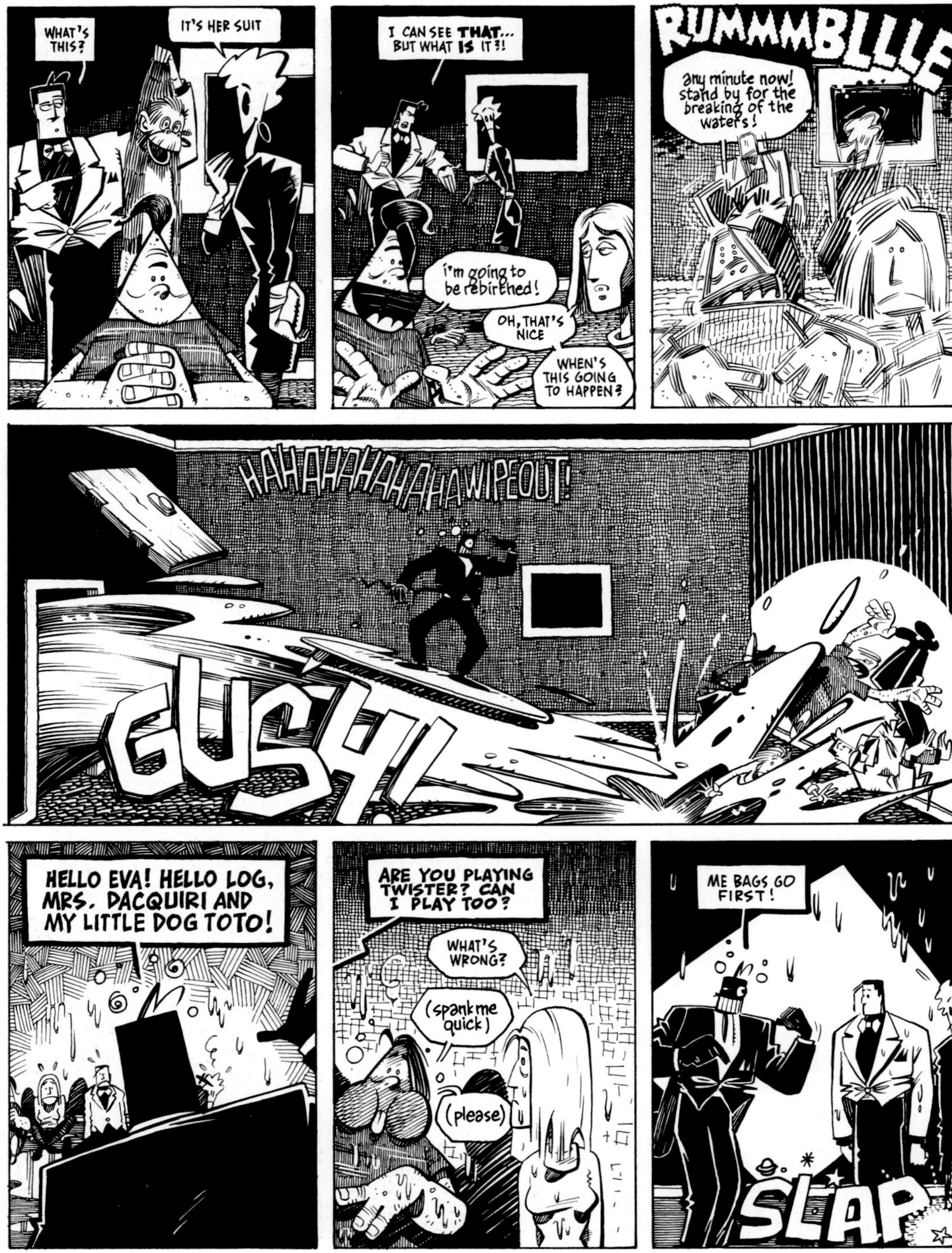
WHAT'S THIS?
IT'S HER SUIT
I CAN SEE THAT... BUT WHAT IS IT?!
i'm going to be rebirthed!
OH, THAT'S NICE
WHEN'S THIS GOING TO HAPPEN?
RUMMMBLLLE
any minute now! stand by for the breaking of the waters!
HAHAHAHAHAHAHAWIPEOUT!
GUSH!
HELLO EVA! HELLO LOG, MRS. DACQUIRI AND MY LITTLE DOG TOTO!
ARE YOU PLAYING TWISTER? CAN I PLAY TOO?
WHAT'S WRONG?
(spank me quick)
(please)
ME BAGS GO FIRST!
SLAP

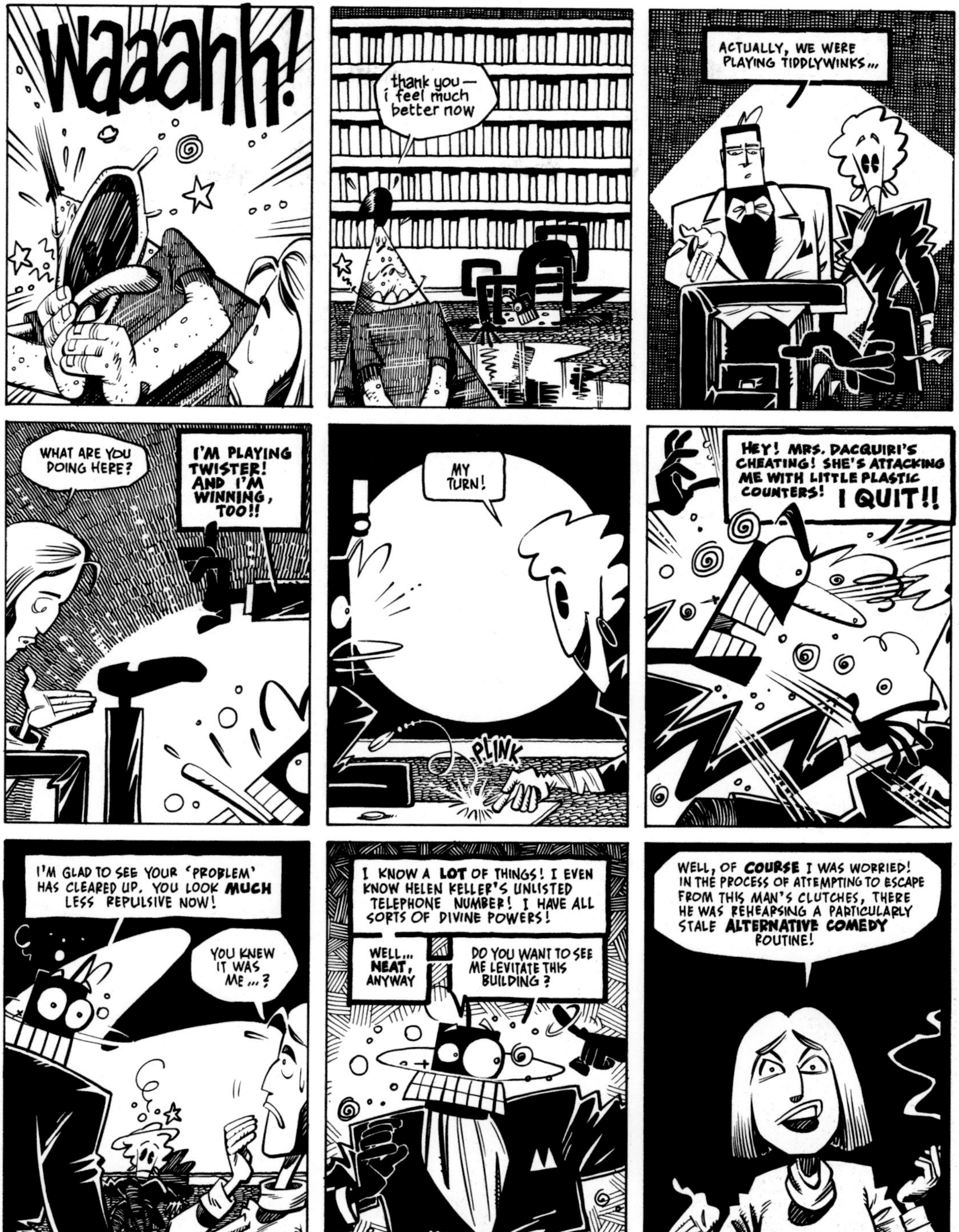
Waaahh!
thank you — i feel much better now
ACTUALLY, WE WERE PLAYING TIDDLYWINKS...
WHAT ARE YOU DOING HERE?
I'M PLAYING TWISTER! AND I'M WINNING, TOO!!
MY TURN!
PLINK
HEY! MRS. DACQUIRI'S CHEATING! SHE'S ATTACKING ME WITH LITTLE PLASTIC COUNTERS! I QUIT!!
I'M GLAD TO SEE YOUR 'PROBLEM' HAS CLEARED UP. YOU LOOK MUCH LESS REPULSIVE NOW!
YOU KNEW IT WAS ME...?
I KNOW A LOT OF THINGS! I EVEN KNOW HELEN KELLER'S UNLISTED TELEPHONE NUMBER! I HAVE ALL SORTS OF DIVINE POWERS!
WELL... NEAT, ANYWAY
DO YOU WANT TO SEE ME LEVITATE THIS BUILDING?
WELL, OF COURSE I WAS WORRIED! IN THE PROCESS OF ATTEMPTING TO ESCAPE FROM THIS MAN'S CLUTCHES, THERE HE WAS REHEARSING A PARTICULARLY STALE ALTERNATIVE COMEDY ROUTINE!

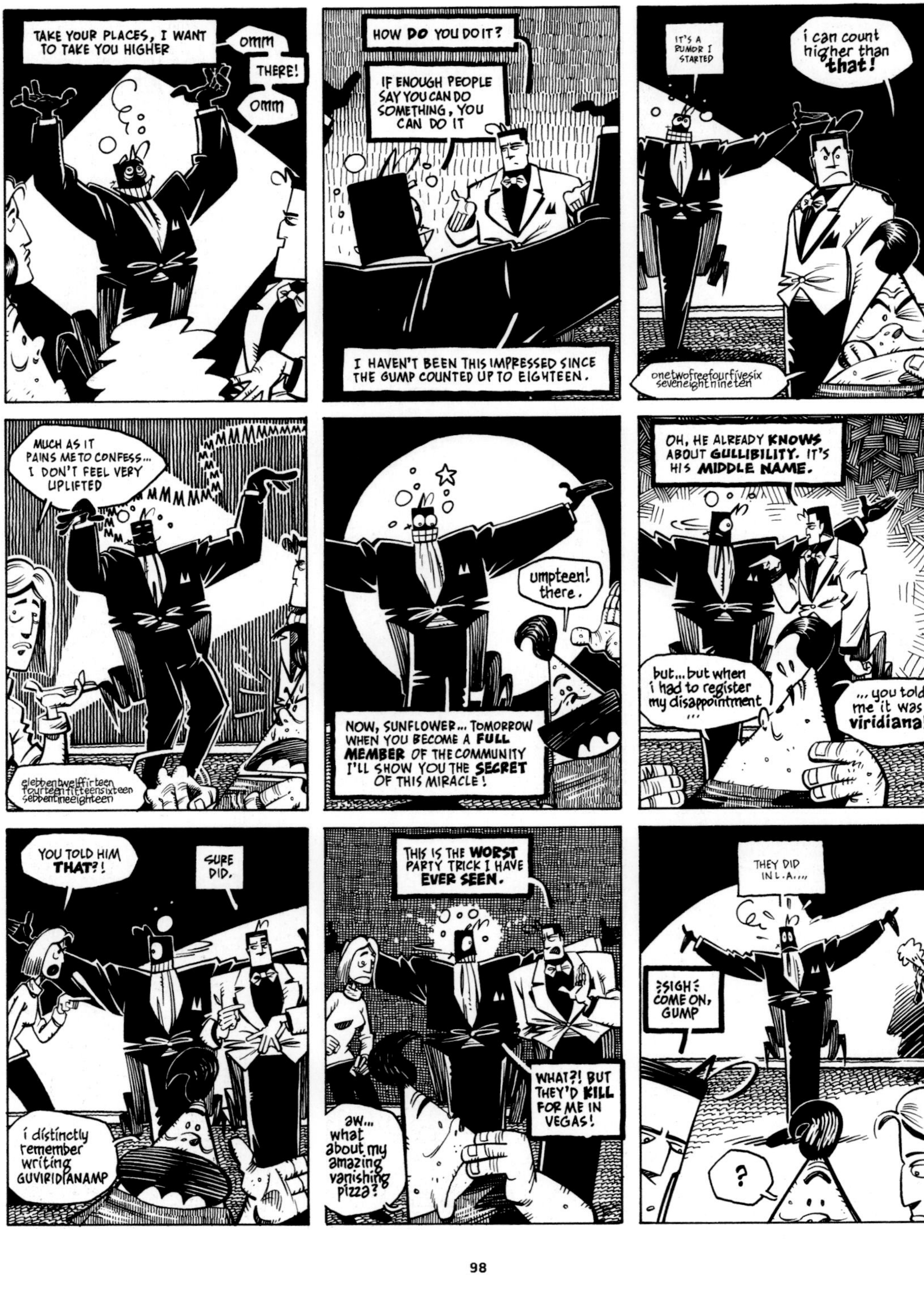

TAKE YOUR PLACES, I WANT TO TAKE YOU HIGHER
omm
THERE!
omm
HOW DO YOU DO IT?
IF ENOUGH PEOPLE SAY YOU CAN DO SOMETHING, YOU CAN DO IT
I HAVEN'T BEEN THIS IMPRESSED SINCE THE GUMP COUNTED UP TO EIGHTEEN.
IT'S A RUMOR I STARTED
i can count higher than that!
onetwofreefourfivesix seveneightnineten
MUCH AS IT PAINS ME TO CONFESS... I DON'T FEEL VERY UPLIFTED
MMMMMMMMMM
elebbentwelffirteen fourteenfifteensixteen sebbenteneeighteen
umpteen! there.
NOW, SUNFLOWER... TOMORROW WHEN YOU BECOME A FULL MEMBER OF THE COMMUNITY I'LL SHOW YOU THE SECRET OF THIS MIRACLE!
OH, HE ALREADY KNOWS ABOUT GULLIBILITY. IT'S HIS MIDDLE NAME.
but... but when i had to register my disappointment ...
... you told me it was viridiana!
YOU TOLD HIM THAT?!
SURE DID.
i distinctly remember writing GUVIRIDIANAMP
THIS IS THE WORST PARTY TRICK I HAVE EVER SEEN.
WHAT?! BUT THEY'D KILL FOR ME IN VEGAS!
aw... what about my amazing vanishing pizza?
THEY DID IN L.A....
SIGH COME ON, GUMP
?

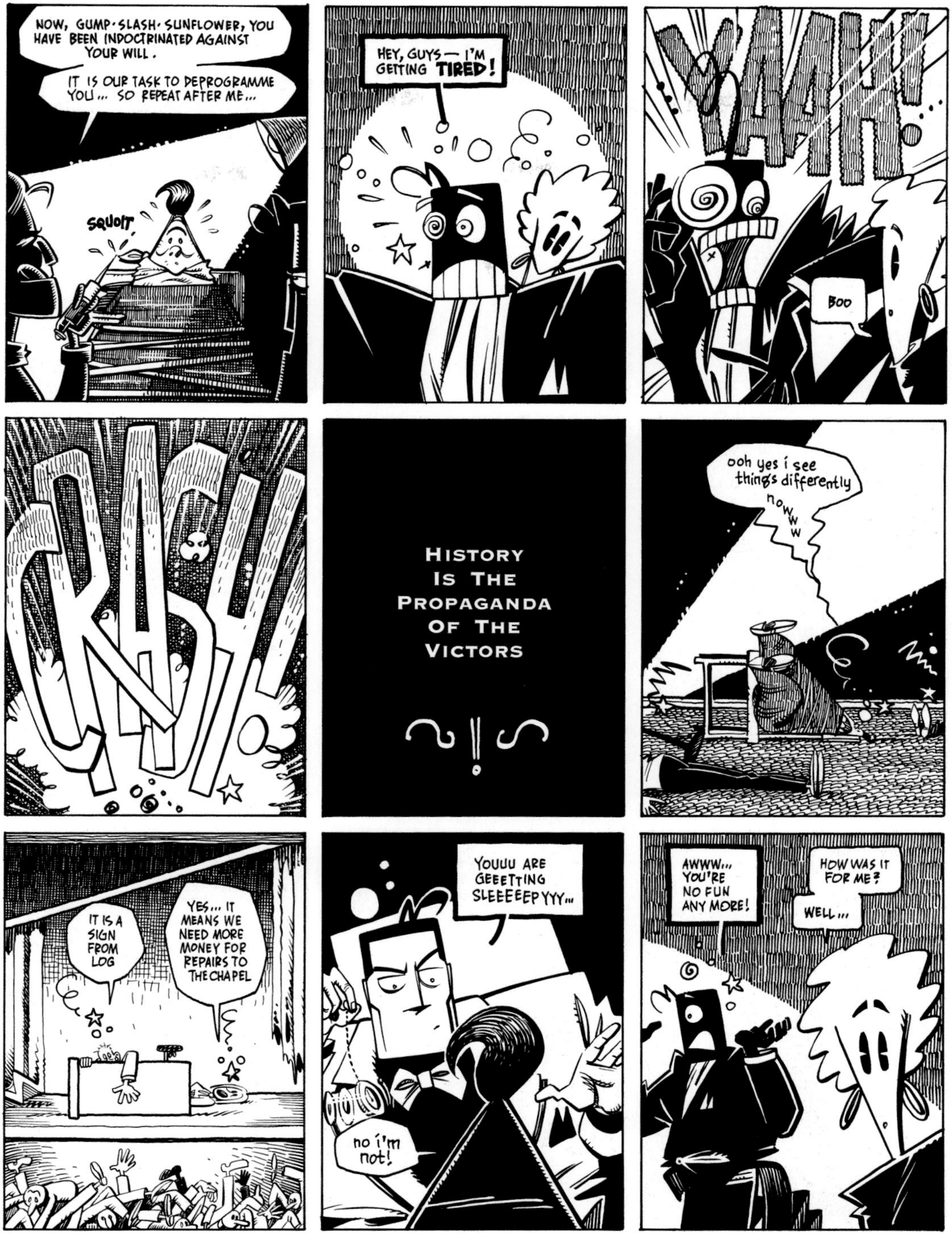
NOW, GUMP·SLASH·SUNFLOWER, YOU HAVE BEEN INDOCTRINATED AGAINST YOUR WILL.
IT IS OUR TASK TO DEPROGRAMME YOU... SO REPEAT AFTER ME...
SQUOIT
HEY, GUYS— I'M GETTING TIRED!
YAAAH!
BOO
CRASH!
HISTORY IS THE PROPAGANDA OF THE VICTORS
ooh yes i see things differently nowww
IT IS A SIGN FROM LOG
YES... IT MEANS WE NEED MORE MONEY FOR REPAIRS TO THE CHAPEL
YOUUU ARE GEEETTING SLEEEEEPYYY...
no i'm not!
AWWW... YOU'RE NO FUN ANY MORE!
HOW WAS IT FOR ME?
WELL...

YES YOU ARE

BWEEP

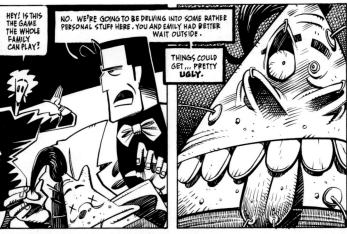

HEY! IS THIS THE GAME THE WHOLE FAMILY CAN PLAY?

NO. WE'RE GOING TO BE DELVING INTO SOME RATHER PERSONAL STUFF HERE. YOU AND EMILY HAD BETTER WAIT OUTSIDE.

THINGS COULD GET... PRETTY **UGLY**.

THAT'S FOR THE TIME YOU...

AND **THIS**...

THKOOM
THKOOM
THKOOM

YES, I THINK WE'RE MAKING **REAL PROGRESS** HERE.

WELL, **I'M** ENJOYING MYSELF...

PWING

ART SEEMED TO KNOW WHAT HE WAS DOING, SO I JUST WAITED OUTSIDE AND SAT ON MY HANDS.

IT WAS THE ONLY WAY TO STOP ME FROM BITING MY **NAILS** AS SIOBHAN WENT THROUGH ALL HER **TATTOOS** ONCE MORE...

GUMP... YOU DON'T HAVE ENOUGH **IRON** IN YOUR DIET

oh

I'VE ALWAYS HATED THOSE SQUIGGLY LITTLE BITS OF PUS AT THE EDGE OF YOUR FACE!

YAROOH!!

WHAM

THE DISCREPANCY
BETWEEN
SIGNIFIER
AND SIGNIFIED
IS
POETRY

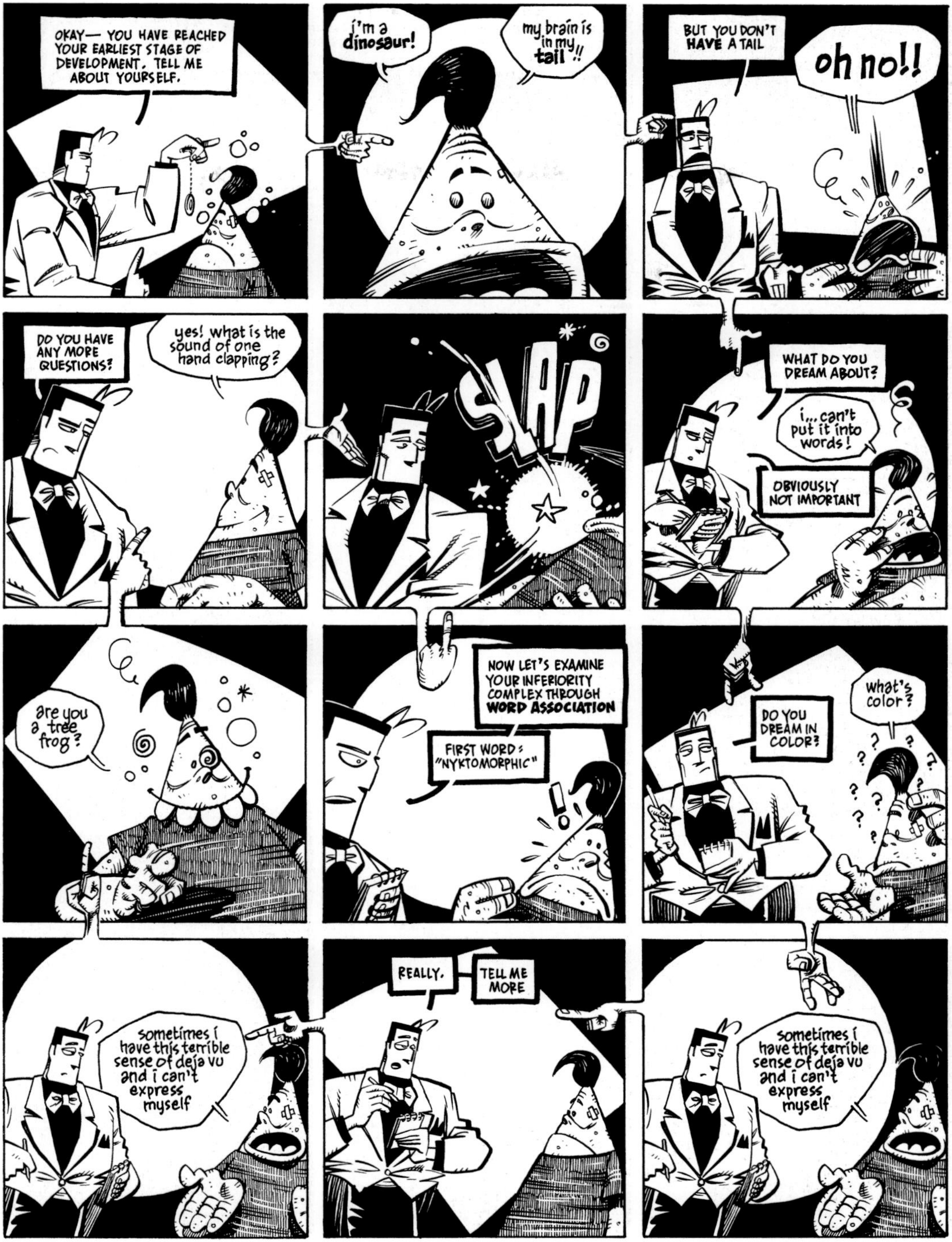

OKAY— YOU HAVE REACHED YOUR EARLIEST STAGE OF DEVELOPMENT. TELL ME ABOUT YOURSELF.
i'm a dinosaur!
my brain is in my tail!!
BUT YOU DON'T HAVE A TAIL
oh no!!
DO YOU HAVE ANY MORE QUESTIONS?
yes! what is the sound of one hand clapping?
SLAP
WHAT DO YOU DREAM ABOUT?
i... can't put it into words!
OBVIOUSLY NOT IMPORTANT
are you a tree frog?
NOW LET'S EXAMINE YOUR INFERIORITY COMPLEX THROUGH WORD ASSOCIATION
FIRST WORD: "NYKTOMORPHIC"
!
DO YOU DREAM IN COLOR?
what's color?
sometimes i have this terrible sense of deja vu and i can't express myself
REALLY.
TELL ME MORE
sometimes i have this terrible sense of deja vu and i can't express myself

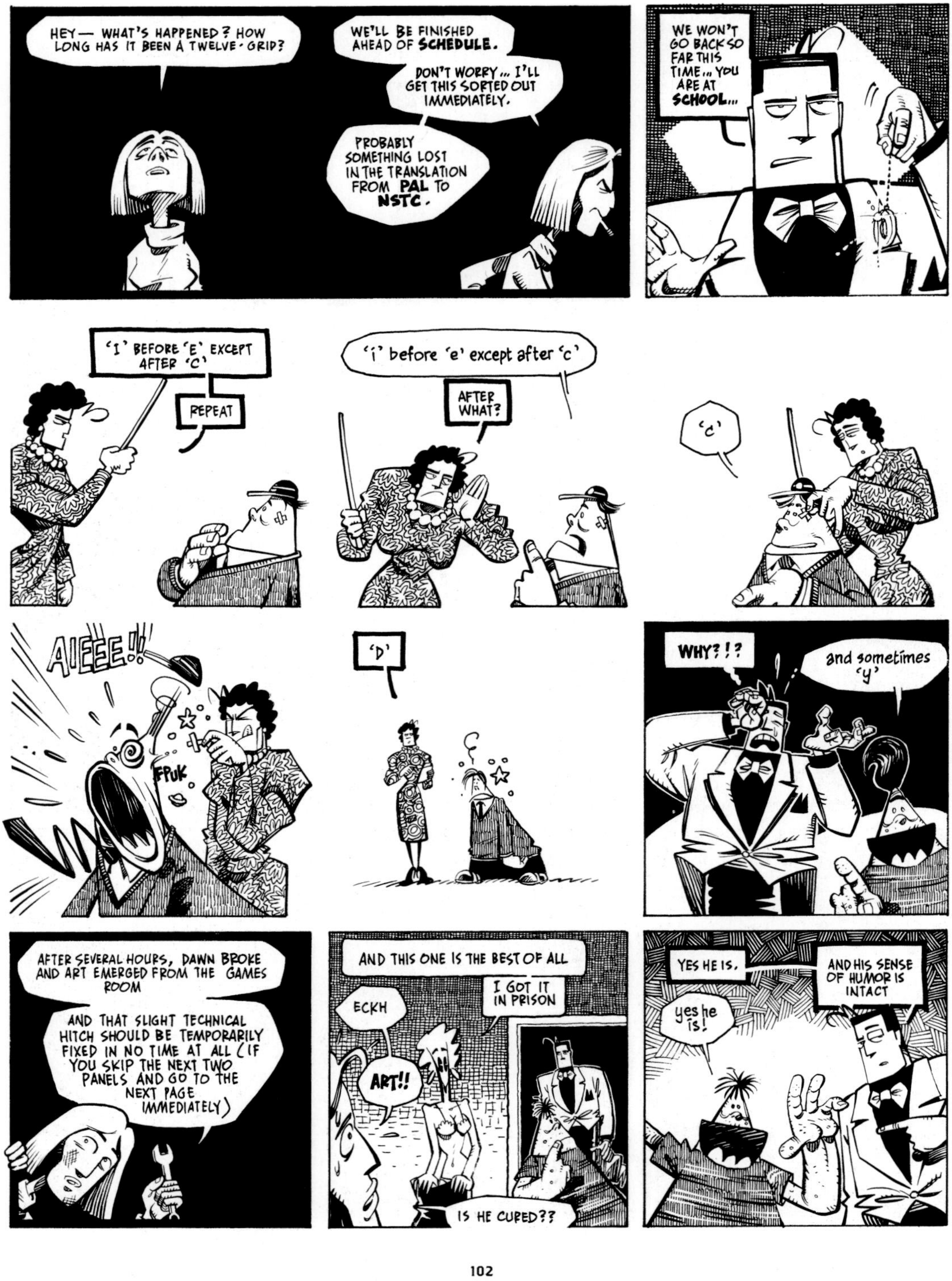

HEY— WHAT'S HAPPENED? HOW LONG HAS IT BEEN A TWELVE-GRID?
WE'LL BE FINISHED AHEAD OF SCHEDULE.
DON'T WORRY... I'LL GET THIS SORTED OUT IMMEDIATELY.
PROBABLY SOMETHING LOST IN THE TRANSLATION FROM PAL TO NSTC.
WE WON'T GO BACK SO FAR THIS TIME... YOU ARE AT SCHOOL...
'I' BEFORE 'E' EXCEPT AFTER 'C'
REPEAT
'i' before 'e' except after 'c'
AFTER WHAT?
'c'
AIEEE!!
FPUK
'D'
WHY?!?
and sometimes 'y'
AFTER SEVERAL HOURS, DAWN BROKE AND ART EMERGED FROM THE GAMES ROOM
AND THAT SLIGHT TECHNICAL HITCH SHOULD BE TEMPORARILY FIXED IN NO TIME AT ALL (IF YOU SKIP THE NEXT TWO PANELS AND GO TO THE NEXT PAGE IMMEDIATELY)
AND THIS ONE IS THE BEST OF ALL
I GOT IT IN PRISON
ECKH
ART!!
IS HE CURED??
YES HE IS.
AND HIS SENSE OF HUMOR IS INTACT
yes he is!

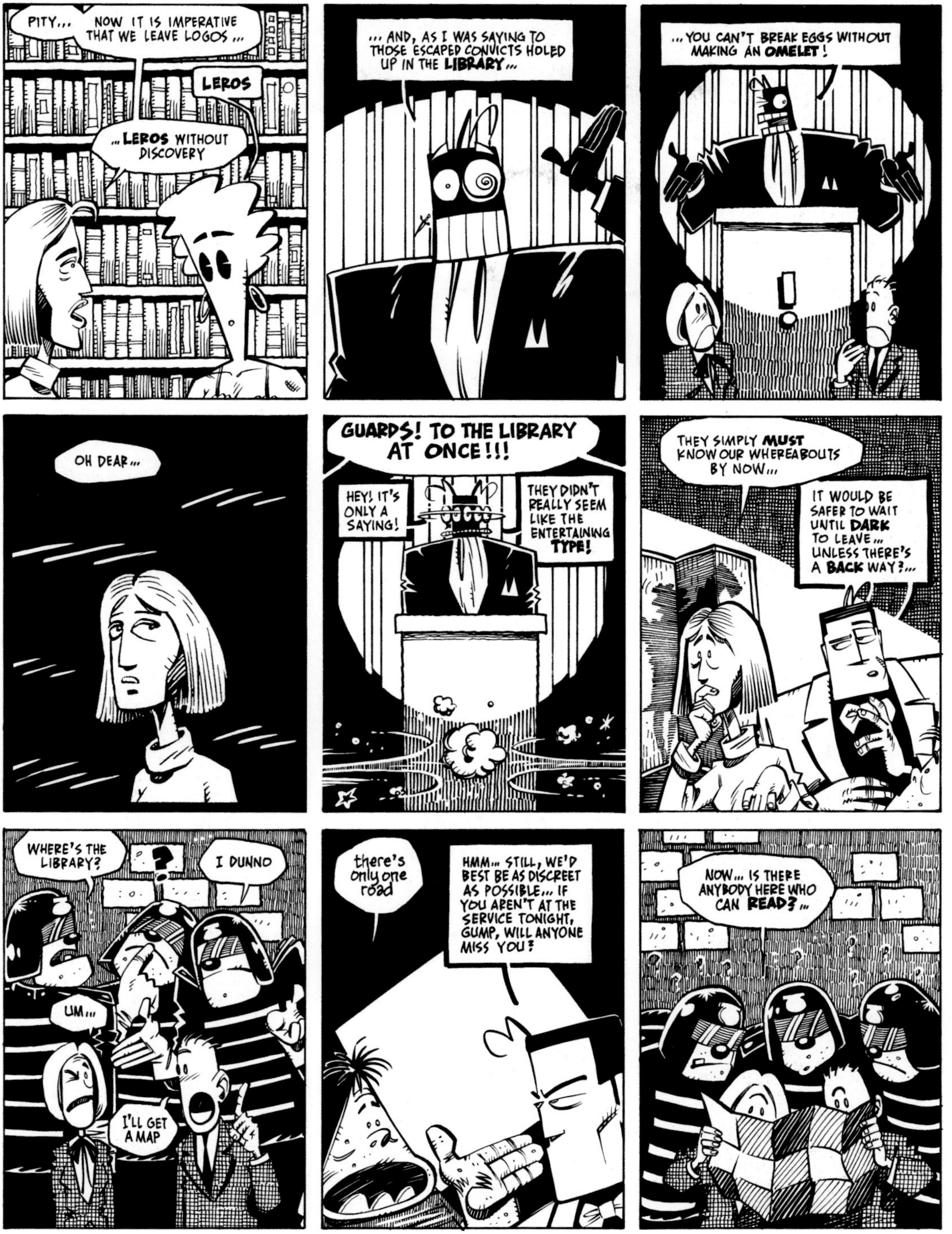
PITY...
NOW IT IS IMPERATIVE THAT WE LEAVE LOGOS...
LEROS
...LEROS WITHOUT DISCOVERY
...AND, AS I WAS SAYING TO THOSE ESCAPED CONVICTS HOLED UP IN THE LIBRARY...
...YOU CAN'T BREAK EGGS WITHOUT MAKING AN OMELET!
OH DEAR...
GUARDS! TO THE LIBRARY AT ONCE!!!
HEY! IT'S ONLY A SAYING!
THEY DIDN'T REALLY SEEM LIKE THE ENTERTAINING TYPE!
THEY SIMPLY MUST KNOW OUR WHEREABOUTS BY NOW...
IT WOULD BE SAFER TO WAIT UNTIL DARK TO LEAVE... UNLESS THERE'S A BACK WAY?...
WHERE'S THE LIBRARY?
?
I DUNNO
UM...
I'LL GET A MAP
there's only one road
HMM... STILL, WE'D BEST BE AS DISCREET AS POSSIBLE... IF YOU AREN'T AT THE SERVICE TONIGHT, GUMP, WILL ANYONE MISS YOU?
NOW... IS THERE ANYBODY HERE WHO CAN READ?...

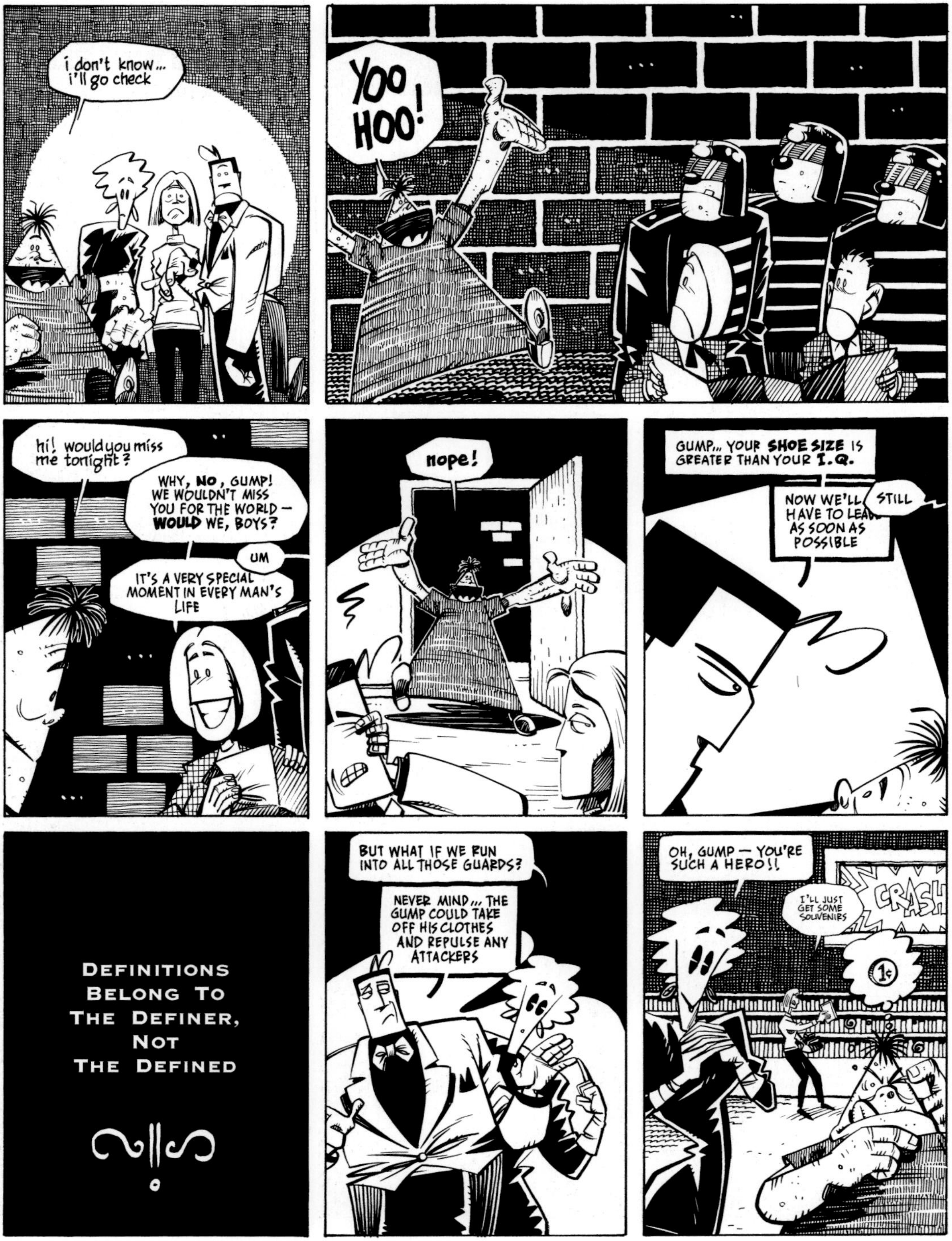
i don't know... i'll go check
YOO HOO!
hi! would you miss me tonight?
WHY, NO, GUMP! WE WOULDN'T MISS YOU FOR THE WORLD— WOULD WE, BOYS?
UM
IT'S A VERY SPECIAL MOMENT IN EVERY MAN'S LIFE
nope!
GUMP... YOUR SHOE SIZE IS GREATER THAN YOUR I.Q.
NOW WE'LL HAVE TO LEA AS SOON AS POSSIBLE
STILL
DEFINITIONS BELONG TO THE DEFINER, NOT THE DEFINED
BUT WHAT IF WE RUN INTO ALL THOSE GUARDS?
NEVER MIND... THE GUMP COULD TAKE OFF HIS CLOTHES AND REPULSE ANY ATTACKERS
OH, GUMP — YOU'RE SUCH A HERO!!
I'LL JUST GET SOME SOUVENIRS
CRASH
1¢

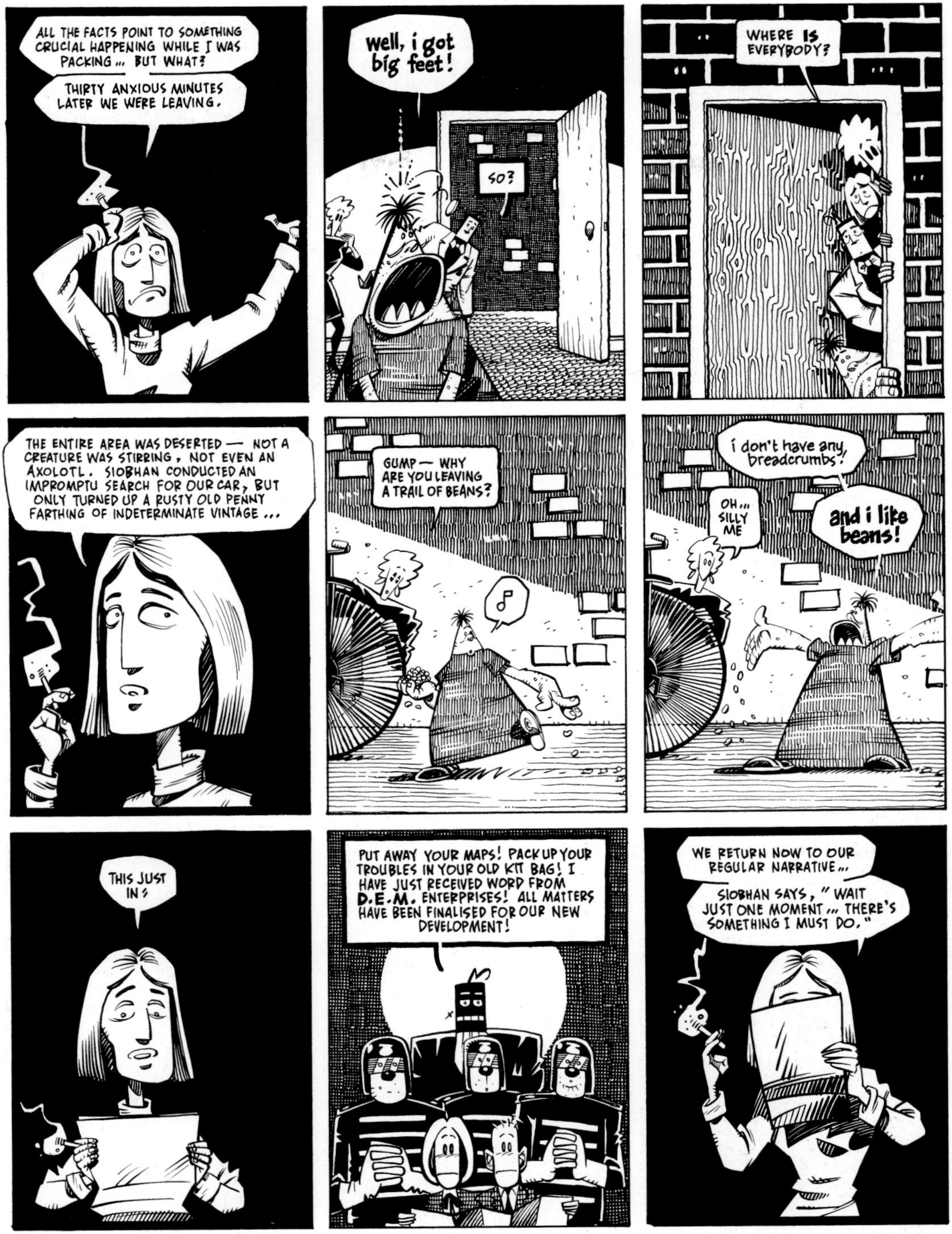

ALL THE FACTS POINT TO SOMETHING CRUCIAL HAPPENING WHILE I WAS PACKING ... BUT WHAT?
THIRTY ANXIOUS MINUTES LATER WE WERE LEAVING.
well, i got big feet!
SO?
WHERE IS EVERYBODY?
THE ENTIRE AREA WAS DESERTED — NOT A CREATURE WAS STIRRING, NOT EVEN AN AXOLOTL. SIOBHAN CONDUCTED AN IMPROMPTU SEARCH FOR OUR CAR, BUT ONLY TURNED UP A RUSTY OLD PENNY FARTHING OF INDETERMINATE VINTAGE ...
GUMP — WHY ARE YOU LEAVING A TRAIL OF BEANS?
i don't have any breadcrumbs!
OH ... SILLY ME
and i like beans!
THIS JUST IN:
PUT AWAY YOUR MAPS! PACK UP YOUR TROUBLES IN YOUR OLD KIT BAG! I HAVE JUST RECEIVED WORD FROM D.E.M. ENTERPRISES! ALL MATTERS HAVE BEEN FINALISED FOR OUR NEW DEVELOPMENT!
WE RETURN NOW TO OUR REGULAR NARRATIVE ...
SIOBHAN SAYS, "WAIT JUST ONE MOMENT ... THERE'S SOMETHING I MUST DO."

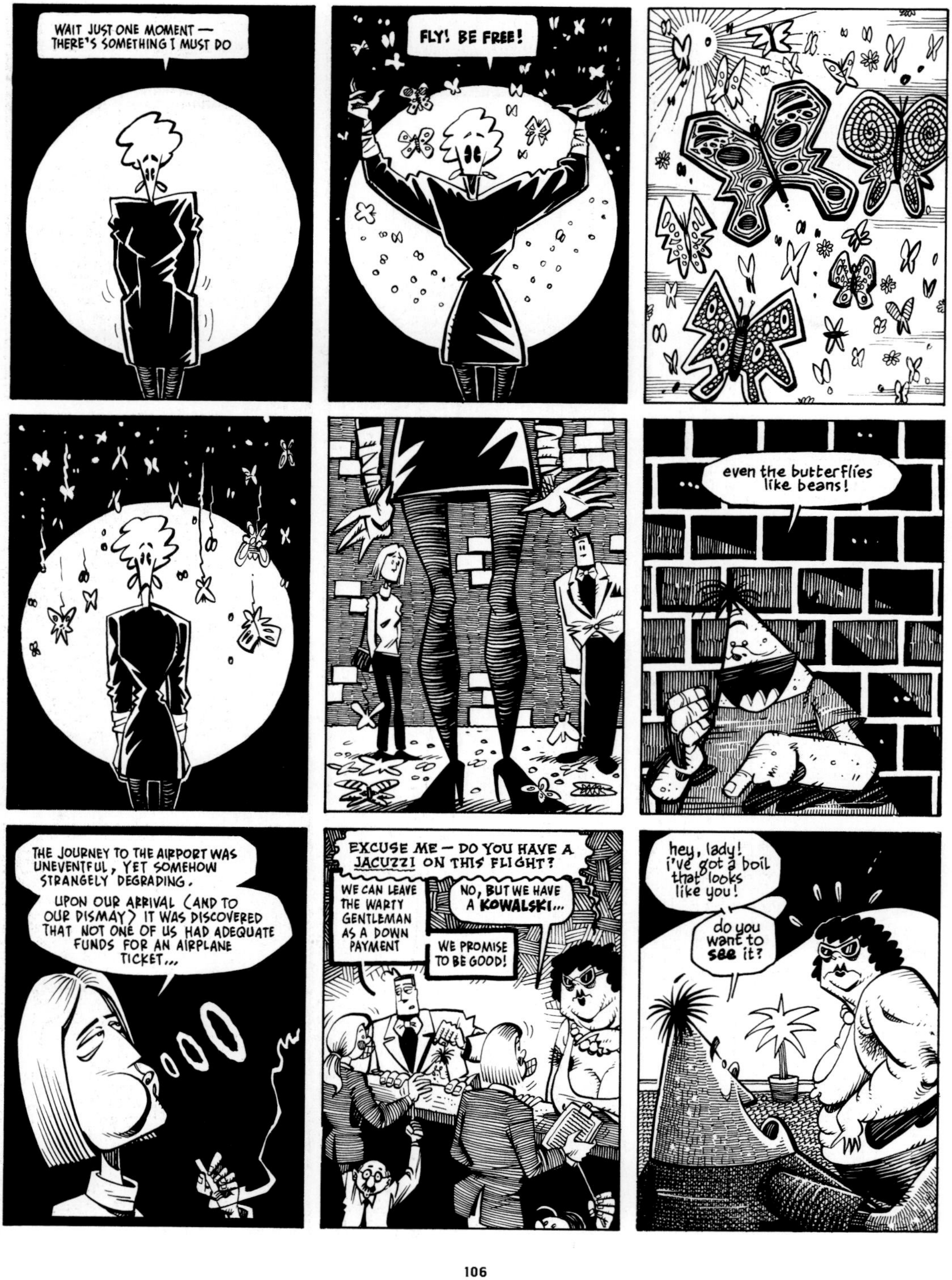
WAIT JUST ONE MOMENT — THERE'S SOMETHING I MUST DO
FLY! BE FREE!
... even the butterflies like beans!
THE JOURNEY TO THE AIRPORT WAS UNEVENTFUL, YET SOMEHOW STRANGELY DEGRADING.
UPON OUR ARRIVAL (AND TO OUR DISMAY) IT WAS DISCOVERED THAT NOT ONE OF US HAD ADEQUATE FUNDS FOR AN AIRPLANE TICKET...
EXCUSE ME — DO YOU HAVE A JACUZZI ON THIS FLIGHT?
WE CAN LEAVE THE WARTY GENTLEMAN AS A DOWN PAYMENT
NO, BUT WE HAVE A KOWALSKI...
WE PROMISE TO BE GOOD!
hey, lady! i've got a boil that looks like you!
do you want to see it?

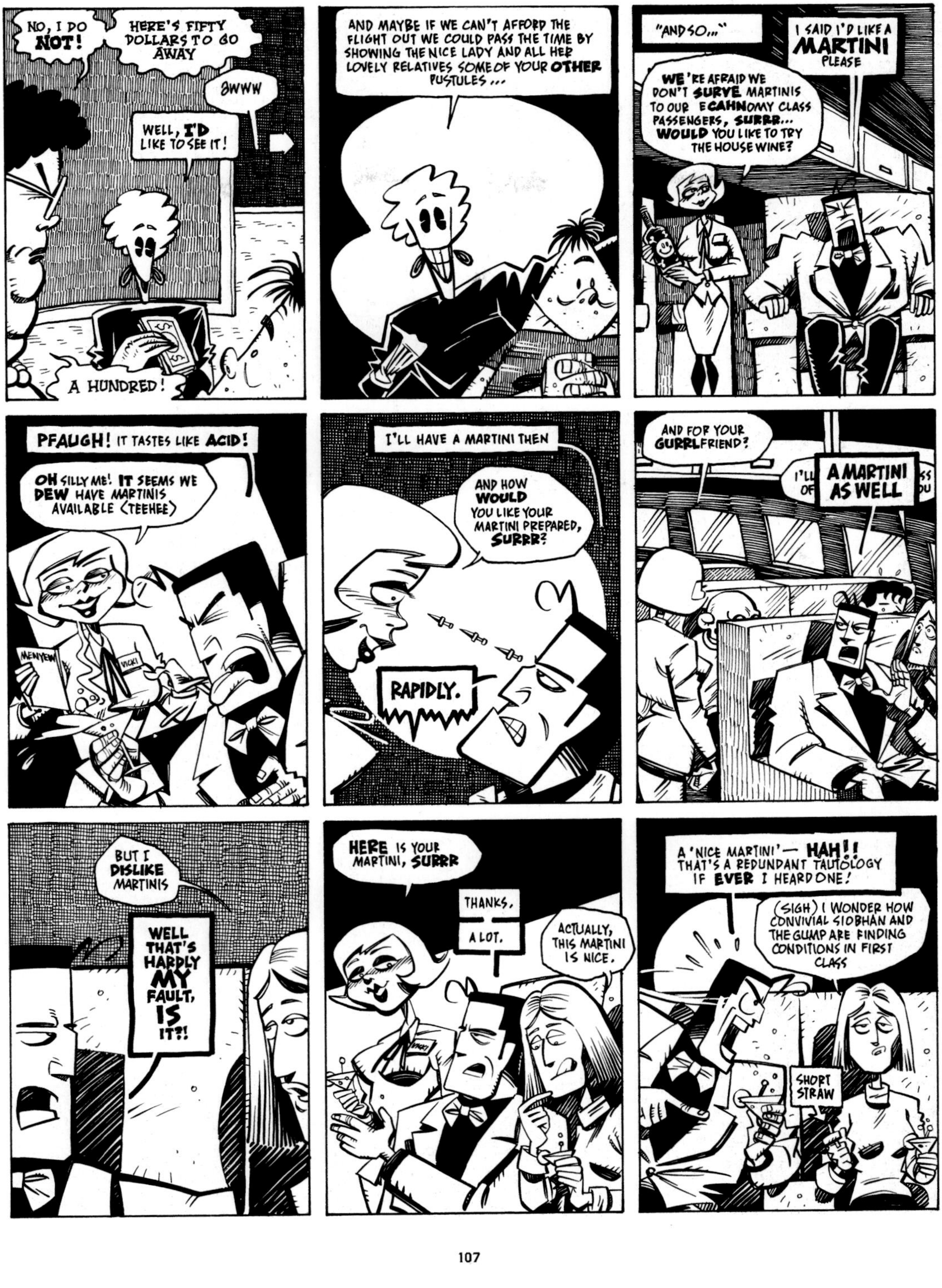

NO, I DO NOT!
HERE'S FIFTY DOLLARS TO GO AWAY
AWWW
WELL, I'D LIKE TO SEE IT!
A HUNDRED!
AND MAYBE IF WE CAN'T AFFORD THE FLIGHT OUT WE COULD PASS THE TIME BY SHOWING THE NICE LADY AND ALL HER LOVELY RELATIVES SOME OF YOUR OTHER PUSTULES...
"AND SO..."
I SAID I'D LIKE A MARTINI PLEASE
WE'RE AFRAID WE DON'T SURVE MARTINIS TO OUR ECAHNOMY CLASS PASSENGERS, SURRR... WOULD YOU LIKE TO TRY THE HOUSE WINE?
PFAUGH! IT TASTES LIKE ACID!
OH SILLY ME! IT SEEMS WE DEW HAVE MARTINIS AVAILABLE (TEEHEE)
MENYEW
VICKI
I'LL HAVE A MARTINI THEN
AND HOW WOULD YOU LIKE YOUR MARTINI PREPARED, SURRR?
RAPIDLY.
AND FOR YOUR GURRLFRIEND?
A MARTINI AS WELL
BUT I DISLIKE MARTINIS
WELL THAT'S HARDLY MY FAULT, IS IT?!
HERE IS YOUR MARTINI, SURRR
THANKS.
A LOT.
ACTUALLY, THIS MARTINI IS NICE.
A 'NICE MARTINI'— HAH!! THAT'S A REDUNDANT TAUTOLOGY IF EVER I HEARD ONE!
(SIGH) I WONDER HOW CONVIVIAL SIOBHAN AND THE GUMP ARE FINDING CONDITIONS IN FIRST CLASS
SHORT STRAW

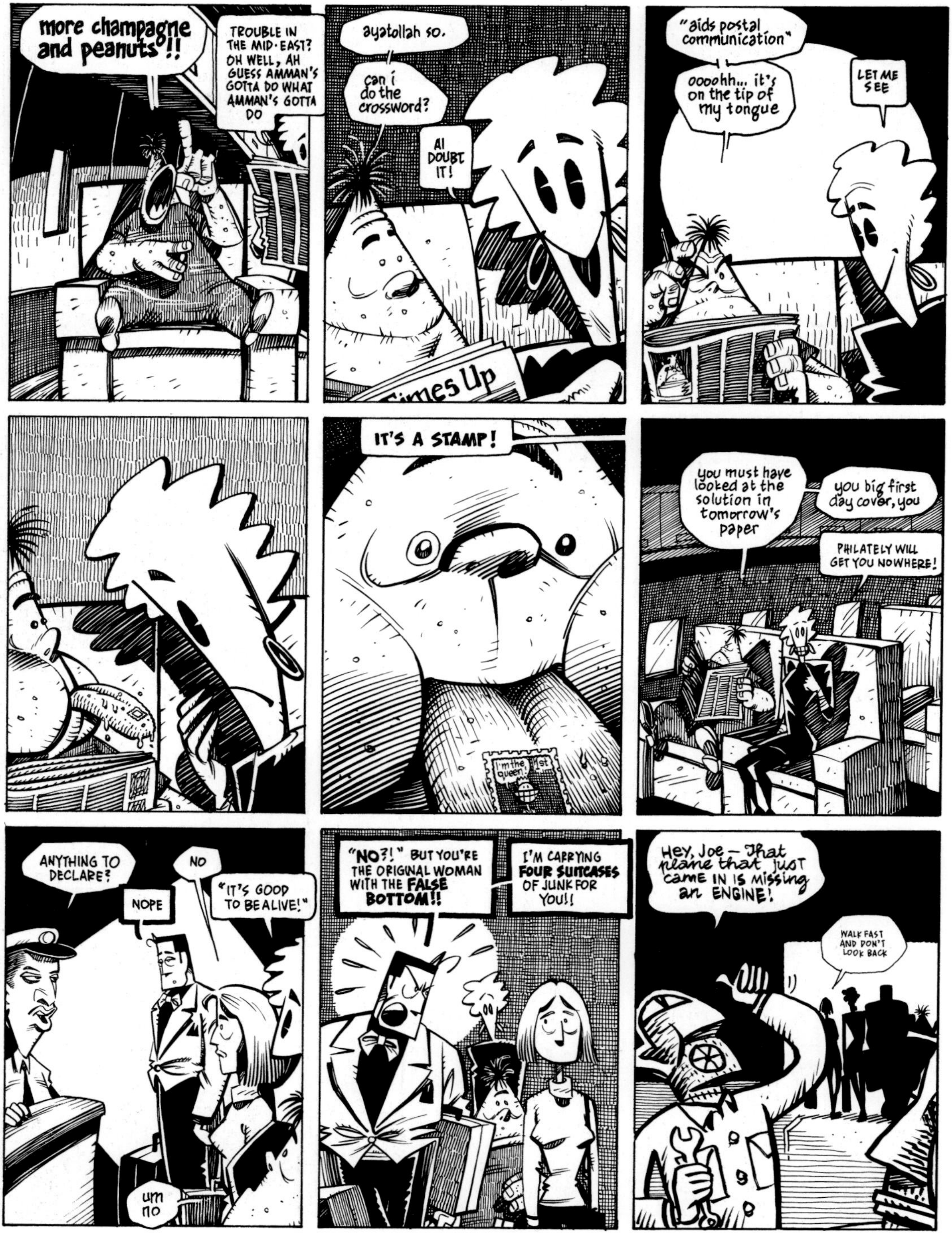

more champagne and peanuts!!
TROUBLE IN THE MID-EAST? OH WELL, AH GUESS AMMAN'S GOTTA DO WHAT AMMAN'S GOTTA DO
ayatollah so.
can i do the crossword?
AI DOUBT IT!
Times Up
"aids postal communication"
ooohh... it's on the tip of my tongue
LET ME SEE
IT'S A STAMP!
you must have looked at the solution in tomorrow's paper
you big first day cover, you
PHILATELY WILL GET YOU NOWHERE!
ANYTHING TO DECLARE?
NO
NOPE
"IT'S GOOD TO BE ALIVE!"
um no
"NO?!" BUT YOU'RE THE ORIGINAL WOMAN WITH THE FALSE BOTTOM!!
I'M CARRYING FOUR SUITCASES OF JUNK FOR YOU!!
Hey, Joe — That plane that just came in is missing an ENGINE!
WALK FAST AND DON'T LOOK BACK

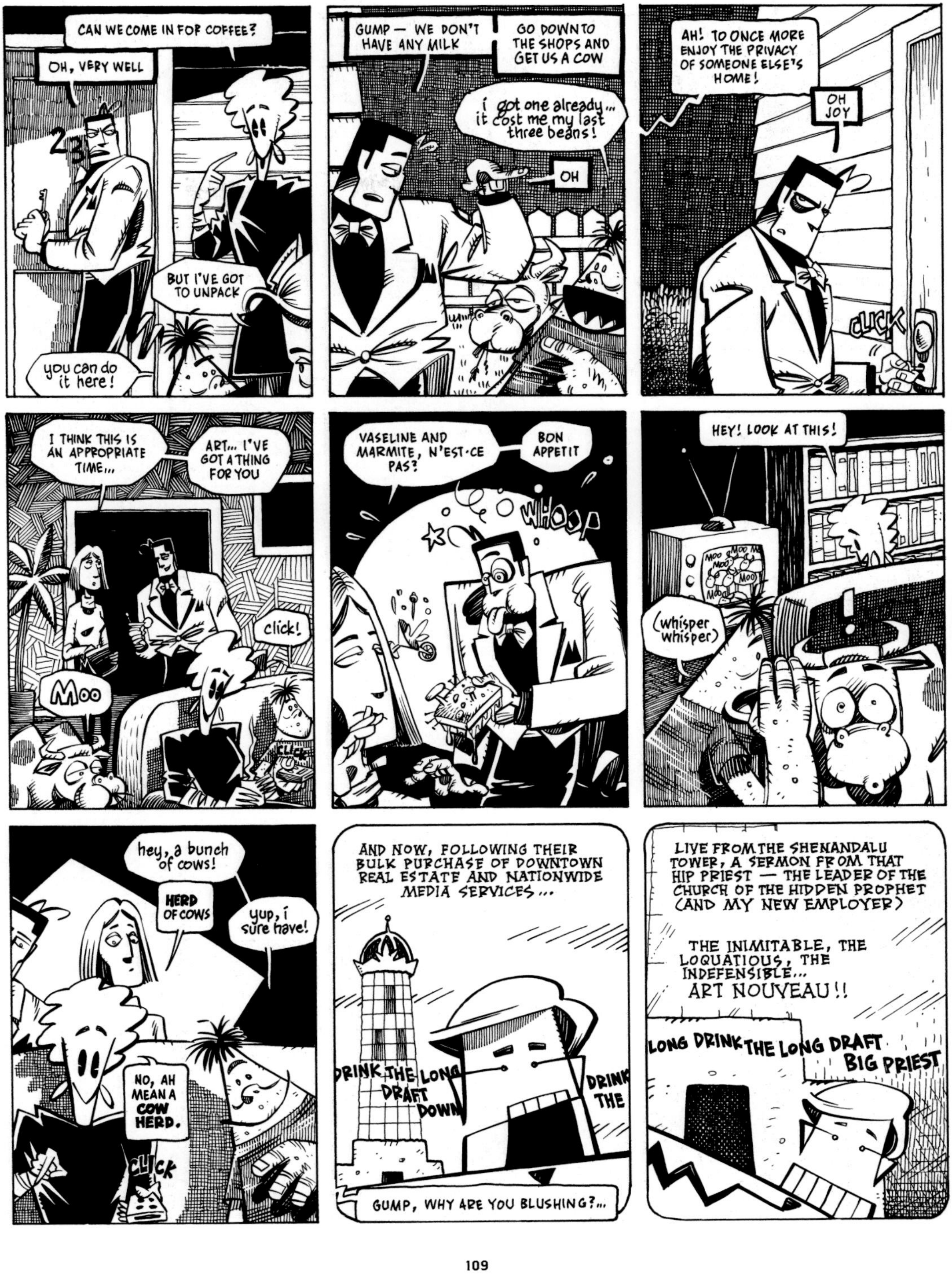
CAN WE COME IN FOR COFFEE?
OH, VERY WELL
BUT I'VE GOT TO UNPACK
you can do it here!
GUMP — WE DON'T HAVE ANY MILK
GO DOWN TO THE SHOPS AND GET US A COW
i got one already... it cost me my last three beans!
OH
AH! TO ONCE MORE ENJOY THE PRIVACY OF SOMEONE ELSE'S HOME!
OH JOY
CLICK
I THINK THIS IS AN APPROPRIATE TIME...
ART... I'VE GOT A THING FOR YOU
click!
MOO
VASELINE AND MARMITE, N'EST-CE PAS?
BON APPETIT
WHOOP
HEY! LOOK AT THIS!
(whisper whisper)
hey, a bunch of cows!
HERD OF COWS
yup, i sure have!
NO, AH MEAN A COW HERD.
CLICK
AND NOW, FOLLOWING THEIR BULK PURCHASE OF DOWNTOWN REAL ESTATE AND NATIONWIDE MEDIA SERVICES...
DRINK THE LONG DRAFT DOWN
DRINK THE
GUMP, WHY ARE YOU BLUSHING?...
LIVE FROM THE SHENANDALU TOWER, A SERMON FROM THAT HIP PRIEST — THE LEADER OF THE CHURCH OF THE HIDDEN PROPHET (AND MY NEW EMPLOYER)
THE INIMITABLE, THE LOQUATIOUS, THE INDEFENSIBLE...
ART NOUVEAU!!
LONG DRINK THE LONG DRAFT
BIG PRIEST

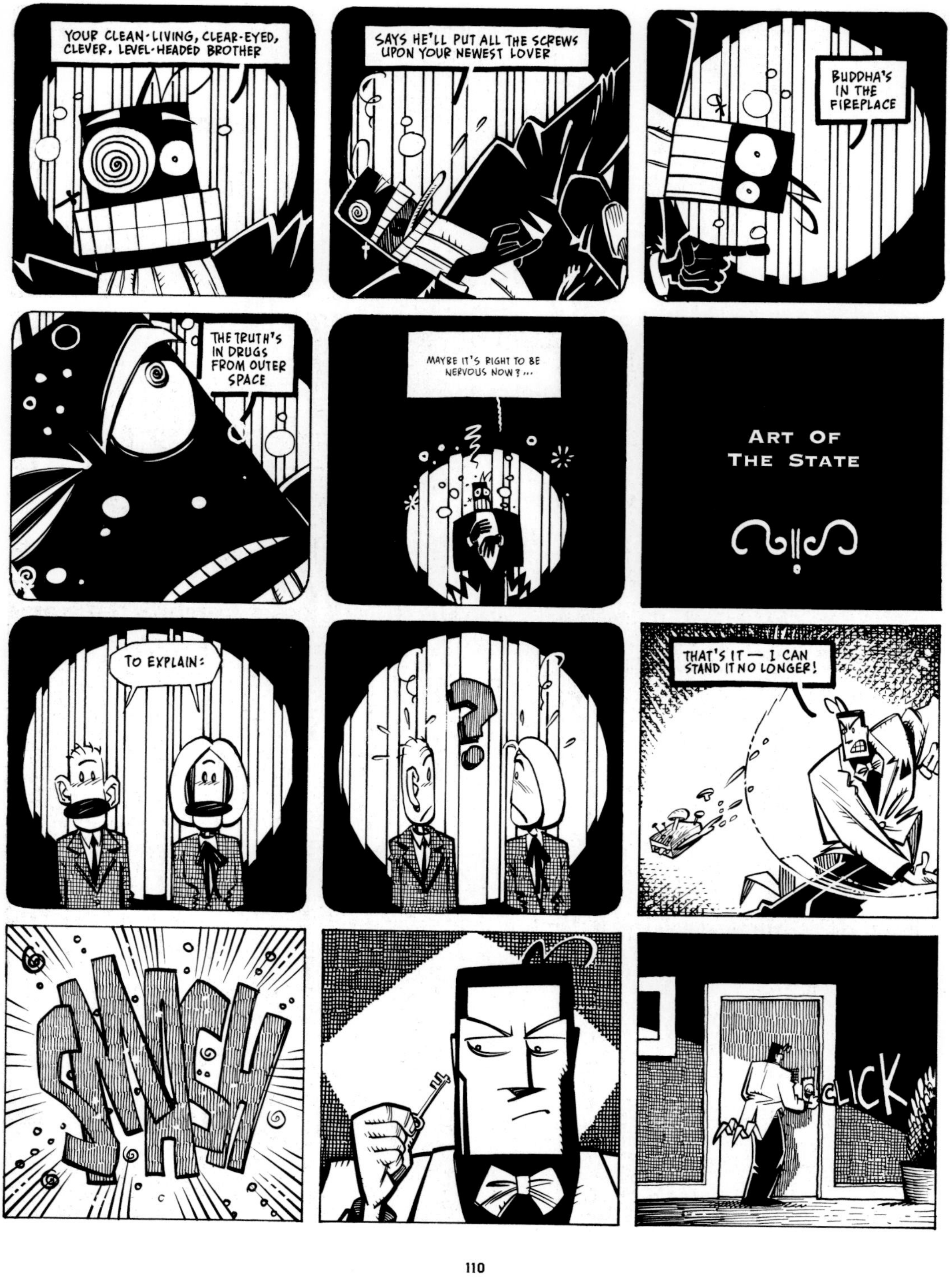
YOUR CLEAN-LIVING, CLEAR-EYED, CLEVER, LEVEL-HEADED BROTHER
SAYS HE'LL PUT ALL THE SCREWS UPON YOUR NEWEST LOVER
BUDDHA'S IN THE FIREPLACE
THE TRUTH'S IN DRUGS FROM OUTER SPACE
MAYBE IT'S RIGHT TO BE NERVOUS NOW?...
ART OF THE STATE
TO EXPLAIN:
THAT'S IT — I CAN STAND IT NO LONGER!
SMASH
CLICK

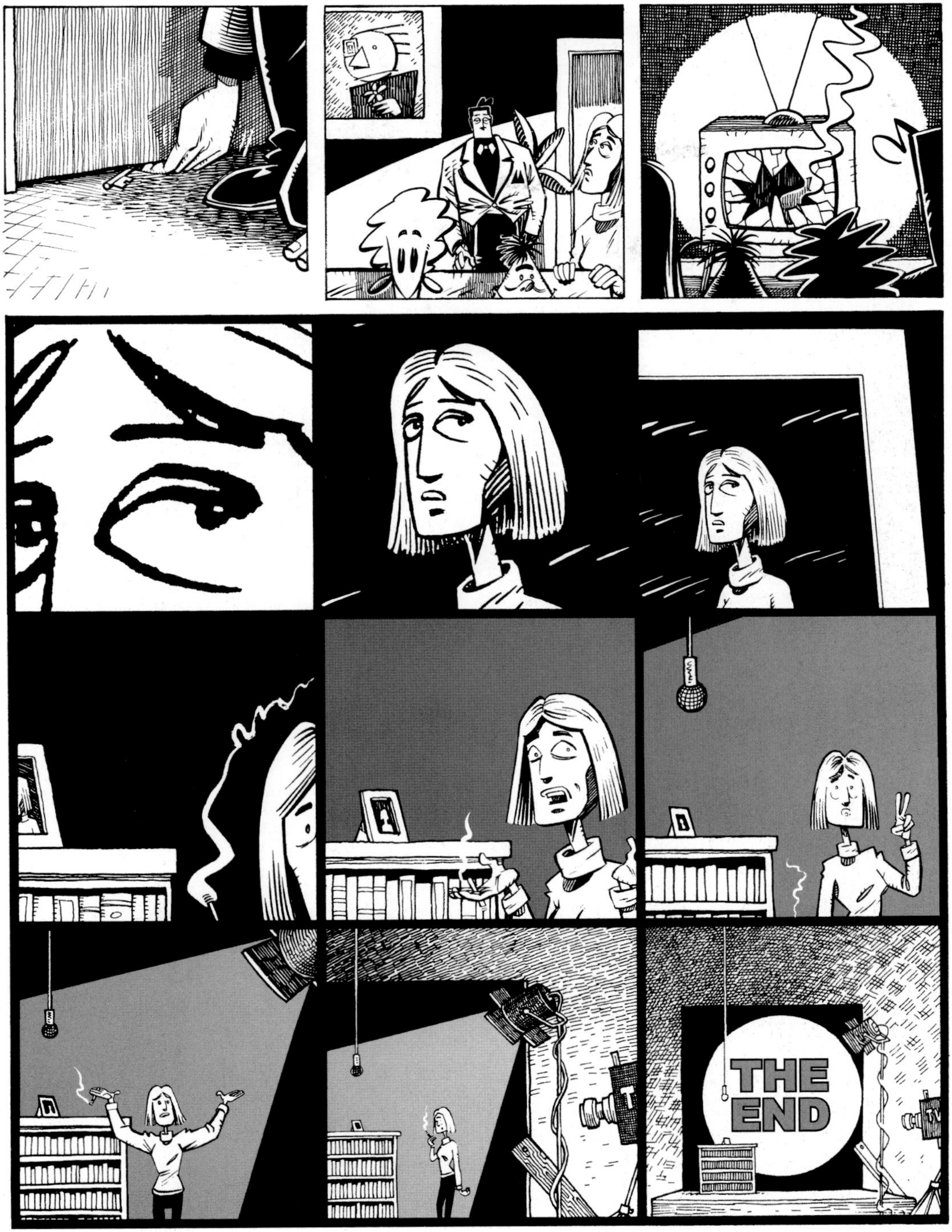
THE
END

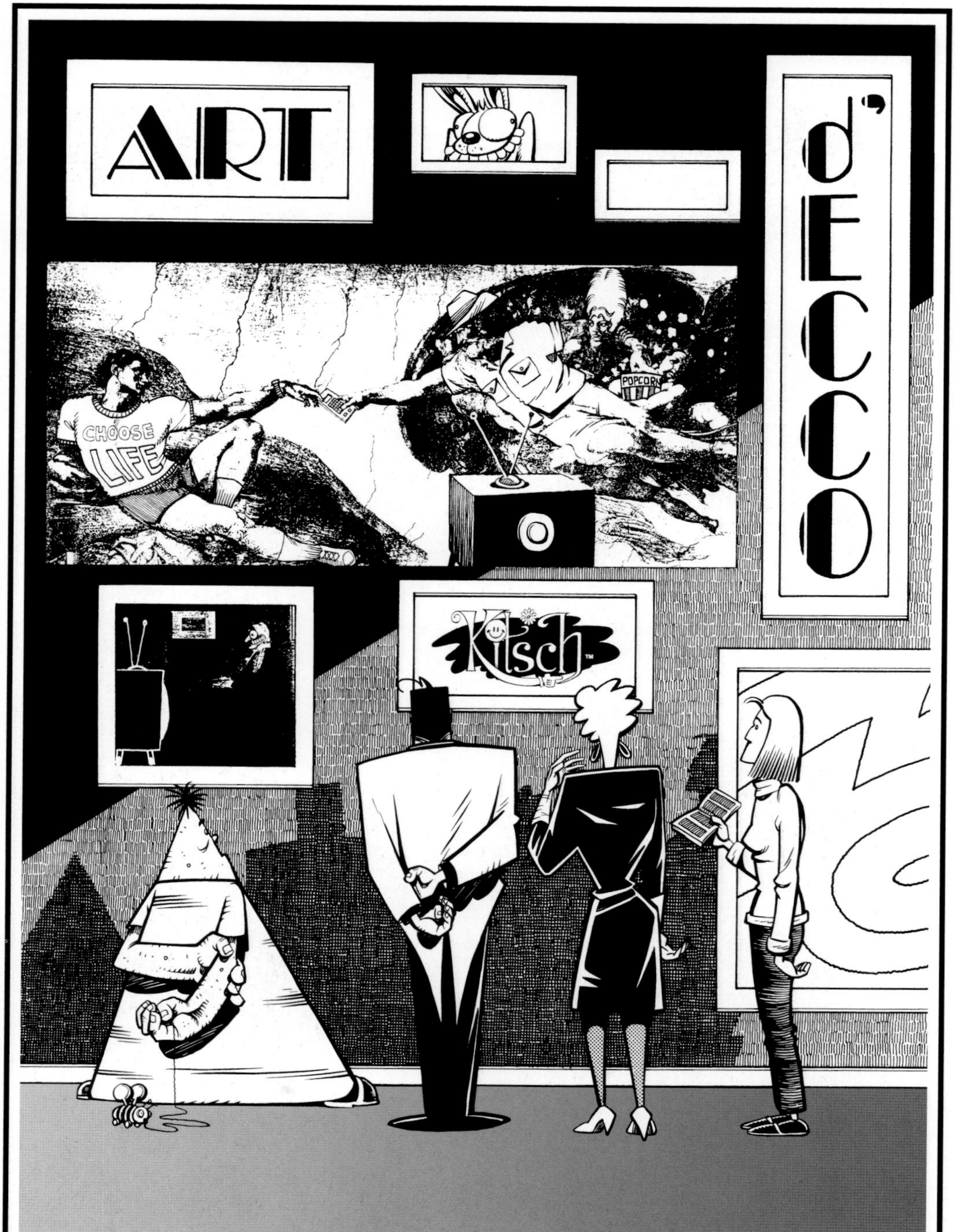
ART
d'ECCO
CHOOSE LIFE
POPCORN
Kitsch™

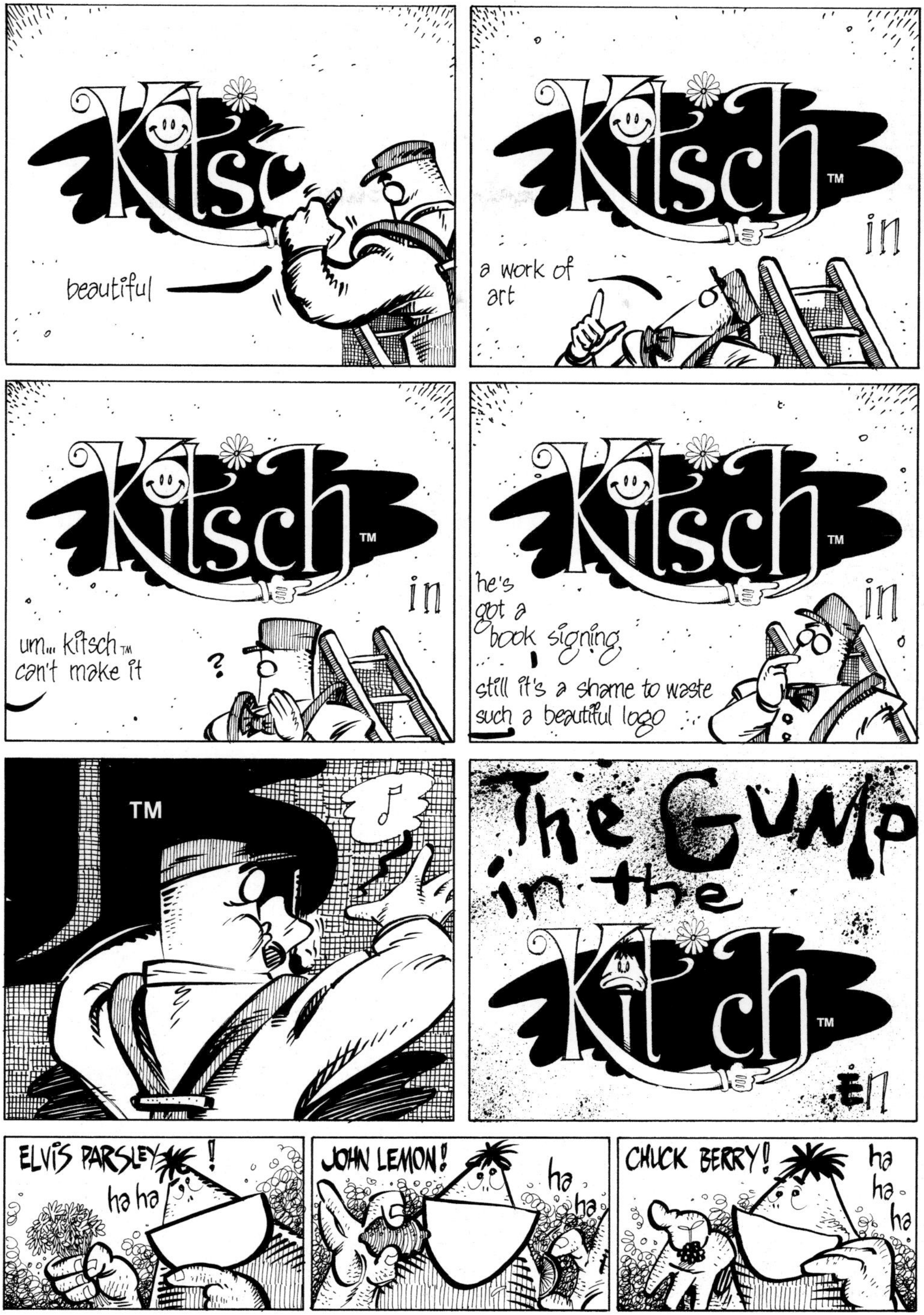

Kitsc
beautiful
Kitsch ™ in
a work of art
Kitsch ™ in
um... kitsch ™ can't make it
?
Kitsch ™ in
he's got a book signing
still it's a shame to waste such a beautiful logo
™
The Gump in the Kitch ™
ELVIS PARSLEY!
ha ha
JOHN LEMON!
ha ha
CHUCK BERRY!
ha ha ha

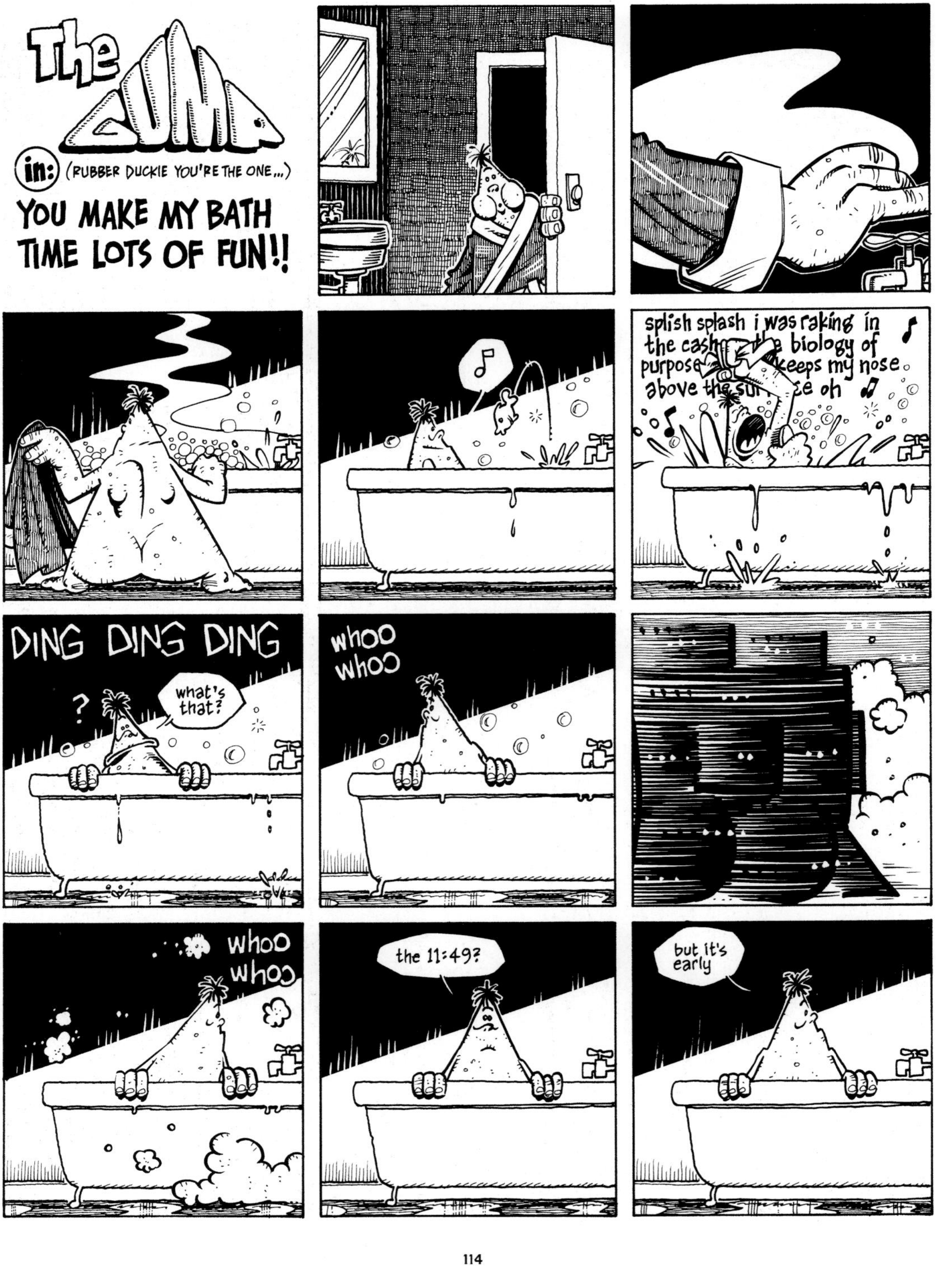
The GUMP
in: (RUBBER DUCKIE YOU'RE THE ONE...)
YOU MAKE MY BATH TIME LOTS OF FUN!!
splish splash i was raking in
the biology of
keeps my nose
above the
DING DING DING
?
what's that?
whoo whoo
whoo whoo
the 11:49?
but it's early

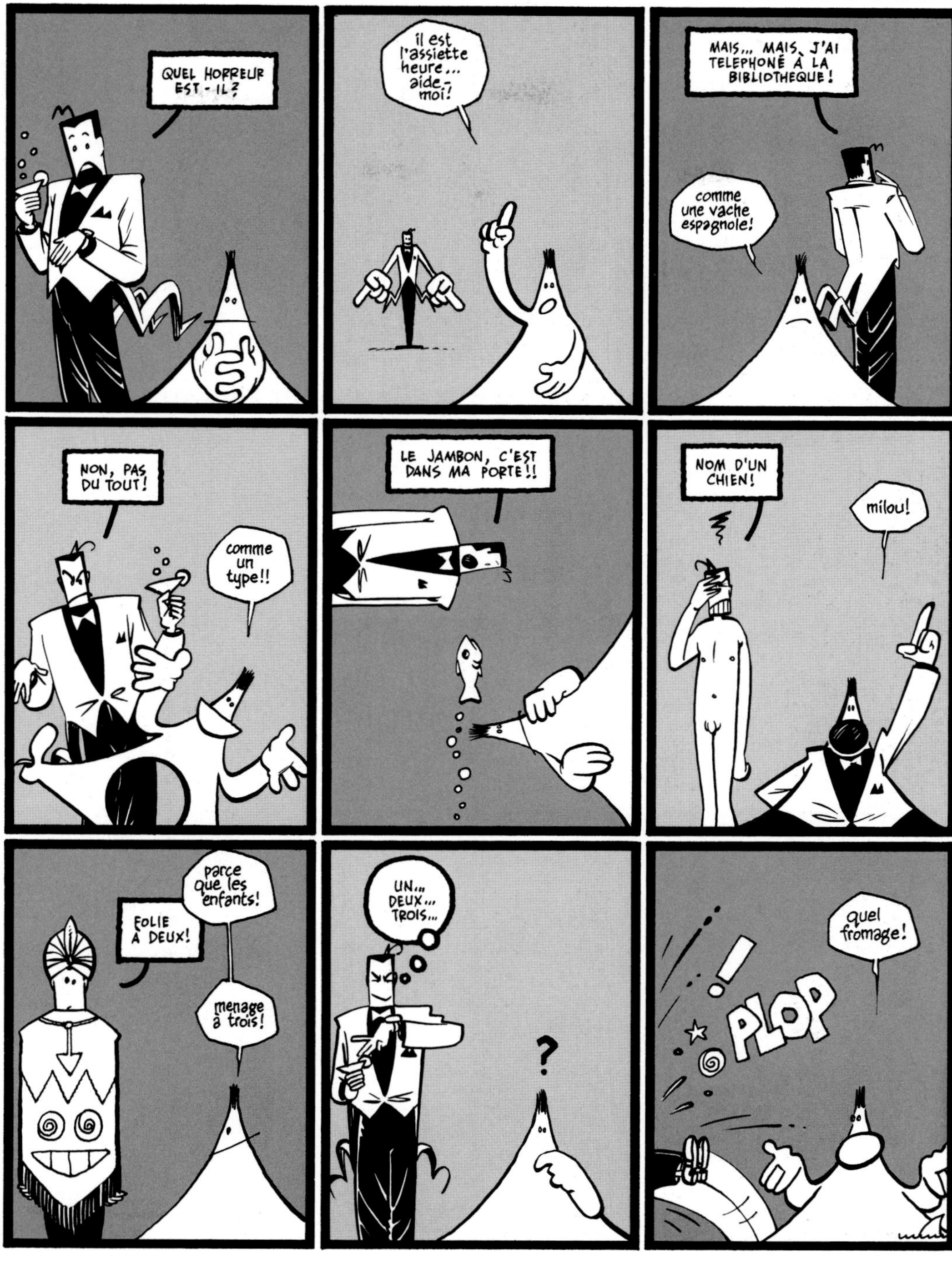
QUEL HORREUR EST-IL?
il est l'assiette heure... aide-moi!
MAIS... MAIS, J'AI TELEPHONÉ À LA BIBLIOTHEQUE!
comme une vache espagnole!
NON, PAS DU TOUT!
comme un type!!
LE JAMBON, C'EST DANS MA PORTE!!
NOM D'UN CHIEN!
milou!
FOLIE À DEUX!
parce que les enfants!
menage à trois!
UN... DEUX... TROIS...
?
quel fromage!
!
PLOP

IN THE LAND OF CATATONIA

HAVING ESCAPED THE DEVIOUS CLUTCHES OF THE CHURCH OF THE HIDDEN PROPHET, OUR INTREPID BAND FLEE SUNNY CATATONIA IN A MARVELLOUS AIRSHIP~

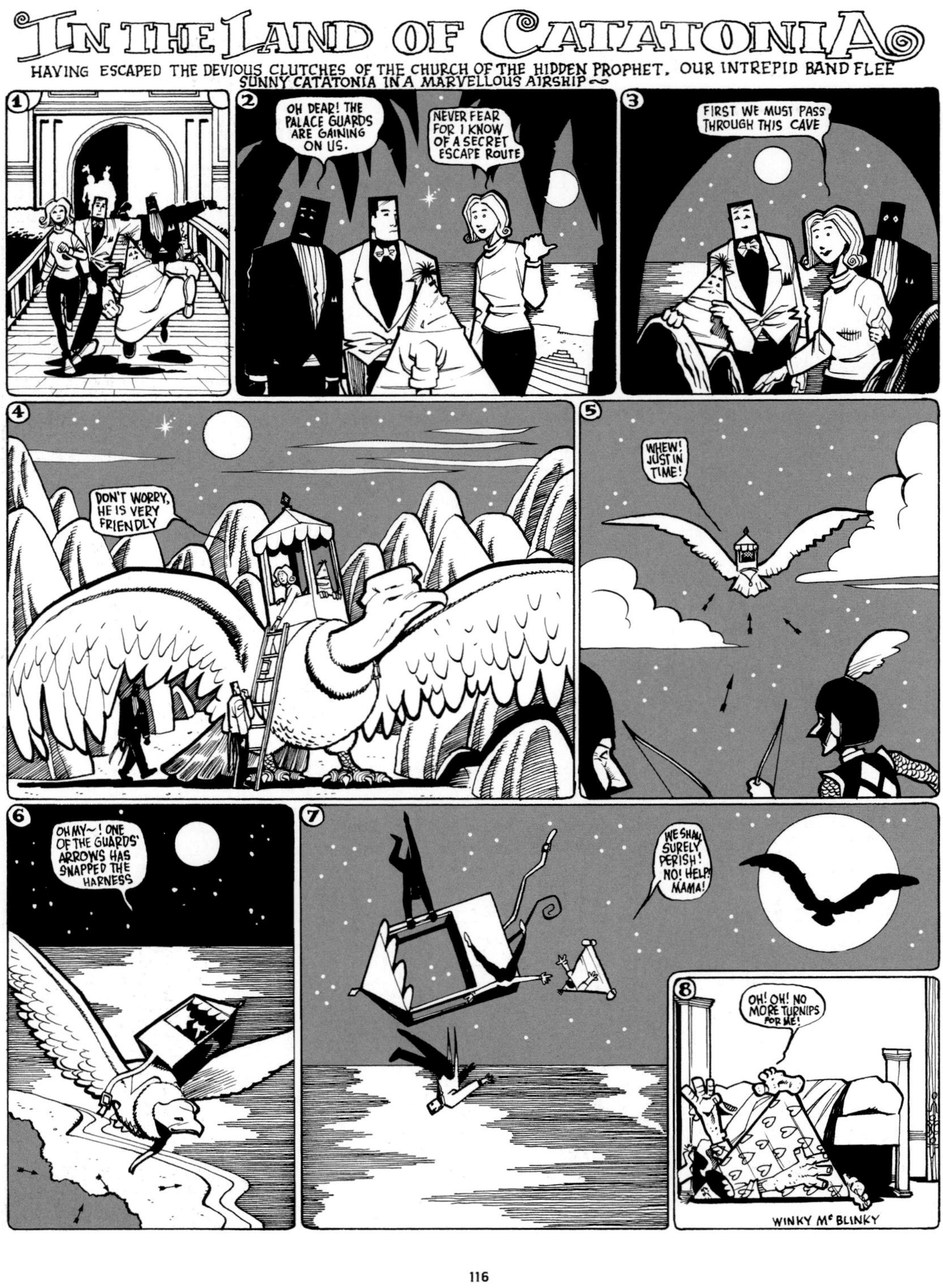
1
2
OH DEAR! THE PALACE GUARDS ARE GAINING ON US.
NEVER FEAR FOR I KNOW OF A SECRET ESCAPE ROUTE
3
FIRST WE MUST PASS THROUGH THIS CAVE
4
DON'T WORRY, HE IS VERY FRIENDLY
5
WHEW! JUST IN TIME!
6
OH MY~! ONE OF THE GUARDS' ARROWS HAS SNAPPED THE HARNESS
7
WE SHALL SURELY PERISH! NO! HELP! MAMA!
8
OH! OH! NO MORE TURNIPS FOR ME!
WINKY McBLINKY

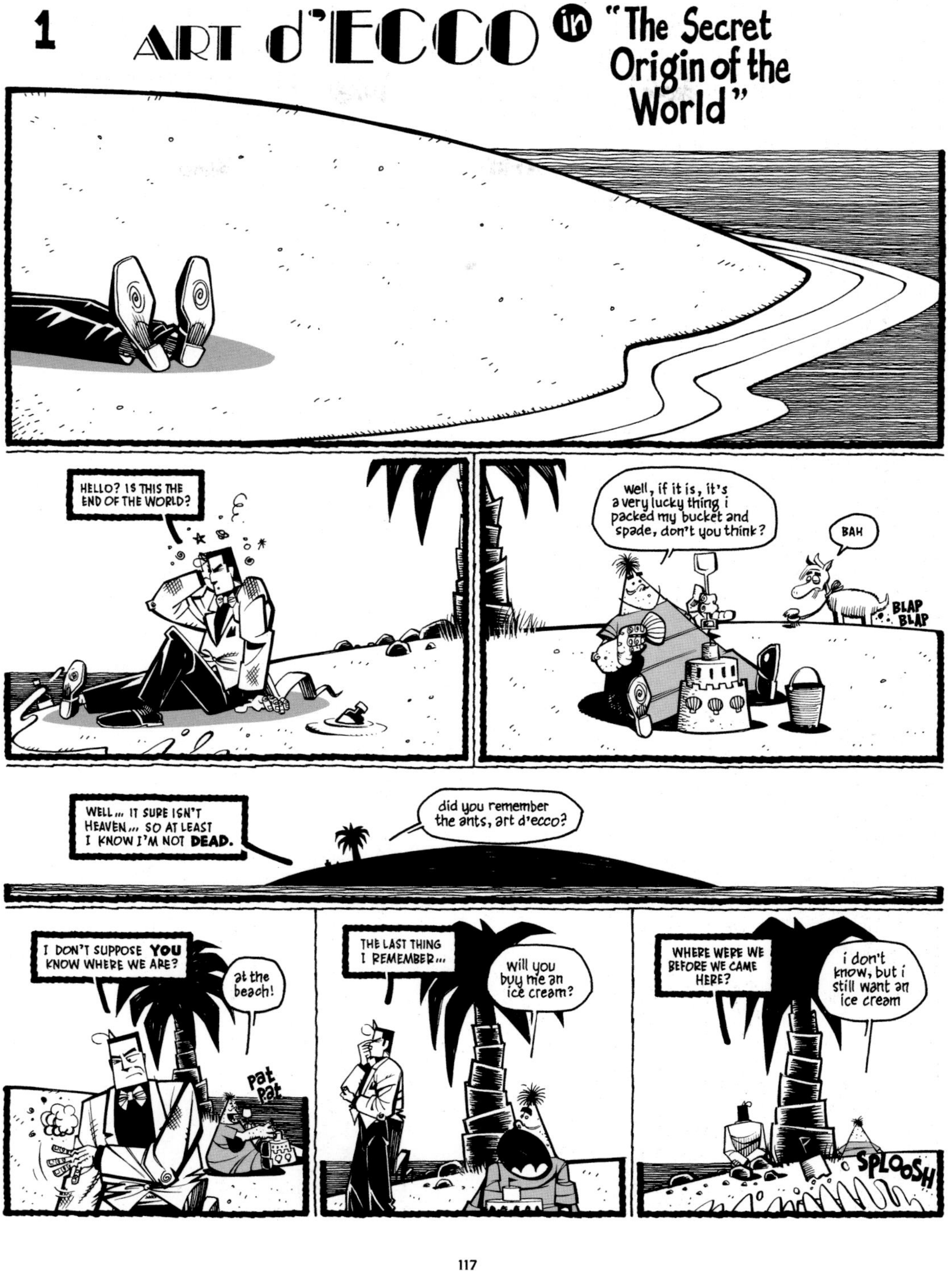
1
ART d'ECCO in "The Secret Origin of the World"
HELLO? IS THIS THE END OF THE WORLD?
Well, if it is, it's a very lucky thing i packed my bucket and spade, don't you think?
BAH
BLAP BLAP
WELL... IT SURE ISN'T HEAVEN... SO AT LEAST I KNOW I'M NOT DEAD.
did you remember the ants, art d'ecco?
I DON'T SUPPOSE YOU KNOW WHERE WE ARE?
at the beach!
pat pat
THE LAST THING I REMEMBER...
will you buy me an ice cream?
WHERE WERE WE BEFORE WE CAME HERE?
i don't know, but i still want an ice cream
SPLOOSH

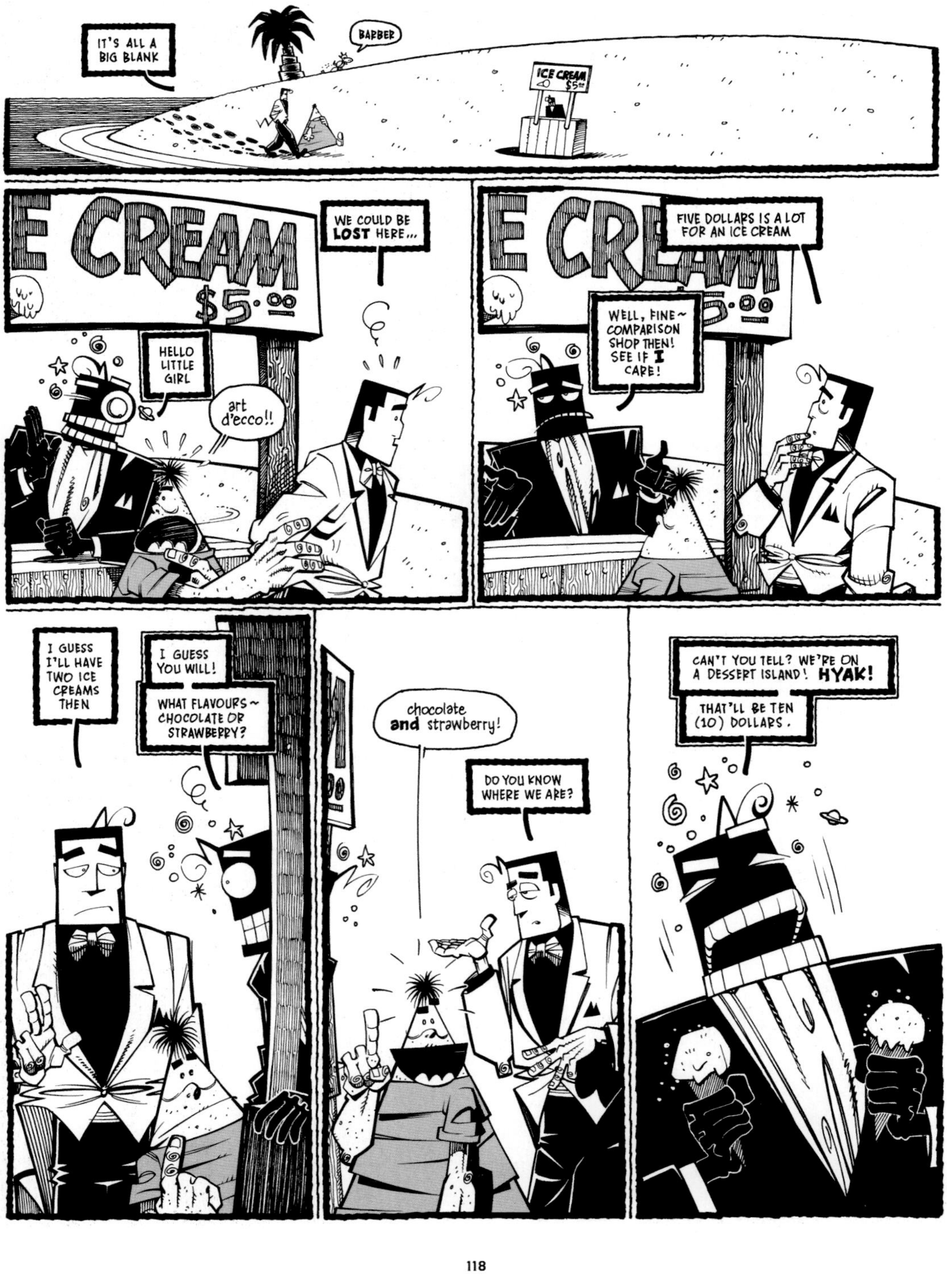
IT'S ALL A BIG BLANK
BARBER
ICE CREAM $5.00
E CREAM $5.00
WE COULD BE LOST HERE...
HELLO LITTLE GIRL
art d'ecco!!
FIVE DOLLARS IS A LOT FOR AN ICE CREAM
WELL, FINE~ COMPARISON SHOP THEN! SEE IF I CARE!
I GUESS I'LL HAVE TWO ICE CREAMS THEN
I GUESS YOU WILL!
WHAT FLAVOURS~ CHOCOLATE OR STRAWBERRY?
chocolate and strawberry!
DO YOU KNOW WHERE WE ARE?
CAN'T YOU TELL? WE'RE ON A DESSERT ISLAND! HYAK!
THAT'LL BE TEN (10) DOLLARS.

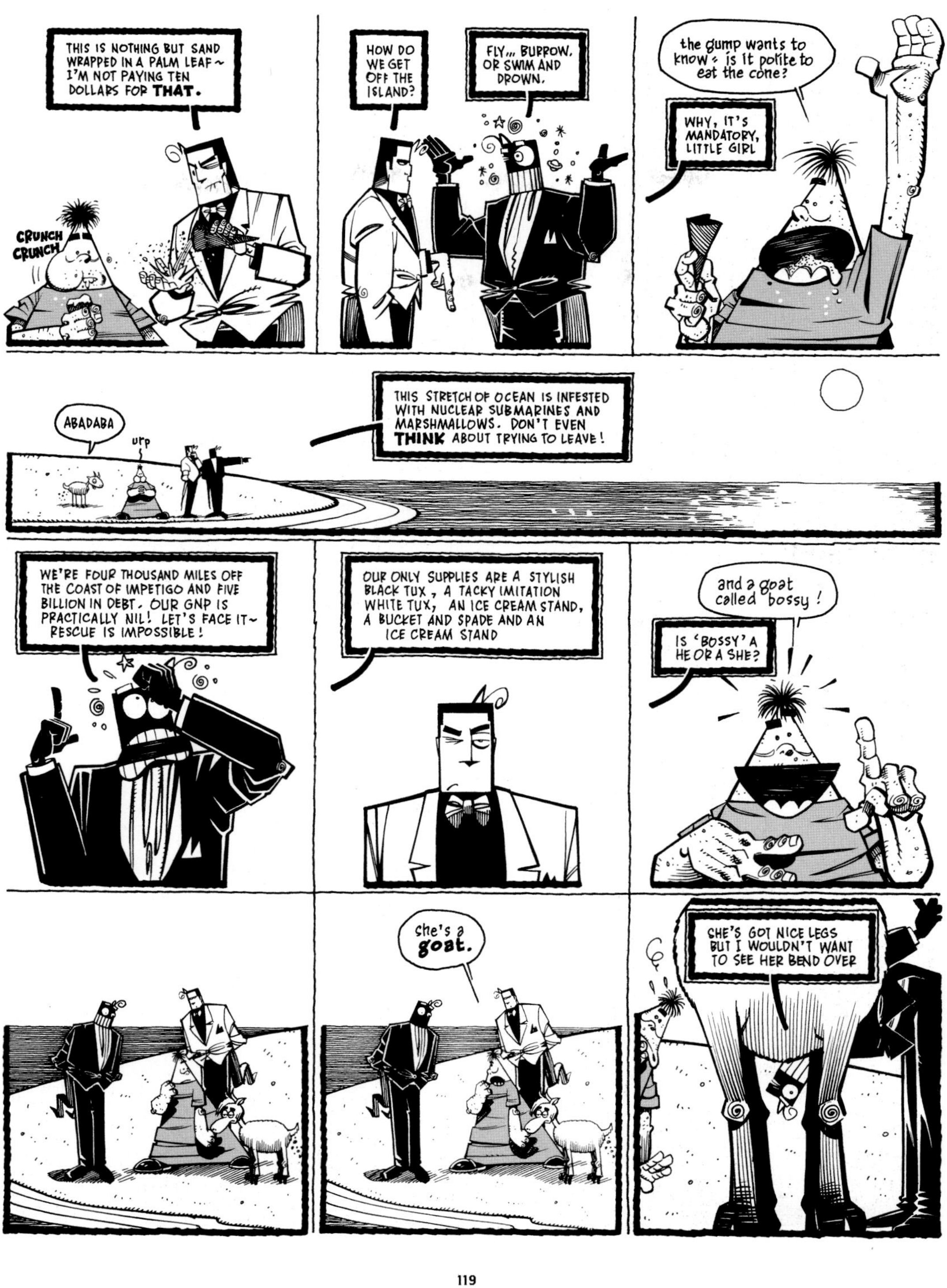
THIS IS NOTHING BUT SAND WRAPPED IN A PALM LEAF ~ I'M NOT PAYING TEN DOLLARS FOR THAT.
CRUNCH CRUNCH
HOW DO WE GET OFF THE ISLAND?
FLY... BURROW, OR SWIM AND DROWN.
the gump wants to know : is it polite to eat the cone?
WHY, IT'S MANDATORY, LITTLE GIRL
ABADABA
urp
THIS STRETCH OF OCEAN IS INFESTED WITH NUCLEAR SUBMARINES AND MARSHMALLOWS. DON'T EVEN THINK ABOUT TRYING TO LEAVE!
WE'RE FOUR THOUSAND MILES OFF THE COAST OF IMPETIGO AND FIVE BILLION IN DEBT. OUR GNP IS PRACTICALLY NIL! LET'S FACE IT ~ RESCUE IS IMPOSSIBLE!
OUR ONLY SUPPLIES ARE A STYLISH BLACK TUX, A TACKY IMITATION WHITE TUX, AN ICE CREAM STAND, A BUCKET AND SPADE AND AN ICE CREAM STAND
and a goat called bossy!
IS 'BOSSY' A HE OR A SHE?
she's a goat.
SHE'S GOT NICE LEGS BUT I WOULDN'T WANT TO SEE HER BEND OVER

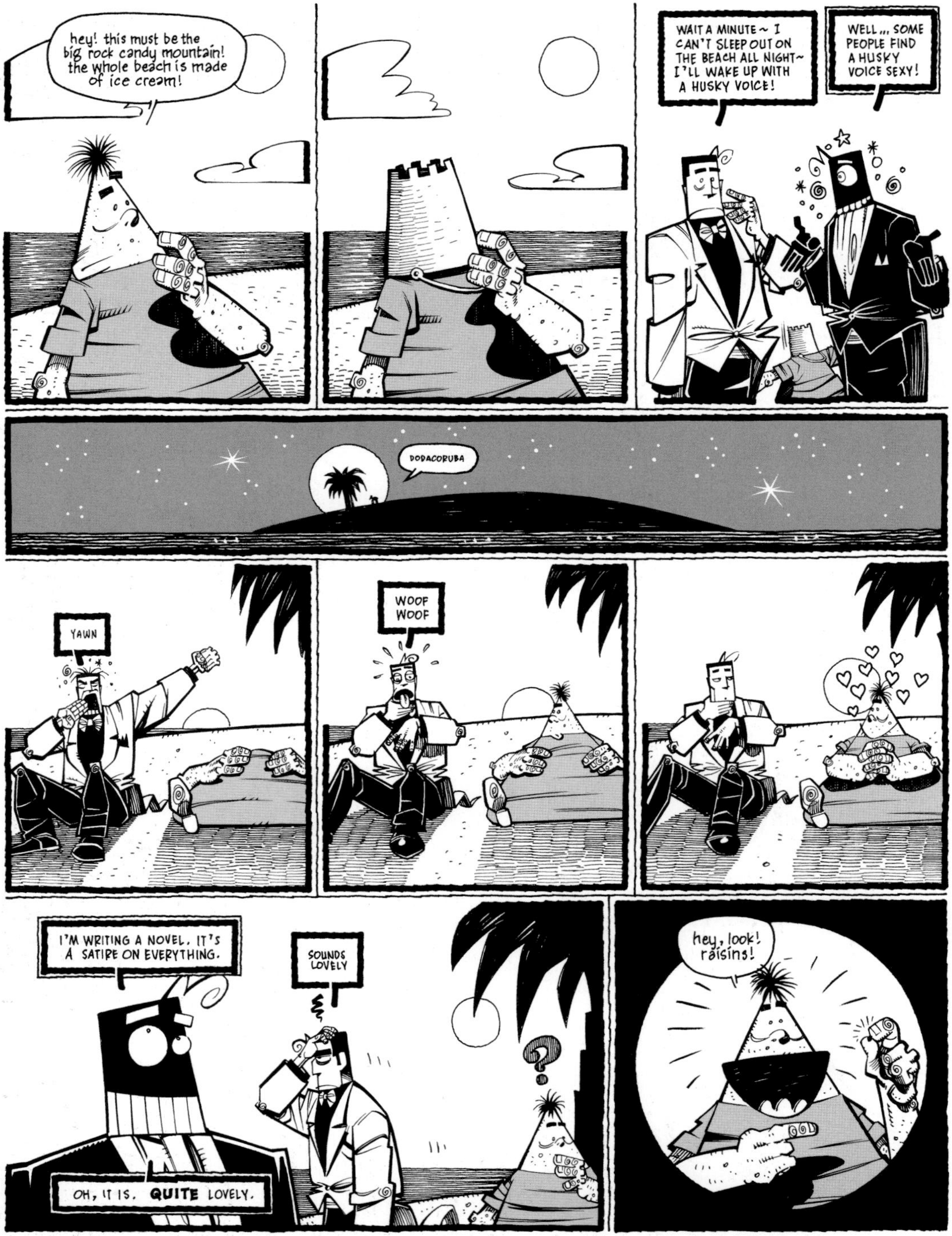
hey! this must be the big rock candy mountain! the whole beach is made of ice cream!
WAIT A MINUTE ~ I CAN'T SLEEP OUT ON THE BEACH ALL NIGHT~ I'LL WAKE UP WITH A HUSKY VOICE!
WELL... SOME PEOPLE FIND A HUSKY VOICE SEXY!
DODACORUBA
YAWN
WOOF WOOF
I'M WRITING A NOVEL. IT'S A SATIRE ON EVERYTHING.
SOUNDS LOVELY
OH, IT IS. QUITE LOVELY.
hey, look! raisins!

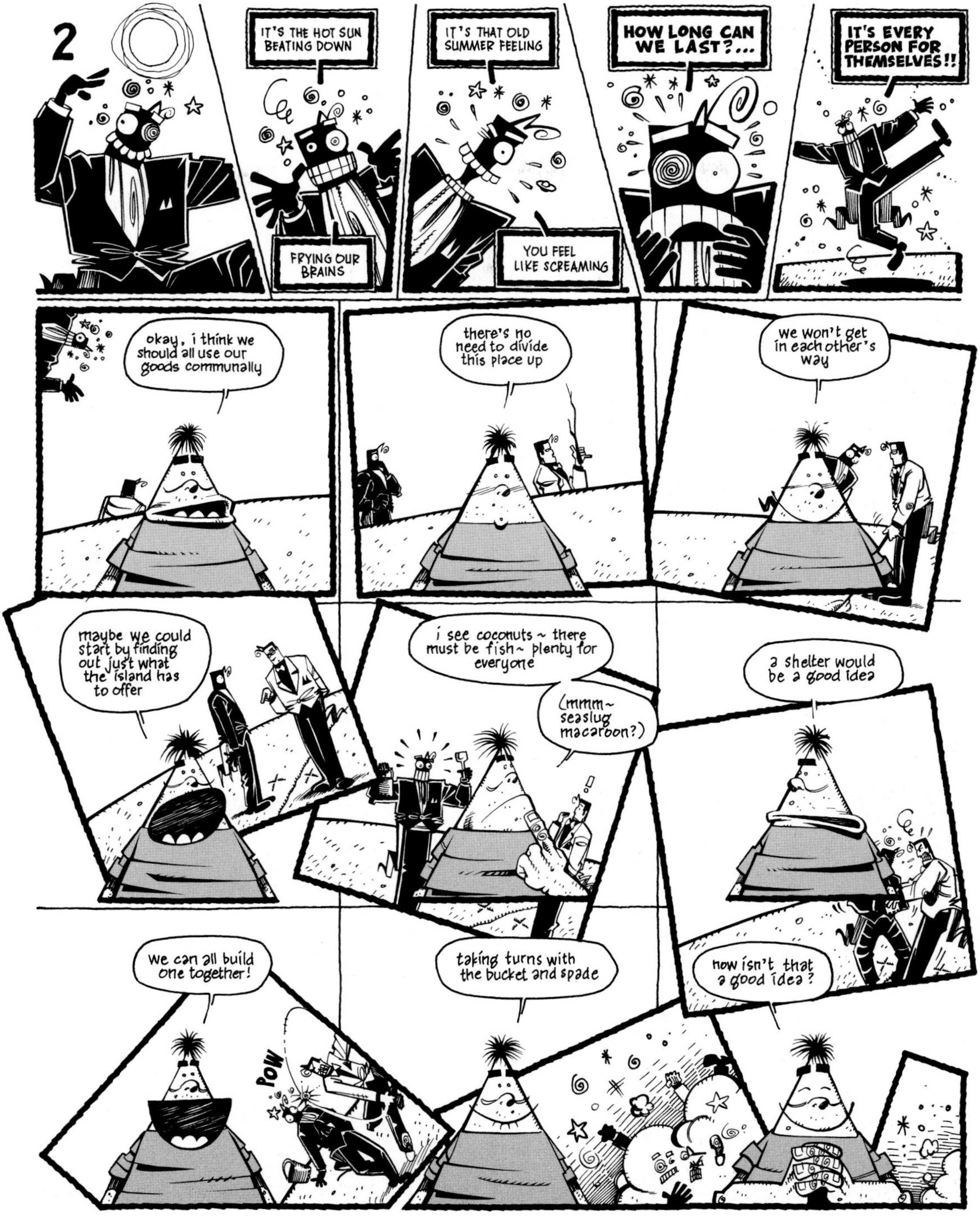
2
IT'S THE HOT SUN BEATING DOWN
FRYING OUR BRAINS
IT'S THAT OLD SUMMER FEELING
YOU FEEL LIKE SCREAMING
HOW LONG CAN WE LAST?...
IT'S EVERY PERSON FOR THEMSELVES!!
okay, i think we should all use our goods communally
there's no need to divide this place up
we won't get in each other's way
maybe we could start by finding out just what the island has to offer
i see coconuts ~ there must be fish ~ plenty for everyone
(mmm~ seaslug macaroon?)
a shelter would be a good idea
we can all build one together!
POW
taking turns with the bucket and spade
now isn't that a good idea?

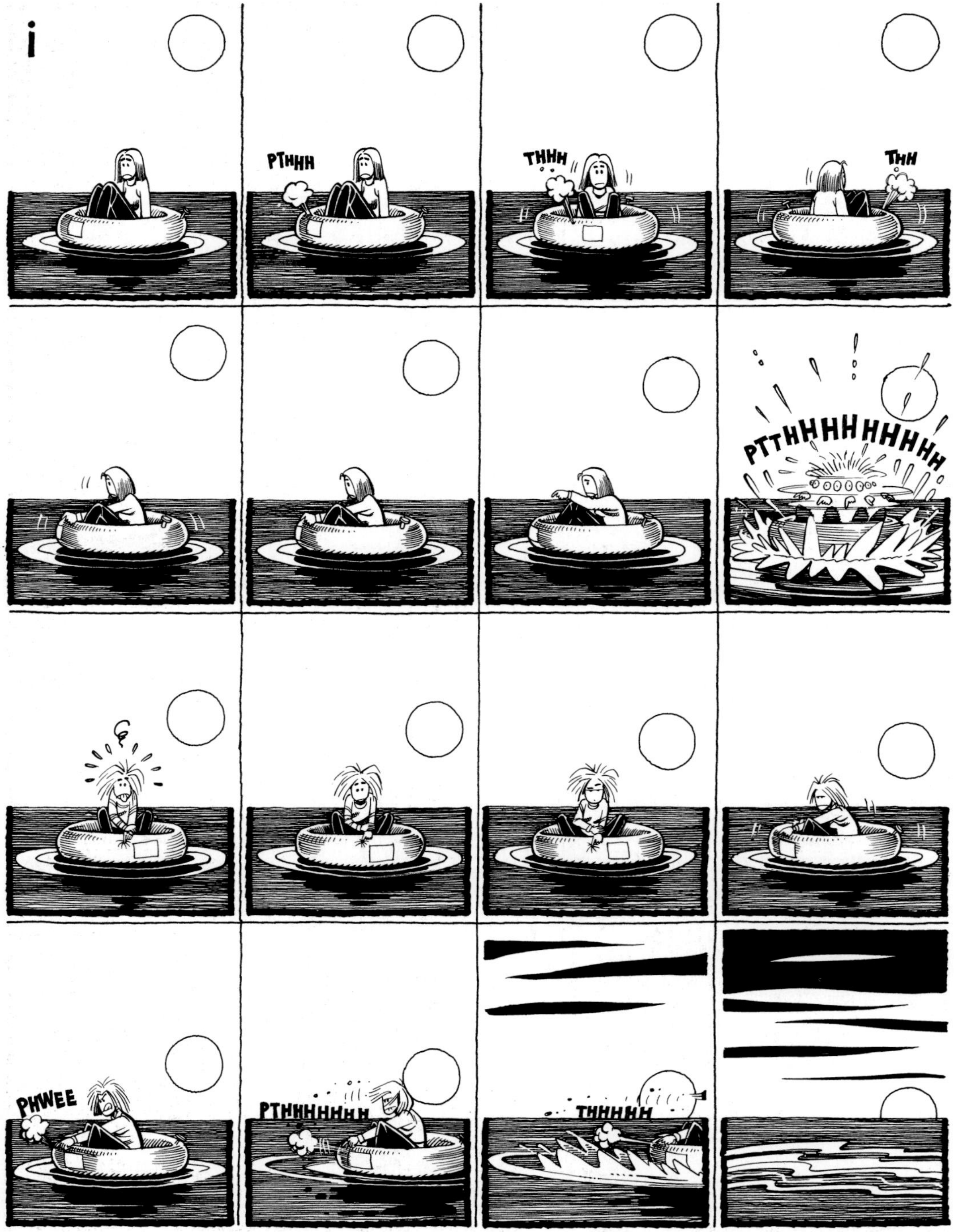
i
PTHHH
THHH
THH
PTTHHHHHHHHHH
PHWEE
PTHHHHHHH
THHHHH

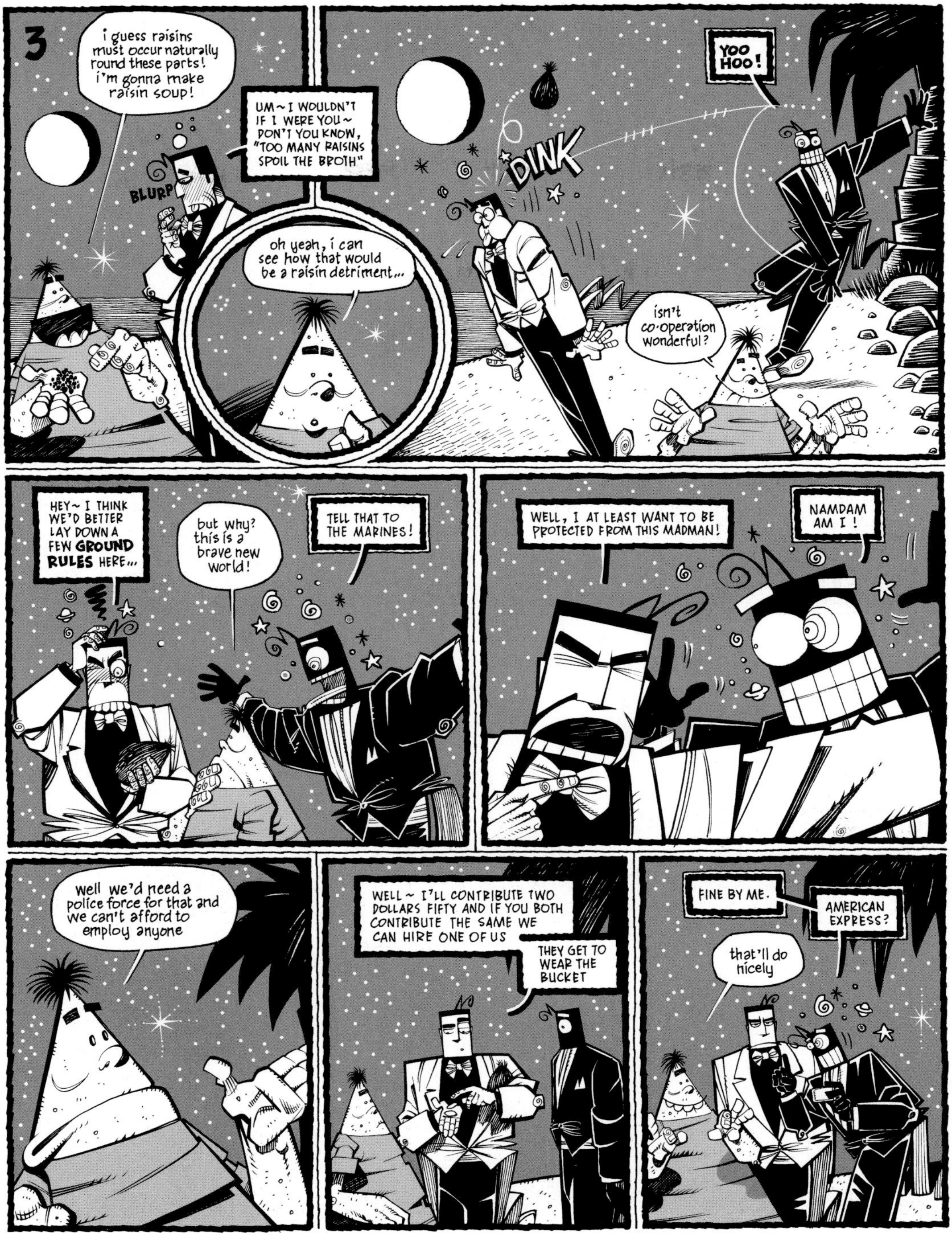
3
i guess raisins must occur naturally round these parts! i'm gonna make raisin soup!
BLURP
UM ~ I WOULDN'T IF I WERE YOU ~ DON'T YOU KNOW, "TOO MANY RAISINS SPOIL THE BROTH"
oh yeah, i can see how that would be a raisin detriment...
YOO HOO!
DINK
isn't co-operation wonderful?
HEY ~ I THINK WE'D BETTER LAY DOWN A FEW GROUND RULES HERE...
but why? this is a brave new world!
TELL THAT TO THE MARINES!
WELL, I AT LEAST WANT TO BE PROTECTED FROM THIS MADMAN!
NAMDAM AM I!
well we'd need a police force for that and we can't afford to employ anyone
WELL ~ I'LL CONTRIBUTE TWO DOLLARS FIFTY AND IF YOU BOTH CONTRIBUTE THE SAME WE CAN HIRE ONE OF US
THEY GET TO WEAR THE BUCKET
FINE BY ME.
AMERICAN EXPRESS?
that'll do nicely

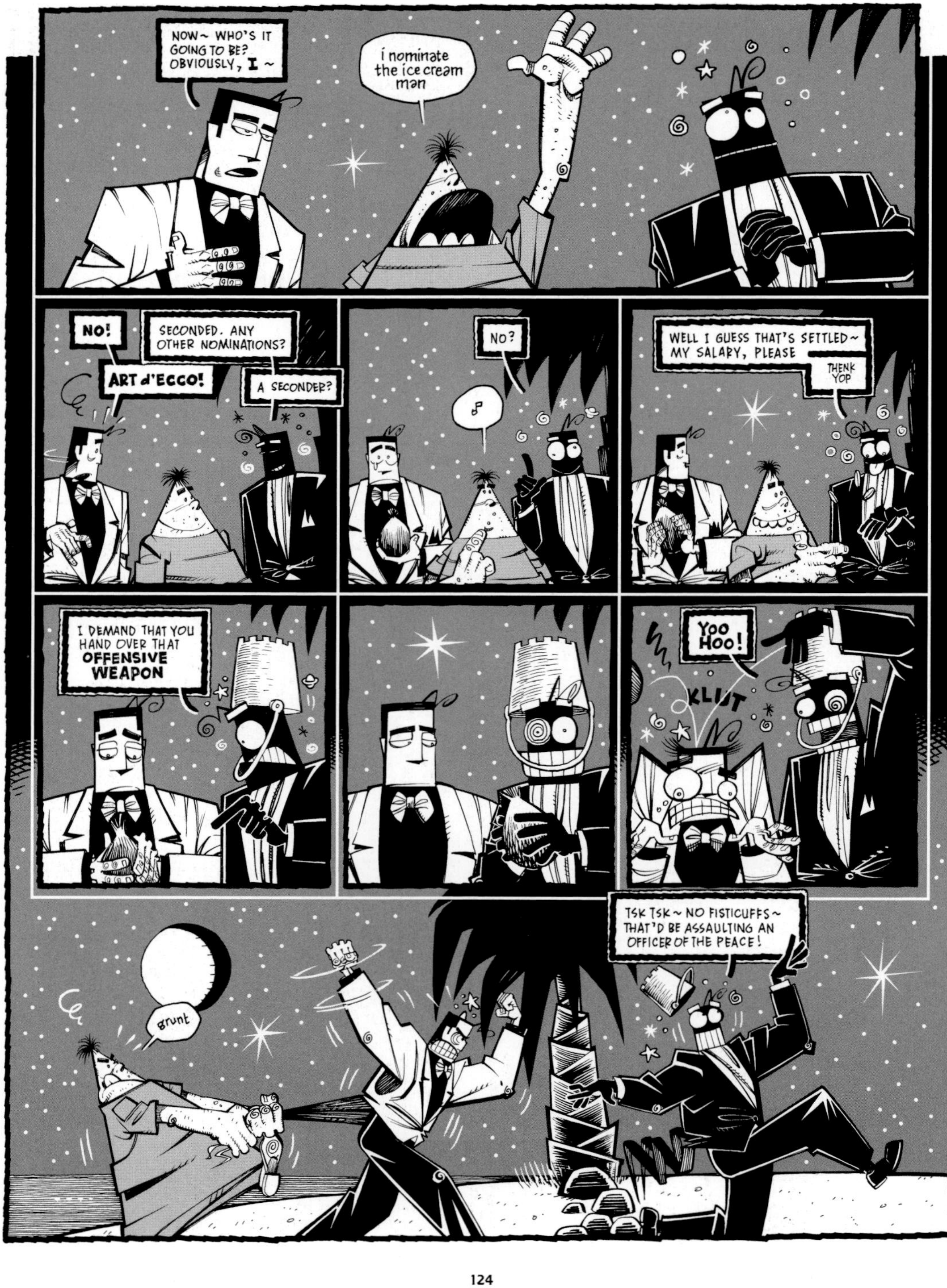
NOW~ WHO'S IT GOING TO BE? OBVIOUSLY, I ~
i nominate the ice cream man
NO!
SECONDED. ANY OTHER NOMINATIONS?
ART d'ECCO!
A SECONDER?
NO?
WELL I GUESS THAT'S SETTLED~ MY SALARY, PLEASE
THENK YOP
I DEMAND THAT YOU HAND OVER THAT OFFENSIVE WEAPON
YOO HOO!
KLUT
TSK TSK~ NO FISTICUFFS~ THAT'D BE ASSAULTING AN OFFICER OF THE PEACE!
grunt

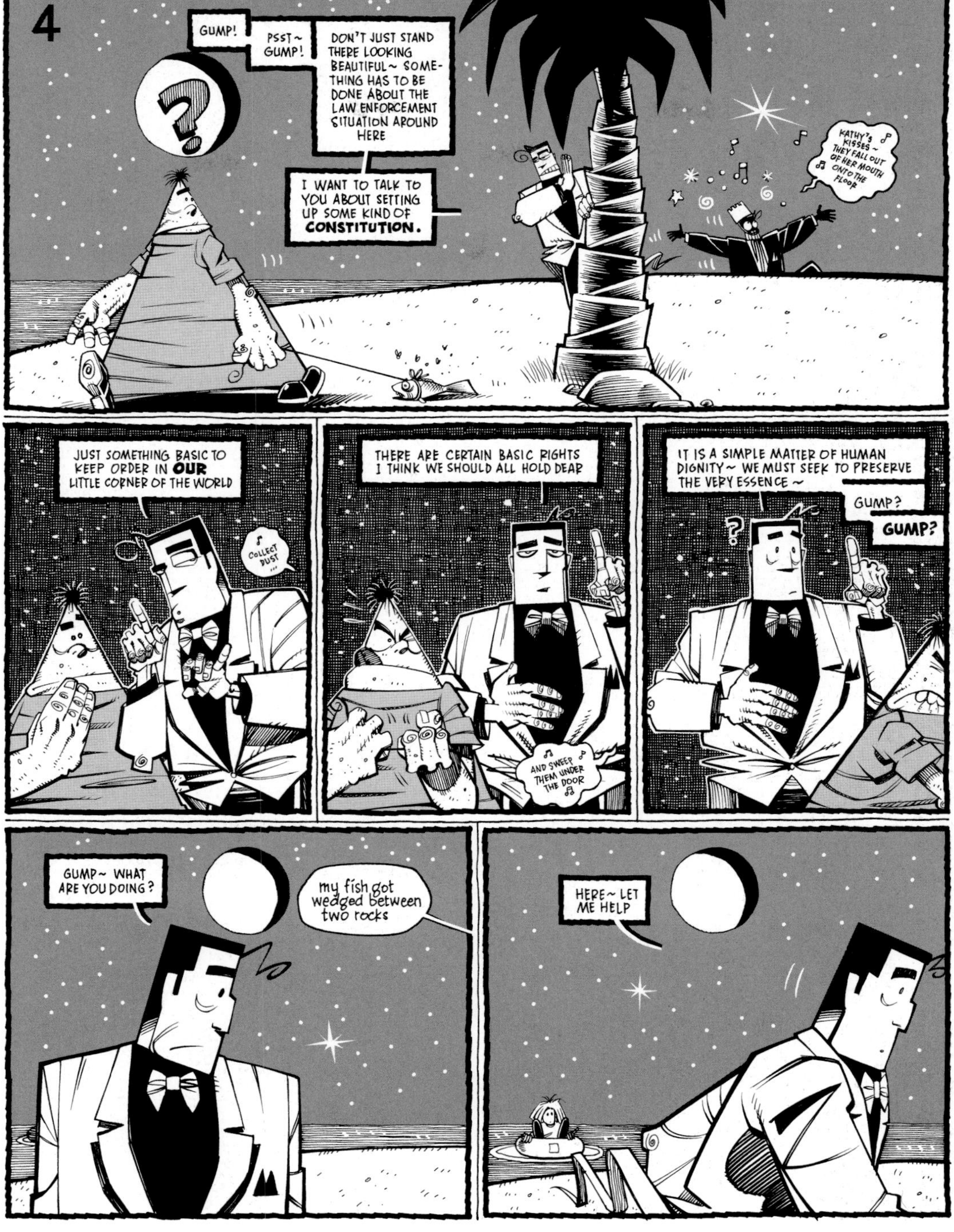
4
GUMP!
PSST~ GUMP!
DON'T JUST STAND THERE LOOKING BEAUTIFUL~ SOMETHING HAS TO BE DONE ABOUT THE LAW ENFORCEMENT SITUATION AROUND HERE
I WANT TO TALK TO YOU ABOUT SETTING UP SOME KIND OF CONSTITUTION.
KATHY'S KISSES~ THEY FALL OUT OF HER MOUTH ONTO THE FLOOR
JUST SOMETHING BASIC TO KEEP ORDER IN OUR LITTLE CORNER OF THE WORLD
COLLECT DUST ...
THERE ARE CERTAIN BASIC RIGHTS I THINK WE SHOULD ALL HOLD DEAR
AND SWEEP THEM UNDER THE DOOR
IT IS A SIMPLE MATTER OF HUMAN DIGNITY~ WE MUST SEEK TO PRESERVE THE VERY ESSENCE~
GUMP?
GUMP?
GUMP~ WHAT ARE YOU DOING?
my fish got wedged between two rocks
HERE~ LET ME HELP

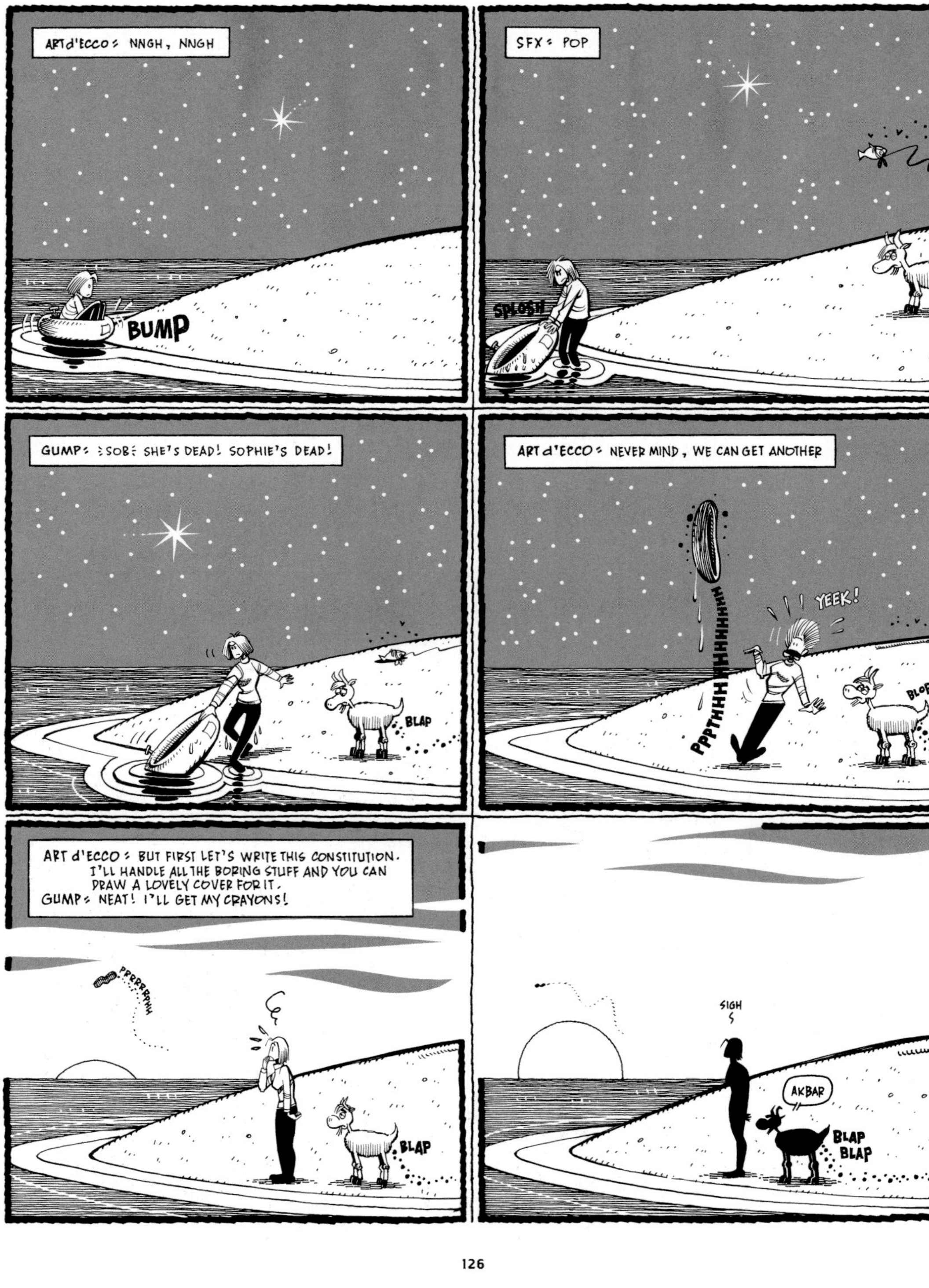
ART d'ECCO: NNGH, NNGH
BUMP
SFX: POP
SPLOSH
GUMP: :SOB: SHE'S DEAD! SOPHIE'S DEAD!
BLAP
ART d'ECCO: NEVER MIND, WE CAN GET ANOTHER
PPPTHHHHHHHHHHHHH
YEEK!
BLOP
ART d'ECCO: BUT FIRST LET'S WRITE THIS CONSTITUTION. I'LL HANDLE ALL THE BORING STUFF AND YOU CAN DRAW A LOVELY COVER FOR IT.
GUMP: NEAT! I'LL GET MY CRAYONS!
BLAP
SIGH
AKBAR
BLAP BLAP

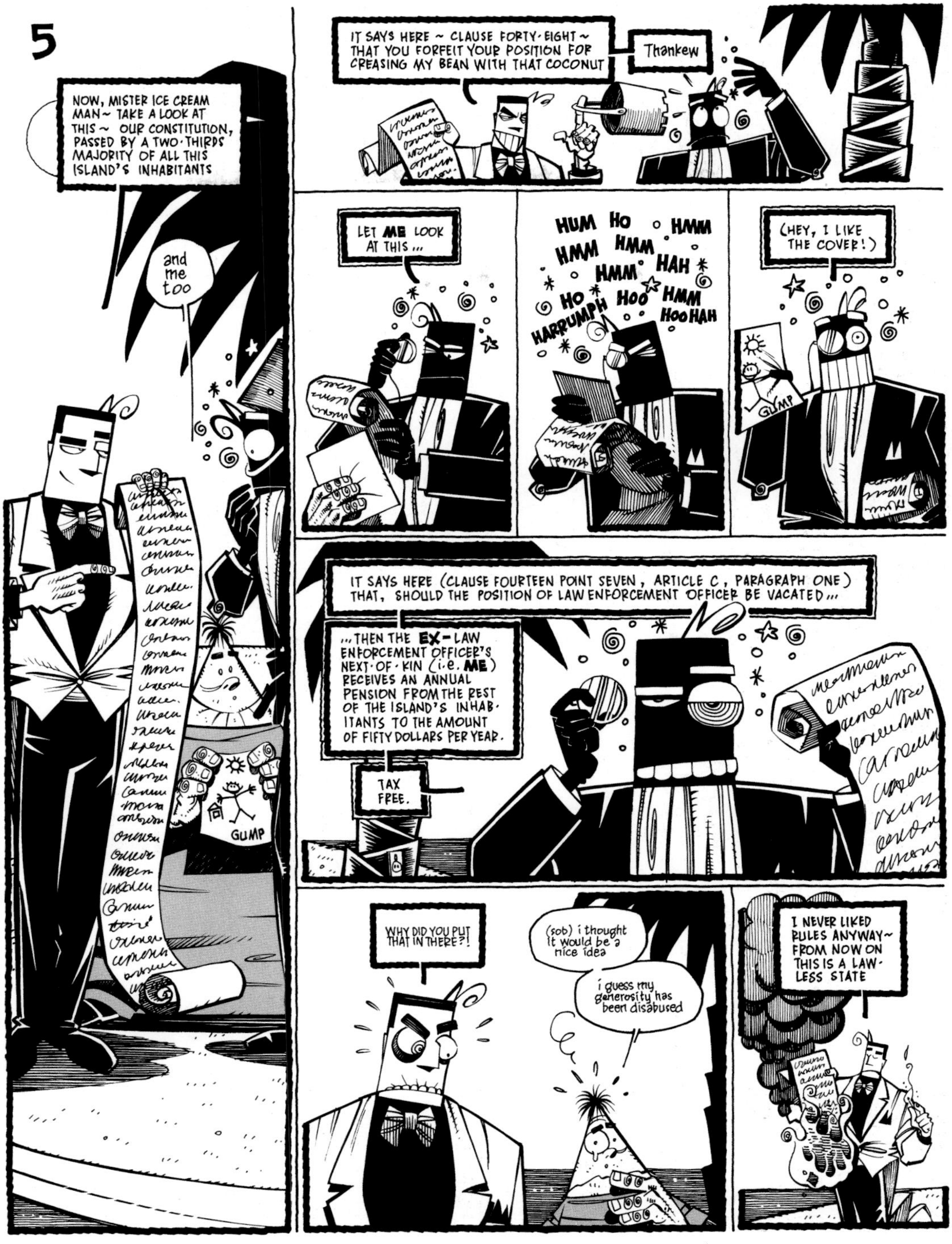
5
NOW, MISTER ICE CREAM MAN~ TAKE A LOOK AT THIS~ OUR CONSTITUTION, PASSED BY A TWO·THIRDS MAJORITY OF ALL THIS ISLAND'S INHABITANTS
and me too
GUMP
IT SAYS HERE ~ CLAUSE FORTY·EIGHT ~ THAT YOU FORFEIT YOUR POSITION FOR CREASING MY BEAN WITH THAT COCONUT
Thankew
LET ME LOOK AT THIS ...
HUM HO HMM HMM HMM HMM HAH HO HARRUMPH HOO HMM HOOHAH
(HEY, I LIKE THE COVER!)
GUMP
IT SAYS HERE (CLAUSE FOURTEEN POINT SEVEN, ARTICLE C, PARAGRAPH ONE) THAT, SHOULD THE POSITION OF LAW ENFORCEMENT OFFICER BE VACATED...
...THEN THE EX-LAW ENFORCEMENT OFFICER'S NEXT·OF·KIN (i.e. ME) RECEIVES AN ANNUAL PENSION FROM THE REST OF THE ISLAND'S INHAB·ITANTS TO THE AMOUNT OF FIFTY DOLLARS PER YEAR.
TAX FREE.
WHY DID YOU PUT THAT IN THERE?!
(sob) i thought it would be a nice idea
i guess my generosity has been disabused
I NEVER LIKED RULES ANYWAY~ FROM NOW ON THIS IS A LAW-LESS STATE

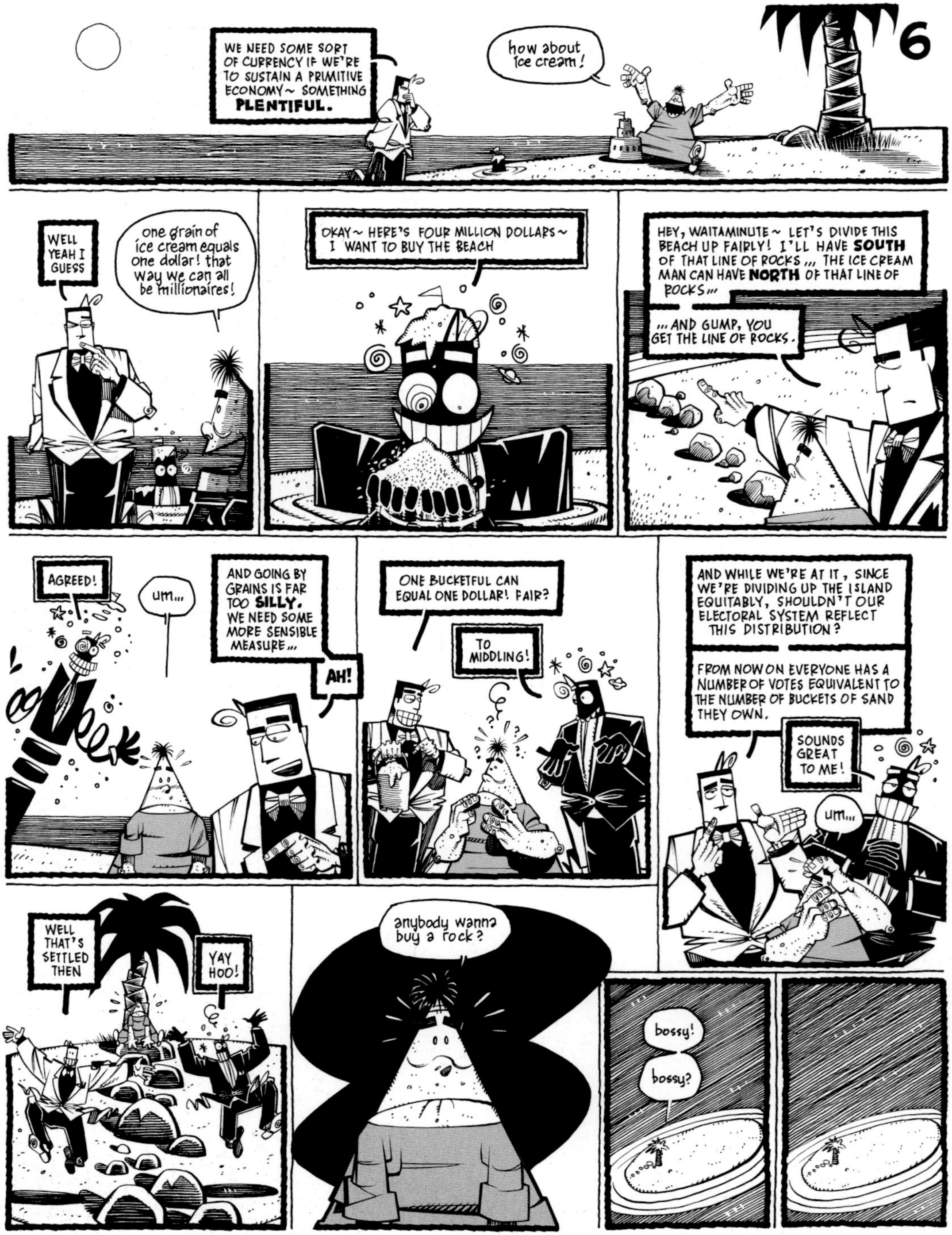
6
WE NEED SOME SORT OF CURRENCY IF WE'RE TO SUSTAIN A PRIMITIVE ECONOMY~ SOMETHING PLENTIFUL.
how about ice cream!
WELL YEAH I GUESS
one grain of ice cream equals one dollar! that way we can all be millionaires!
OKAY~ HERE'S FOUR MILLION DOLLARS~ I WANT TO BUY THE BEACH
HEY, WAITAMINUTE~ LET'S DIVIDE THIS BEACH UP FAIRLY! I'LL HAVE SOUTH OF THAT LINE OF ROCKS,,, THE ICE CREAM MAN CAN HAVE NORTH OF THAT LINE OF ROCKS,,,
,,, AND GUMP, YOU GET THE LINE OF ROCKS.
AGREED!
um,,,
AND GOING BY GRAINS IS FAR TOO SILLY. WE NEED SOME MORE SENSIBLE MEASURE,,,
AH!
ONE BUCKETFUL CAN EQUAL ONE DOLLAR! FAIR?
TO MIDDLING!
AND WHILE WE'RE AT IT, SINCE WE'RE DIVIDING UP THE ISLAND EQUITABLY, SHOULDN'T OUR ELECTORAL SYSTEM REFLECT THIS DISTRIBUTION?
FROM NOW ON EVERYONE HAS A NUMBER OF VOTES EQUIVALENT TO THE NUMBER OF BUCKETS OF SAND THEY OWN.
SOUNDS GREAT TO ME!
um,,,
WELL THAT'S SETTLED THEN
YAY HOO!
anybody wanna buy a rock?
bossy!
bossy?

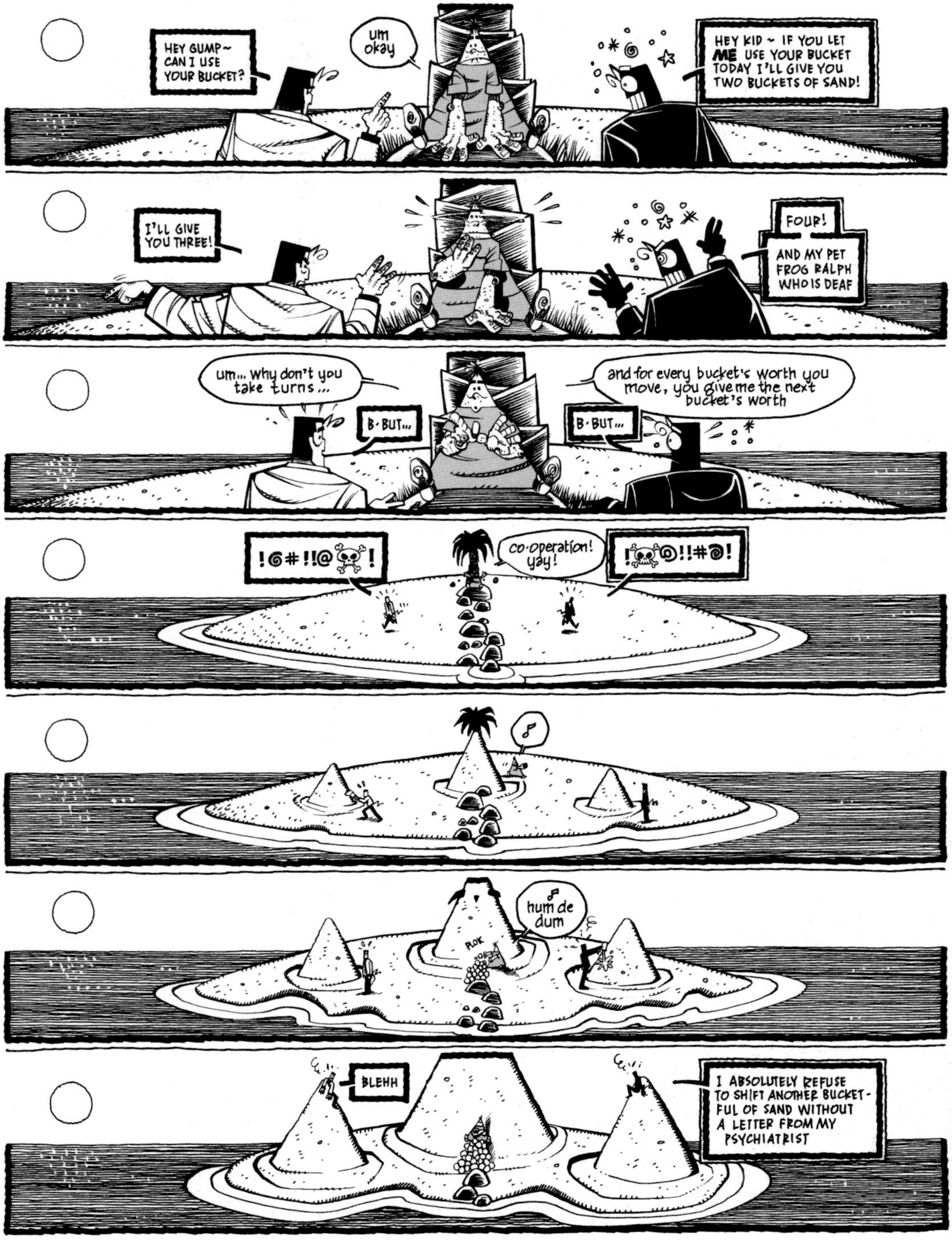
HEY GUMP ~ CAN I USE YOUR BUCKET?
um okay
HEY KID ~ IF YOU LET ME USE YOUR BUCKET TODAY I'LL GIVE YOU TWO BUCKETS OF SAND!
I'LL GIVE YOU THREE!
FOUR!
AND MY PET FROG RALPH WHO IS DEAF
um... why don't you take turns...
B·BUT...
B·BUT...
and for every bucket's worth you move, you give me the next bucket's worth
co·operation! yay!
hum de dum
PLOK
BLEHH
I ABSOLUTELY REFUSE TO SHIFT ANOTHER BUCKET-FUL OF SAND WITHOUT A LETTER FROM MY PSYCHIATRIST

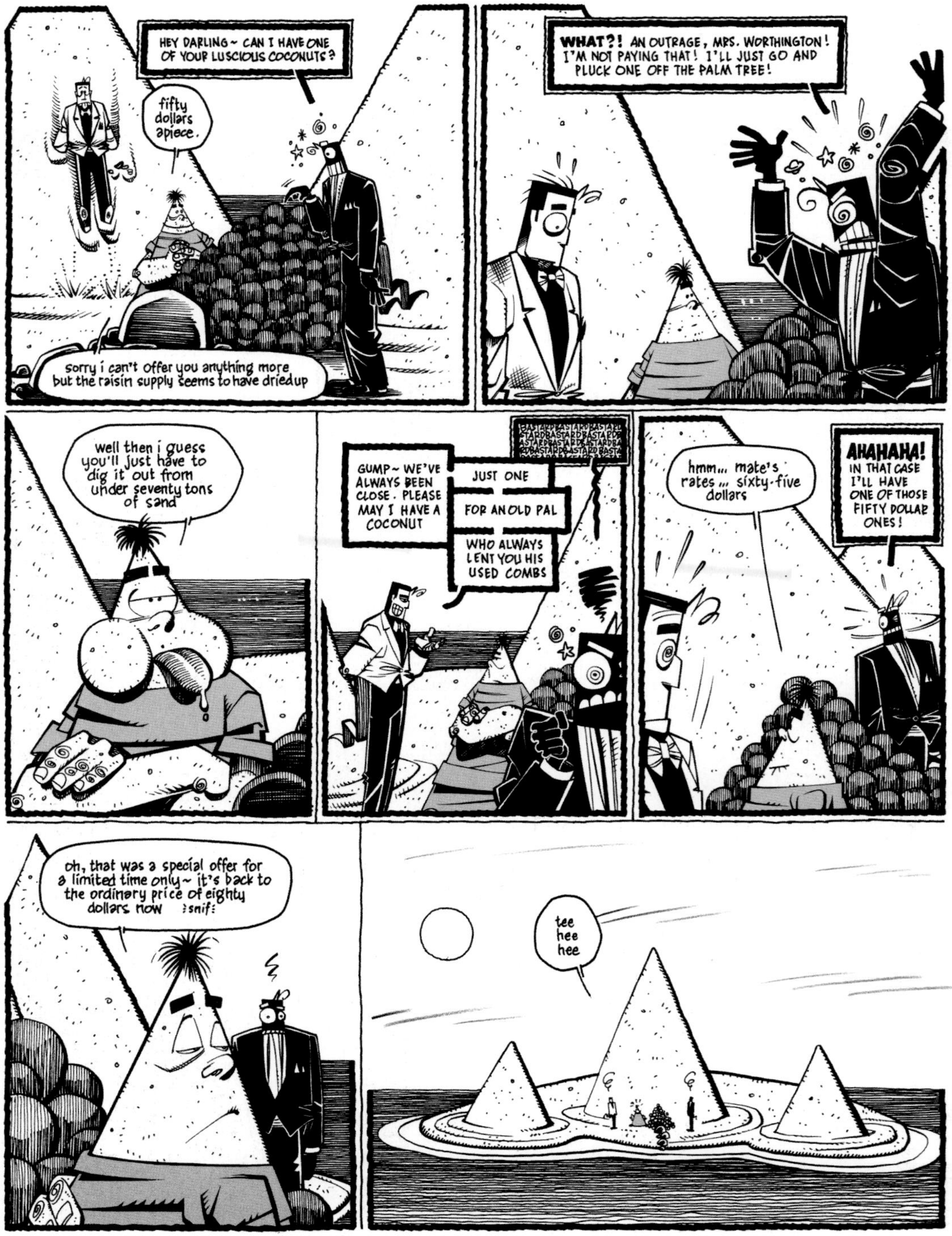
HEY DARLING ~ CAN I HAVE ONE OF YOUR LUSCIOUS COCONUTS?
fifty dollars apiece.
sorry i can't offer you anything more but the raisin supply seems to have dried up
WHAT?! AN OUTRAGE, MRS. WORTHINGTON! I'M NOT PAYING THAT! I'LL JUST GO AND PLUCK ONE OFF THE PALM TREE!
well then i guess you'll just have to dig it out from under seventy tons of sand
GUMP ~ WE'VE ALWAYS BEEN CLOSE. PLEASE MAY I HAVE A COCONUT
JUST ONE
FOR AN OLD PAL
WHO ALWAYS LENT YOU HIS USED COMBS
BASTARDBASTARDBASTARD
STARDBASTARDBASTARDB
ASTARDBASTARDBASTARDBA
RDBASTARDBASTARDBASTA
hmm... mate's rates ... sixty-five dollars
AHAHAHA! IN THAT CASE I'LL HAVE ONE OF THOSE FIFTY DOLLAR ONES!
oh, that was a special offer for a limited time only ~ it's back to the ordinary price of eighty dollars now
snif
tee hee hee

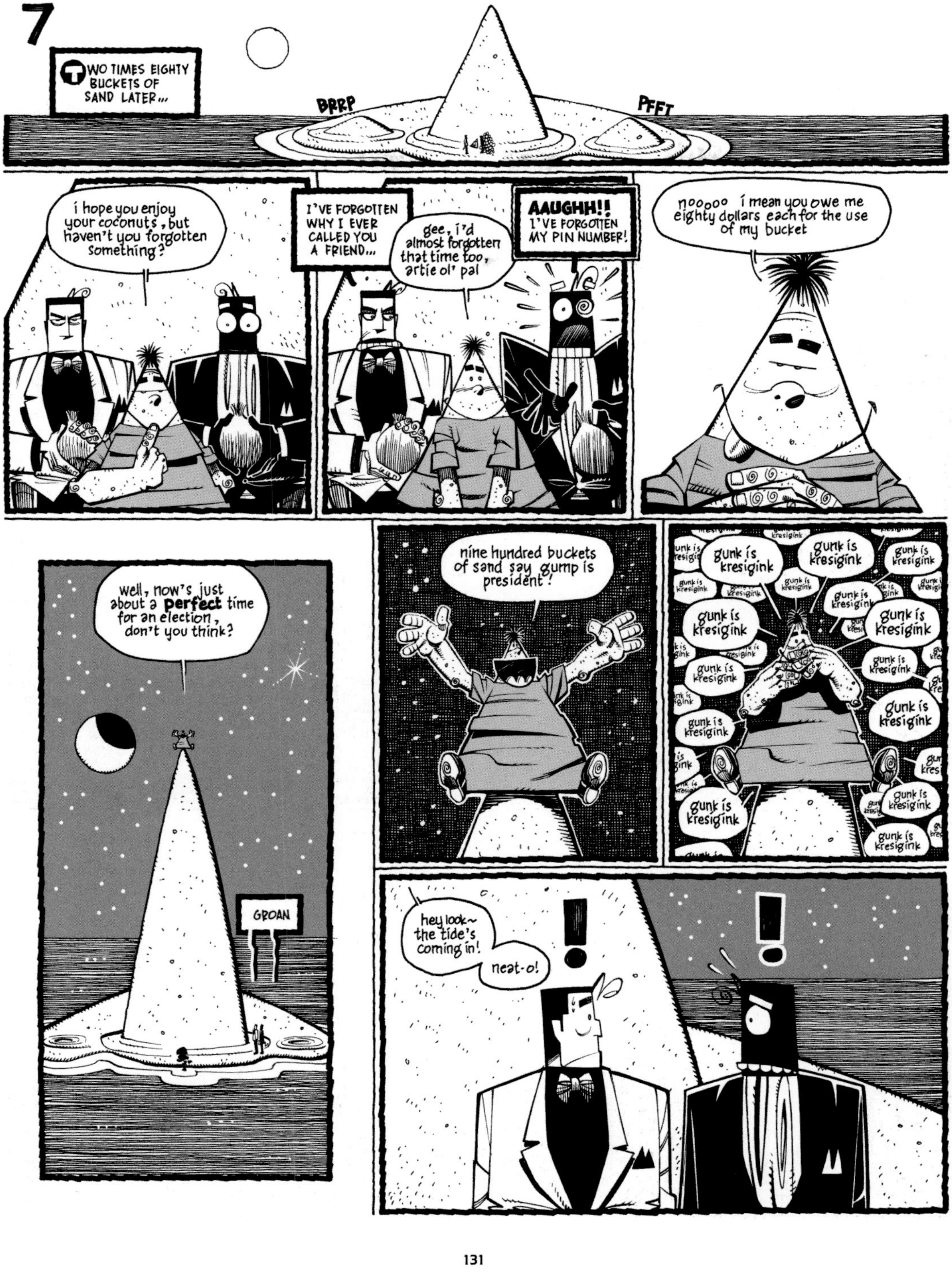
7
TWO TIMES EIGHTY BUCKETS OF SAND LATER...
BRRP
PFFT
i hope you enjoy your coconuts, but haven't you forgotten something?
I'VE FORGOTTEN WHY I EVER CALLED YOU A FRIEND...
gee, i'd almost forgotten that time too, artie ol' pal
AAUGHH!! I'VE FORGOTTEN MY PIN NUMBER!
nooooo i mean you owe me eighty dollars each for the use of my bucket
well, now's just about a **perfect** time for an election, don't you think?
GROAN
nine hundred buckets of sand say gump is president!
gunk is kresigink
hey look~ the tide's coming in!
neat-o!
!
!

8

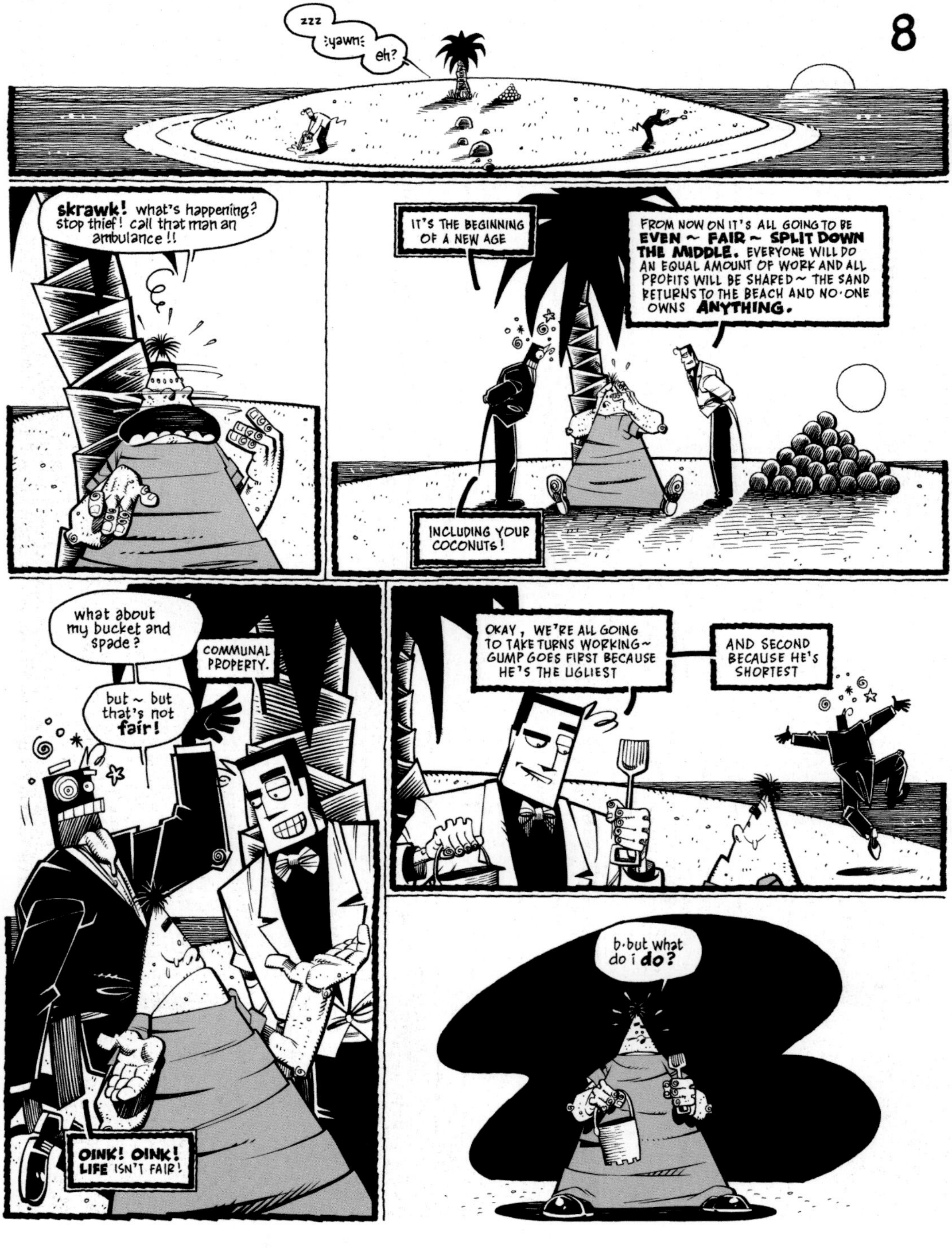
zzz
:yawn:
eh?
skrawk! what's happening? stop thief! call that man an ambulance !!
IT'S THE BEGINNING OF A NEW AGE
FROM NOW ON IT'S ALL GOING TO BE EVEN ~ FAIR ~ SPLIT DOWN THE MIDDLE. EVERYONE WILL DO AN EQUAL AMOUNT OF WORK AND ALL PROFITS WILL BE SHARED ~ THE SAND RETURNS TO THE BEACH AND NO·ONE OWNS ANYTHING.
INCLUDING YOUR COCONUTS!
what about my bucket and spade?
COMMUNAL PROPERTY.
but ~ but that's not fair!
OINK! OINK! LIFE ISN'T FAIR!
OKAY, WE'RE ALL GOING TO TAKE TURNS WORKING~ GUMP GOES FIRST BECAUSE HE'S THE UGLIEST
AND SECOND BECAUSE HE'S SHORTEST
b·but what do i do?

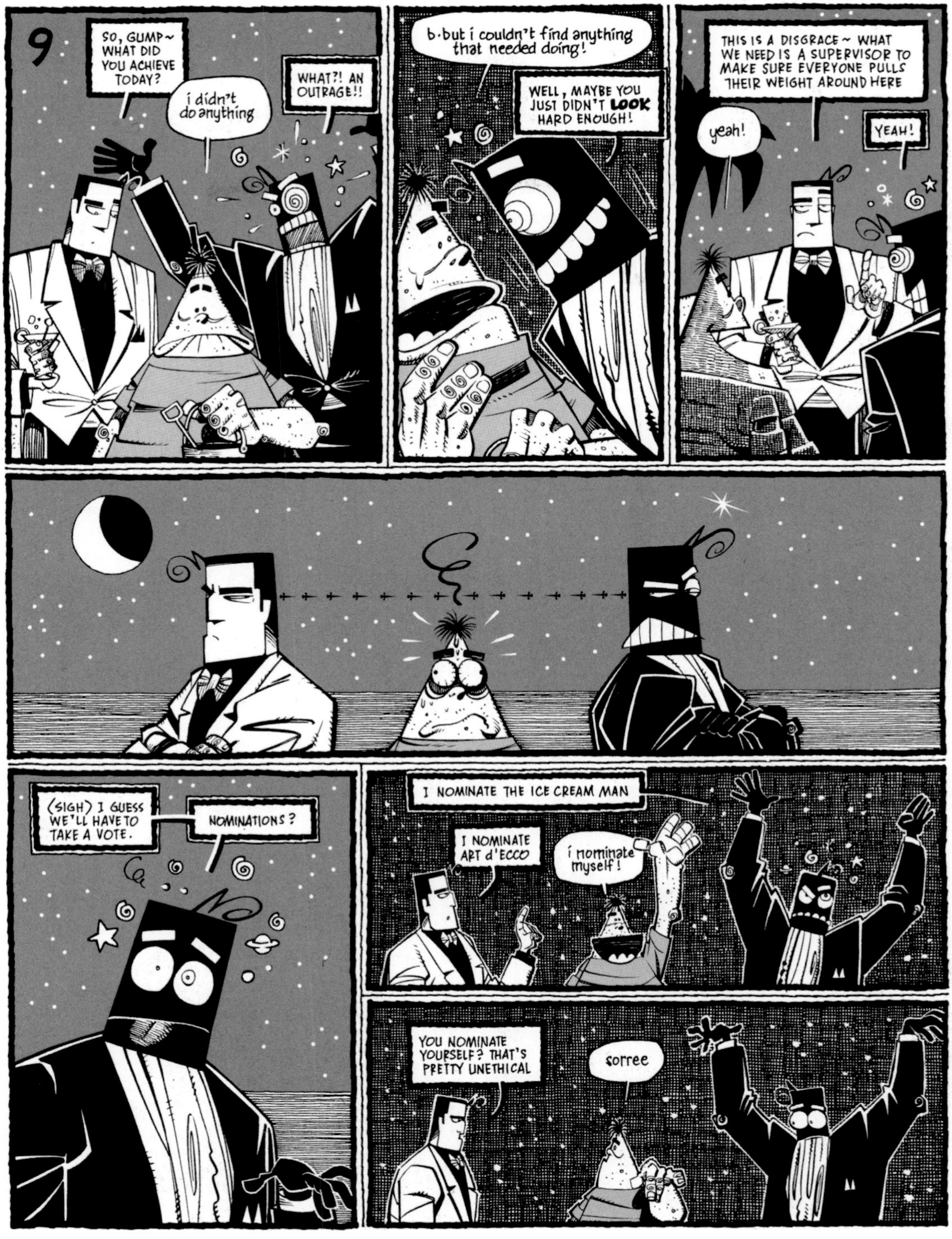
9
SO, GUMP~ WHAT DID YOU ACHIEVE TODAY?
i didn't do anything
WHAT?! AN OUTRAGE!!
b-but i couldn't find anything that needed doing!
WELL, MAYBE YOU JUST DIDN'T LOOK HARD ENOUGH!
THIS IS A DISGRACE~ WHAT WE NEED IS A SUPERVISOR TO MAKE SURE EVERYONE PULLS THEIR WEIGHT AROUND HERE
yeah!
YEAH!
(SIGH) I GUESS WE'LL HAVE TO TAKE A VOTE.
NOMINATIONS?
I NOMINATE THE ICE CREAM MAN
I NOMINATE ART d'ECCO
i nominate myself!
YOU NOMINATE YOURSELF? THAT'S PRETTY UNETHICAL
sorree

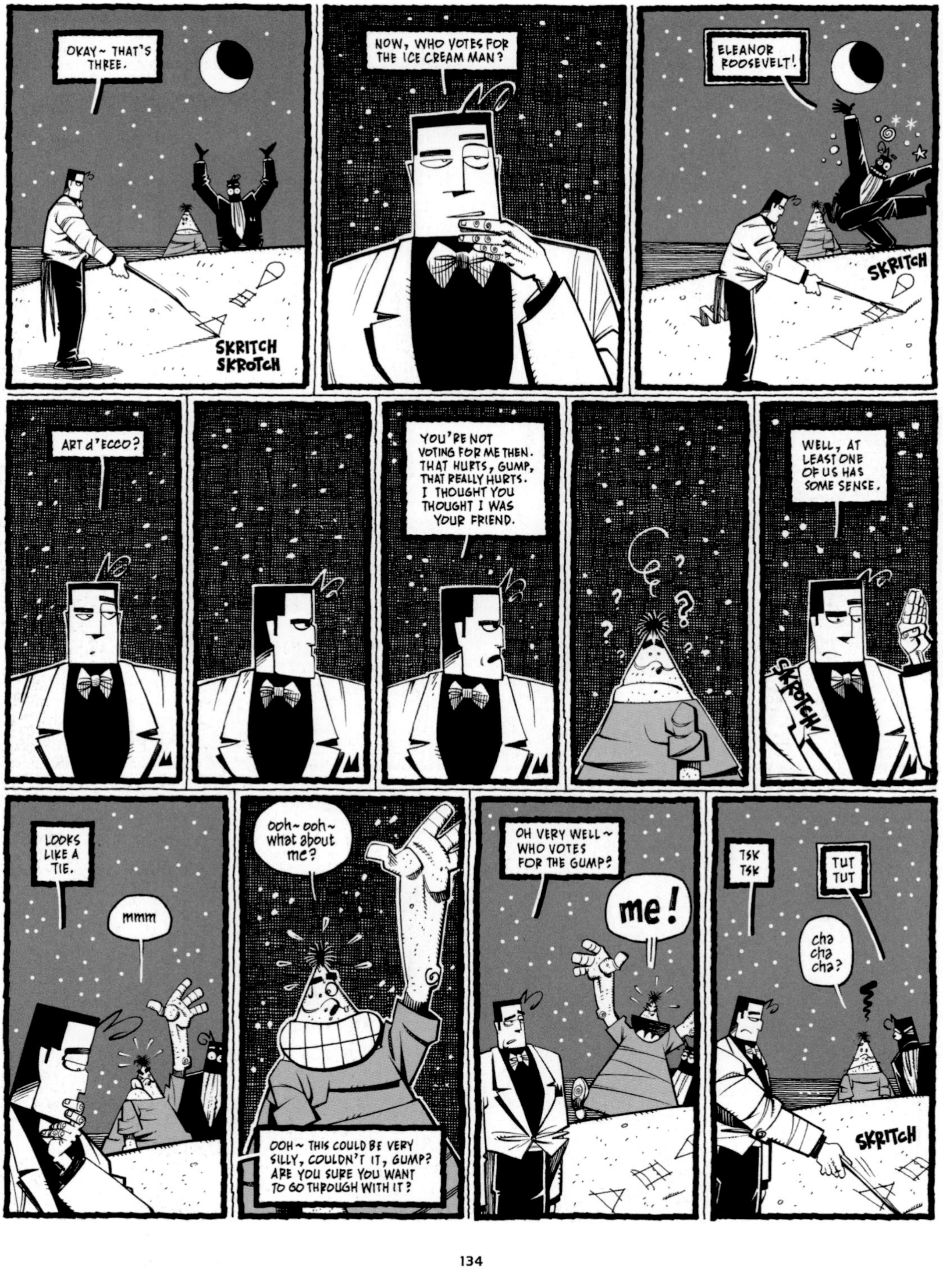
OKAY ~ THAT'S THREE.
SKRITCH SKROTCH
NOW, WHO VOTES FOR THE ICE CREAM MAN?
ELEANOR ROOSEVELT!
SKRITCH
ART d'ECCO?
YOU'RE NOT VOTING FOR ME THEN. THAT HURTS, GUMP, THAT REALLY HURTS. I THOUGHT YOU THOUGHT I WAS YOUR FRIEND.
WELL, AT LEAST ONE OF US HAS SOME SENSE.
SKROTCH
LOOKS LIKE A TIE.
mmm
ooh~ ooh~ what about me?
OOH~ THIS COULD BE VERY SILLY, COULDN'T IT, GUMP? ARE YOU SURE YOU WANT TO GO THROUGH WITH IT?
OH VERY WELL ~ WHO VOTES FOR THE GUMP?
me!
TSK TSK
TUT TUT
cha cha cha?
SKRITCH

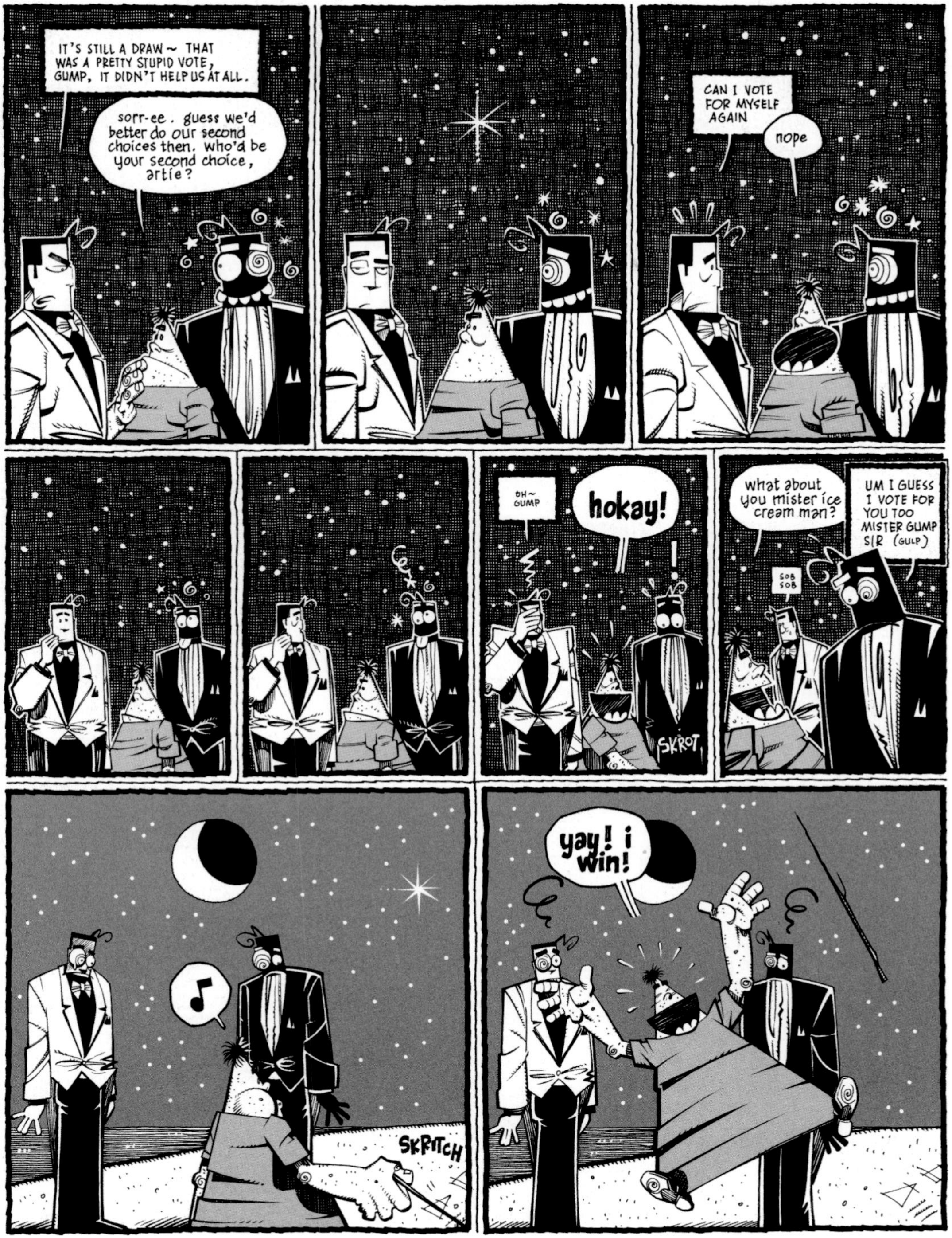
IT'S STILL A DRAW ~ THAT WAS A PRETTY STUPID VOTE, GUMP, IT DIDN'T HELP US AT ALL.
sorr-ee. guess we'd better do our second choices then. who'd be your second choice, artie?
CAN I VOTE FOR MYSELF AGAIN
nope
OH~ GUMP
hokay!
!
SKROT
what about you mister ice cream man?
UM I GUESS I VOTE FOR YOU TOO MISTER GUMP SIR (GULP)
SOB SOB
SKRITCH
yay! i win!

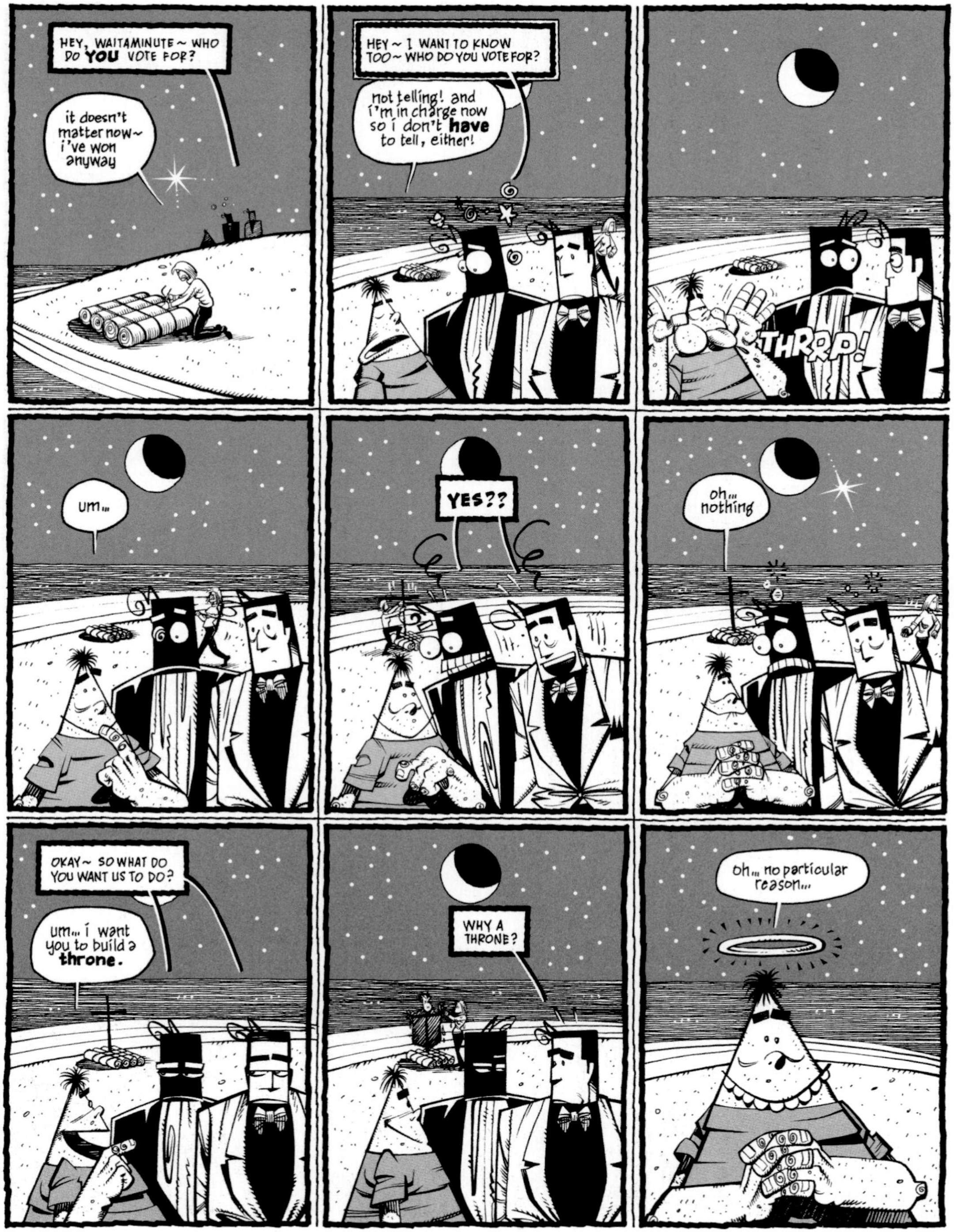

HEY, WAITAMINUTE ~ WHO DO YOU VOTE FOR?
it doesn't matter now~ i've won anyway
HEY ~ I WANT TO KNOW TOO ~ WHO DO YOU VOTE FOR?
not telling! and i'm in charge now so i don't have to tell, either!
THRRP!
um...
YES??
oh... nothing
OKAY ~ SO WHAT DO YOU WANT US TO DO?
um... i want you to build a throne.
WHY A THRONE?
oh... no particular reason...

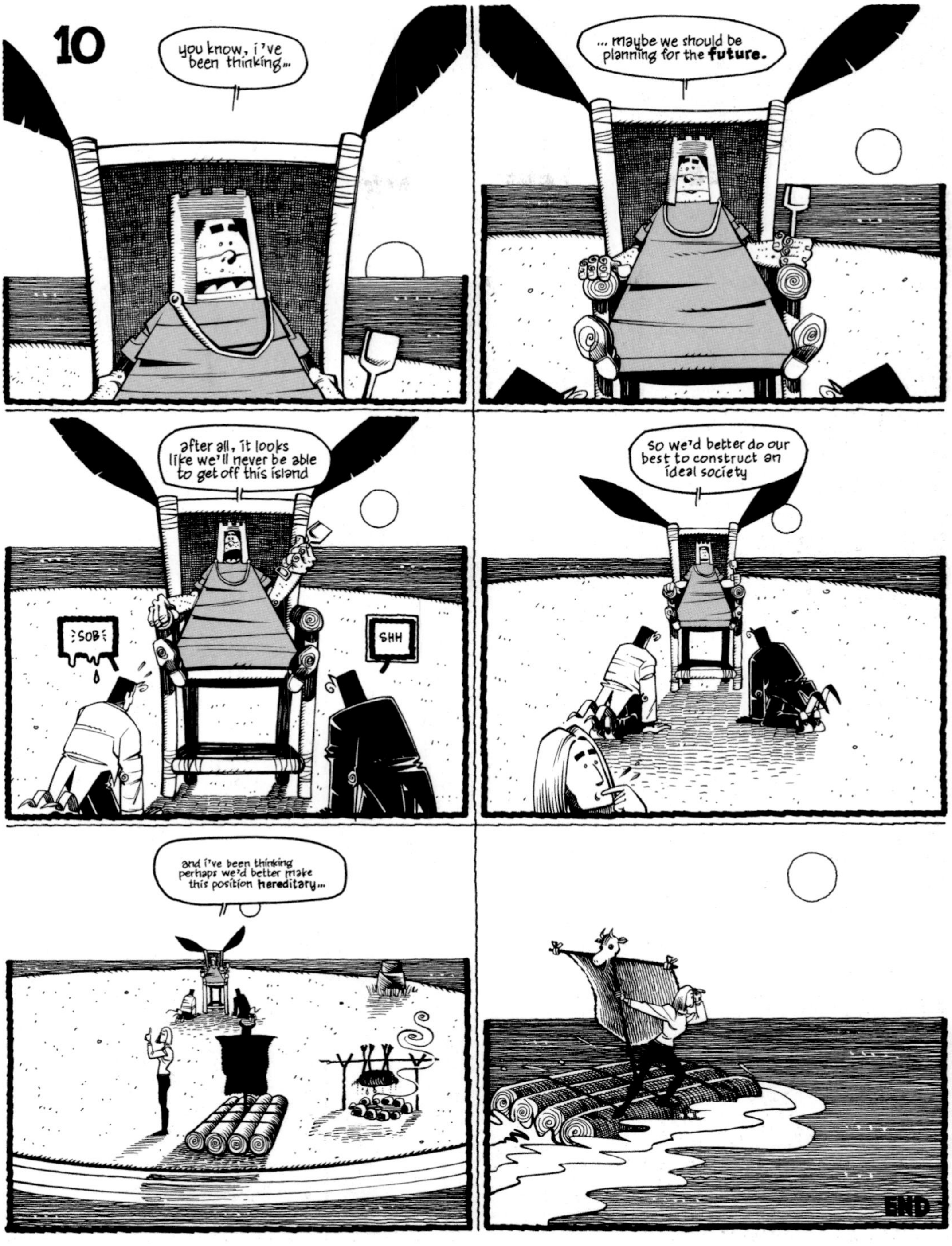
10
you know, i've been thinking...
... maybe we should be planning for the **future.**
after all, it looks like we'll never be able to get off this island
SOB
SHH
so we'd better do our best to construct an ideal society
and i've been thinking perhaps we'd better make this position **hereditary...**
END

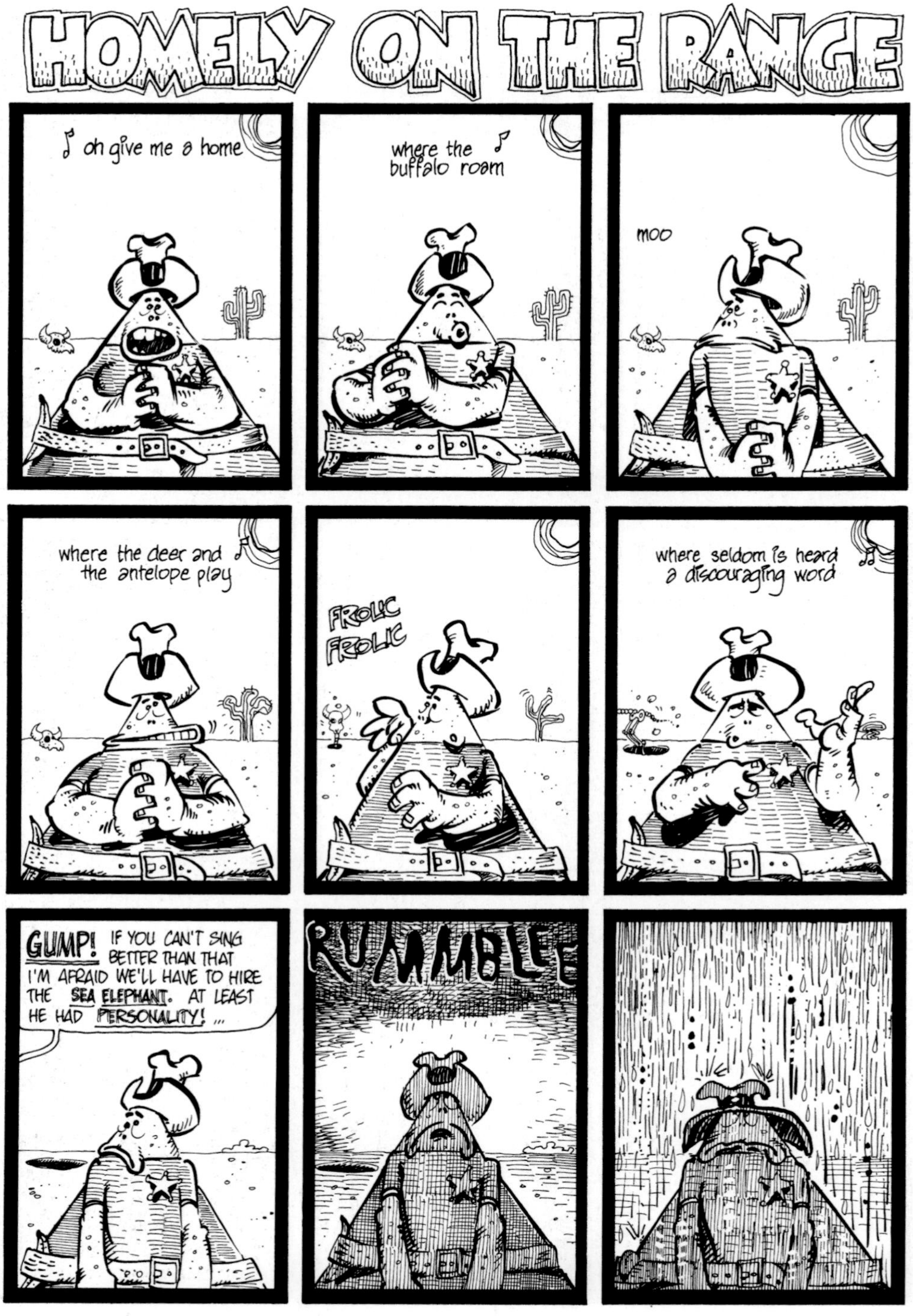
HOMELY ON THE RANGE
oh give me a home
where the buffalo roam
moo
where the deer and the antelope play
FROLIC FROLIC
where seldom is heard a discouraging word
GUMP! IF YOU CAN'T SING BETTER THAN THAT I'M AFRAID WE'LL HAVE TO HIRE THE SEA ELEPHANT. AT LEAST HE HAD PERSONALITY! ...
RUMMBLEE

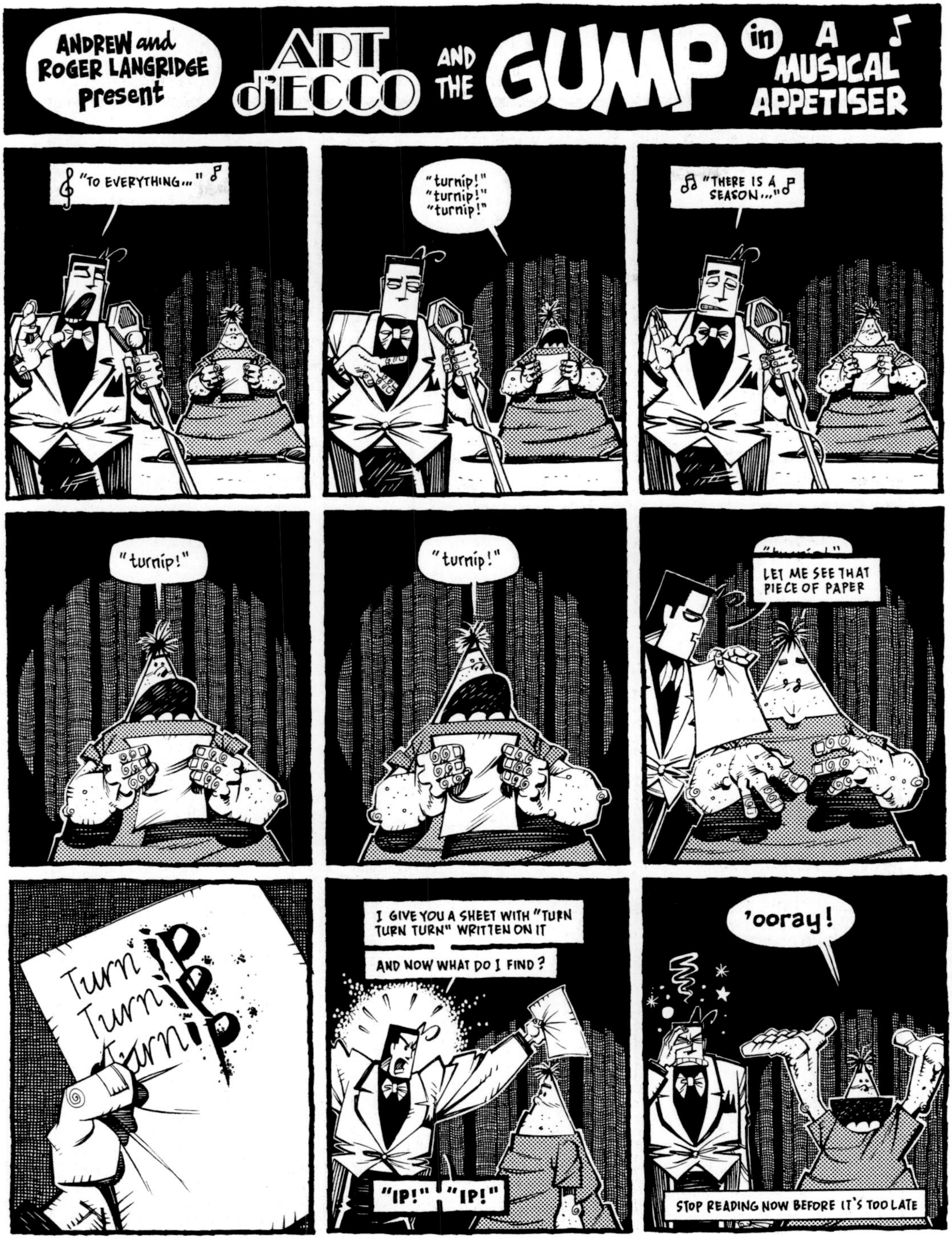
ANDREW and ROGER LANGRIDGE Present
ART d'ECCO AND THE GUMP in A MUSICAL APPETISER
"TO EVERYTHING..."
"turnip!" "turnip!" "turnip!"
"THERE IS A SEASON..."
"turnip!"
"turnip!"
LET ME SEE THAT PIECE OF PAPER
Turn ip Turn ip Turn ip
I GIVE YOU A SHEET WITH "TURN TURN TURN" WRITTEN ON IT
AND NOW WHAT DO I FIND?
"IP!" "IP!"
'ooray!
STOP READING NOW BEFORE IT'S TOO LATE

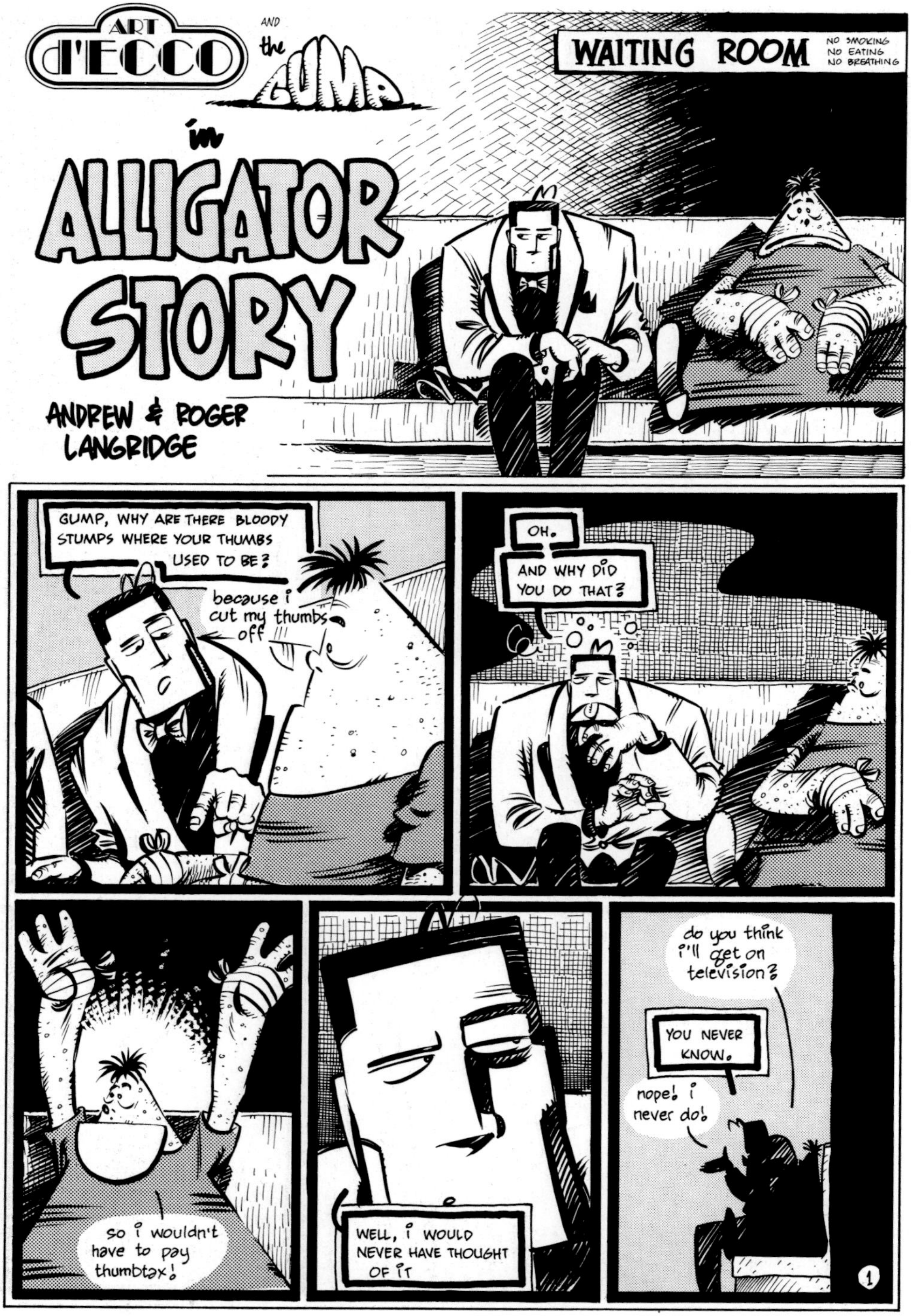
ART d'ECCO
AND
the GUMP
in
ALLIGATOR STORY
ANDREW & ROGER LANGRIDGE
WAITING ROOM
NO SMOKING
NO EATING
NO BREATHING
GUMP, WHY ARE THERE BLOODY STUMPS WHERE YOUR THUMBS USED TO BE?
because i cut my thumbs off
OH.
AND WHY DID YOU DO THAT?
so i wouldn't have to pay thumbtax!
WELL, i WOULD NEVER HAVE THOUGHT OF iT
do you think i'll get on television?
YOU NEVER KNOW.
nope! i never do!
1

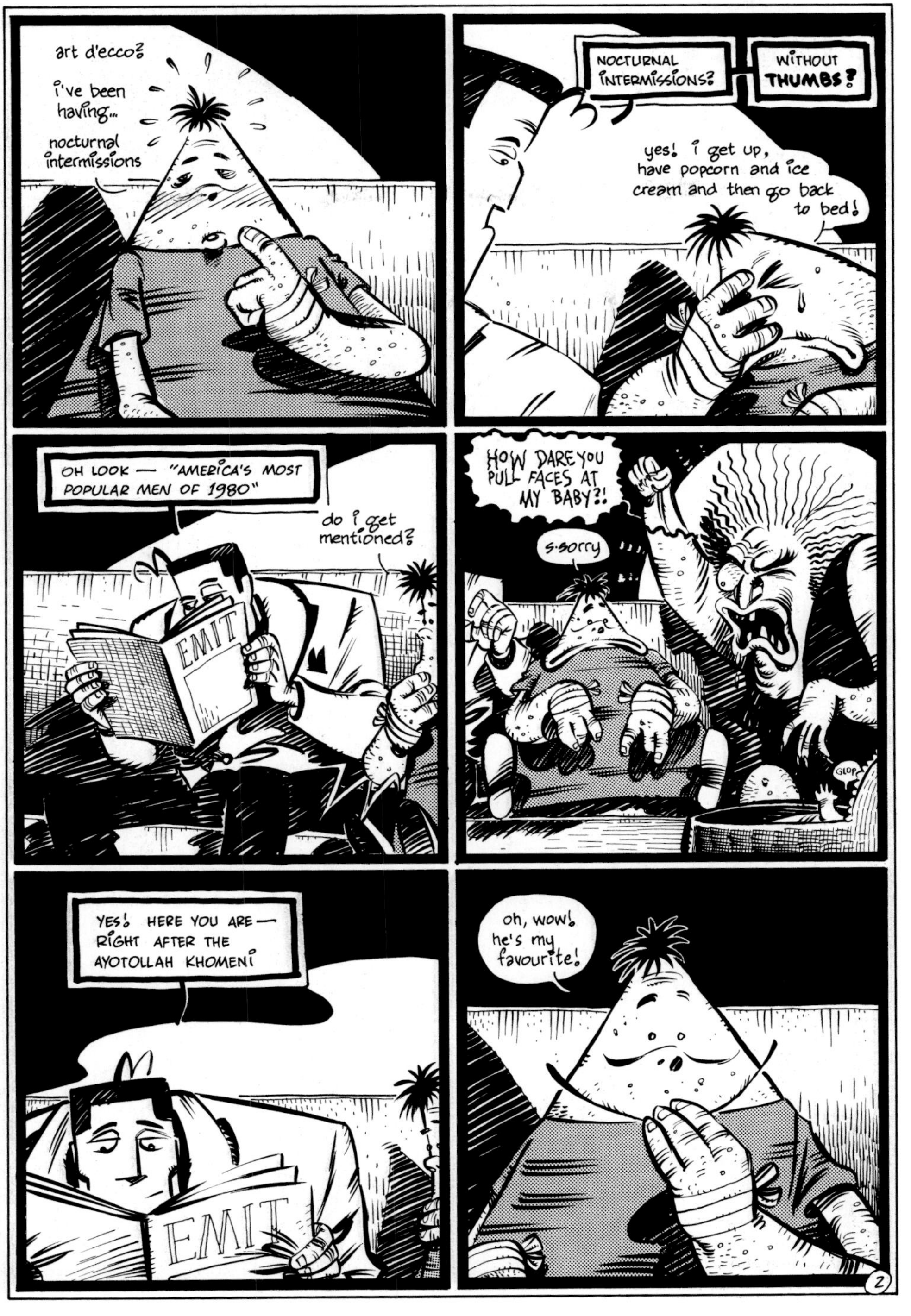
art d'ecco?
i've been having...
nocturnal intermissions
NOCTURNAL INTERMISSIONS?
WITHOUT THUMBS?
yes! i get up, have popcorn and ice cream and then go back to bed!
OH LOOK — "AMERICA'S MOST POPULAR MEN OF 1980"
do i get mentioned?
EMIT
HOW DARE YOU PULL FACES AT MY BABY?!
s-sorry
GLOP
YES! HERE YOU ARE — RIGHT AFTER THE AYOTOLLAH KHOMENI
EMIT
oh, wow! he's my favourite!
2

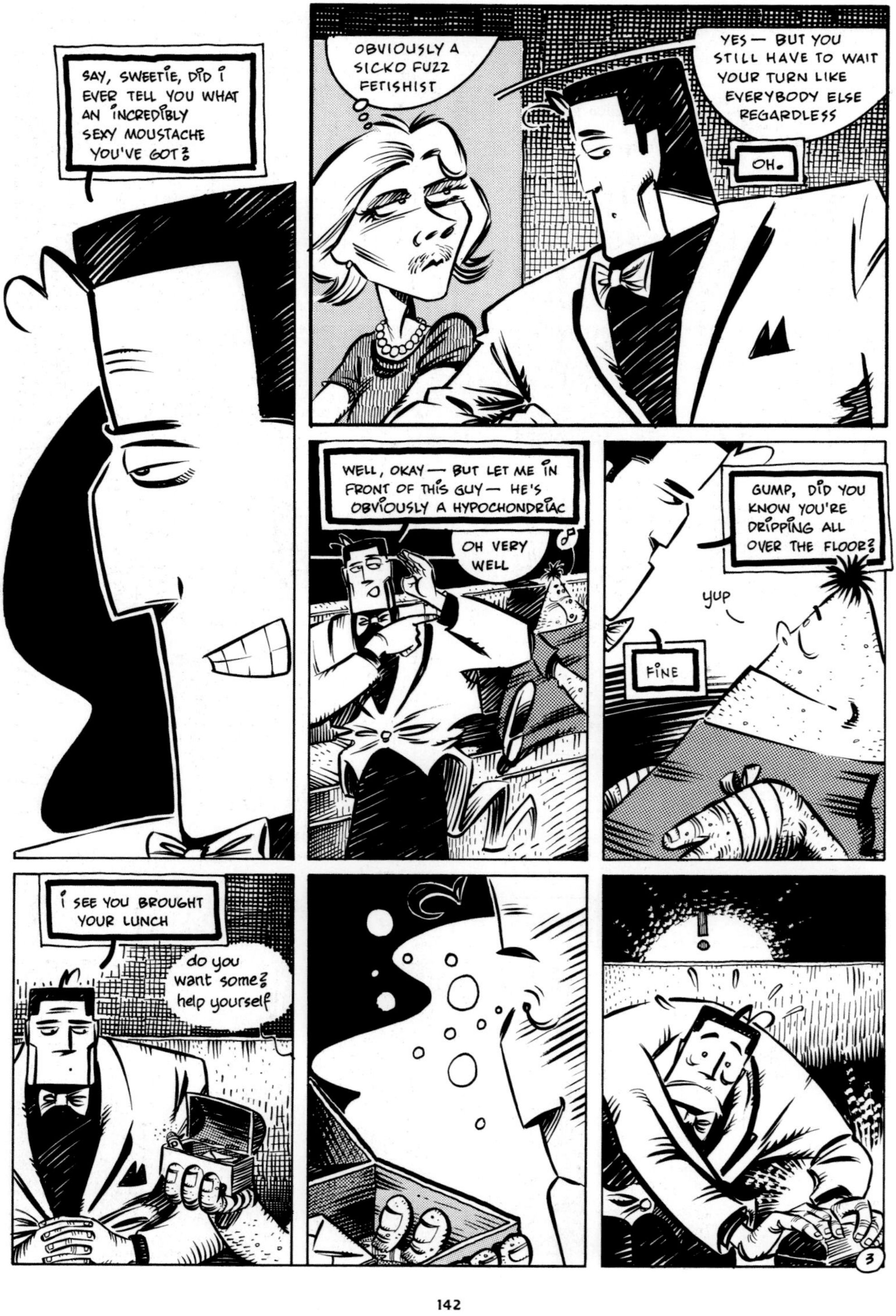
SAY, SWEETIE, DID I EVER TELL YOU WHAT AN INCREDIBLY SEXY MOUSTACHE YOU'VE GOT?
OBVIOUSLY A SICKO FUZZ FETISHIST
YES — BUT YOU STILL HAVE TO WAIT YOUR TURN LIKE EVERYBODY ELSE REGARDLESS
OH.
WELL, OKAY — BUT LET ME IN FRONT OF THIS GUY — HE'S OBVIOUSLY A HYPOCHONDRIAC
OH VERY WELL
GUMP, DID YOU KNOW YOU'RE DRIPPING ALL OVER THE FLOOR?
YUP
FINE
I SEE YOU BROUGHT YOUR LUNCH
do you want some? help yourself
3

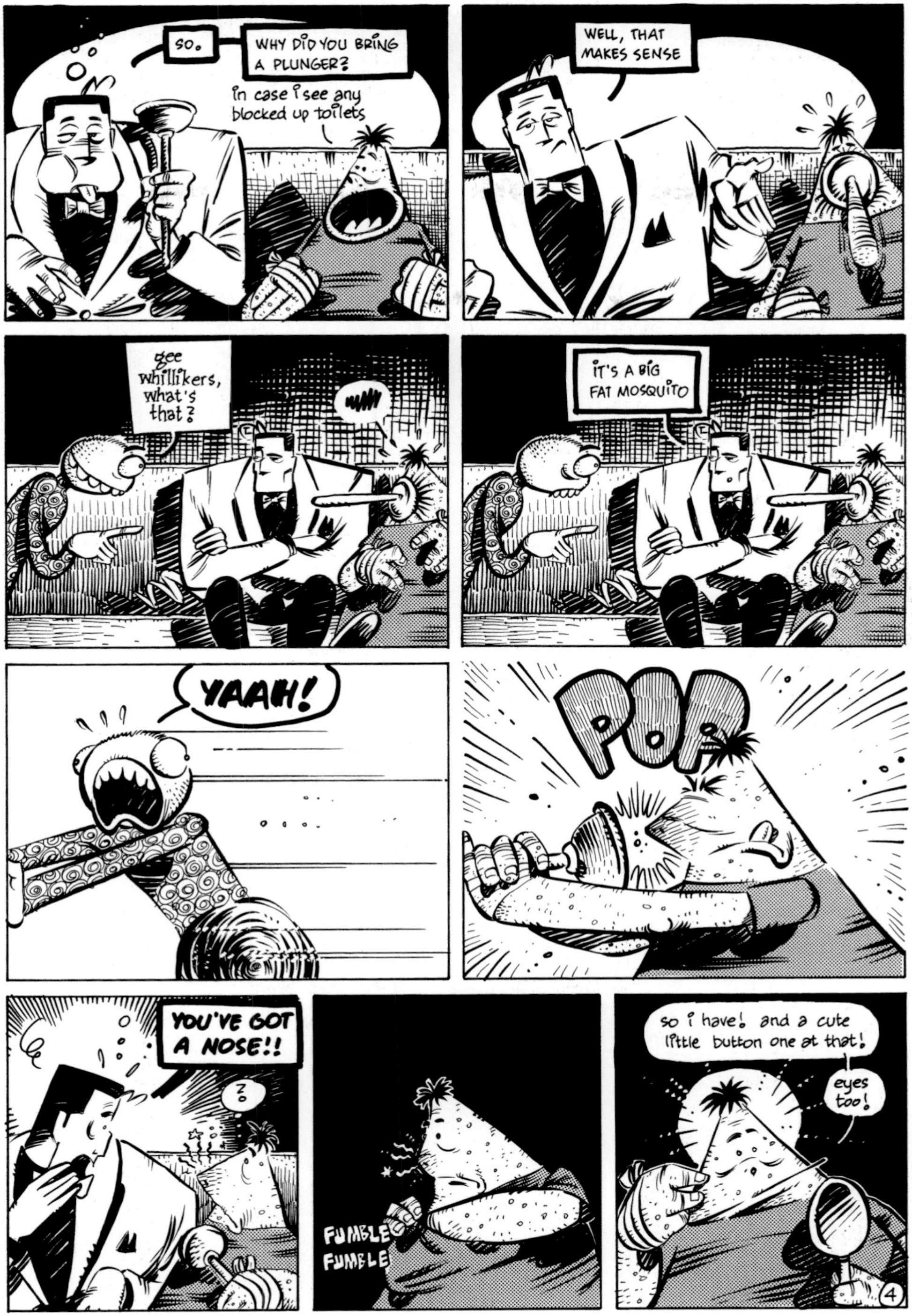
SO.
WHY DID YOU BRING A PLUNGER?
in case i see any blocked up toilets
WELL, THAT MAKES SENSE
gee whillikers, what's that?
IT'S A BIG FAT MOSQUITO
YAAH!
POP
YOU'VE GOT A NOSE!!
FUMBLE FUMBLE
so i have! and a cute little button one at that!
eyes too!
4

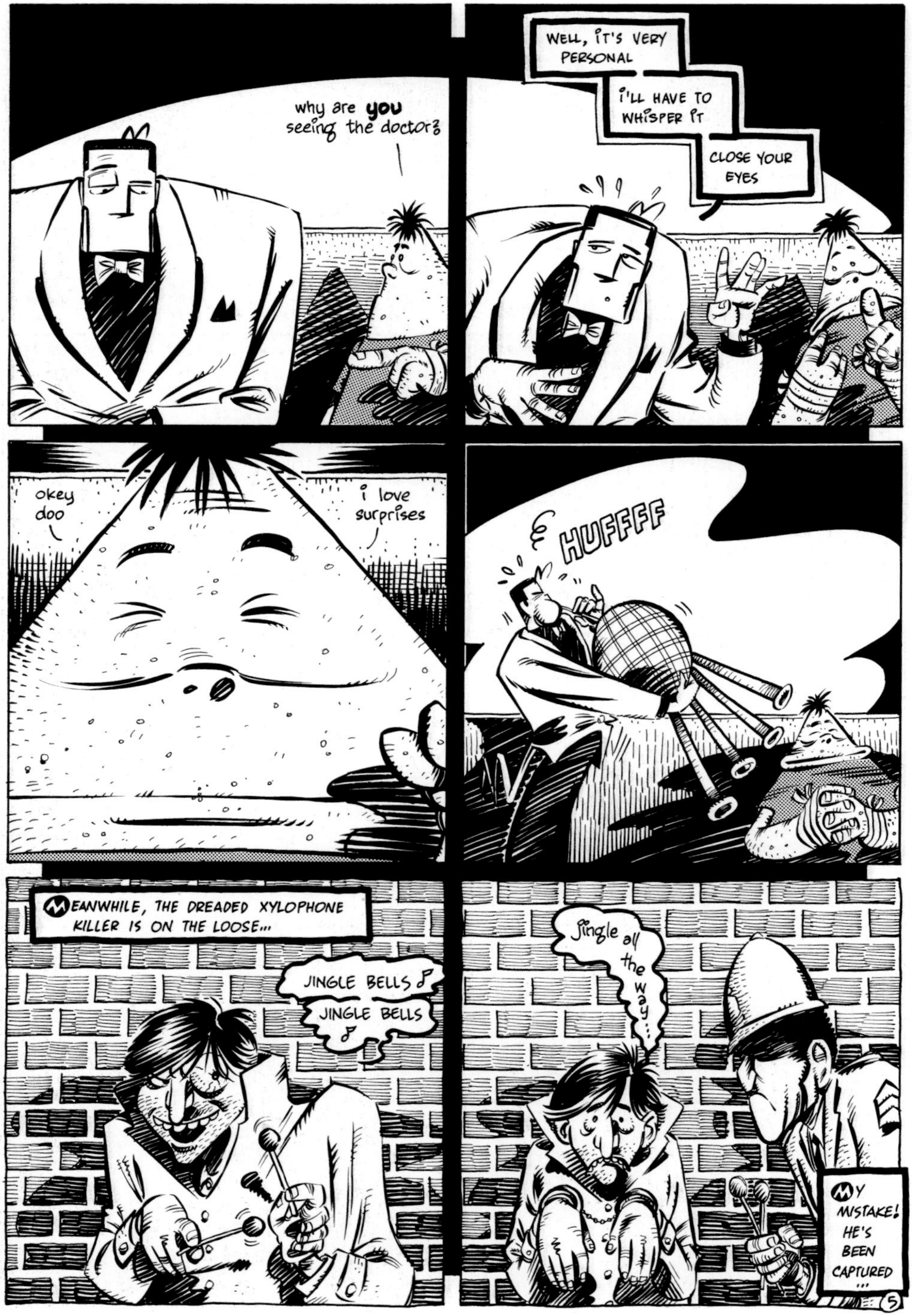
why are you seeing the doctor?
WELL, IT'S VERY PERSONAL
I'LL HAVE TO WHISPER IT
CLOSE YOUR EYES
okey doo
i love surprises
& HUFFFF
MEANWHILE, THE DREADED XYLOPHONE KILLER IS ON THE LOOSE...
JINGLE BELLS
JINGLE BELLS
jingle all the way...
MY MISTAKE! HE'S BEEN CAPTURED ...
5

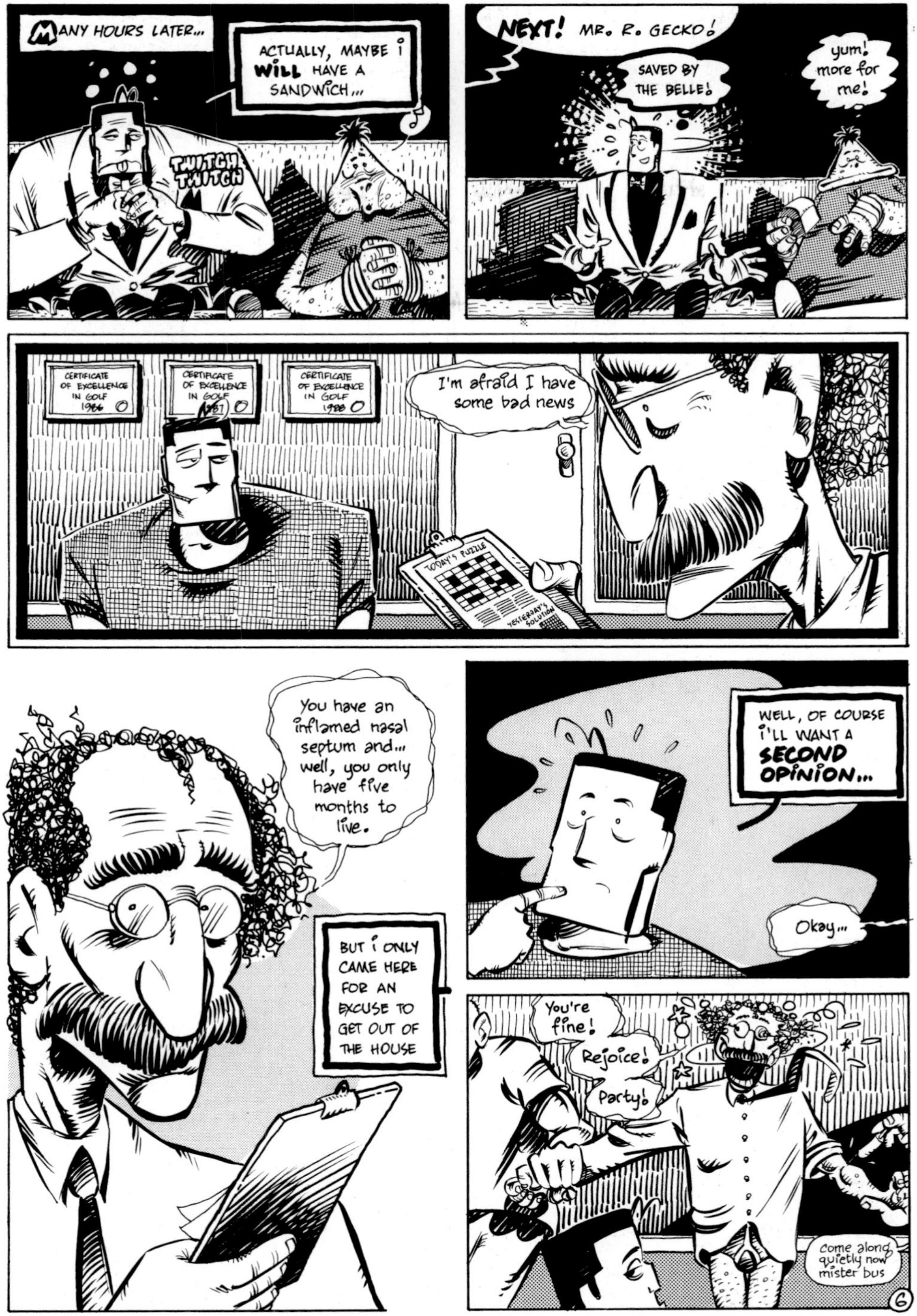
MANY HOURS LATER...
ACTUALLY, MAYBE I WILL HAVE A SANDWICH...
TWITCH TWITCH
NEXT! MR. R. GECKO!
SAVED BY THE BELLE!
yum! more for me!
CERTIFICATE OF EXCELLENCE IN GOLF 1986
CERTIFICATE OF EXCELLENCE IN GOLF
CERTIFICATE OF EXCELLENCE IN GOLF 1988
I'm afraid I have some bad news
TODAY'S PUZZLE
YESTERDAY'S SOLUTION
You have an inflamed nasal septum and... well, you only have five months to live.
BUT I ONLY CAME HERE FOR AN EXCUSE TO GET OUT OF THE HOUSE
WELL, OF COURSE I'LL WANT A SECOND OPINION...
Okay...
You're fine!
Rejoice!
Party!
come along, quietly now mister bus
6

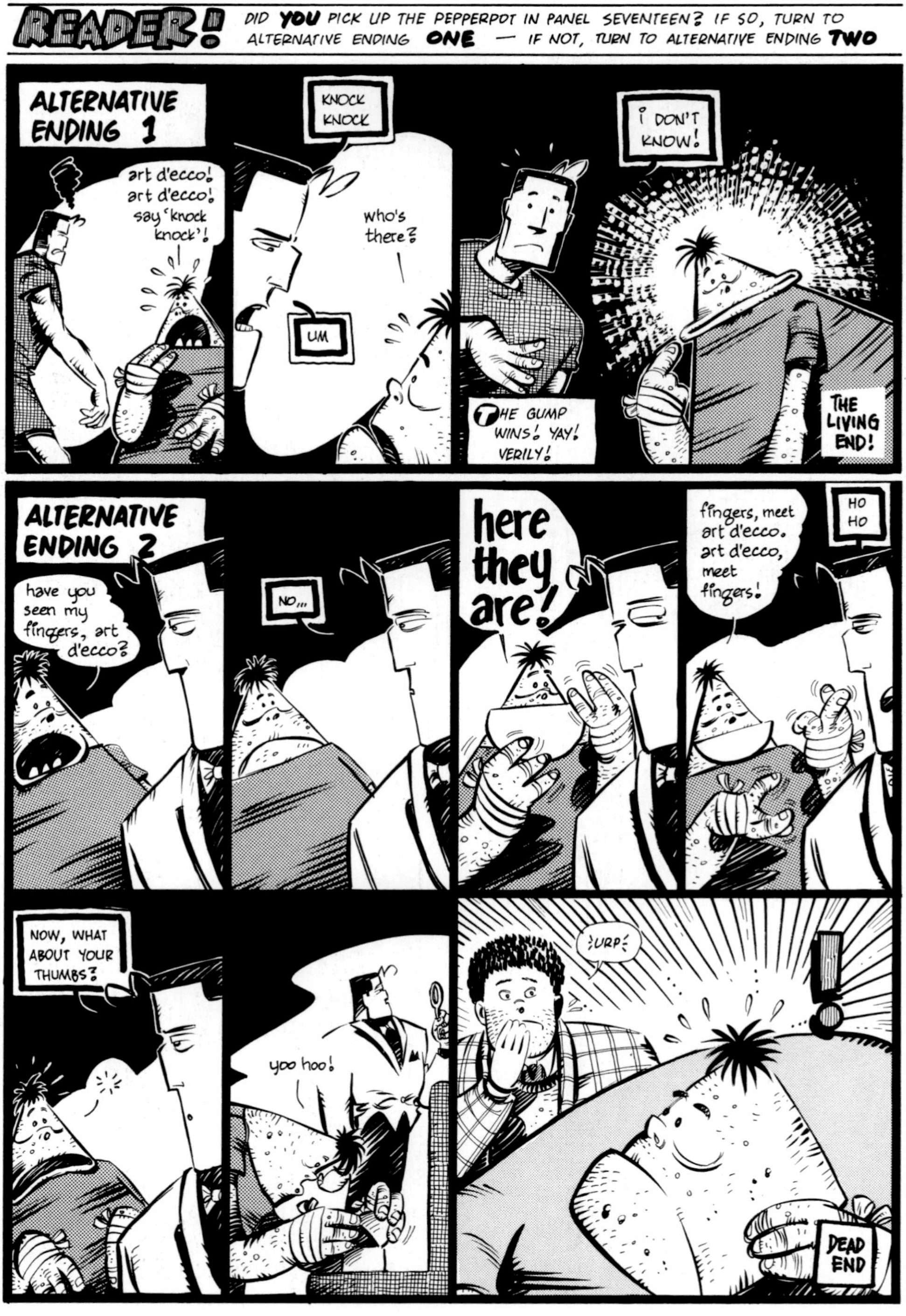
READER!
DID YOU PICK UP THE PEPPERPOT IN PANEL SEVENTEEN? IF SO, TURN TO ALTERNATIVE ENDING ONE — IF NOT, TURN TO ALTERNATIVE ENDING TWO
ALTERNATIVE ENDING 1
art d'ecco! art d'ecco! say 'knock knock'!
KNOCK KNOCK
who's there?
UM
I DON'T KNOW!
THE GUMP WINS! YAY! VERILY!
THE LIVING END!
ALTERNATIVE ENDING 2
have you seen my fingers, art d'ecco?
NO...
here they are!
fingers, meet art d'ecco. art d'ecco, meet fingers!
HO HO
NOW, WHAT ABOUT YOUR THUMBS?
yoo hoo!
URP
DEAD END

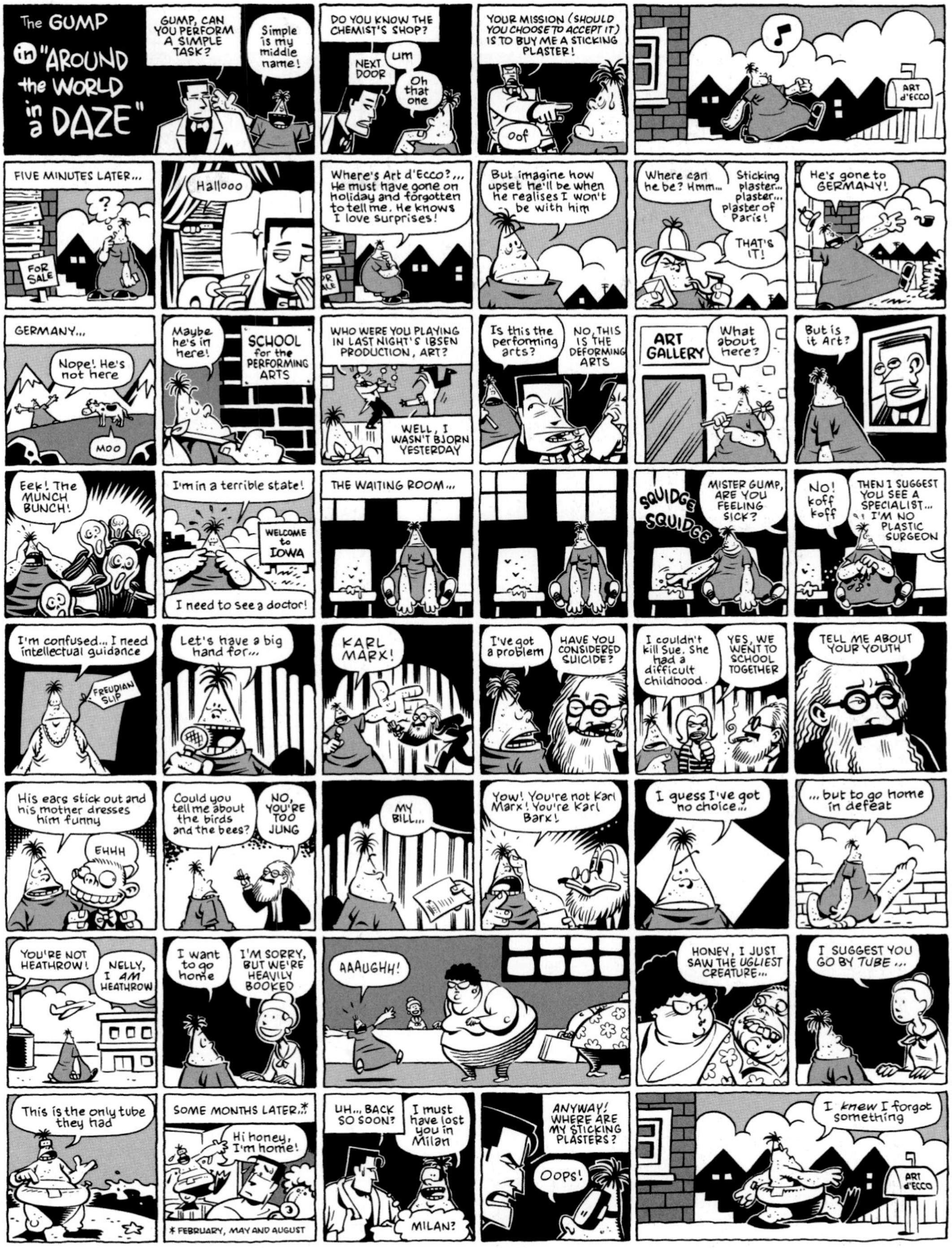
The GUMP in "AROUND the WORLD in a DAZE"
GUMP, CAN YOU PERFORM A SIMPLE TASK?
Simple is my middle name!
DO YOU KNOW THE CHEMIST'S SHOP?
um
NEXT DOOR
Oh that one
YOUR MISSION (SHOULD YOU CHOOSE TO ACCEPT IT) IS TO BUY ME A STICKING PLASTER!
Oof
ART d'ECCO
FIVE MINUTES LATER...
?
FOR SALE
Hallooo
Where's Art d'Ecco?... He must have gone on holiday and forgotten to tell me. He knows I love surprises!
But imagine how upset he'll be when he realises I won't be with him
Where can he be? Hmm...
Sticking plaster... plaster... plaster of Paris!
THAT'S IT!
He's gone to GERMANY!
GERMANY...
Nope! He's not here
MOO
Maybe he's in here!
SCHOOL for the PERFORMING ARTS
WHO WERE YOU PLAYING IN LAST NIGHT'S IBSEN PRODUCTION, ART?
WELL, I WASN'T BJORN YESTERDAY
Is this the performing arts?
NO, THIS IS THE DEFORMING ARTS
ART GALLERY
What about here?
But is it Art?
Eek! The MUNCH BUNCH!
I'm in a terrible state!
WELCOME to IOWA
I need to see a doctor!
THE WAITING ROOM...
SQUIDGE SQUIDGE
MISTER GUMP, ARE YOU FEELING SICK?
No! koff koff
THEN I SUGGEST YOU SEE A SPECIALIST... I'M NO PLASTIC SURGEON
I'm confused... I need intellectual guidance
FREUDIAN SLIP
Let's have a big hand for...
KARL MARX!
I've got a problem
HAVE YOU CONSIDERED SUICIDE?
I couldn't kill Sue. She had a difficult childhood.
YES, WE WENT TO SCHOOL TOGETHER
TELL ME ABOUT YOUR YOUTH
His ears stick out and his mother dresses him funny
EHHH
Could you tell me about the birds and the bees?
NO, YOU'RE TOO JUNG
MY BILL...
Yow! You're not Karl Marx! You're Karl Barx!
I guess I've got no choice...
... but to go home in defeat
YOU'RE NOT HEATHROW!
NELLY, I AM HEATHROW
I want to go home
I'M SORRY, BUT WE'RE HEAVILY BOOKED
AAAUGHH!
HONEY, I JUST SAW THE UGLIEST CREATURE...
I SUGGEST YOU GO BY TUBE...
This is the only tube they had
SOME MONTHS LATER...*
Hi honey, I'm home!
* FEBRUARY, MAY AND AUGUST
UH... BACK SO SOON?
I must have lost you in Milan
MILAN?
ANYWAY! WHERE ARE MY STICKING PLASTERS?
Oops!
I knew I forgot something
ART d'ECCO

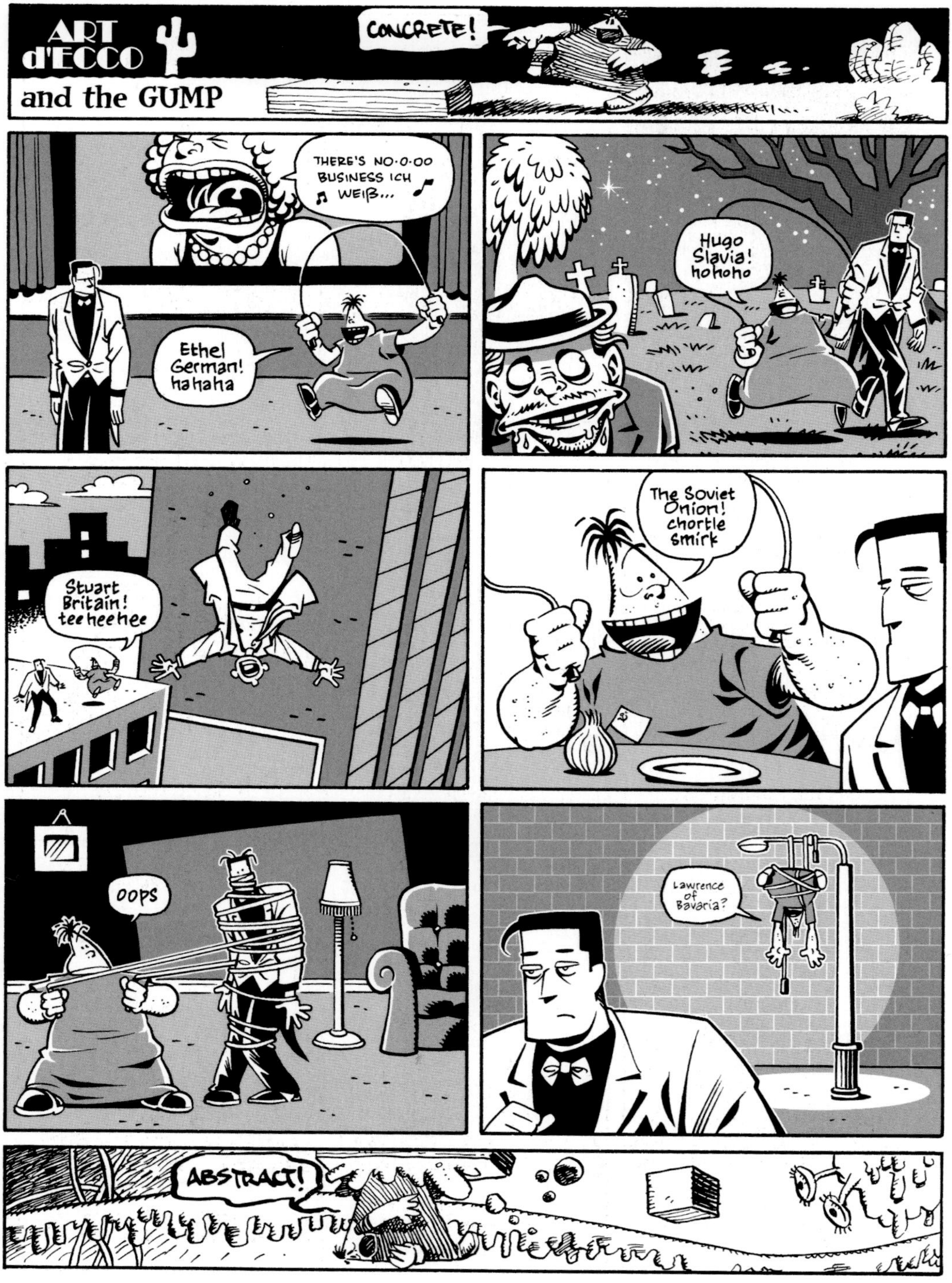
ART d'ECCO
and the GUMP
CONCRETE!
THERE'S NO-O-OO BUSINESS ICH WEIß...
Ethel German! hahaha
Hugo Slavia! hohoho
Stuart Britain! teeheehee
The Soviet Onion! chortle smirk
OOPS
Lawrence of Bavaria?
ABSTRACT!

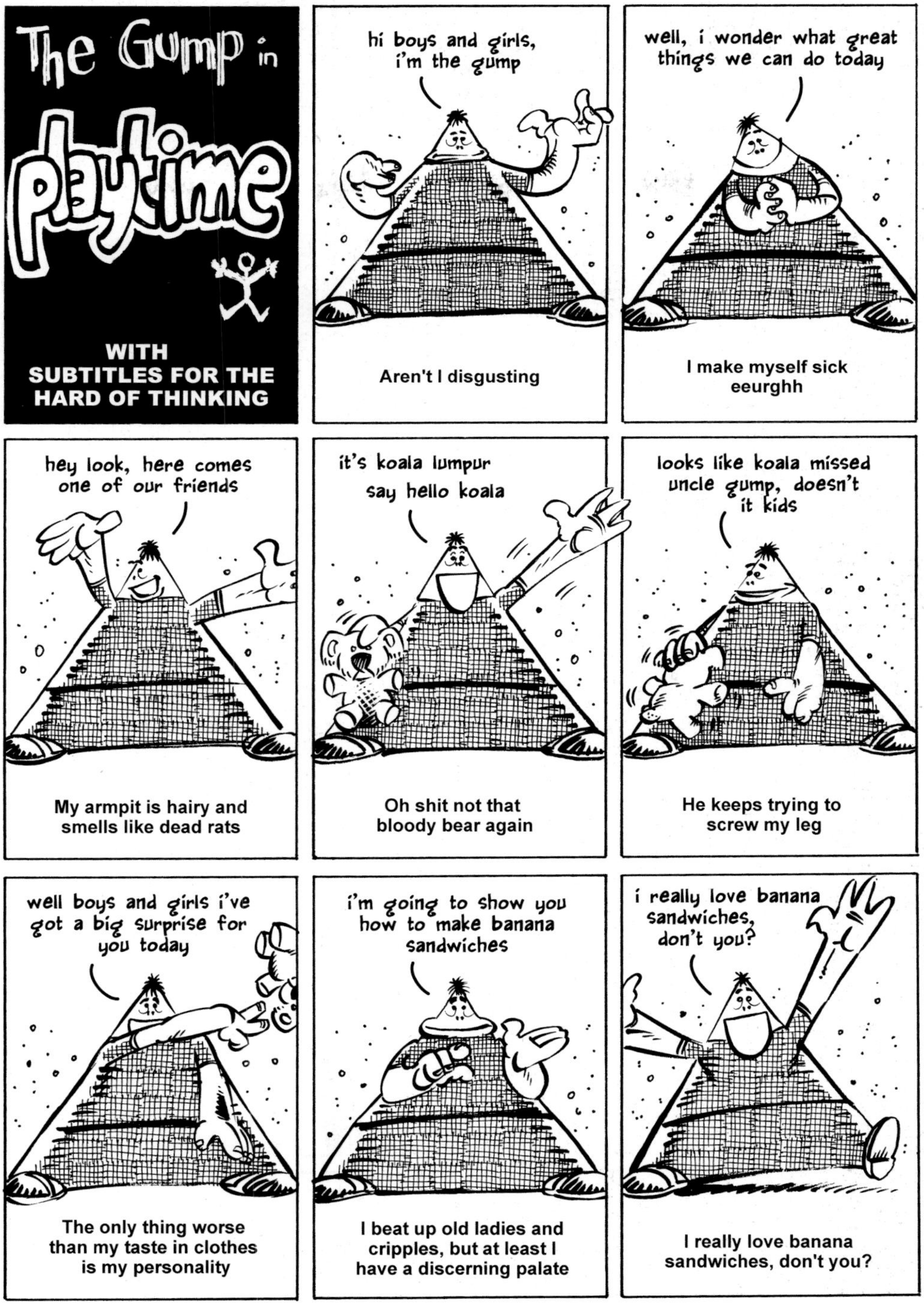
The Gump in
playtime
WITH SUBTITLES FOR THE HARD OF THINKING
hi boys and girls, i'm the gump
Aren't I disgusting
well, i wonder what great things we can do today
I make myself sick eeurghh
hey look, here comes one of our friends
My armpit is hairy and smells like dead rats
it's koala lumpur
say hello koala
Oh shit not that bloody bear again
looks like koala missed uncle gump, doesn't it kids
He keeps trying to screw my leg
well boys and girls i've got a big surprise for you today
The only thing worse than my taste in clothes is my personality
i'm going to show you how to make banana sandwiches
I beat up old ladies and cripples, but at least I have a discerning palate
i really love banana sandwiches, don't you?
I really love banana sandwiches, don't you?

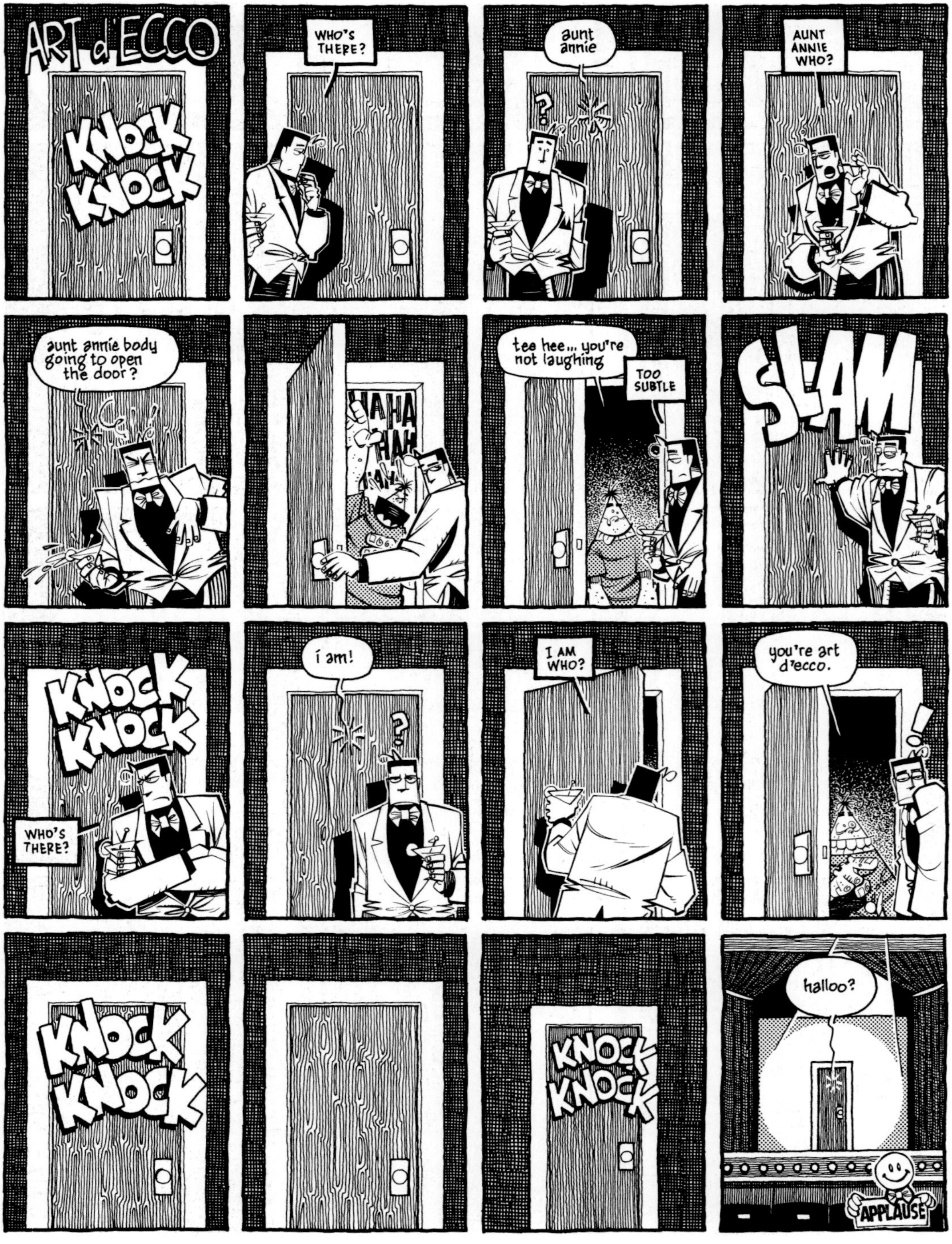
ART d'ECCO
KNOCK KNOCK
WHO'S THERE?
aunt annie
AUNT ANNIE WHO?
aunt annie body going to open the door?
HAHA HAH
tee hee... you're not laughing
TOO SUBTLE
SLAM
KNOCK KNOCK
WHO'S THERE?
i am!
I AM WHO?
you're art d'ecco.
KNOCK KNOCK
KNOCK KNOCK
halloo?
APPLAUSE

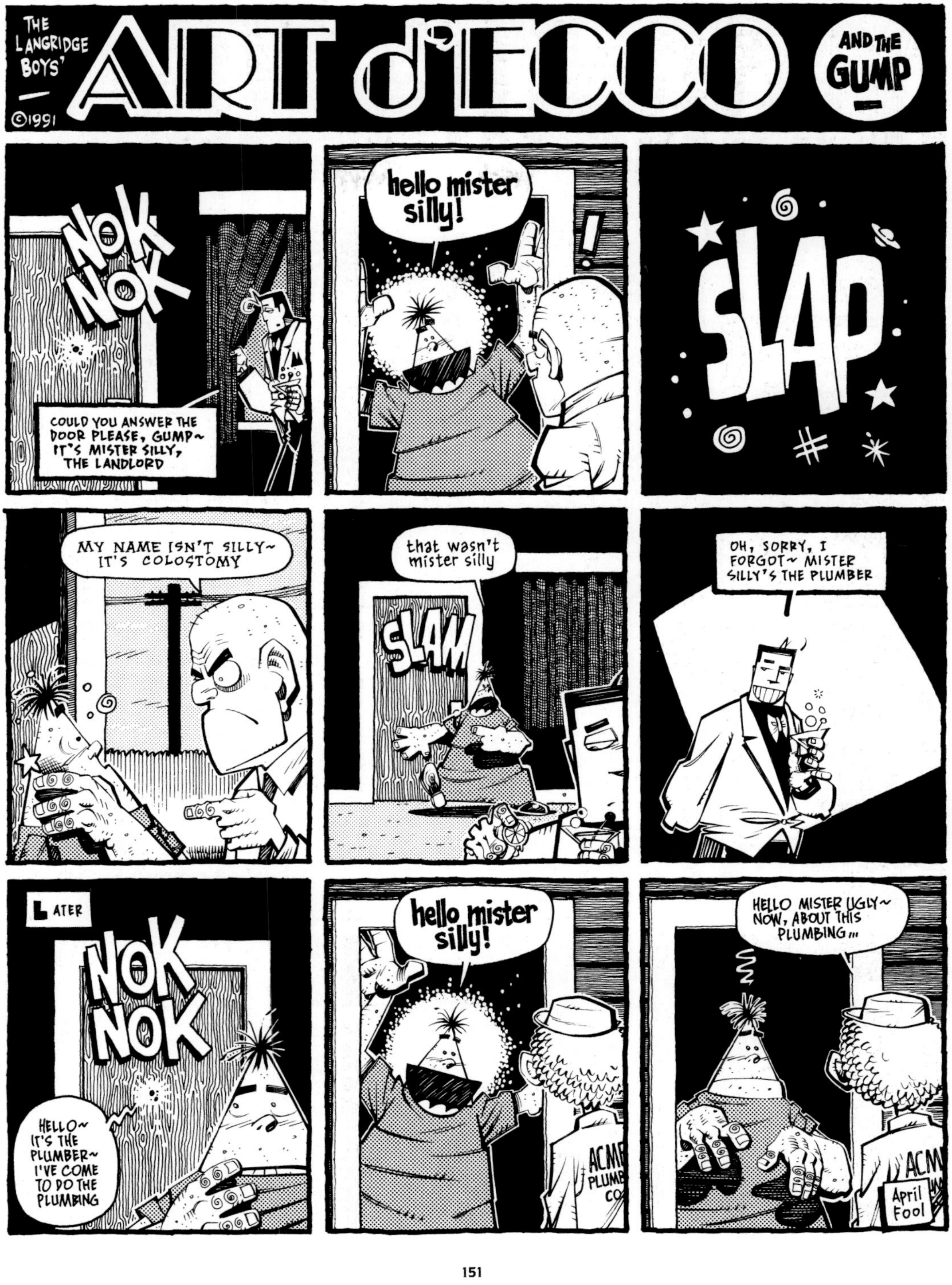

THE LANGRIDGE BOYS'
ART d'ECCO
AND THE GUMP
©1991
NOK NOK
COULD YOU ANSWER THE DOOR PLEASE, GUMP~ IT'S MISTER SILLY, THE LANDLORD
hello mister silly!
!
SLAP
MY NAME ISN'T SILLY~ IT'S COLOSTOMY
that wasn't mister silly
SLAM
OH, SORRY, I FORGOT~ MISTER SILLY'S THE PLUMBER
LATER
NOK NOK
HELLO~ IT'S THE PLUMBER~ I'VE COME TO DO THE PLUMBING
hello mister silly!
ACME PLUMB CO
HELLO MISTER UGLY~ NOW, ABOUT THIS PLUMBING...
ACM
April Fool

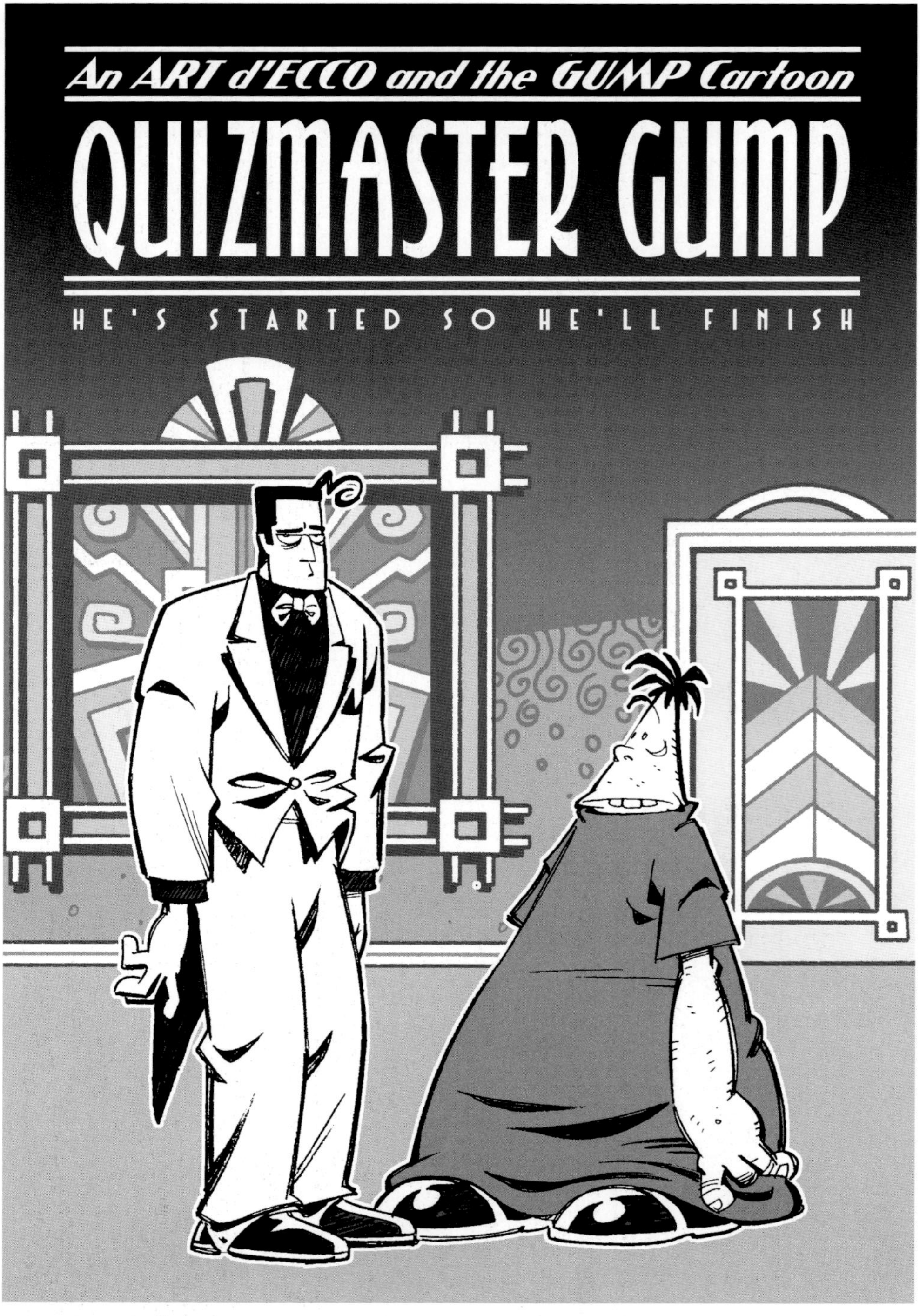
An ART d'ECCO and the GUMP Cartoon
QUIZMASTER GUMP
HE'S STARTED SO HE'LL FINISH

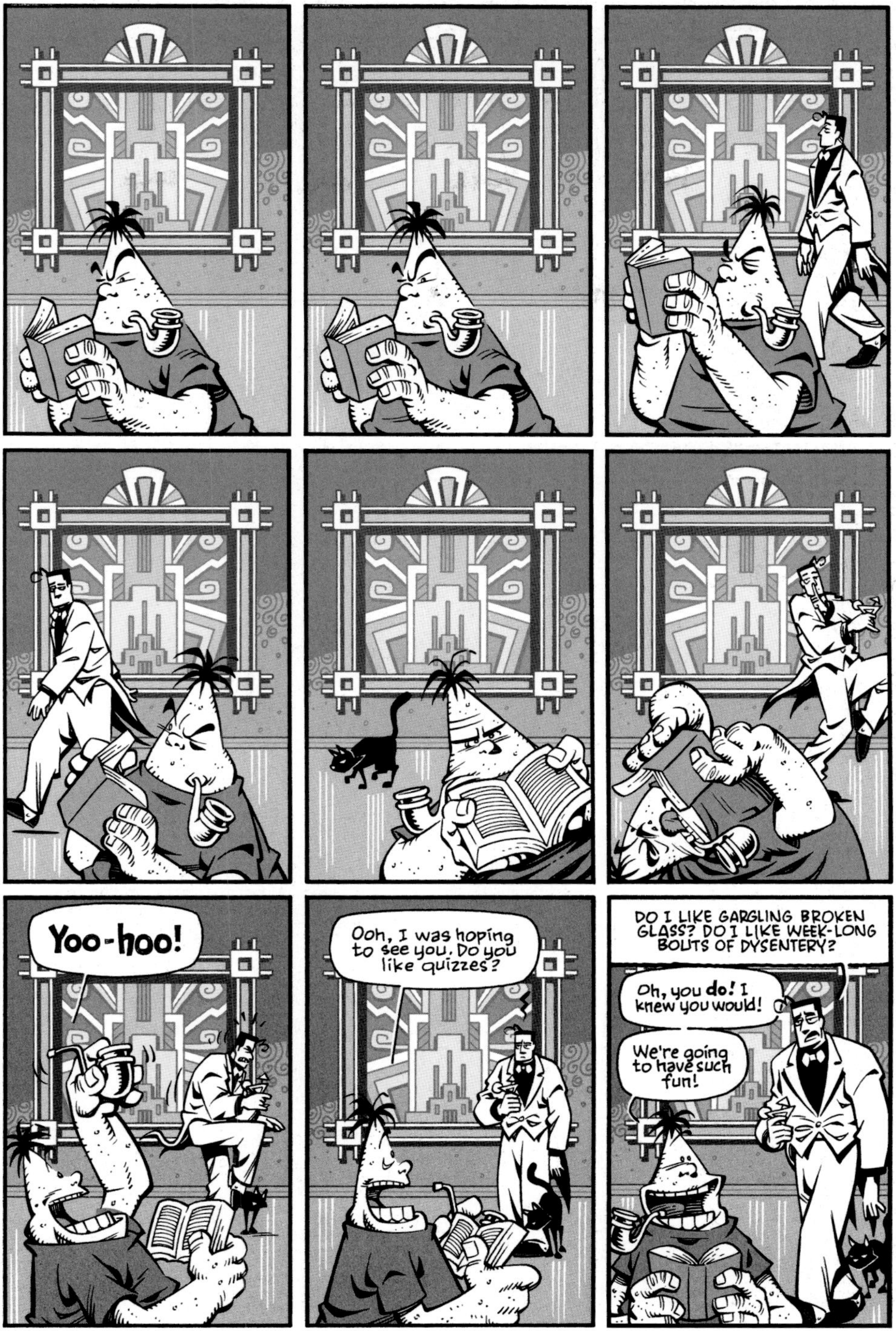

Yoo-hoo!
Ooh, I was hoping to see you. Do you like quizzes?
DO I LIKE GARGLING BROKEN GLASS? DO I LIKE WEEK-LONG BOUTS OF DYSENTERY?
Oh, you do! I knew you would!
We're going to have such fun!

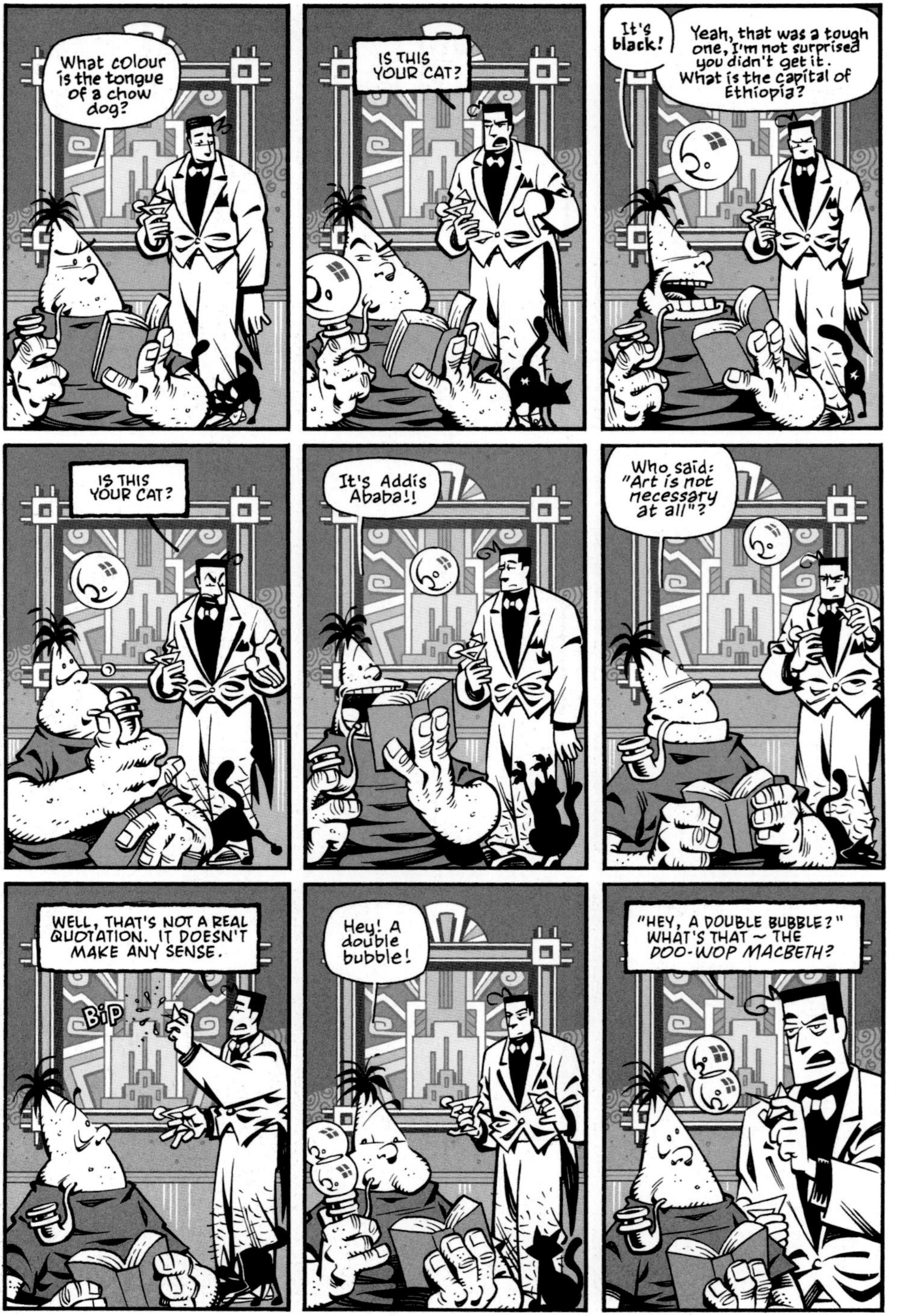
What colour is the tongue of a chow dog?
IS THIS YOUR CAT?
It's black!
Yeah, that was a tough one, I'm not surprised you didn't get it. What is the capital of Ethiopia?
IS THIS YOUR CAT?
It's Addis Ababa!!
Who said: "Art is not necessary at all"?
WELL, THAT'S NOT A REAL QUOTATION. IT DOESN'T MAKE ANY SENSE.
BIP
Hey! A double bubble!
"HEY, A DOUBLE BUBBLE?" WHAT'S THAT ~ THE DOO-WOP MACBETH?

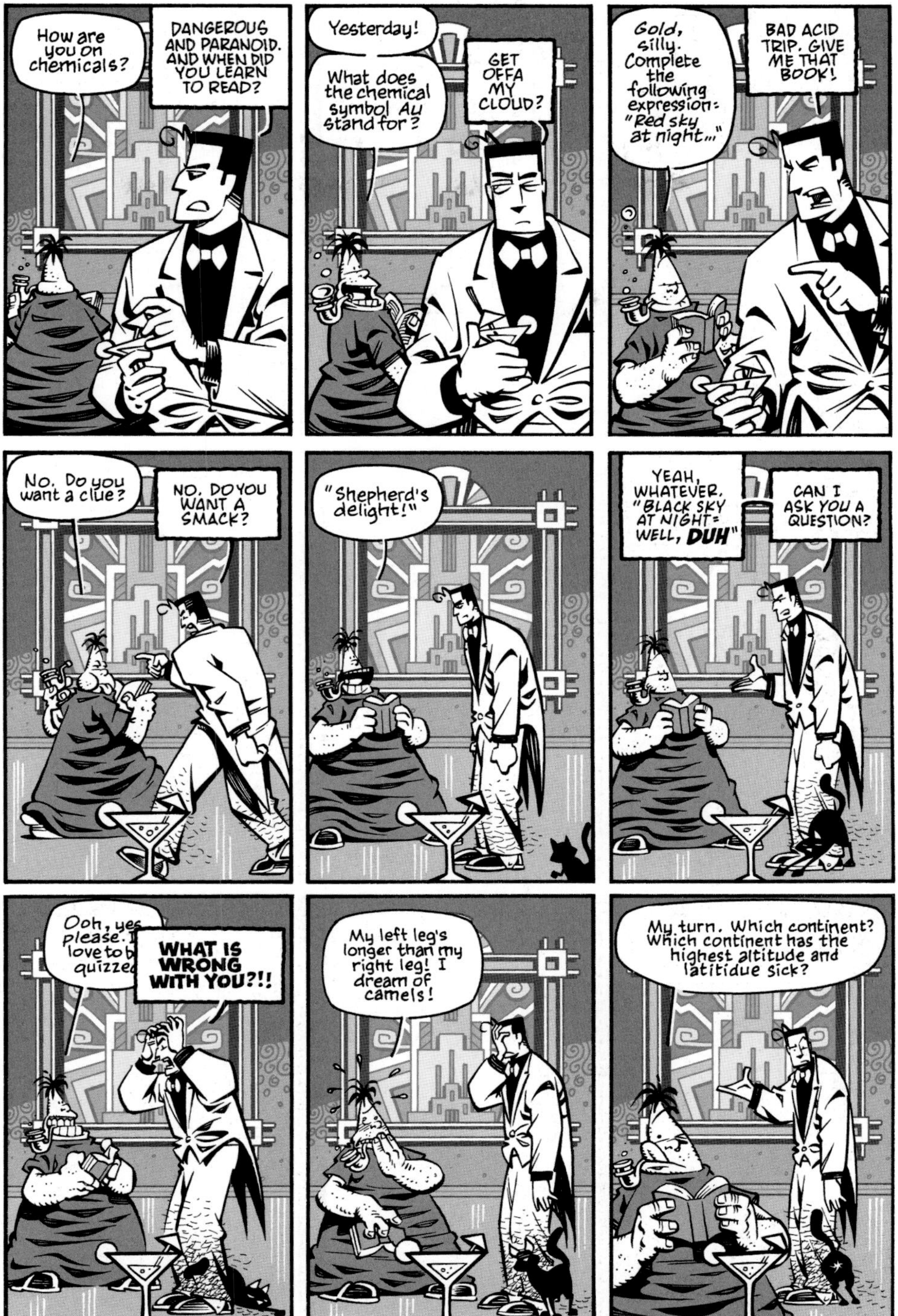
How are you on chemicals?
DANGEROUS AND PARANOID. AND WHEN DID YOU LEARN TO READ?
Yesterday!
What does the chemical symbol Au stand for?
GET OFFA MY CLOUD?
Gold, silly. Complete the following expression: "Red sky at night..."
BAD ACID TRIP. GIVE ME THAT BOOK!
No. Do you want a clue?
NO. DO YOU WANT A SMACK?
"Shepherd's delight!"
YEAH, WHATEVER. "BLACK SKY AT NIGHT= WELL, DUH"
CAN I ASK YOU A QUESTION?
WHAT IS WRONG WITH YOU?!!
My left leg's longer than my right leg! I dream of camels!
My turn. Which continent? Which continent has the highest altitude and latitidue sick?

Which planet of the Solar System is smaller than the moon?
SO, ADDIS, IF THAT REALLY IS YOUR NAME, WHAT ARE YOU GOING TO DO ABOUT MY TROUSERS?
What's the most important thing about the U.S.S. Missouri?
MROWWRR
IT LOVED COMPANY?
Nope, Japan surrendered on it.
CAN I ASK YOU ANOTHER QUESTION?
Ooh! Yay! Pick me!
HAVE YOU SEEN MY MARTINI?
It's in the next panel.
AHA!
STUPID CARTOONIST
But that wasn't a quiz question.
You're not really playing quiz with me.
I was only trying to bring a little sunshine into your life!

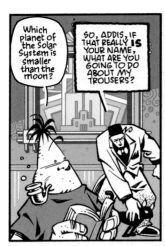

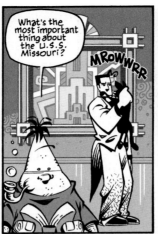

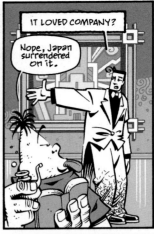

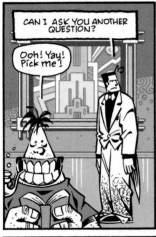

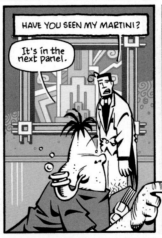

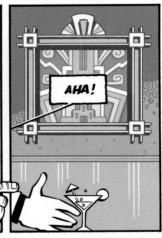

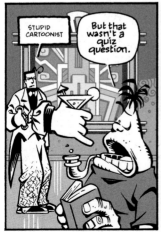

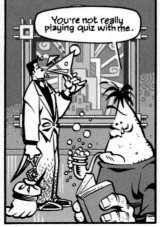

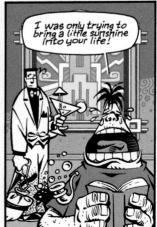

I give so much! What do I ever get in return?
WELL, I GAVE YOU A POKE IN THE EYE WITH A SHARP STICK THE OTHER DAY
AND I LET YOU KEEP THE SHARP STICK
That's true.
AND I GAVE YOU THAT REMAINDERED YOKO·IN·A·BOX LAST CHRISTMAS.
That's true too.
EEEEEEEEEEEEEEEEEEEEEEEEEEEEEEE
But I can't get her back in the box.
WOW. THOSE REALLY WERE LONG-LIFE BATTERIES.
OKAY, QUIZMASTER, LIGHT UP MY LIFE. ONE LAST QUESTION.
In the famous equation e=mc², what is the constancy?
"WHAT IS THE CONSTANT 'C'?"
Sorry, I misheard.
I DON'T CARE
What is the constant 'C'?
I DON'T CARE
"Turn upside down for answer"

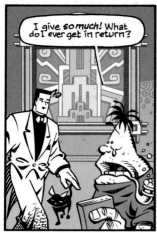

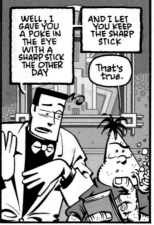

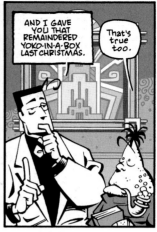

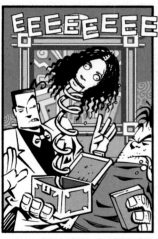

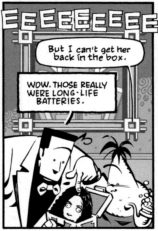

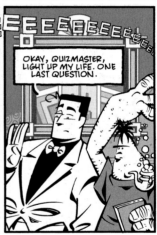

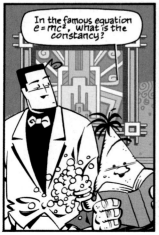

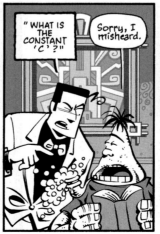

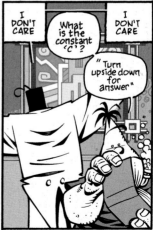

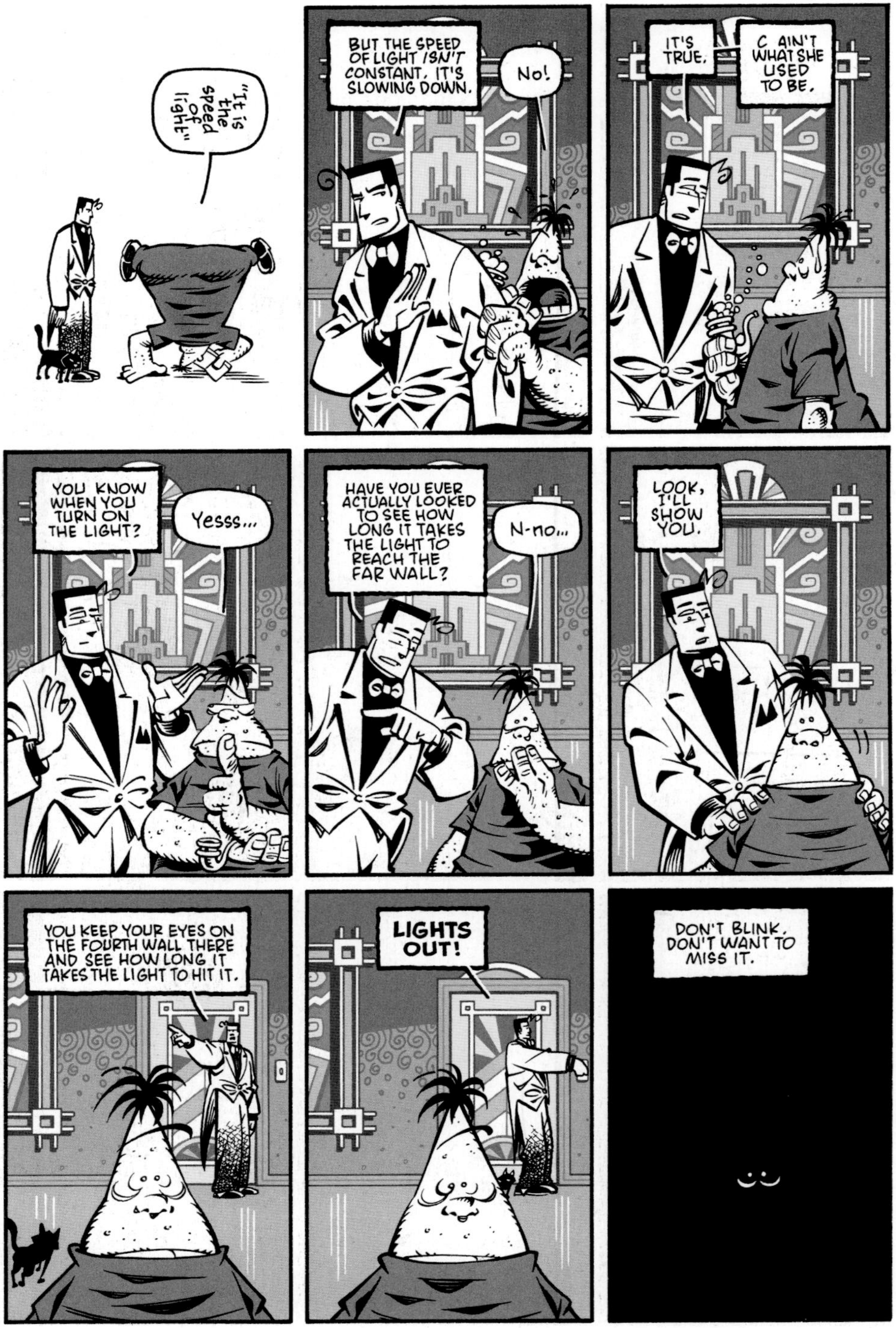
"It is the speed of light."
BUT THE SPEED OF LIGHT ISN'T CONSTANT. IT'S SLOWING DOWN.
No!
IT'S TRUE.
C AIN'T WHAT SHE USED TO BE.
YOU KNOW WHEN YOU TURN ON THE LIGHT?
Yesss...
HAVE YOU EVER ACTUALLY LOOKED TO SEE HOW LONG IT TAKES THE LIGHT TO REACH THE FAR WALL?
N-no...
LOOK, I'LL SHOW YOU.
YOU KEEP YOUR EYES ON THE FOURTH WALL THERE AND SEE HOW LONG IT TAKES THE LIGHT TO HIT IT.
LIGHTS OUT!
DON'T BLINK. DON'T WANT TO MISS IT.

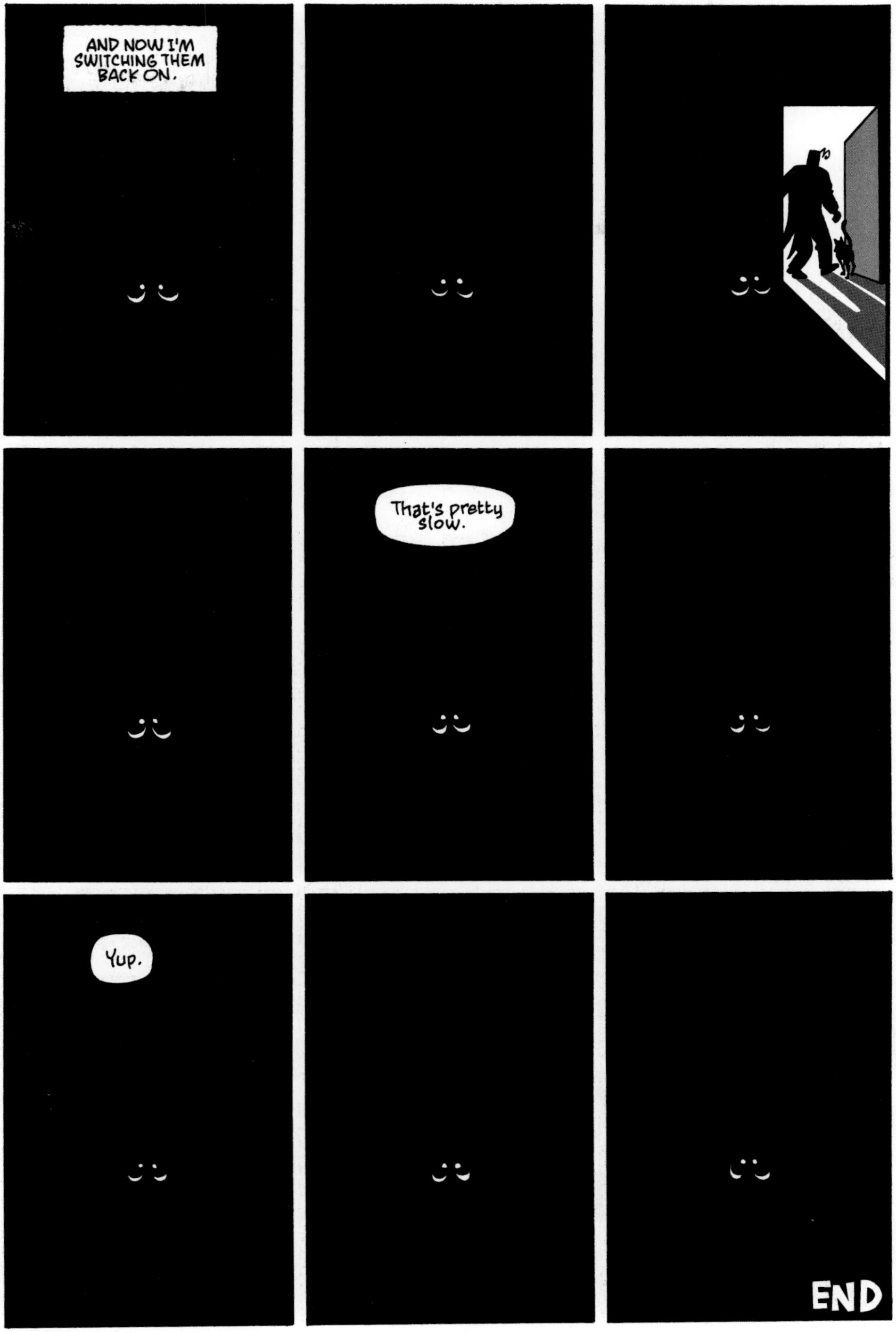
AND NOW I'M SWITCHING THEM BACK ON.
That's pretty slow.
Yup.
END

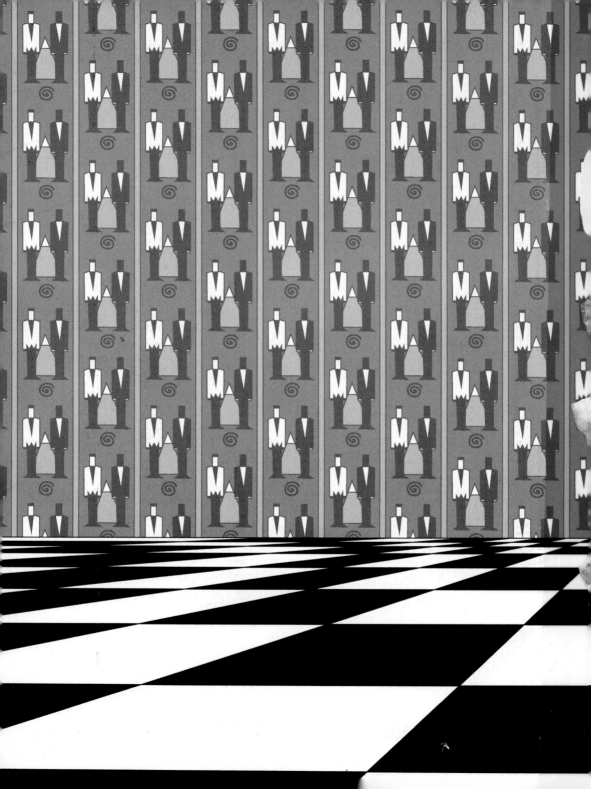